SOMOZA

SOMOZA

And the Legacy of
U.S. Involvement in Central America

BERNARD DIEDERICH

WATERFRONT PRESS
Maplewood, New Jersey

Published by

WATERFRONT PRESS
52 Maple Ave.
Maplewood, N.J. 07040

ISBN 0-943862-42-6 (Paperbound)

Published earlier (1981) in a clothbound
edition by E.P. Dutton, New York.

Printed in the United States of America, 1989

CONTENTS

Photographs follow page 188 of text

PREFACE

They were as anachronistic as the quaintly antiquated American slang which they laced with obscenities, portraying a 1930s B-picture tough-but-nice-guy image. They were the archetypal *caudillos,* the Latin strongmen who paid lip service to democracy and killed and tortured in its name to save the "free world" from communism.

Their little manias set them apart from their contemporaries. They deemed themselves less sanguinary and more enlightened than such autocrats as Trujillo of the Dominican Republic, Batista of Cuba or Pérez Jiménez of Venezuela.

Yet in the final analysis the Somozas of Nicaragua were the same breed of tyrants that has for so long dominated Latin America.

After the founder of the dynasty was assassinated in 1956, there was a period of relative liberalization—totalitarian rule wasn't good for business—but the third and last clan member to take control, Anastasio Somoza Debayle (Tacho II), drove the country into a popular insurrection. Despised and hated by the great majority of his people, he was defended only by a few. In Nicaragua there was his praetorian National Guard. In the United States there were his few congressional backers who still argued that he was the bulwark against communism.

Yet it was he who was most responsible for the Somozas' fall from power. No one else. It was his contempt for his own people that destroyed him. I was among those who chronicled his fall, but my first glimpse of the Somoza clan went back to 1952 when the old patriarch, Tacho Somoza García, visited Haiti on his return from the Dominican Republic, the fiefdom of fellow despot Generalissimo Rafael Leonidas Trujillo Molina.

With a straight face the heavy-jowled Tacho told a press conference he hoped all of Latin America would adopt his political doctrine. He explained his simplistic philosophy: not permitting the rich to abuse labor and not allowing labor to abuse the rich. Communism was the only real menace, he said, and it was important to be strong in order to prevail against the Marxists. In essence, the Somoza doctrine didn't change for the next twenty-seven years. In practice, however, all it meant was that only the Somozas had the right to abuse whom they liked—all in the name of anticommunism.

I caught my first whiff of the dictatorship (they continually disputed the label) in 1967, when Tacho II was engineering his "election" as president. It was the acrid stench of National Guard tear gas on Roosevelt Avenue clearing out the opposition which had seized the Gran Hotel across from the National Palace. The guard had already put down an anti-Somoza demonstration three days earlier, leaving forty dead. The demonstrators were protesting the election of another Somoza.

In those days I met most of the main actors in the Nicaraguan tragedy. Tacho II at El Retiro, his Spanish-style residence, entertained the foreign press early one morning with whiskey and soda (he drank bloody marys) and conveyed the image of a genial businessman enhanced by his colloquial American English and glib openness.

The electoral charade that Tacho II—like his father—orchestrated to earn his exemption from the dictator label was laughingly called the election of "guaro and nacatamales," the favorite booze and food handed out as rewards to compliant voters.

The earthquake in December 1972 shattered Managua and also produced the first serious fissures in the regime. Ten thousand died, but reconstruction awakened Somoza and his cronies' greed to the fullest.

Just prior to the earthquake, United States Ambassador Turner B. Shelton had been instrumental in bringing billionaire recluse Howard Hughes to Managua, giving newsmen a chance to see to what depth of subservience this envoy had fallen as a courtier to both Somoza and Hughes.

The 1974 "Christmas Party" raid of the Sandinistas brought us all back to Managua. The story made both Somoza and the Sandinistas front-page news.

The years that followed were never the same for either. At first the battles between the National Guard and the Sandinista guerrillas were fought in far-off rural areas with only casualty figures filtering through. By 1977 the Sandinistas were no longer just noms de guerre, but flesh and blood. National Guard repression made headlines that year, and the January 10, 1978, murder of Somoza's archenemy, newspaper publisher Pedro Joaquín Chamorro, ignited a revolution. The single most important act that brought the Sandinistas to the attention of the world was the August 22, 1978, capture of the National Palace in Managua, which made the leader of the raid, Comandante Cero, Eden Pastora, the best known Sandinista.

The Nicaraguan people held Somoza responsible for Chamorro's murder, and their repudiation of the family grew to such intensity that it finally swept the Somozas from power. As an irony of history it was the killing of another newsman, American Broadcasting Company TV correspondent Bill Stewart, that accelerated the collapse. Stewart's execution by a National Guardsman, filmed by his crew, shocked the world. It was graphic testimony to what was happening in Somoza's Nicaragua.

A U.S. congressman, onetime friend of Somoza, warned at the end that there would one day be an inquiry into who lost Nicaragua. It was a nonquestion. As with so many dictators before him, Somoza's downfall was inevitable.

This book is dedicated to the journalists who covered the last of the Somoza years. It is essentially a newsman's view of Nicaragua and the Somozas. Many of the incidents and events in this book I personally witnessed; others were covered by my colleagues in the area. Wherever possible I have tried to let events speak for themselves.

BERNARD DIEDERICH
Mexico City, July 1, 1980

ACKNOWLEDGMENTS

I wish to acknowledge the help of Robert Oskam who suggested this book on the Somozas, John Stanton who reported on Nicaragua for *Time* in 1948 and the assistance of other newspeople, especially June Erlick, Joseph Harmes, Heidi Holland and Susan Lynd. And the forbearance of my family who suffered my bringing a third dictator into our home.

The others:

Papa Doc: The Truth About Haiti (with Al Burt)
Trujillo: The Death of the Goat

SOMOZA

CHAPTER 1

A Folksy Dynasty

"I'm enjoying the hell out of getting together with you guys," Anastasio Somoza Debayle slurred in English to the little group of foreign newsmen on Sunday evening, June 3, 1979.

He'd descended from a cocktail party on the ninth floor of the Intercontinental Hotel and accepted the newsmen's invitation to continue the party in the hotel's Cabaña restaurant. Changing from vodka to wine, he was obviously still elated from his trip to the southern front, where he had met with his favorite battle commander, Major Pablo Emilio Salazar, alias Comandante Bravo. Now he wore a business suit. Earlier in the day he had been photographed in green camouflage fatigues, as befit the supreme commander of the armed forces of Nicaragua, studying field maps and discussing strategy, his West Point ring with its acorn-size diamond sparkling on his left hand.

In an expansive and genial mood he spoke out to the same newsmen he had complained about the day before. Then he had accused the press of covering events in his country in an unbalanced manner. Now he teased the reporters, saying that they would not publish what he said. But anything Somoza said was news. In the week preceding, the Sandinista National Liberation Front (FSLN) had launched what they called their "final offensive against the Somoza dynasty"—against his rule —and the world press was at his doorstep.

Outside the hotel, the city was morguelike. The entire country was closed down by a national strike demanding Somoza's ouster from power. Nicaragua was at war.

One of the reporters asked Somoza if he had had a good time at the cocktail party. "I sure did, they cut me down and I cut them down. Listen, you know freedom is not only for the press. It's also for the man who is being interrogated. So there we are."

There was laughter all around. "You know you guys think that I am an inaccessible sonofabitch and then you get defeated because I am an accessible sonofabitch that will talk to you all and put you in your place. But you haven't got the gumption to print what I say."

A reporter objected that "sometimes the language gets a little unprintable." To

1

which Somoza replied, "No, no, let's not talk about the language, let's talk about the implementation of the goddamn words."

He commented that he hadn't seen any of the people from ABC television that night, although he had seen their film of his activities earlier that day. He supposed they were now busy sending the videotape out via satellite. "What the fuck do you think. We've got a satellite station here," he bragged.

Somoza continued his monologue. "I'm enjoying the hell out of getting together with you guys, because you know something? You are just human beings like I am—you're a bunch of shits. You know, we ought to clear the air. Forget about me being president. Let's just be men and then we should get together and say, all right, what the fuck is good for this goddamn undeveloped country and what is good for these bastards who are trying to make hay in situations that are not realistic."

Somoza was cast in the macho image of his father, who had previously built up a reputation for cultivating intimate audiences with almost burlesque performances. But this kind of drunken chat with newsmen, though very much part of the Somoza style, was reserved for foreigners. His scorn and contempt for his own people didn't allow such intimacy with them, not even with his closest aides.

Somoza's father, Anastasio (Tacho I) Somoza García, was well known for his Falstaffian charm. The son, Tachito, inherited many of his father's mannerisms; the ability to charm, but especially the old man's toughness. And Tachito—Tacho II —was more violent. As with his father, his mastery of English was one of his greatest assets, even though his Americanisms became outdated.

If the first Tacho had not spoken English, the history of Nicaragua might have been written differently. Tacho I might never have come to the attention of the Americans, and might never have been placed on the first rung of the ladder of power as *jefe director* of the Guardia Nacional, January 1, 1933. He charmed the Americans with the use of their own vernacular. And charm paid a big dividend for the Somozas; the dividend was Nicaragua.

Despite early years spent in the United States, Anastasio Somoza García was very much the nineteenth-century *caudillo* (strong man). He understood the reasons behind the tragic civil wars that had torn his country apart for over a hundred years. He knew the importance of developing strategic alliances in order to gain and maintain power. History had shown that he who had the guns and commanded from the Presidential Palace on La Loma de Tiscapa controlled the country. And by the time Tacho became a man, the American presence in Nicaragua was so strong that only by winning the support of the United States could one hope to rule Nicaragua.

The history that led to the virtual American occupation of Nicaragua is a violent one. In September 1821, the Captain-Generalship of Guatemala, as Central America was known, obtained its independence from Spain almost without bloodshed. For a short time, the provinces of Central America united with Mexico. In what is now Nicaragua, the city of León had been a stronghold of opposition to Spanish colonialism, although many León citizens welcomed the liberal reforms instituted by the Bourbon monarchy. This earned the hatred of rival city Granada, whose Conservatives envisioned a highly centralized government in an aristocracy-dominated nation free of the Spanish, the Mexicans or of any Central American federation. In 1823 the Granadinos repelled a force sent from León to subdue them and succeeded in establishing an independent republic of Nicaragua within the territory the nation comprised as a federation member. Guatemala, Honduras, El Salvador and Costa Rica soon followed suit. In 1824 the former colonies joined together to form the United Provinces of Central America.

The ill-starred Central American federation dissolved in 1838 without ever being able to impose complete control over the Nicaraguans. During the period from 1824 to 1842 differences between the Liberals of León and the Conservatives of Granada accounted for seventeen major battles and eighteen different heads of state, with the Liberals usually holding the upper hand. When in 1845, the Conservatives, aided by the governments of El Salvador and Honduras, drove the Liberals from power, it gave León a chance to rebel.

One of the many subsequent Liberal uprisings was led by Tacho's great-uncle, Bernabé Somoza, Nicaragua's most notorious bandit. Tacho, secure in the presidency, enjoyed regaling visitors at the Casa Presidencial with tales about his illustrious relative.

"He was so handsome that when he played the guitar women shivered and swooned," Tacho would say. "He could put himself in the yoke and pull like an ox." Once Bernabé killed twenty men with a machete over a cockfight. But, calling to mind that he was subsequently hanged (July 17, 1849), Tacho sighed, "Remembering him, I always try now to avoid provocation. God knows, nobody wishes bloodshed less than I."[1]

According to Tacho, his great-uncle had had the best intelligence service in the country. His agents—the wives of most of his foes. Bernabé's chief rival was legitimist (Conservative) leader Fruto Chamorro, who commanded the loyalty of his men —not his women—to the point that at a word from Chamorro, one soldier reportedly threw himself into a river to be chewed up by freshwater sharks.

On one occasion when Bernabé's men were fleeing the small town of Rivas, Bernabé himself tarried in bed with Fruto Chamorro's mistress. Impatient to reach her side, Chamorro, who was leading the charge against Somoza, was shocked and indignant to find his enemy there usurping his prerogative. The conclusion to this story, a favorite of Tacho Somoza's, inevitably caused him to shake with laughter.

Bernabé Somoza was a Liberal. He was also a declared enemy of the English, who threatened the young nation's territorial integrity. He hoped to gain control of Nicaragua and govern with the aid of the Americans. But he did not have sufficient charm to convince the Americans that he was not a bandit. That was the chief difference between him and his great-nephew. Lacking outside support, Bernabé Somoza was hanged. Fruto Chamorro later became Nicaragua's first chief of state with the title of president (1853–55).

When gold was discovered in California in 1849, the British, who had taken advantage of the unsettled conditions in Nicaragua to expand their holdings on the east coast, suddenly found themselves in direct conflict with the United States. That year Cornelius Vanderbilt, together with several other New York investors, received permission from the Nicaraguan government to establish a company to ferry passengers and goods bound for the California goldfields across Nicaragua. A successful freight and passenger service developed that was several days shorter and safer than the trip across the Isthmus of Panama. The Nicaraguan government was supposed to be paid $10,000 a year plus 10 percent of the transit company's profits. However the financier juggled the books to show that the "accessory transit company" in Nicaragua operated at a loss, while another company for his oceangoing vessels made large profits. So, the Nicaraguan government got nothing.

When England tried to take over Vanderbilt's terminal in San Juan del Sur a diplomatic crisis ensued. That was resolved in April 1850. The Clayton-Bulwer treaty signed between the United States and England provided that any crossing of Nicaragua by water or rail would be jointly controlled by the United States and England and all tolls divided between them. Neither power bothered consulting the Nicaraguans.

This event marked the first time that foreign powers would use Nicaragua— theoretically an independent nation—simply as a piece in a much larger global jigsaw puzzle. The issue in 1849 was geopolitics. Later it would be international communism, and the Somozas would relish their role as the United States' Central American bulwark against the Red Menace.

In the interim, the Liberals and Conservatives had not paused in their contest for supremacy. The entire country was in bedlam. In an effort to avert further senseless bloodshed, Conservative dictator Laureano Pineda in 1851 moved the capital to the then-small city of Managua, situated roughly halfway between León and Granada. Unfortunately, the move only provided another military objective for the antagonists. The Liberals managed in a brief insurgency to have the capital returned to León. But when the president of Honduras sent his army to Nicaragua to support Pineda, it ended the Liberal uprising and granted Managua permanent claim as the seat of government.

By May 1854, the Liberals were ready to make yet another try at unseating the Conservatives. Fruto Chamorro had been elected "supreme director" in 1853 to serve a term of two years (between 1847 and 1855 thirteen leaders of the Nicaraguan government were known as "supreme directors"), but the ambitious Conservative managed to change the constitution in 1854, extending his term to four years. In addition he changed his title to president and vastly increased the powers of the office.

Early in 1855 the Liberals came to the conclusion that without outside help, their struggle was useless. So they invited an American, William Walker, to lead an army of mercenaries against the Conservatives in return for land and gold.

Walker was an adventurer. The 1850s were the heyday of the United States' policy of Manifest Destiny, a period when aggressive expansionism was applauded. Texas had been annexed in 1845, California became part of the Union in 1848, and the United States became obsessed with the desire for even more land. Any means by which this desire could be satisfied was considered justified.

Walker initially became interested in a scheme to colonize Mexico's Sonora and Lower California (Baja California). Backed by recruits from the saloons of San Francisco, Walker landed in La Paz in November 1853, hauled down the Mexican flag, named himself president and declared Lower California a free and sovereign state, independent of and owing no allegiance to Mexico. The young lawyer-journalist attracted worldwide attention in January 1854, when he further proclaimed himself president of Sonora, simultaneously declaring it independent of Mexico. Public sentiment in the United States seemed to be overwhelmingly in favor of Walker's venture. Supported by a handful of men, he had liberated two Mexican states, albeit without the knowledge or consent of the inhabitants.

But the conquest was short-lived. Mexican volunteers, led by a notorious guerrilla fighter named Guadalupe Melendres, and the Mexican army chased Walker and what was left of his forces back across the border in May 1854.

However, Walker was more than willing to do battle again. He welcomed the opportunity presented in Nicaragua. On June 16, 1855, accompanied by fifty-eight well-armed soldiers of fortune and supported by 110 Liberal troops, he landed in Corinto and began his conquest of Nicaragua.

His force was increased by an additional two hundred recruits shortly thereafter. Led by Walker, the Liberals won battle after battle. In mid-October 1855 Walker attacked Granada. When he also seized the Vanderbilts' lake steamer, the Conservatives surrendered unconditionally. Now he controlled both León and Granada. On October 23 a peace treaty was signed. Patricio Rivas, a moderate Legitimist (Conservative), was named provisional president of Nicaragua; William Walker became the new commander in chief of the army. Within four months after landing in Nicaragua, Walker had virtually taken over as dictator of the nation. In June 1856, after a disagreement with President Rivas, Walker held an election that made him president of Nicaragua.

Walker's spectacular military achievements were due entirely to the contrast between the two contending armies. The men under Walker were well armed and well equipped; they were in many cases professional soldiers fighting for a promised reward of gold and land. The Conservative government army, on the other hand, was made up of conscripts who fought in a war that meant nothing to them but hardship. They received no training, were given no uniforms and were armed with outdated weapons. They were sent into battle by officers who told them to charge or be shot dead where they stood. They were forced to loot to supplement their rations.

Walker's reign was turbulent. Other Central American governments were disturbed by his avowed intention to take over all of the region. The British resented his presence in what they considered their domain. The Liberals and the Conservatives both had been betrayed by him. And Cornelius Vanderbilt, whose ferrying business Walker had ruined, was also determined to see the adventurer's downfall.

Costa Rica, supported by troops from El Salvador, Honduras and Guatemala and armed with guns supplied by Vanderbilt and the English, declared war on Walker.

By December of 1856 he could no longer defend his stronghold at Granada, so Walker ordered the old colonial city destroyed. This act of vandalism earned him the undying hatred of all Central Americans. Fighting lasted until May 1, 1857, when Walker surrendered to the United States Navy. He returned to New Orleans a hero. But two subsequent attempts to return to Central America ended in failure. He was finally executed by a firing squad in Honduras on Sept mber 12, 1860.

The Liberals had been compromised by the fact that they had invited Walker to Nicaragua, and from 1857 to 1893 a succession of Conservative leaders peacefully took turns at being president. Then, in July 1893, Liberal General José Santos Zelaya ousted the Conservatives from office. This set off a new period of instability that would result in Tacho Somoza's coming to power a few decades later.

The first mention of a Somoza in Nicaragua is of José de Lozada y Somoza, a parish priest in Subtiava, an Indian barrio of León. He is recorded as having also served as auxiliary vicar general to the bishop of León in 1752.

But the immediate family can be traced only as far back as Fernando Somoza Robelo, a doctor and goldsmith whose name was engraved on a silver plaque dated 1810 on a church in Masaya. Somoza Robelo married Juana Martínez and fathered four children—Bernabé, Francisco, Anastasio and Manuela.

Anastasio Somoza Martínez had two children with wife Isabel Reyes—Anastasio and Francisco. Julia García became the wife of Anastasio Somoza Reyes and had four children by him—Josefina, Anastasio (Tacho I), Amalia and Julio.

Anastasio Somoza Martínez, Tacho I's grandfather and Bernabé's brother, was killed serving in the artillery at a siege of Granada in 1854. Another great-uncle was killed that same year, run through by a sword, when a new Liberal president of Honduras sent his troops in to fight on the side of the Nicaraguan Liberals. They soon withdrew when Conservative government troops from Guatemala invaded Honduras. During their stay the Hondurans had captured León but failed in an attempt to seize Granada. It was after their withdrawal that the Liberals had been quick to embrace Walker.

Tacho I was fond of bragging years later, when he was in power, that these events, along with Bernabé Somoza's fate, had convinced his own father, Anastasio Somoza Reyes, to avoid politics all his life. He also attributed the elder Somoza's distaste for politics to the effects of the conduct of his brother, Francisco, who habitually waged war against General Zelaya. Whenever General Zelaya couldn't find Francisco, he would throw brother Anastasio (Tacho's father) in jail instead. Because of this family history, Tacho went so far as to claim that he was a "Liberal from four ribs"—from all of his ancestors.

Yet Tacho's principal "rib," his father, served as a Conservative senator from the department of Carazo for eight years, and in 1914 was elected vice-secretary of the Senate, according to that year's September 17 issue of the official *Gazette*. Anastasio Somoza Reyes also signed the Bryan-Chamorro treaty in 1916—hardly the activities of a man never involved in politics. He even sent Tacho, born in San Marcos in 1896, to school in Granada, the stronghold of the Conservatives, naming Diego Manuel Chamorro (onetime Conservative president of Nicaragua) as the boy's guardian! While there, young Tacho attended the Instituto Nacional del

Oriente. Tacho later joked that "Chamorro gave me so many instructive lectures, I decided I wanted to be a Liberal and so I persuaded my father to send me to León."

The rivalry between León and Granada, at the core of political unrest and upheaval in Nicaragua since 1821, was based on pronounced regional differences. The great families of Granada, with their strong attachment to Hispanic culture and traditions, considered themselves an aristocracy. They were gentlemen farmers who supported the Catholic church and the ideas of monarchical Spain. Their Conservative life-style carried over into the quiet, colonial architecture of the city. The Liberals, by contrast, held sway in the thriving commercial center of León. Here, the elite promoted ideas compatible to growth of trade, and enterprise was king. León's Liberal party was inclined to accept the ideals of the American and French revolutions.

General José Santos Zelaya is credited with contributing more to the modernization of Nicaragua than any other president. Soon after taking office he set about to secure his borders. In December 1893, he armed 1,600 Honduran Liberal refugees. The following March, a combined force of these refugees and 3,000 Nicaraguan troops crossed the border into Honduras and put a Liberal president in office. His next target was the Mosquito (Atlantic) Coast, where British influence was still strong. With aid of pressure from the United States, the English were forced to withdraw in 1894. Once Zelaya felt his country free of threat from the outside, he openly turned his regime into a dictatorship. To protect himself from internal uprisings, he modernized the armed forces, creating a military academy and arming his troops with machine guns, and organized a small navy of five vessels to patrol Nicaragua's waterways.

Zelaya's newly revamped army suppressed all opposition to his rule. It quickly quashed Conservative revolts in 1896, 1899 and 1903. Zelaya maintained the legal mandate to power through a series of rigged elections. In one election rural voters were reportedly given their choice of three candidates, "José, Santos or Zelaya."[2] So of course General José Santos Zelaya won by a landslide.

In 1902, the United States decided to construct its transisthmian canal through Panama, a decision that shocked Zelaya and Nicaragua, since it had been generally assumed that the route would be through Nicaragua. General Zelaya favored foreign investment and had granted unusual concessions to American capitalists. He had long cherished the dream that a canal would make Nicaragua the leading power in Latin America, and that he would become a world leader. When the Americans decided to put the canal in Panama, it destroyed this dream and caused relations between the two countries to deteriorate.

Zelaya turned to other nations for support. In January 1909 he negotiated a loan with a London banking syndicate. The dictator was also said to be ready to offer Japan exclusive rights to construct a canal across his country. He canceled some of the American business concessions, which led to sharp diplomatic exchanges. Because the United States considered that it had a right to determine and guide policy in Central America, Zelaya came to be regarded a serious threat.

Although Nicaragua enjoyed some prosperity and improvement under the dictator's rule, cruel and often unjustified suppression of any form of opposition earned him the hatred of most of his countrymen. Despised at home and abroad, it was only a matter of time before his enemies banded together to crush him. On October 10, 1909 anti-Zelaya Liberals led by General Juan J. Estrada and Conservative forces led by General Emiliano Chamorro and Adolfo Díaz launched an assault on Bluefields, the capital of the Mosquito Coast. The United States had been warned of the attack which they concealed from Zelaya. The American consul at Bluefields established contact with the Conservatives and declared his faith in the revolution's speedy conclusion, stating the many advantages Zelaya's ouster would have for the United States.

Zelaya reacted swiftly to the rebellion and sent three thousand men against the insurgents. Estrada's expectation of a mass uprising by his countrymen proved illusory, so he asked for American intervention to protect the lives and property of foreigners in Bluefields. The United States complied by landing four hundred Marines.

In an attempt to keep government troops from landing in the port, the rebel Liberal general also hired two American soldiers of fortune to blow up Zelaya's ships. Mines exploded but failed to keep Zelaya's army from landing, and the Americans were promptly captured, tried and executed. The executions gave the United States all the justification necessary to break diplomatic relations with Zelaya and establish unofficial contact with Estrada. Realizing that with American support the rebels would soon be in power, Zelaya resigned on December 17, 1909, in order to avoid being removed.

The Liberal-controlled Congress appointed a new president, but the United States refused to recognize the new government. Estrada continued his military campaign under American protection. The United States Navy declared Bluefields a neutral zone on grounds that any fighting or bombardment would cause danger to foreign lives and property. After occupying the port the Americans handed over the principal source of government revenue, collection of customs, to the Conservatives.

The Liberals' demoralized army withdrew to the interior of the country where desertion thinned its ranks while the Conservative army swelled, boosted by the moral and material support of the Americans.

Then General Estrada was appointed president. He promised to hold free elections as quickly as possible, to work with the United States to secure a loan to stabilize Nicaragua's economy, and to punish those responsible for the execution of the two Americans. He stated that all threat to American business in Nicaragua was ended.

It was rumored that American interests had contributed one million dollars to the revolution. The United States sent a special agent to help form a stabilized government amenable to American interests. He negotiated an accord with President Estrada and Conservative party leaders that called for Estrada to serve as president for two years. Adolfo Díaz was chosen as vice-president, General Luis Mena was made minister of war and Emiliano Chamorro gained control over the

Constituent Assembly. On December 31, 1910, the United States recognized the new government. Their mission completed, the Marines were withdrawn from Nicaragua.

The new coalition government split immediately on the question of what collateral should be used to secure a loan from American businessmen. Mena opposed this loan and hoped to use the issue to make himself president. But the minister of war had two strong enemies, Chamorro and José María Moncada, an anti-Zelaya Liberal, who was the minister of the interior. Mena was able to rid himself of Chamorro by convincing President Estrada that the general would use the Constituent Assembly to pull off a bloodless coup. Estrada dissolved the Assembly and had Chamorro exiled.

With Chamorro out of the way Estrada sought a way to neutralize the power that Mena had over the army. The president's plan was to reduce the army to an internal police force and to use American advisers to keep the military professional. Eventually the United States adopted the idea, which was the seed from which the National Guard under the Somozas grew, but not in time to neutralize Mena.

When an explosion destroyed the main arsenal in Managua in February 1911, it sent Estrada into a panic. He assumed that Zelaya supporters were ready to rebel. The president declared martial law, but then resigned in favor of Vice-President Díaz and went into exile. Mena continued as war minister, and the United States recognized the Díaz government. Without supporters of his own, he became a figurehead ruler for the United States. On July 29, 1912, troops loyal to Mena attacked the army garrison on La Loma (the Hill) where the heart and brains of the Somoza power structure would one day be housed. The American minister (as ambassadors were called in the first part of the century) intervened however and persuaded Mena to order a withdrawal. The war minister, however, continued his rebellion against the puppet regime. On August 4, at the request of President Díaz, a small force of sailors left the U.S.S. *Annapolis* for Corinto and rushed to the president's aid in Managua. An entire battalion of United States Marines disembarked at Corinto ten days later and soon still another American force occupied Bluefields. By October there were 2,700 Marines in various parts of Nicaragua.

The Marines suppressed Mena's rebellion and forced him to surrender his troops and flee into exile. Following the end of the uprising, the bulk of the American forces were withdrawn from Nicaragua but a 100-man contingent remained until August 1925, to maintain the peace. During this period Emiliano Chamorro returned from exile and helped draw up the Bryan-Chamorro treaty, which gave the United States exclusive rights to construct an interoceanic canal across Nicaragua in return for a payment of three million dollars. Tacho's father, as a Conservative senator, was one of the signers of this treaty.

The Americans supervised what was termed the most honest election in the country's history in 1924. Carlos Solórzano, a moderate Conservative, was elected president. Dr. Juan B. Sacasa, a Liberal, became vice-president. While this was going on a new world was opening up for the twenty-eight-year-old Tacho Somoza.

The hot-blooded youth's sexual activity at nineteen had changed the course of his life. The maid in the Somoza home became pregnant, and Tacho confessed. Seducing a maid was not an uncommon act in Latin America but Tacho's family worried about him getting into deeper trouble; he had always been a problem child. Tacho's senator father was making only a modest living from the coffee they raised on their farm near San Marcos. Tacho's mother, Julia García de Somoza, had inherited the farm. A strong person and a hard worker who supervised the picking of the coffee—some of the best in the region of Carazo—she also sold milk in the little town nearby. Tacho's cousin, Dr. Víctor Román y Reyes, a successful coffee farmer, could well afford to help his young relative. He sent him to Philadelphia in 1916, where he had a brother, Dr. Desiderio Román y Reyes, practicing medicine. Because the maid's son looked so much like Tacho, Julia saw to it that he was brought up a healthy lad. Much later in life Tacho recognized his bastard son, José Somoza Rodríguez. Even though semi-illiterate he rose to general in the Somoza guard and was known as Papa Chepe.

In wartime Philadelphia Tacho studied bookkeeping and advertising techniques at the Pierce Business School. He also became very interested in baseball averages—he was an ardent fan of both the Phillies and the Athletics. Later, under his rule, baseball became the national sport of Nicaragua.

Tacho liked to say, "I met the girl of my dreams on a blind date." One night Tacho accompanied his uncle, Dr. Román y Reyes, to the hospital to see a young woman from Beechwood (now Beaver) College in Jenkintown, Pennsylvania, whose appendix the doctor had removed. She was the sophisticated daughter of a well-known Liberal from León, Dr. Luis N. Debayle, who had family connections with most of the important wealthy families of Nicaragua. Salvadora Debayle was also the granddaughter of Roberto Sacasa, one of Nicaragua's Conservative presidents. Because of the war in Europe, her family had felt it safer for Salvadora to leave the Belgian convent she had been attending and take up her studies in the United States. To ambitious young Tacho, Yoya, as she was known, fulfilled all the requirements he desired in a young wife. Her credentials were excellent. The trouble was, his were not. But in Philadelphia every afternoon he waited under the clock at Wanamaker's department store to take Yoya to tea, to the movies or dancing. Just to be near the woman he intended to make his wife, he stayed on in Philadelphia after his classes had ended, working as a bookkeeper at the Graham-Paige advertising agency on Broad Street.

Returning to Nicaragua in 1919, Tacho garnered a little money and opened a store near the Debayle home—to impress her family and continue wooing Yoya. Yoya was an attractive, fashion-conscious woman. As young debutantes she and her sisters caused a stir in Granada society when they appeared at a ball there with their underarms shaved. She was not highly intelligent but she was politically shrewd. The Debayle family had decided she should marry an up-and-coming young dentist from an aristocratic Liberal family. There was bitter opposition when instead she announced her determination to marry Tacho, who was now declaring himself a loyal Liberal.

It was said that Nicaragua's top surgeon objected to seeing his children grow up and would have opposed any suitor. But gossip at the time was that the doctor, a learned and cultured man who was a close friend of both France's Georges Clemenceau (premier of France, 1906–09; 1917–20) and Nicaraguan poet Rubén Darío, objected in particular to the provincial Somoza, who had his uncouth side and was of doubtful character. Even more damaging, he had questionable Liberal credentials. Old Dr. Debayle, who had two sons follow him into medicine, was not easily persuaded, but Tacho finally won out and just in time—the store was failing.

Tacho and Yoya were married in León on August 31, 1919, in Dr. Debayle's house. An extravagant church wedding followed the next day in the León cathedral with Bishop Monseñor Simeon Pereira y Castellon officiating. Tacho's father, who had enjoyed a good coffee crop, gave Yoya a diamond necklace and presented the couple with five hundred dollars and a share of his coffee harvest, which Tacho quickly sold to finance their honeymoon—a ten-month cruise to, and trip through, the United States. Upon their return the newlyweds moved into an old, high-ceilinged, colonial-style house in León opposite the San Juan de Dios Church.

Since Tacho's parents were soon having more than their usual financial difficulties because of a series of bad crops, forcing them to mortgage the San Marcos farm, and as the bride's family was not inclined to offer aid, the young bridegroom had to take care of himself. Tacho, who bragged he could strip down any engine, opened an agency for Lexington motorcars. The failure of the motor agency was natural because Nicaragua at the time had few roads, "the roads such as they have being only beaten paths through the woods where mule-drawn carts have cut two deep ruts in the ground. These roads, even in the dry seasons, are almost impassable, and in the rainy seasons are given up entirely for the pack trains."[3] When the Lexington business failed, Tacho tried numerous other jobs.

Tacho loved sports. He was a baseball fanatic. He had brought boxing gloves back from the United States as well as a book of rules, and introduced boxing to Nicaragua, refereeing bouts in León. He also refereed football games. At the same time he worked for a while in León as an electric meter reader.

He also held a job inspecting privies for the Rockefeller Foundation's Sanitation Mission to Nicaragua. Even today, in many modest homes in Nicaragua the toilet is a wooden seat with a hole in it under which is dug a pit that soon fills with water. It is not only unsanitary, but is a prime breeding place for mosquitoes. Oil is customarily poured on the water to kill the mosquito larvae. Because he carried a long, batonlike flashlight which he used to check out the interiors of the latrines, Tacho was soon being called "El Mariscal," the field marshal, behind his back.

Somoza tired of such mundane pursuits. According to former city officials in León, he and a boyhood friend, Camilio González Cervantes—later brought into the National Guard and made military attaché at the embassy in Washington—became involved in a get-rich-quick scheme counterfeiting córdoba notes, Nicaragua's currency. It required the intervention of Tacho's old guardian, Diego Manuel Chamorro, to keep him from going to prison. A friend who had a print shop was also involved. This printer, once Tacho came to power, got the contract to print checks for the government Bank of Nicaragua.

By 1926, Somoza was the father of three children by Salvadora, all born in their colonial home. There was a son, Luis, and a daughter, Lilian. On December 5, 1925, his younger son, Anastasio (called Tachito, and who was to become Tacho II), was born. By now weary of trying to make a conventional living to support his growing family and a failure as a counterfeiter, Tacho decided to take a stab at politics. He had met some of the country's leading politicians through his wife's family and was not overly impressed by the caliber of these men. When General José María Moncada (whose grandmother was Somoza's great-aunt, Manuela, sister of old Bernabé) called the Liberals to arms to overthrow Conservative General Emiliano Chamorro, Tacho promptly joined the rebels. Some said at the time that he acted to win his spurs as a Liberal.

On August 20, 1926, Tacho briefly emulated some of his fighting ancestors when he invaded his hometown of San Marcos, near the family farm. His troops were recruited from the poor peasants of the region, who captured the town simply by trudging into it. Tacho quickly adopted the title "General." But his little force was quickly scattered and the new general was promptly captured by the Conservative forces and brought before none other than President Chamorro. Chamorro had really earned his generalship as Nicaragua's leading revolutionary of the time. He was to lead more revolutions and revolts than any other Nicaraguan—and later even against Somoza. He couldn't stomach the new "General" Somoza, who had been the ward of his uncle, but neither could he take him seriously. He handed Tacho three hundred dollars with instructions to go to the war minister's home and remain there until the troubles were over. He might get hurt otherwise. Instead Somoza took the money and went to Costa Rica where he represented the Liberal rebels, from a safe distance.

When United States authorities attempted to negotiate an end to the fighting between the Liberals and Conservatives in October 1926, Tacho was quick to return to Nicaragua. He attached himself to General Moncada's staff and soon assumed importance beyond his years because of the easy manner in which he could communicate with the Americans. On August 27, 1926, the Marines had landed at Bluefields to protect "American lives and property."

The United States Marines were in Nicaragua in force again. When the United States became a world power after the Spanish-American War it began to concern itself with territorial prerogatives in policy toward Latin America. The point was to keep European powers out of the area. While the ostensible reason for American intervention was to protect American lives and property and the rights of United States creditors, the main concern was maintaining security in the Caribbean and Central America. That meant keeping in power governments that were favorable to United States interests.

Each time the United States intervened in Latin America the invaded country's strategic proximity to the Panama Canal was cited. Also publicized, virtually to the point of preaching missionary work, was the fact that the country's finances would be reorganized and a responsible armed force created to ensure democracy and constitutional order. The United States Marine Corps became pistol-packing zealots carrying the faith to the infidels. Ironically, the Marines' actual legacy to Nicaragua was one of the most long-lived repressive regimes in Latin American history.

The Marines stayed only briefly at Bluefields in 1926. After Chamorro was overthrown, Díaz was installed. It was at Díaz's urging that the Marines returned again on January 6, 1927, appearing in Managua at the renewed outbreak of the Liberal uprising.

Tacho's real chance came when President Calvin Coolidge sent former Secretary of War Henry L. Stimson to resolve the Nicaraguan crisis. Stimson arrived on April 15, 1927. After meeting Tacho, the American noted in his diary how impressed he was by Tacho's manners, his friendly disposition and his English. So he took Somoza in tow as a translator. Before long, the young Nicaraguan was so closely identified with American interests that he was called "El Yanqui."

Tacho learned a lot from the Marines and from Stimson. Handsome, smiling, bowing from the waist, Somoza was the perfect Latin gentleman. Tray in hand, he served whiskey to the Zelaya's relatives and other venerable statesmen who in later years he tossed casually into jail for days or weeks at a time.

When Moncada became president in 1928, Tacho again became his personal aide. The new president loved the ladies. Nocturnal visits to homes around town from which husbands were absent were his favorite pastime. When Moncada was being a "good president" in the Marine Corps' eyes (that is, furthering United States policy), the military aide charged with his safety would always be a nice, obliging lieutenant, who would assign a couple of tough boys to drift along behind the president, somewhere in the shadows, to guard the chief executive discreetly. But when the president was "bad" his aide would be Lieutenant Fred Osbourne, a stickler for spit, polish and ceremony. Hardly would Moncada have sneaked into the house of his choice than a couple of platoons of the presidential guard would come clumping down the street, drums beating out their steps. They would stand at parade rest in front of the house while Lieutenant Osbourne, sword at side, slowly paced up and down the street, ready to render presidential honors when a furious Moncada—two steps away from an apoplectic stroke—emerged.

"My God, Tacho," he'd yell at Somoza the next morning, "we've got to do something."

It was Tacho's wife, Salvadora, who came up with the answer—medals. Nice big gold Nicaraguan Legion of Merit medals for the top Marine officers, silver ones for the majors and captains, bronze for lieutenants. For a while they had copper medals for enlisted men, but later gave them certificates—let 'em go out and buy their own medals. Lieutenant Osbourne faded away. Wives of Marine Corps officers were soon coming to Tacho, begging for silver medals instead of bronze ones. They sought his aid in moving their husbands from one post to another. And top officers who had just received gold medals could scarcely turn down a request from the genial Tacho.

Somoza's relationship with the wife of the American minister Matthew Hanna has often been speculated upon. That both Hanna and his wife were seduced by

Tacho's charm is a matter of record. It was certainly an important boost to have Hanna's voice raised in Somoza's favor when a Nicaraguan commander of the guard was being chosen. Tacho's political career flourished as he adroitly exploited opportunities for influence. All these opportunities he pursued for the country's sake, he told Salvadora. Certainly, his star never seemed brighter.

When President Moncada suddenly dismissed him in disgrace the shock, therefore, was all the greater. Somoza had been given $75,000 and sent to the Segovia mountains to repay landowners for property destroyed in revolutionary fighting. A misunderstanding arose. When he returned, Moncada greeted him, hot with anger, "Listen, Tacho, you are not a thief, you are a pickpocket. Get out of here."

Somoza went to his mother's San Marcos farm and waited. He had friends to speak for him now—Marine officers and American diplomats. Even old Dr. Debayle, still cold to him personally, went to the president on his behalf. Moncada relented and called him back but exiled him to Costa Rica as a consul. In the end Somoza's command of English restored him to full favor. Moncada needed his talent. He was called back to Managua and made undersecretary for foreign affairs.

In the troublesome days just after a great earthquake destroyed Managua on March 31, 1931, Tacho made himself appear invaluable by fomenting taxi and truck driver strikes, and then demonstrating that he was the only one who could settle them. And during the crisis itself he managed to be helpful as a go-between with the Marines. In six seconds the quake all but flattened the capital. The Casa Presidencial, built in 1929 by President Moncada, was badly damaged. Every telephone, telegraph and electric wire in the city was down. The water main had ruptured. Hundreds lay dead and dying. What was left of the city began to burn. The fledgling National Guard and the United States Marine Corps used dynamite to keep the blaze from spreading from the downtown area and consuming the rest of the city. Even so, the fire burned for five days.

Many believed the destruction was so great that the city was doomed to be forever abandoned. Conservative Granada and Liberal León prepared to battle bloodily again for the right to be the capital. Somehow, probably because of the presence of the Marines, Managua held on.

Somoza's luck continued. His wife's uncle, Juan Bautista Sacasa, was elected president in the fall of 1932. Shortly thereafter, Tacho, with his family, moved into Campo de Marte, the military camp built by President Zelaya in 1903. They lived in an old wooden house that had once been inhabited by Zelaya. Tachito, his son, was only seven and was put in the Instituto Pedagógico run by the Christian Brothers, which was across the street from the Campo de Marte and the Carcel Hormiguero (Ant Hole Prison). There one of his classmates was Pedro Joaquín Chamorro Cardenal, son of the publisher of La Prensa. The Chamorros were Conservatives and at school Tachito and Pedro became rivals. "We fought often and I always beat him. He never forgot and hated me all his life because I won in the schoolyard," Tachito recounted years later.

Tachito became a barracks brat, accustomed to the harsh language of the soldiers and to their servility toward him. The obsequious guardsmen, especially the raw recruits, were his to command. His father, however, was having a little trouble adjusting to military life. But as he was the favored candidate for *jefe director* of the guard, a politically astute guard sergeant, Francisco Gaitán, took Tacho in hand and taught him to salute and to march. For this, when Tacho finally took over power, Gaitán was promoted to colonel and eventually chief of staff of the guard.

With order reestablished to its satisfaction, the United States finally withdrew the last of the Marines from Nicaragua on January 2, 1933. The Marine Corps left Nicaragua two deadly legacies: the National Guard they created and trained and the man who was later referred to as "the last Marine," Anastasio Somoza García (Tacho I), who was immediately appointed *jefe director* of the guard at the age of thirty-seven.

The Marines' departure also left an undefeated revolutionary hero for Latin Americans, Augusto César Sandino, with sympathizers even in the United States. Sandino, a former Liberal forces commander in the revolt against Chamorro in the mid-1920s, had become a top-ranked general under Moncada. In 1927 the young general, born in 1895, began a six-year war against the Marines and what he called the "illegal" National Guard.

By a strange quirk of history, Sandino and Tacho had similiar backgrounds, odd for two people who were ultimately so different. They were virtually the same age and grew up at the same time a few miles apart in the cool, lovely coffee-growing hills south of Managua. Both came from middle-class families—Somoza from a farm near San Marcos, Sandino from the sleepy village of Niquinohomo. There is no evidence that they ever met as children, not even on the train that linked their hometowns with Managua, but it could have happened. They attended the same school in Jinotepe but at different times.

By the time they reached manhood, however, their differences were far more important than their commonalities. Sandino was an idealist and a dreamer. Somoza was a realist and a hustler. Sandino was short and skinny; Somoza was wide and heavy. Sandino was half Indian; Somoza was much whiter. Sandino was illegitimate; Somoza claimed illustrious ancestors. Most important, perhaps, Somoza spoke English and Sandino did not. When the Marines were in Nicaragua and forever after, this made all the difference.

Sandino was a lifelong Liberal and the roots of his fight had nothing to do with anti-Americanism per se—he objected to the Conservative government the United States had put in power. But with the Americans backing the Conservative government, Sandino was forced to fight the Yanks when Moncada, called a Liberal "traitor" by many, became president in 1928. American dominance of Nicaraguan politics finally led Sandino to an explicit rejection of American imperialism and his historic struggle became a working model for guerrilla action by worldwide revolutionary movements for the next fifty years. It also marked the first time American intervention experienced defeat in Latin America.

While Sacasa and Moncada had agreed to a government compromise to end the war, Sandino had not.

Sandino dismissed all the married men in his army and went to the hills. . . . His men reverently called him San Digno (The Worthy Saint). When he went into battle he hung extra cartridge belts around his neck, shined up his puttees and stuck a jungle flower into his shovel-shaped cowboy hat.

The Nicaraguan Government could not stop him. Five thousand U.S. Marines chased him for five years, killed nearly 1,000 of his followers, reported him dead a score of times, but never laid hands on him. U.S. newspapers uniformly called him "bandit." But what Sandino wanted, and what he finally got in January 1933, was the withdrawal of all U.S. Marines from Nicaragua.[4]

Acting on the assumption that they could establish a totally nonpolitical armed force in this politically oriented country, the Americans created the National Guard on May 12, 1927. In theory, the guardsmen were drawn equally from the ranks of Liberals and Conservatives, ensuring that neither got the upper hand, and they were under the command of United States Marine officers. The guard was to be a well-trained, well-armed, internal police force dedicated to preserving law and order and protecting the democratic process. It would thereby become a deterrent to the kind of internal strife that previously had wracked the nation. In reality, the Marines created a monster that was to plague Nicaragua for forty-two years. Under the apt guidance of the Corps' "amigo" Tacho, the guard became known as the "best-armed, best-drilled, worst-conceived, most vicious little army in Central America." The guard adhered to one of its original precepts: it was totally nonpolitical to the end. Its one and only loyalty was to Somoza himself.

In July 1935, Arthur Bliss Lane, the American minister to Nicaragua himself —who had succeeded Hanna in 1934 and had tried to stop Somoza's presidential bid—wrote to Millard Beaulac, who had been the American chargé d'affaires in Managua during the guerrilla conflict. Lane pointed out what a mistake the creation of the guard had been. He referred to the armed force as a "Nicaraguan-North American hybrid" that constituted the "biggest stumbling block to the progress of Nicaragua." He summed up the problem by saying:

> The people who created the National Guard had no adequate understanding of the psychology of the people here. Otherwise they would not have bequeathed Nicaragua with an instrument to blast constitutional procedure off the map. Did it ever occur to the eminent statesmen who created the National Guard that personal ambition lurks in the human breast, even in Nicaragua? In my opinion, it is one of the sorriest examples of our part, of our inability to understand that we should not meddle in other people's affairs.[5]

Tacho inherited the problem of Sandino, who had defied every effort on the part of the Marines to crush him. Refusing to lay down his arms after the Marine-enforced peace accord of 1927, he had taken two hundred men into the hills to become one of the most successful guerrilla fighters in Latin America in this century. Viewing him as an obstacle to United States interests, President Coolidge sent six thousand Marines to Nicaragua with the orders: "Get Sandino dead or alive."[6]

In his first battle against the Marines at Ocotal on the morning of July 16, 1927, Sandino learned a lesson that was to profit him throughout his campaign. He had ordered his two-hundred-man force to attack the Marines, who, armed with rifles and machine guns, were barricaded behind the strong adobe walls of the city hall buildings. The National Guardsmen were behind barricades across the plaza. Although the guerrillas had the advantage of numbers—two hundred men plus a large group of sympathizing townspeople who fought on their side against the thirty-nine Marines and forty-eight guardsmen—they were unable to breach the defenses of their enemy.

Three all-out attempts to take the heavily fortified positions left the streets strewn with the bodies of Sandinistas. Gradually, the battle settled down to a siege, with both sides holding their ground. Firing continued throughout the morning and into the afternoon. About 2:30 P.M., a formation of five DeHavilland biplanes appeared over Ocotal. The planes formed a column and made reconnaissance flights, quickly locating concentrations of Sandinistas. And then began the first organized dive-bombing attack in history—long before the Nazi Luftwaffe was popularly credited with the "innovation."

One after the other, the planes peeled out of formation at 1,500 feet, fixed machine guns blazing as they dived to 300 feet, where they dropped their bombs. As the planes climbed, the rear gunner mowed down Sandinistas as they scrambled for cover. The air attack lasted only forty-five minutes, but that was enough for the guerrillas, who fled into the surrounding jungles. Sandino lost over a hundred men in this fiasco. Only one Marine was killed, and one was wounded. The guard's casualties were even lighter, only three wounded.

The Battle of Ocotal was the only major defeat that Sandino's troops ever suffered. He learned his lesson well that day. From that time forward, Sandino used "hit-and-run" tactics. The Marines found themselves repeatedly caught in ambushes that lasted only a few minutes. By the time they regrouped to launch a counter-attack, the Sandinistas had vanished. The ambushes were conceived not to destroy the enemy, but to inflict as much damage as possible with minimum risk to the guerrillas. Sandino split up his command into small, fast-moving patrols that could live off the land and sometimes he combined them into large groups to attack outnumbered Marine and guard patrols.

Early on, Sandino recognized the value of good relations with the populace, many of whom were part-time Sandinistas. The people of the countryside kept him supplied with provisions, sheltered his soldiers and most important of all, kept him informed of every move the Marines and guard made. Although the Marines continued to use air power against the guerrillas, they were never again able to inflict much damage. Sandino proved to the world that a "people's army" could resist every effort of the most modern military machine.

As soon as the United States removed its troops from Nicaraguan soil in 1933, President Juan Bautista Sacasa, for whom Sandino had formerly fought, succeeded in making up with the guerrilla leader. But Somoza and the guard were distressed by the terms of the truce, which gave Sandino control of a 36,800-square-kilometer area in the Segovia mountains. The guerrilla leader was allowed to maintain an armed force of 100 men to protect this territory, in which he planned to establish agricultural cooperatives. Sacasa further promised to begin various public works projects in the area and to give the Sandinistas first preference of employment. In addition, the guerrillas were given amnesty for any political or criminal offenses committed since May 4, 1927.

In return, Sandino declared that his crusade for the liberation of Nicaragua was ended, and he officially allowed his army to be disarmed on February 22, 1933. That spring Sandino published a "Manifesto to the Peoples of the Earth and in Particular the People of Nicaragua." In this manifesto he stated his intentions to give "moral support to Sacasa during his administration" but declared that he was "independent of the government."

The National Guard could not forgive Sandino for remaining undefeated. Tacho could not forget that Sandino was a threat to all of his ambitions. Relations between the two deteriorated rapidly after August 20, when the guard opened fire on Sandinistas who were driving cattle near Yali. Five Sandinistas, all of them well within their own territory, were killed and one guardsman was wounded. Somoza said officially that the incident was a mistake and ordered the guard to cooperate with the Sandinistas in maintaining order and peace in the area. But, said Tacho, the Sandinistas' position of being a state within a state could no longer be tolerated.

Somoza not only opposed issuing Sandino more arms, he demanded that the Sandinistas surrender all weapons to the guard. Sandino replied that he would never turn his guns over to the "unconstitutional" National Guard. He called for the disbanding of the guard, which, he protested, had been created by an act of "foreign intervention." He then suggested that his men protect President Sacasa against all comers, including Somoza and his guard.

By this time Sacasa was living under a state of virtual siege in the Presidential Palace on La Loma, where he had surrounded himself with the presidential guard. Although the president felt that he had more to fear from the National Guard, over which he had no control, than from Sandino, he was still afraid to give Sandino more arms. Tension finally reached such a high level that in February Sacasa invited Sandino to come to Managua to work out an agreement acceptable to both him and the guard.

Sandino was welcomed warmly by Somoza when he arrived on February 16, 1934. By February 21, the ex-guerrilla leader had signed the new agreement and was ready to return to his headquarters in the mountains. Pleased to have everything settled so quickly, President Sacasa gave a farewell dinner at the palace that night in honor of Sandino, who was leaving the capital the next morning.

Accompanied by his co-host of the evening, agriculture minister Sofonias Salvatierra, Sandino drove into the city. When his car came abreast of El Hormiguero prison, a truck blocked the street, and soldiers ordered Sandino, his father, Don Gregorio, his generals Juan Pablo Umanzor and Francisco Estrada and minister Salvatierra out of the car and into the building. Across the street in the Campo de Marte, where he was attending a poetry recital, Somoza refused to accept a call from

Sandino. Sandino's fate had already been sealed. Along with his two generals, he was taken by truck to the nearby airfield and executed. From the prison Don Gregorio and Salvatierra heard the shots.

Sandino's brother Socrates was less trusting. When soldiers arrived that same evening to arrest him at Salvatierra's house, where he was spending the night, he resisted. Killed along with Socrates was Salvatierra's brother-in-law, Rolando Murillo.

The next morning, the official announcement stated simply that after he left the Presidential Palace, unknown men had fallen upon Sandino and machine-gunned him to death.

> The death of Sandino, hero and symbol of Latin Americans' resentment against what they call "The Colossus of the North," sent a pang of sorrow and dismay from the Rio Grande to the Horn.[7]

Somoza admitted that he had issued the order to have Sandino murdered after receiving the approval of the American minister. The minister hotly denied any involvement in the plot and the State Department issued a statement disclaiming any part in Sandino's death.

Tacho wasted little time in ruthlessly destroying the now leaderless Sandinista movement. The very next morning a large guard force attacked the Sandinistas' stronghold in the mountains.

The guerrilla problem was quickly solved, and Somoza now gave full attention to plotting ways and means by which he could become the new president. His first move was to have part of the constitution rewritten so that he could legally be elected in November. Later he formally resigned his post as head of the guard for the same purpose, although all orders still originated with him.

By the time Somoza felt strong enough to move against Uncle Juan, the country was no longer upset. The Nicaraguan upper class was happy to be rid of the bothersome guerrilla Sandino, who had disrupted business and destroyed their property; Sacasa had proven a weak and ineffectual leader. The only armed forces still loyal to the president were the presidential guard stationed at La Loma and a garrison of troops commanded by Major Ramón Sacasa, the president's cousin, at Fortín de Acosasco in León.

On May 29, 1936, Tacho led two thousand handpicked guard troops to León and surrounded the *fortín*. Somoza demanded the immediate surrender of the garrison. Major Sacasa refused. A flurry of messages was exchanged between Managua and the *fortín*. The president ordered Somoza to withdraw his troops and return to the capital. Tacho's response to the order was an order of his own—his troops attacked the fort.

Sunday morning, May 31, in Managua the guns at the Campo de Marte shattered the silence; a few shots flew up to La Loma in the direction of the Presidential Palace. One of the guns on La Loma responded. On a golf course between the two rival power centers, a few Americans and Nicaraguans crouched in the sandtraps, waiting until a legation car, flying the United States flag, drove in and took them out.

All day the guns fired back and forth, taking care not to hit anything. By nightfall Juan Bautista Sacasa had agreed to an informal armistice in Managua, but fighting continued in León.

Then, tiring of the delay, Tacho announced that if the *fortín* at León did not halt all resistance immediately, he would order the guard to attack the Presidential Palace. Sacasa was beaten. He submitted his formal resignation on June 6. Julián Irías was appointed acting president.

Irías lasted three days. On June 9, 1936, Somoza's choice, Dr. Carlos Brenes Jarquín, was appointed interim president until the November elections, in which Tacho stood as the candidate of the Nationalist Liberal party, which he founded as an offshoot of the old Liberal party. The elections made Tacho's control over Nicaragua legal. He became president on January 1, 1937.

CHAPTER 2

Tacho I

Friend and foe watched in awe as Tacho Somoza began manipulating power from the nation's highest office on January 1, 1937, something he would become proficient at during the next decade. He resigned from the presidency, but first appointed an acting president for the interim period: himself. Then he had the constitution rewritten and new elections called. He was re-elected with 99 percent of the vote for a longer term of office: eight years.

He sent his son Tachito to St. Leo's Prep School near Tampa, Florida, for a short time before enrolling him at La Salle Academy on Long Island, New York, along with his brother, Luis. In Tampa Tachito met his first cousin and future wife, Hope Portocarrero. She was six years old. He was ten.

Two years later, in the first week of May 1939, Tacho and Yoya made an historic trip to Washington, D.C. It was to be the high point of Somoza's rule. He used the trip repeatedly to underline his closeness to Washington. Although President Franklin Delano Roosevelt gave the chunky general what was described as the swankiest military reception in Washington history, it was, in fact, just a dress rehearsal for the visit of royalty, King George and Queen Elizabeth of England. "The fact that it was a rehearsal did in no manner diminish its splendor for the Somozas—and the notion that they came before the royal couple added pleasure. It was as handsome a performance as a Latin American heart could desire, a gesture that was intended to honor all Good Neighbors as well as Nicaragua."[1]

President Roosevelt received a State Department memo briefing him on Somoza. It elicited the famous comment, also applied to dictator Rafael Trujillo of the Dominican Republic, "He's a sonofabitch, but he's ours."

For years, Tacho told stories about the time he slept in the White House. United States taxpayers paid for his fare from New Orleans to Washington to New York's World Fair and back. In return, Somoza gave FDR a complete issue of Nicaraguan stamps and an eight-foot-long table, inlaid with a design of Nicaraguan hardwoods and gold depicting Teddy Roosevelt and a map of the Panama Canal, and FDR and a much larger map of Nicaragua and the proposed canal there.

Tacho addressed the United States Congress and urged authorization of the construction of a Nicaraguan canal as a continental defense measure. When a representative denounced him as a "South American dictator," Tacho brushed the epithet off with customary good humor.

Somoza returned to Nicaragua with more than pleasant memories. He had the stamp of approval of FDR, father of the Good Neighbor Policy, and two million dollars in credit from Roosevelt—arranged by the Bank of Manhattan Company and guaranteed by the Export-Import Bank. As to being a dictator, Tacho said, "I once told FDR about democracy in Central America. Democracy down here is like a baby —and nobody gives a baby everything to eat right away. I'm giving 'em liberty— but in my style. If you give a baby a hot tamale, you'll kill him."[2]

Tacho Somoza came to power after the Depression had eased in its worldwide effect. Business was booming, even in this backward Central American nation. Coffee, cattle, rice and lumber prices were high. A Good Neighbor health project and the Pan American highway poured dollars into Nicaragua, now something of a client-state of the United States.

For thirteen-year-old Tachito and his fifteen-year-old brother Luis at La Salle on Long Island, the fallout from their father's reception by FDR made them into lifelong disciples of Roosevelt. Overnight, they grew in stature before their class-mates, no longer just rich and spoiled sons of some banana republic dictator, no longer hailed as "spics," as Tachito later in life reported some Americans had called them.

As the major countries of the world were either preparing for war or already at war, President Somoza announced: "I consider every Nicaraguan aviator and soldier as a potential fighting man for the U.S."[3] The United States constructed large airfields at Managua and Puerto Cabezas and a naval base at the port of Corinto. The men who manned them contributed more cash to the country's economy.

All this was a disaster for ordinary Nicaraguans—it drove prices up far beyond their means. But for the small upper class and the politicians, these were good times.

The war offered a golden opportunity for Tacho. At the beginning of World War II, all German and Italian properties were seized and auctioned. Julio Balke, a German, owned choice real estate around Managua, and owed $150,000 to the Bank of London. Tacho sent guardsmen to the National Bank of Nicaragua to withdraw $150,000, which was placed in a steel box and taken to the auction. The guardsmen kept other bidders for the Balke land away, and by paying the minimum outstanding debt, Somoza added property worth a million to his private fortune. He never paid the $150,000 back to the National Bank of Nicaragua.

He bought Montelimar, an estate stretching twenty miles along the Pacific and deep enough inland to embrace forty thousand acres, for $9,000. Nobody else wanted it. Nobody else had the government machinery to build roads and railroads to it, or the pull to buy a sugar refinery in Cuba and an alcohol distillery in Honduras for a quarter of their worth, and have them transported free of charge to Nicaragua by companies anxious to please the boss.

Tacho could boast that there were more millionaires in Nicaragua than there had ever been. They should, he told them, love him. But they hated him more than any president before him. The main reason was that Somoza had made himself the wealthiest of all. His starting salary as head of the National Guard had been forty-eight dollars a month. In just a few short years, Nicaragua was his, lock, stock and barrel. Before long, he could smugly report that nice things befall the presidents of Nicaragua in the course of events. One of those nice things was the way in which the whole country came across financially.

" 'Coming across' has always been the leitmotif of the Somoza regime. Cattlemen pay through import and export levies, marketing and slaughtering licenses. Gold-mine operators pay through special 'taxes.' Those who deal in mahogany, cinchona bark, milk, hides, tallow, cement and liquor pay in devious but nonetheless painful ways. Nicaraguans quip about an alphabetical list of Somoza rackets running from A to Z; they say that X stands for rackets unknown to the public."[4]

Tacho included the family in his get-rich and hold-power schemes. He brought his brother Julio into the National Guard, where he was eventually given the rank of colonel. Julio, who died in 1944, was an arbitrary man with a reputation for having "*malas pulgas*," "bad fleas"—meaning quick to take offense and quick to retaliate. When he spotted an article in the newspaper *Estrella de Nicaragua* that he didn't like, he canceled the offending newsman's license. When he was head of the department of Carazo, he gave orders that people considered his enemies were not to be permitted to enter the Jinotepe movie theater, the major public diversion of the city.

Tachito at age sixteen was named second lieutenant of the guard, in preparation for his appointment to United States Military Academy at West Point. In July 1942 he received his captain's bars and was named military instructor with the first presidential battalion, a title he carried when he entered West Point in 1942.

Tacho suppressed a student and citizen antigovernment demonstration in 1944 by shooting some and putting more than two hundred others in jail. When the society women of Managua marched to protest the arrest of their sons and husbands, Tacho kept the guard in the barracks and sent a mob of prostitutes against the protesters. "They pressed around the horrified ladies, slapped them and spat at them."[5] The march broke up in confusion and later Somoza invited one of the madams of a cut-rate brothel to the Presidential Palace as a reward for services rendered. "I played this by ear," Tacho later explained. "I don't really like to arrest these people. Their wives and mothers come up here begging me to let them out and sometimes I have to loan them money to tide them over. But this is the way you run a country like this."

In 1946, *The New York Times* reported:

> It had been agreed between Nicaragua and the U.S. that the Corinto naval base would be turned over to Nicaragua after the war. Surplus vehicles, furniture, plumbing, medical supplies, etc., which the Foreign Liquidation Commissioner had priced at $106,400, had accumulated on the base.
>
> Under the original terms, the Nicaraguan government had an option to purchase. President Somoza said he wished to take up the option, but asked, in view of the

country's need for foreign exchange, whether the U.S. would accept a piece of land. He knew, of course, that the United States wanted a new site for its embassy, which is situated in rented quarters.

The site was agreed upon and the property formally evaluated at $106,400 or $14 a square vara (33.06 square inches).

President Somoza then went to Carlos Palazio, owner of the property, and, as a private buyer, squeezed it from him at $2 a square vara.

He then resold the property to his Government at the price agreed upon.[6]

Foreign gold mining firms and lumber concessionaires found ways to help the president against the day he should retire. Somoza said he got a lot of good properties by "smart" buying. "My father taught me that it was wiser to buy from the heirs," he grinned. "They rarely know the true value of their inheritance." He applied this advice to the British-owned La Fundadora plantations. "I offered the heirs the first silly price that popped into my head, $25,000. Then I added $800 to make it look serious. By God, those people in England didn't know what they had. They took my offer, and I'm sure the $800 did it. The first year's crop brought me $28,000."[7]

Tacho had a lot of schemes. He smuggled cattle into Costa Rica until the 1948 revolution there stopped that. Then he cornered the meat market. No one could move cattle without a government permit. These were very slow in coming, so a desperate rancher usually wound up selling his stock to Somoza at low prices. Tacho then exported the cattle via government aircraft and made a tremendous profit.

In the summer of 1946, Tachito, a trim twenty-one-year-old captain, returned from three years at West Point to begin his military career at Campo de Marte. A month after his return he was promoted to the rank of major, the youngest ever in the guard. Even though Luis had gone into the study of agronomy at Louisiana State University, he also was commissioned by his father in the guard. But Luis always showed more interest in cows than in the Campo de Marte.

Tachito returned from the discipline of the Point to a slipshod dictatorship which his father was running out of his pocket. After the exciting World War jitterbug days in the United States, Managua was a "very dull place." Tachito suffered culture shock in those early months. After the spic and span of West Point, he was appalled at the slovenly Campo de Marte. Even though Tachito eventually learned to accept the situation, the decade spent in the United States during the formative years from eleven to twenty-one left a deep imprint on him. Spanish had become his second language. He came home thinking and acting like an American. "Except for four years all my studies were in the U.S. and I knew the U.S. better than my own country," he recalled in an interview years later. His values and interests were American, which didn't ingratiate him with the officer corps of the guard. The guard brass saw him as an upstart, quick-tempered, spoiled and *muy creido* (presumptuous). While many of these same officers had attended American military courses and were Marine-trained, they didn't all believe in the superiority of United States military tradition, having witnessed the Corps' inability to defeat Sandino. But they were careful not to voice their feelings lest Tacho react against them. In those days, a few recalled years later, "Tachito would have been happier to have continued his career in the United States."

Tachito, just beginning to learn the business, had come home from West Point full of ideas about the nonpolitical nature of a good army. That nonsense was quickly drilled out of his head.

> Tachito once said, "Papa, you had better abandon the Presidency while the leaving is good. The people are in an ugly mood, and we have enough money."
>
> Papa, furious, struck Tachito, shouting, "Remember, as an officer of the National Guard you're under military discipline. I'll put you under arrest."
>
> Salvadora, the President's wife, intervened. Cried she, "Don't strike him for speaking the truth. If your own family can't tell you what's going on, who will?"
>
> Said daughter Lilian, "He's right—I've just come from the U.S. and the atmosphere is most hostile."
>
> Tachito was not arrested.[8]

Tacho loved the bawdy side of life. He could hear the mounting anger against him coming out of his radio. In hot and sticky Managua the radio stations kept their windows wide open. Consequently all broadcasting was accompanied by the noises of the street outside. Frequently hot and foul arguments floated in from the sidewalks and into the microphones. More and more Tacho heard sudden shouted references to himself—juicy, uncomplimentary references.

He replied with his own accusations. The opposition, he declared, was busy buying arms abroad, with dollars taken out of Nicaragua. This had an adverse effect on the economy. To save the economy, he would sell the opposition all the arms it wanted from the National Guard stores—and for córdobas.[9]

But sometimes things got beyond him. He promised the attractive young wife of one of his foes that her husband would be out of jail by nightfall. He wasn't. Salvadora had seen her coming from his office. Nicaragua was very much a family business. The high command of the Somoza dictatorship was always Tacho and Salvadora.

One visitor at the beginning of 1947 noted that the Nicaraguan people were so poor and ill fed that, to keep them in place, all it took were some two thousand guardsmen armed with sharp bayonets to stick them occasionally. Ailing bank accounts were becoming endemic. Over the years Somoza had muscled in on every economic activity in the nation. After only ten years in office, his private fortune was estimated at $120 million.

There was significant opposition to his rule. General Emiliano Chamorro spent more than a year in Guatemala trying to get a revolution going against Somoza. No one had a better right. From the days of old Fruto, a hundred years before, the Chamorro family had dominated Nicaraguan revolutions. After an unhappy beginning—as a youth Emiliano had been forbidden to eat at the table with his brothers because the cook, not his father's wife, called him son—he had carried the family name farther than any of the others. He had exceeded Fruto himself, the first

Chamorro president of Nicaragua; Alejandro, chief of the Conservative supremacy; Pedro Joaquín and Diego Manuel, both presidents. Emiliano had led sixteen revolutions.

Don Emiliano was the last of the true *caudillos*, a leader by the sheer force of his personality. The Nicaraguan peasants believed him blessed by God. They were convinced that if the general pressed a certain spot on his neck, he could walk invisible among his enemies. After ten years of exile from the country, he could still remember their names when he met them, and even the illnesses their wives had suffered. That was the reason that, when Conservative leaders gathered, they spoke very tentatively, for in the end, just one vote counted, Don Emiliano's. Don Emiliano spoke for the peasants and without them the Conservative party was just a small group of wealthy families.

"I'm a pacifist—in the newspapers. I am also a fatalist—what comes, will come." Privately, the old general went a good deal further. "We voted Somoza out of office and our votes weren't counted. We watched Somoza throw his own fraudulently elected president out of office and the other nations of the world did nothing. Now we must act for ourselves." Once General Chamorro had but to be in this mood and a revolution would have popped up almost automatically.[10]

In January 1947, he was ready. More than $20,000 had been invested in acquiring rifles, hand grenades, submachine guns. They were tucked away in two gasoline trucks and started on their journey through Mexico to meet the little boat that would carry them on to Nicaragua's east coast, traditionally the revolutionary starting point. This was, more or less, the way one went about it; that was the way it had been done in 1908 and 1912. But this time the Mexican police grabbed the whole cargo just south of Mexico City. The revolution was nipped in the bud.

In 1947, at the end of his eight-year term, constitutionally unable to stand for reelection, Tacho once again proved himself an apt political contortionist. His actions, once again, kindled old political emotions. Nothing in Nicaraguan history has been so hotly denied nor more substantially true than that Tacho made a deal when he nominated the crusty old goateed Liberal Leonardo Argüello for president. In the February elections, Somoza declared him the winner despite the fact that more than 75 percent of the people voted against him and in favor of the Conservative candidate.

The plan was for Somoza to continue as head of the National Guard, staffing its key posts with his most trusted officers. When all was arranged, Tacho would leave the country for a long-delayed operation at the Mayo Clinic in Rochester, Minnesota, temporarily placing his interests in the hands of trusted officers. (Tachito was too young to take over and hold the realm together.)

Meanwhile two distinguished exiles had returned. Old General Chamorro was first. Then came the dark, burly, independent Liberal party leader, General Carlos Pasos.

Pasos, once a good Somoza man and like him a Liberal, fell out with the dictator in 1944. Nicaragua, Pasos felt, could do with a little more democracy; after a time the Liberals called a convention to talk about it. Some of the cautious ones went to Tacho to get his views. They got them. "Tell Carlos Pasos that I know that twice last night at the home of Castro Wassmer he read the speech he has prepared, and if he insists on reading it at the convention, let him not forget to come armed. I am not the man to let myself be overthrown by speeches. There'll certainly be some gunplay there."[11]

There was no gunplay, because Pasos did not make his speech. He went to jail for three weeks instead, and was later exiled.

Argüello was inaugurated on May 1, 1947. On May 2, he began reorganizing the National Guard, shipping Somoza's buddies to outlying posts. He in effect slapped Somoza's face by sending Tachito, the inspector general and commander of the presidential guards, to the province of León. On May 6, Argüello announced his appointees for the cabinet, eight of whom had voted against him in the election and whose politics ranged from mild to outright anti-Somoza. He kept his promise and made Somoza head of the guard, but every time Tacho transferred a second lieutenant, Argüello countermanded the order. The president seemed to ignore the fact that Somoza was literally sitting atop the only official arms depot in the nation.

The cellar beneath the guard officers' club, which Somoza converted into his La Curva Palace, was stacked to the ceiling with arms and ammunition. The only thing that held Tacho in check was what he and every other Nicaraguan believed to be a fact: Chamorro and Pasos, unarmed at the time of the February elections, now had support.

Somoza steamed with rage. His guard, the best so-called military force between Mexico and Panama, and supposedly utterly loyal to him, was beginning to break up. Among the officers, men were being identified as Somocistas, Argüellistas and legalistas. The last group was composed of the worried majority who wished some way could be found around the problem. Tacho started calling in his officers, demanding personal pledges of loyalty. He failed to keep appointments, charging that plots were afoot to kill him. Then Argüello issued an order giving Tacho twenty-four hours to get out of the country. Somoza called the Casa Presidencial pleading for seventy-two hours, and was asked to step up the hill and talk it over. That was an appointment he failed to keep; he claimed eight machine guns had been planted in the bushes in front of the house to kill him. There were reports that a plane was warmed up at the airport ready to hustle him out of the country, which was really what Argüello wanted.

Somoza became more uncertain and worried as the crisis mounted. On Friday, May 23, 1947, he made known his intention of leaving the country. But there could be no guarantees sufficiently strong for General Somoza to leave the country voluntarily. He required not only guarantees for his life and property, but also guarantees that the National Guard, the railroad workers and other governmental employees would continue to work his ranches. Profits would depend on that.

So on Saturday, he called in the Conservatives and urged them to join him in a revolution against Argüello. Tacho warned them that the president was appointing Pasos's men to key guard posts and argued that soon Pasos would be controlling the armed forces. Every move Tacho made was promptly reported to the president, even the fact that he, Somoza, had ten million córdobas (two million dollars) stashed away with the ammunition in the cellar.

Sunday night the cabinet met to discuss the situation. Some were worried, but not aged Argüello. "The cards are stacked against Somoza and he knows it," the president said. "He'll quietly leave the country tomorrow."

Then the president went to bed.

That night, apparently on an impulse, Somoza struck. Tacho led twenty-five men to the Palacio de Communicaciones and seized the telephone and telegraph offices. Then, supported by one medium tank, he ordered his men to take the National Palace. The men on duty there were sitting around talking to their commander. When they looked outside they saw the cannon on the tank pointing at the building. They all surrendered without a fight, save the twenty-seven-year-old commander. This worthy officer rushed out the back door and took cover in the Guatemalan embassy.

With a radio microphone in one hand to instruct the tank crew and a telephone in the other to demand surrenders, Somoza directed his little army about the city, taking one potential resistance point after another. By 3:00 A.M. he had Congress in session to declare Argüello mentally incompetent and had the entire two-thousand-man National Guard on the roads moving into Managua, where there were córdobas for some officers, threats for others, and praise for a few. Then Tacho went up the hill and woke up President Argüello to tell him he had joined the ranks of the unemployed. He would, however, house him—in a cell in "the hole," the dungeon in the presidential offices.

Elsewhere in the city people of influence were sprinting to the nearest foreign legation. Among those on the run were the chief of staff of the guard, the police chief of Managua and various cabinet ministers.

By daylight, Tacho had raked in all the chips. He had wagered his life on a long shot and won. Not one bullet had been fired, not one drop of blood had been shed. He had realized the big risk he was taking but the stakes were high—control of the country. Somoza walked away from the table with Nicaragua in his pocket—again.

Somoza did bow to pressure from the entire diplomatic corps in Managua to free Argüello. The stubborn old president, who took refuge in the Mexican embassy, refused to resign and refused to leave Nicaragua. He sent Tacho a bold note saying, "I would rather die like Sandino [murdered on orders from Somoza] than like Sacasa [who died in bed in exile]." But in the end, Argüello did die in bed in exile in Mexico in December 1947.

Political liberty? Nicaraguans had been free to vote as they liked in the election in February 1947, but it was Somoza who decided that the man who lost at the ballot box was actually the winner. "When asked about charges that he had tyrannized Nicaragua, Tacho replied: 'These little countries are like children. When a boy's sick, you've got to force castor oil down him whether he likes it or not. After he's been to the toilet a few times he'll be all right.' "[12]

Tacho had forced President Leonardo Argüello down Nicaragua's throat, then sugarcoated the affair by decking Managua out splendidly for the inauguration. The

Vatican and even far-off Poland sent delegations to the inauguration. Twenty-six days later Somoza chased Argüello out of the Presidential Palace and into exile in Mexico.

All through the 1947 summer, old General Emiliano Chamorro had watched Somoza's struggle from the wide veranda of the Managua Club, overlooking the Plaza de Armas. The situation was unstable politically and economically. People were not paying their bills. Dollars which a few months earlier had cost five córdobas on the black market were now up to twelve. Now and then old Chamorro probed to see how shaky Tacho's hold was. His friends raided guard outposts for arms. They even persuaded a few guardsmen to abandon their posts and take to the hills. But mostly Chamorro just sat on the veranda and smiled. When asked if he planned an all-out drive to oust Somoza, the old general's only answer was "maybe."

Before the year was over, Tacho had installed two more puppet presidents. The first new president was Lacayo Sacasa, a fat, florid man with a fringe of white hair who poured sweat as he lolled in comfortable liquidity in the same chair from which Somoza had ruled the nation. To a few friends who dropped in to help pass the sticky hours he remarked that his power was increasing daily—now that he, Sacasa, was boss, Somoza was sending a car for his very own use and he would no longer have to depend on taxis or horse-drawn coaches. A few soldiers of the presidential guard —not many, but a few—were beginning to recognize him and salute him as he passed. His great laugh rolled through the almost empty Casa Presidencial as he told how people downtown were calling him "La Muñeco Gordito" (the fat puppet).[13]

But no one was taking President Lacayo Sacasa seriously, least of all President Lacayo Sacasa. The great political winds that had blown him from his comfortable home and rolled him up the hill to the Presidential Palace were still blowing and might send him back at any minute. However, he felt comfortably sure that no matter how the storm raged, his bulky padding and engaging good humor would save him any unpleasant consequences. Meanwhile, though he might well have been checked into "the hole" or even been shot, since the boss was pretty jittery, he was content to play president.

Sacasa was not the only fake in Nicaragua at the time. There was the boss himself. He was described as tired, nervous and with great dark circles under his eyes, but he had never looked so strong.

At 3:00 A.M. on May 26, Somoza woke President Lacayo Sacasa from a sound sleep, informed him that he had just ceased to be president and sent the ex-president down to "the hole" to finish his nap.

By taking over the government of his successor by force Tacho placed the United States in an awkward position. To recognize Somoza's regime would be to condone an irresponsible and undemocratic coup. But to refuse to recognize him would mean a departure from the general diplomatic practice of recognizing any government that was clearly in power and that promised to live up to its international obligations.[14]

The United States decided on a course of nonrecognition, as did most nations, hoping that international disapproval might force Tacho to hold new elections.

Instead, Somoza placed another puppet in the Presidential Palace, this time one he was sure he could control: his favorite uncle, Víctor Román y Reyes, who had sent him to school in the United States.

> Dictator Anastasio Somoza passed the word: one nation after another was recognizing the government of his uncle, President Víctor Román y Reyes, which he put in power last August without an election. He listed them: Costa Rica, Honduras, the Dominican Republic of Fellow-Dictator Rafael Leonidas Trujillo, Brazil, Bolivia, Peru, Paraguay. If enough of the American republics gave him the right hand of fellowship, he felt that the U.S. would follow. That would again make him a member in good standing in the Pan American nations' club.
>
> Tacho was right about Costa Rica, Honduras and Trujillo land, but the other countries hastily denied any such intentions. At week's end, the Foreign Office lamely admitted that it had all been a mistake. Tacho had cabled New Year's greetings to the American republics and when Brazil, Bolivia, Peru and Paraguay sent him best wishes in return, he had mistaken them for notes of recognition.[15]

Maurice Berbaun, the young United States chargé d'affaires in Nicaragua at the time, asked Tachito, "When is your father leaving?" Tachito weepingly related the question to his father. Tacho called Berbaun on the phone and said, "This is my country. Where do you want me to go? You come and take me out." When Berbaun left Nicaragua he gave Somoza a signed photo which read: "To the most able politician I have known, with all my admiration."

By September Chamorro was set for a second try at revolution. The rebel tradition was that with a few men and a few arms one could capture a small outpost, and then a still larger one, until finally one rode triumphantly into the capital. The first outposts were carefully selected—Nuelle de Bueyes, in the Bluefields area, and La India mine, across the lake from Managua. At these places it turned out that tradition had not taken into account a defending general who so expected his small outposts to be taken that he left them poorly armed. Nor did tradition consider the use of airplanes and trucks that moved whole platoons of well-armed troops against small forces before they could establish momentum. So some of Chamorro's men died; many more went to prison. Another uprising was aborted.

The autumn of 1947 found loud political rumblings along the line of little volcanic countries stretching southward from Mexico. In Nicaragua, Somoza, supported by only a hard core of the guard, most of whose officers felt that their personal fortunes and their very lives depended on his fate, faced a powerful coalition of rival *caciques*. In Guatemala, Juan José Arévalo, the Liberal reformer, still had the backing of the overwhelming majority of common people, but was confronted with trouble from the armed forces.

In Managua, Somoza struck savagely. Pedro José Zepeda, at one time Sandino's emissary to Mexico, was clapped into jail. So were most of the town's leading newspapermen, including Dr. Pedro Joaquín Chamorro of *La Prensa*.

"You know I have been good to my foes," Tacho said, his eyes dancing. "You know I wish General Chamorro well out of the country." He laughed, then shot a quizzical glance and asked, "Tell me, do you really believe Chamorro would run this place one bit differently than I run it?"[16]

Unlike Chamorro, Tacho delighted in cheap, gaudy things. A jukebox, with all its flashing lights, occupied a place of honor in the reception hall of his palace, next to a fourteen-foot stuffed alligator on the floor. His favorite sport was cockfighting, although he sometimes liked to have a calf thrown into the Tipitapa River and then watch the freshwater sharks fight over it.

Nor was he always happy simply rummaging around in the disorderly pile of papers on his desk, looking for his collection of dirty pictures to show visitors. He sometimes took his cabinet and friends to his ranch to watch bulls servicing cows. They sat on the corral fence and rooted like football fans for a home team defending its own five-yard line.

Callers to Tacho's office were likely to come away a little dazed after hearing two or three specimens from his collection of dirty stories, followed by a good-bye pat on the back with the admonition: "Be good, and if you can't be good, be careful, and if you can't be careful, goddammit, at least be sanitary."

Police state? There were no police in Nicaragua, just the army—but army permits were required to go from one city to another. In Managua in 1948, every street corner was under observation and the movements of all important people were charted. Telephone calls were monitored, private mail was opened, and the local press was under strict censorship. Managua stringers for foreign news organizations not only had facts removed from their stories, but had to stand by when untrue statements were substituted. They were refused the right to inform their editors that dispatches had been tampered with.[17]

Men disappeared from the streets in Nicaragua. They paused briefly at La Aviación prison at the edge of the Taca airfield, just outside Managua, for brutal questioning. Then they were taken to a prison camp on Great Corn Island off the Atlantic coast to nurse their wounds.

On three occasions in 1947 the Nicaraguan equivalents of the National Association of Manufacturers and the United States Chamber of Commerce could have held their meetings at La Aviación—each had a quorum present there. Members were dragged into jail whenever Somoza felt nervous and let out again when he felt better.

Tacho teased the opposition with false reports that the other American republics had decided to recognize Uncle Víctor. He mocked them with false reports that airplanes the opposition had purchased had been seized in the United States. Then Tacho got down to serious business.

From the hill above Managua where he sat in his palace, searchlights swept the city night after night. Machine guns, fired into the lake, clattered warnings. His armored force—three MIs and a Fiat tankette, rumbled about. One night the town echoed with sustained firing from La Aviación. The next morning rumors spread through town: eight prisoners, who were being tortured at the jail, had been lined up and executed the night before. National Guardsmen confessed to their friends that they had seen it. Men close to Somoza whispered that Tachito was the man responsible. In a rage against the prisoners he had lost his head and ordered the executions. By the third day the entire town was convinced of the story, certain that the days when prisoners were put into jail and then either sent to Great Corn Island or released, were gone. The old man on the hill had lost all his geniality and was in a murderous mood.

The shooting at La Aviación was actually occasioned by the escape of Luis H. Scott, an ex-hardware merchant who managed to flee to Guatemala. (Scott had been arrested when a large amount of dynamite was found hidden in his home.)

At La Curva, General Somoza chuckled at the rumors: "Stories that people have been killed are usually more effective than actually killing people," he said. "If you'd like to go out to the prison and count noses you may," he told a visiting newsman. "Except for Luis Scott, who escaped, they are all there." In fact no one had been killed at the prison on that day, although prisoners had been tortured with a device used to give electric shocks to the testicles.

Nicaragua's foreign minister Luis Manuel Debayle paddled around town. A revolution wasn't really necessary, he said. If General Somoza got the correct guarantees for his life and property, he would be willing to leave. Tacho was ill. He needed an operation. He was not enjoying all this tension. Inside and outside of jail, everyone waited for Scott and others from Guatemala City to arrive to overthrow the government.

They never came. Instead, two Liberator aircraft came from the United States. They had been purchased by agents ostensibly for a revolution in Venezuela—the United States had guaranteed that no bombers would be sent to Managua. And from the Dominican Republic, Dictator Rafael Trujillo sent two C-46s loaded down with additional guns for the National Guard. General Chamorro had waited too long—his moment was gone.

The United States had its eyes fixed on Europe, concerned with such things as political liberty, the emergence of police states, the growth of communism, and the persistence of the fascist remnants there. Tacho Somoza, not ungrateful that the United States was involved elsewhere, didn't really worry. "They are like little balls to juggle while walking a slack rope," he explained, referring to political freedoms. "At first you are a little nervous, but after a while you get used to the rope's motion. Then you can do it blindfolded."

Tacho had not been so happy in weeks. Laughter filled the air as Somoza padded around a new blond mahogany table, a gift from officers of the guard. The jukebox and stuffed alligator that had occupied places of honor in the second-floor reception room in his palace in Managua were shoved out of the way, and billiard balls were clicking. The hard-faced armed men who guarded his every move grinned at his triumphant cries when his shots came off and added to his jeers when his son Tachito missed.

Once Somoza flubbed badly and a frown crossed his face, almost immediately to be replaced by a smile. "I wonder what the old gentleman is thinking now?" he cried. The last words of his sentence were almost lost in the laughter of the guards. He meant Chamorro.

A stub-winged two-engine A-20 low-level attack bomber had been sitting on the runway at the Guatemala City airport. There had been a lot of talk about a smashing blow at the very center of Somoza's power, a blow so spectacular that it would persuade a considerable number of wavering, utterly corrupt guard officers to change sides hurriedly. Tacho's intelligence people had relayed the talk to Managua, where Somoza believed it to such an extent that he stopped sleeping in his own bed. He took to staying at different locations nightly, sometimes at friends' homes and at other times at his San Juan ranch. These were the days when Somoza's foreign minister offered gold medals to newsmen in return for their giving the "correct view" of the situation, as Tacho had once given medals to the Marines. As nervous as Tacho was, he kept his eye on all important work. He would delegate a little to Tachito. But only his wife, Salvadora, was part of his political brain trust—no one else was allowed any but the most minor powers. His wife was tough, in her way, and once remarked when Tacho was said to be contemplating quitting, "I prefer to be the widow of a president than the wife of an exile."

No message went through the cable offices without one of the Somozas' signatures; no one spoke on international phones without their people listening. Those were days of repression. A new wave of arrests began with a January raid on a "secret meeting" of the "communist party," actually the Nicaraguan Socialist party (PSN) formed in 1944. Twenty-six persons were taken into custody, including the leader, tall, smooth Armando Armado, the Nicaraguan who once served as secretary to Mexico's famous socialist leader Lombardo Toledano. Somoza cried: "My opponents should remember that we, the *gente decente*, are only 6 percent; if trouble arises, the 94 percent may crush us all."[18]

There were a number of odd facts behind the arrests of the "communists." First, Somoza himself had originally encouraged the creation of the Socialist party in an effort to cut into the Conservative and Independent parties' followings among the city workers and rural people. Tacho used the same tactic with the Fascist blueshirts in the hope that they would split the Conservative leadership lined up against him. Second, as recently as November 1947, Tacho had given the party a printing press and had arranged for the party to receive a loan from the National Bank in return for a promise that it would stand aside in the event that the Conservatives and Independents revolted. But apparently Somoza decided the Socialists were more valuable in jail than outside of it. This mass arrest served to kick off a communist witch-hunt, even though most of the so-called communists happened to be well-known capitalists. One of those jailed used to play poker with Tacho. Every time he lost a pot, he would lean over the table and mutter, "Come the revolution . . ." The repeated remark was evidently not appreciated.

By month's end, Tacho had some three hundred Nicaraguans, mostly prominent citizens, behind bars. Another hundred or so had gone into hiding in foreign embassies. At La Aviación prison a newsman found some seventy-five rather prosperous, usually sleek businessmen jammed into three cells where an open trench served as their toilet. They slept on wooden planks and were filthy from the lack of water. The prisoners numbered among them Carlos Pasos, owner of the country's largest textile mill; Mariano Morales, whose shirt-making company competed with Manhattan in Central America; Salvador Mendieta, the gentle, fuzzy rector of the Free (and only, since Somoza had closed down the other) University of Managua; Carlos Cardenal, merchant and realtor; and Ernesto Salazar, whose air service to outlying mines ran into difficulties when Tacho had his landing fields plowed up. Morales bowed formally and said to the newsman, "Say the word and we will call a meeting of the Chamber of Commerce or the National Association of Manufacturers."

Tacho's land assets, acquired one way or another, began to reach staggering acreage. But Nicaraguans were not too disturbed. By the end of 1947, General Somoza owned everything in sight, except for an airport and two small farms, from Managua to the Tipitapa River. On both sides of the Tipitapa River was his 20,000-acre San Juan cattle ranch. He also owned eighty of the largest pieces of real estate up against the eastern jungles of Nicaragua.

Not until the general began moving in on other businesses did anger begin welling up. Somoza controlled the railroads; ranchers found that if they wanted to move their cattle to market, they had to sell to Tacho. He controlled the ports and through them the country's exports of corn, chicken and rice. "We Nicaraguans are a Spanish and Indian mixture, and that's dynamite," said Tacho. "Give us a finger and we take a hand. Give us a hand and we take an arm."[19]

Wherever Nicaraguans looked, they found the general. He was their partner or their competitor in business, frequently both. His Fábrica Montelimar was the country's largest distillery, he was partner in the only brewery, he owned bars and cafes in every city of the republic. The only factories for the manufacture of soap, perfume, shoe polish and toothpaste belonged to him. Tacho also owned the largest flour mill and the largest bakery. The cement factory, the electric plants in Chinandega, Tipitapa and Bluefields were his. He manufactured transmission belts, ice, ice cream and matches.

It went even further. Somoza's Nicaragua was run like an occupied country. In those days, in most Latin American nations, the army was a phantom force that only became visible when it overthrew the government. It then disappeared back to its bases. The only contact the citizenry had with the men with the guns was when the army decided it was time for another coup d'état. But in Nicaragua, the army was always present. It mixed aggressively into people's lives.

Since the days when the United States Marines began training the incipient National Guard, the guard had been assigned all police duties and therefore doubled as the de facto police force. Its officers, especially the colonels, took their graft where they could find it and any woman of the lower class who happened to strike their fancy. The enlisted men, especially the sergeants, had almost as many rights. A private on the streets of Managua could insult and slap one of the town's leading lawyers and not worry about punishment. When the United States Army pointed out that two enlisted guardsmen were stealing generators from American vehicles, the men were punished—with only four days of double duty.

In typical dictator fashion, Somoza sent two lieutenants of the guard to the Guatemalan embassy in Managua demanding the surrender of two refugees. When the chargé d'affaires refused, even with a pistol stuck in his stomach, to turn over the refugees, he was told that the guard was tired of protecting his legation from the just wrath of the Nicaraguan people and that protection would be withdrawn. That night forty municipal employees in civilian dress attacked the legation. When they found Managua's entire diplomatic corps meeting inside, Somoza called off the attack. Unfortunately it was too late to save one white-suited diplomat from being manhandled. It turned out to be Franco Spain's ambassador to Tacho's government.

Somoza maintained a bizarre sense of humor about his own repressive actions. Once, when a Conservative accosted Tacho at a party and demanded to know why he had been placed under house arrest for two months, Somoza told him, "I did it to please your wife. She told me she couldn't keep you home at night."[20]

Unlike Dominican dictator Trujillo, Somoza killed only as a last resort. A spell in jail usually brought the enemy around. If jail failed, the guard had the little electric device known as *la maquinita* (the little machine). A wire was wrapped around the prisoner's scrotum; if he was stubborn the current was turned on. There were Nicaraguan exiles in Guatemala who cried in their sleep about the "Little Machine." "Oh hell," snorted Tacho, "that damned thing isn't so bad. I've tried it myself— on my hand."[21]

Physically the middle-aged dictator looked undertrained and overstuffed in February 1948. But his boasts about his strength, his horsemanship, his swimming, his farming, his pool-shooting, his poker-playing and his business ability were not altogether idle. When he played cards, he never lost. "It's fantastic the luck I have. . . . It's that way with anything I want to try—I'm the champ. I'm the champ shot of the Guardia Nacional, didja know that? Pistol or rifle. Jeez, I never miss, it seems."[22]

Though recurrent malaria and stubborn amoebae in his intestines had put Somoza past his physical peak, he still set a tough pace. At parties he had begun limiting himself to three scotch and sodas, but he could still shake a light foot in the rumba, tango, bolero or samba. If he felt like it, he would dance the whole night through at La Curva, then adjourn the party to a Somoza ranch for another six or eight hours.

Tachito did a little sparring in the guard and even acted as second during a boxing match in 1948, which pleased his sports-loving father. The younger Somoza was doing his best to ingratiate himself with veteran officers of the guard, but they still didn't trust him. He was having difficulty managing them, even though he drank with them and went with them to the best brothels as just one of the boys.

Tacho was up each morning around six, breakfasting on steak and cornflakes while aides read him guard telegrams and reports on the country. After that, he went to a desk piled high with guard business and with his own business affairs, mainly cattle and coffee.

Tacho spent hours talking with pleaders, politicians and hangers-on. If he agreed to a proposal he would give the order then and there for it to be carried out. If he said he would think it over, he would forget about it. If he asked for a memo, he would never read it.

When his office work was done, he would go to check on his Mercedes ranch down the lakeshore from Managua. "I'm no *político*," Tacho claimed, without batting an eyelash. "I'm a farmer."[23] Tacho loved to make that claim. His son, Tachito, was to utter the same phrase to the author thirty years later.

In the late 1940s, the son of one of Lyndon Johnson's lawyers met a Nicaraguan student at the University of Texas in Austin who was the Nicaraguan consul as well as a student and bartender, the latter a task at which he spent most of his time. United States companies were then just beginning heavy prospecting, and the youths tried to work up a plan to get an interest in some oil leases in Nicaragua and make a quick fortune. They finally hit on the idea of bringing Somoza to Austin and treating him as guest of honor. Although they could not make him an honored guest of the city or give him a key to the city, they had political ties in the Texas state capital and they compiled fancy printed books and other memorabilia to give the general. Tacho accepted the invitation eagerly.

When Tacho arrived at the Austin city limits aboard a train, the youths met him with a caravan of Cadillac convertibles and other cars and drove him into town. Tacho was resplendent in a white uniform with the presidential sash draped over his shoulder. He was wined and dined for days at parties and lake outings.

One of the secretaries at the Austin *American Statesman* newspaper who had spent most of her time helping organize details of Somoza's visit wanted to meet the president. It was agreed. She was blond and good-looking, and Somoza was persuaded to see her over dinner one night in his hotel. Late the following day the Texan hosts went to see what had happened to the general in his hotel and encountered weary guards outside Somoza's door. They asked what had happened, where was Somoza? "He's still in his room," one of the guards replied. "That damned blonde went in there last night and they haven't left since."

The general finally left Austin but, because of later personal fallings-out, the boys never got their lease to search for oil in Nicaragua.

CHAPTER 3

Assassination

By the end of February 1948, talk of guarantees for Tacho to quit were forgotten. "It took," Tacho bragged repeatedly, "twenty thousand lives for the Liberals to get into power. It will take forty thousand to get us out of here." The Somoza dynasty was securely established.

The early 1950s were good years for the Somozas. When Uncle Víctor died, Tacho felt so secure that he did not even bother with an ornamental president. He assumed the title again.

The war was on in Korea. President Truman's interest in Latin America was scant. Tacho used his credentials as the friend of FDR at every opportunity. He sometimes forgot that Republicans didn't share his enthusiasm for the New Deal leader. He named the main street of Managua Roosevelt Avenue and at the beginning of this avenue built a monument honoring the United States president. A small bronze plaque at the base read: From Somoza to Roosevelt.

In late 1950, New Mexico's Senator Dennis Chávez decided that a trip to Central America might convince a congressional commission to approve enough funds for the completion of the Pan American highway. When the United States solons dropped in to see Tacho they found that the highway had been cleverly planned to wind its way by his best ranches. He also wanted United States assistance in the construction of the Rama highway, which would link the Atlantic and Pacific coasts. Tacho told the congressmen, "The U.S. is obligated to build the Rama road. I got a letter from President Roosevelt agreeing to build it." A Republican senator lost his temper and exploded. "That agreement has no value," he shouted.

In those days the United States customarily doled out road-building money to appease right-wing dictators but the senator was worried about the impression that would arise with United States tax money paying for Nicaraguan roads when Nicaragua had no income tax.

The Republican said, "Mr. President, we have the most perfect income tax system ever devised. We reach everyone. What kind of income tax do you have?"

"Why, Senator," Tacho replied, "if I started an income tax these people would shoot me."[1] The issue ended in a standoff but much later Nicaragua got United States funds for roads.

Despite Tacho's avowed anticommunism, he put business before ideological considerations when civil war broke out in neighboring Costa Rica in March 1948. Journalist Otilio Ulate's election to the presidency had been annuled by a compliant congress backing ex-president Rafael Angel Calderón Guardia, who had the support of the Costa Rican communists. Even historians credit José Figueres Ferrer, Don Pepe, as he later became known, with saving Costa Rica from communism by leading a civilian uprising to seat the legally elected Ulate. Tacho aided Calderón Guardia by airlifting some four hundred Guardia soldiers to San José. His ulterior motive: For years he had reaped huge profits smuggling cattle into Costa Rica and his business associates were corrupt officials and even members of Calderón Guardia's family. Calderón Guardia sought refuge in Nicaragua on losing the war and the triumphant Figueres won the undying enmity of Tacho.

Just nine days after Costa Rica officially disbanded its army in December the spunky Figueres, heading the provisional government, had to call his nation to arms to ward off an invasion from Nicaragua by an exile force armed with mortars and automatic weapons. Calderón Guardia issued his proclamation of war from Managua as Tacho went on the record: "I'm told Calderón Guardia invaded Costa Rica— but that's his affair. We're guarding our frontier."[2] The invasion force, trained in Nicaragua, failed miserably, but Tacho had his National Guard waiting in reserve ready to pounce if the Caribbean Legion, a force of Caribbean exiles who helped Figueres win his war, entered the battle. The legion formed initially to overthrow dictator Rafael Trujillo of the Dominican Republic also had Tacho in its sights.

The Organization of American States induced Nicaragua and Costa Rica to sign a friendship treaty in Washington in March 1949. It was also the Caribbean Legion's death certificate. But Tacho was not certain that the Legion was really dead, and when rumors continued to circulate that they had him targeted, he let it be known he was ready to fight. During the closing days of 1950 Tacho attacked the Legion verbally from his trophy-cluttered parlor at La Curva palace. "People say I've got the best intelligence service in Latin America. That's a lot of hooey. I just got a lot of friends, but they tell me plenty. I know more than the FBI. And if that gang of ragged bums in Costa Rica thinks I don't know they're getting ready to take a poke at me, they're sure in for one hell of a surprise."[3]

But while he kept a watchful eye on Costa Rica, he also had problems at home. In November he uncovered a plot in which six air force mechanics at Xolotlán Military Airfield had been bribed to subdue the sentries and hand over the airfield to civilian rebels. He quickly snuffed the plot out and threw the little fish, as he called them, into La Curva dungeons. Tacho gloated, "The big fish I haven't pulled in— yet. I like to let 'em wiggle on the hook a while."

He sent a message by a friend to Figueres next door. "Pepe, if you love Costa Rica, and I pray to God you do, then don't shoot. I'm not a nervous man, but gunfire sure disturbs me."[4]

Tacho wallowed in his blustering humor and jokes. Managua lawyer Francisco Ibarra Mayorga, a bitter Somoza critic who had been exiled and jailed earlier, found he was barred from leaving Nicaragua to attend the Inter-American Conference of

Democracy in Havana in May 1950. The lawyer ignored Tacho's objections by simply slipping across the Sapoa River into Costa Rica. When he was ready to return, the Nicaraguan consulate in Costa Rica refused him permission to re-enter the country. Finally, hoping to spend Christmas with his family, he appealed directly to Somoza, who replied, "You can return—the same way you left."

When a bearded cult leader from southern California showed up in Managua and offered to deliver, by supernatural relevation, the invasion plans of Tacho's enemies in Costa Rica, Somoza told him, "Hell, I had those plans before the ink was dry."

Tachito, meanwhile, when he wasn't playing billiards with his father, was spending a lot of time sitting around the editorial office of *Novedades*. This was the paper started in 1936 by his father to combat *La Prensa*, the paper of the opposition Chamorros. Tachito's interest was not journalism but a beautiful young staffer, Berta Zambrano, who wrote the social column for the newspaper. She was from a middle-class family of Niquinohomo, the birthplace of Sandino. Her job entailed covering the social activities of the Somozas and their friends, who were now Managua society. Berta was the love of Tachito's life. When he wasn't in the newspaper offices with her, he escorted her to parties, even to Montelimar. But Tacho decided that the young girl was below Tachito's station in life. The family worried that Berta might bewitch Tachito. When Tachito tried to defend his love for Berta, he was physically attacked by his father, who hit him in the mouth and loosened a tooth. The romance ended abruptly when Berta went off to Mexico, where she wed a well-known radio announcer. Berta and Tachito remained friends, and for years she shipped the latest records from Mexico to Somoza's Radio X in Managua as part of a business deal.

To Tacho a good marriage was of the utmost importance for his heirs. Although Tachito spread his affection among a number of young ladies, his father was still determined he should marry into a good family. Recalling his own courtship which was at times, he said, as difficult as any political battle he had ever fought, he had become class-conscious and wanted "well-bred" partners for his children, especially for his sons. He intended that the Somoza name would be around for a long time in Nicaragua and healthy grandchildren were essential. Tacho had a girl in mind for Tachito, but she remained in Europe.

Then the old man learned of Hope's almost lifelong interest in Tachito. Years previously, when the boys were en route to the military academy in Long Island, they had spent a brief time in Tampa, where they stayed with Uncle Nestor and polished up their English. Nestor's daughter, Hope, had developed a childhood crush on her cousin Tachito.

"At age six, as a tomboyish little girl with dark braids who longed for the curly blonde femininity of Shirley Temple, Hope made up her mind that her first cousin Tachito would be her husband because he offered to protect her on the way to a Tampa grocery store. She decided, 'This man is for me.' "[5]

After attending Miss Harris's Girls' School in Miami, Hope went on to several other finishing schools and to Barnard College in New York as well as Georgetown

University Foreign Service School. In the North after 1943 she often spent time with her cousin Lilian at the Washington embassy, where Tachito and Luis were also guests. She was a modern young girl and liked to dance. When she returned home in the early hours of the morning during her visits to Washington, Lilian would reprimand her. She wouldn't catch herself a man if she behaved that way. Hope startled her cousin with the announcement that she was going to marry Tachito.

Hope had grown into an attractive brunette, extremely well groomed, and Tacho agreed she would make a good wife for Tachito. "She's got class," old Tacho liked to say and indeed, refinement was Hope's forte. No woman dressed as smartly as Hope, at least in Nicaragua. Yoya was all for the match. There was some concern that the offspring of such close blood relatives might suffer mental or physical defects. But for old man Tacho, the good blood of the Debayles overruled this consideration. Tachito was attracted to Hope as well, and on December 20, 1950, they were married in style at the new Palace of Communications, only a short walk from the Managua cathedral. It was the social event of the year. The buffet tables were laden with food and champagne and dancing went on until dawn on all three floors of the palace. They went to South America for their honeymoon. By this time Tachito had become chief of the general staff.

Tacho I was by then feeling secure enough to move away from Managua to play farmer. He had always sought to be a patriarch and make Nicaragua his parochial pasture. Posing as a farmer was one of the things he loved best. In February 1951, he went off to his 25,000-acre Montelimar sugar plantation on the Pacific coast. "From now on and until further notice," he told his cabinet, "the presidential house will be at Montelimar. You can come and see me there."

In baggy khaki trousers, a gray stetson and a diamond-clasped blue silk neckerchief, he'd stand on a platform in the sugar mill's cane-unloading yard and bellow orders through a microphone to the arriving truckers and oxcart drivers. Cabinet officers got something of the same treatment. When the foreign minister tried to discuss a bomb that had been thrown harmlessly against the Nicaraguan embassy in San José, Costa Rica, Tacho said, "I love to make these guys [the ministers] eat a little dust." Then he added, "It's good for their inflated egos."

Like most dictators, Tacho had nothing but contempt for his lackeys. He was even in the habit of calling the American diplomats "boy." In his book, *Inside Latin America*, published in 1941, John Gunther notes that once the "boy's" wife, Mrs. Meredith Nicholson, complained mildly that there was no good milk in Managua. The next day she had a cow at her doorstep, a gift from Somoza.

Somoza was fond and proud of Montelimar. In 1948 he ground the first bag of Montelimar sugar. "That was the happiest day of my life," he recalled later. "I just pulled out my ole pistol and tried to blast the roof off the world." In 1951 he harvested 2,600 acres and by 1953 hoped to double output and start making big money on the mill. "Every president ought to have a job [like this], keeps him out of mischief," Tacho said.

In 1950 Tacho took a young mistress. One day in 1951 she imprudently visited him at the Casa Presidencial. She was quickly ushered into Tacho's presence. Fortunately, few had any idea of the relationship, not even the suspicious Yoya. He had previously had an affair with a Spanish lady, who suddenly left town pregnant. But extramarital affairs were all part of the Latin American macho tradition.

If Somoza hadn't had enough problems at home to keep him occupied, he most probably would have been heavily into mischief in the rest of Central America. His old enemy Guatemalan President Juan José Arévalo, who had been recalled from exile in Argentina to the presidency of Guatemala following the 1944 revolution, retired in March 1951, after surviving twenty-eight plots, some of which may have had a little backing from Tacho. Arévalo ended his six-year term and democratically handed the government to his successor. The new president was thirty-seven-year-old Colonel Jacobo Arbenz, son of a Swiss pharmacist and onetime defense minister under Arévalo.

Guatemala under "spiritual socialist" Arévalo and now Arbenz, was experimenting with a social revolution, something as foreign to Tacho as an auto without bulletproof plating. (Tacho drove around in a bulletproof limousine and was always well protected fore and aft by squads of bodyguards.)

In May 1951 Somoza had himself inaugurated for a new term of office. He tried to make it a solemn occasion. Foreign dignitaries were invited. They had to wear top hats in the sizzling heat in Managua's baseball stadium.

There was genuine interest on the part of the spectators as to how Tacho was going to manage the inauguration protocol. He was already wearing the blue and white presidential sash, which he had taken back when Uncle Víctor died. Despite Somoza's preference for rumpled khakis, rumors abounded in Managua that Tacho had purchased a new uniform for $10,000. Some even whispered the uniform had neon lights. Others said he would pass the sash of high office around his back and put it back on again, like a juggler.

The new uniform didn't appear, but Tacho was suitably impressive in a gold-braided formal bandleader's outfit, dark blue in color with large gold epaulets. The left breast and part of his protruding stomach were encrusted with medals. It was the same uniform, aides noted, that Somoza had worn at the wedding of son Tachito to Hope Portocarrero.

As the spectators watched attentively, Tacho removed the presidential sash and handed it to an aide, who in turn placed it over the breast of Senate President Mariano Argüello Vargas. Then the Senate president again draped the sash across Tacho's chest. Thoroughly pleased with himself, Tacho had the guard band march twice in front of the reviewing stand. A dozen air force planes roared over the spectators. There was a twenty-three-gun salute.

The following month Tacho gave a clue to his lack of interest in education in his country, where the illiteracy rate was close to 80 percent. That rate was to remain unchanged during most of the dynasty. He closed the University of Granada (300 students) saying, "One university is enough." With only the University of León to maintain, he reasoned, the state would have more money for elementary schools. "I prefer to open 150 new schools rather than to help educate . . . more lawyers, who at present are a menace to law and order." When the students protested he declared a state of siege and called out the National Guard.

Intimates reported that Tacho raged against President Harry Truman when the latter dispatched the undersecretary of state to San José to award President Otilio Ulate the white and gold Legion of Merit in the highest grade for "exceptionally meritorious conduct" in office. It was also announced that the United States Congress had earmarked a million dollars for work on the northwestern Costa Rican section of the Pan American highway. Tacho didn't get a medal or his Rama highway.

But when demagogue Joseph McCarthy began his communist witch-hunting in the United States and the winds of the Cold War began to ruffle the feathers of reformers, Tacho began to feel more relaxed and secure. He beat the anticommunist drum even louder.

In August 1952 Tacho went to the Dominican Republic to attend the August 16 inauguration ceremonies of Hector Trujillo, who was sitting in for his brother dictator Rafael Trujillo. Tacho, who didn't think of himself in the same league as the "tough dictators," told his aides, "Let's get the hell out of here. I can't stand this damn dictatorship." He also felt put down by Trujillo's sense of self-importance and a protocol that put visitors in second place. Tacho hated "the fancy dress of this monkey."

En route home, Tacho and his official party spent three days with President General Paul Magloire in Haiti. Accompanied by his son Luis, then a colonel and president of Congress, he complimented Magloire on his combating of communism and said he had worked out a formula in his country to solve labor problems: "I place myself between the two groups," he said, "and guard against the rich abusing labor through their advantages of wealth and labor abusing the rich through their advantages of numbers."

In Haiti he startled newsmen by expressing the hope that his political doctrine would eventually become a continental doctrine. "With the communist menace," he said, "it is essential to be strong because one or the other will win—communism or democracy."

At the Port-au-Prince press conference Tacho also explained that he had brought an "era of peace" to the Nicaraguan people by reaching an accord with the political opposition through a proportional distribution of government posts. His own Nationalist Liberal party had two-thirds representation and the minority Conservative party one-third.

While Tacho was away playing statesman, son Tachito, as chief of staff of the National Guard, was keeping things quiet at home. He was also having a lively time with his friends, including a Chilean consul. They visited whorehouses together where they frequently boozed all night, much as he had done years before. (Two years after his return from West Point, Tachito, a young blade about town, had fathered a baby girl, whom he recognized as his illegitimate child and christened Patricia. As soon as she was old enough Patricia was sent abroad to a series of schools.) Though Tachito was devoting more of his time to the guard, he was still considered a wild one. There were girls and drinks, brawls and bawdy games, which he obviously preferred to Hope's refinements. But he did take on some superficial polish as the years went by.

Then West Point graduate General Dwight D. Eisenhower took office in Washington in January 1953. John Foster Dulles, his secretary of state, noted that the Truman Administration had fallen into a "policy of neglect" toward southern neighbors. "There is a very strong, well-organized communist movement in most Latin American republics," he testified to the Senate Foreign Relations Committee in January 1953. "There is also a fascist movement in Argentina which has tentacles elsewhere. At the present time, in my opinion, there is . . . a working alliance between the fascist and the communist elements to agree on at least one proposition, that is hatred of the Yankee—to destroy the influence of the so-called Colossus of the North, in Central and South America. That is making considerable progress."

Dulles added, "I have the feeling that conditions in Latin America are some-what comparable to conditions as they were in China in the mid-thirties, when the communist movement was getting started."[6]

In March, Spruille Braden, former United States ambassador to Argentina, pointed to Guatemala as the neighborhood Red Menace. "In Guatemala, next door to the Panama Canal, party members, fellow travelers, demagogues, gunmen and killers have joined with opportunists, extreme nationalists, some of the military and a few misguided idealists, to make a beachhead for international communism. . . . [This] gives them a springboard for a military attack against the U.S. and an ideal depot from which to dispatch subversive and espionage agents and to expand their operations into all the Americas. . . .

"Our very survival as a nation may be threatened if this situation is permitted to continue and grow. I pray the new administration will attack this danger, rapidly, intelligently and energetically."

That same week the Guatemalan Congress, after overriding five members of the anticommunist opposition in a three-hour debate, voted to observe one minute of silence in memory of Joseph Stalin. No other Latin American legislature made such a gesture. The action was noted in Washington.

Also in March 1953, Dulles took time out to tell Latin Americans at the OAS meeting in Washington that the hemisphere's regional security pacts were impor-tant to the defense against Soviet aggression. Communist infiltration in the Ameri-cas must be guarded against, he told the OAS assembly, which included Tacho's son-in-law, Guillermo Sevilla-Sacasa. "We, here, can generate the right kind of moral force to help solve the problems of the whole world."

The right-wing dictators took comfort in the words and actions of Eisenhower, Vice-President Richard Nixon, and Dulles. At home, things went on much the same. Tacho's old pal Eddie Monterrey, who had given the coup de grace to Sandino and been rewarded for years of good service to the chief by being commissioned a colonel and given a lonely, unprofitable military district in the north, angered Somoza by grumbling too much about Tachito being the Crown Prince. Monterrey was thrown into jail by Tachito, while Somoza talked of a possible plot. Eddie's crime, after years of loyalty, was disrespect for an heir apparent who was taking on more of his father's characteristics every day, even the physical ones. Tacho had been a slim young cadet when he left West Point, but heavy eating and drinking since his return was making him fleshy. With age his hairline receded and his girth increased, following the longtime family tendency to obesity. All the Somozas had a flabbiness about them.

In September 1953, fifty-seven-year-old Tacho set out with a party of twenty for a seven-week tour of South America. In Río, President Getulio Vargas greeted the portly Somoza at the airport with a twenty-one-gun salute. A little overcome with his welcome, Tacho said, "I am the first Central American president to visit Brazil. It has been the ambition of my life."

But unused to following protocol, Tacho kept President Vargas waiting sixty-five minutes for dinner. Subsequently the plan to sign a treaty, or at least a pact of affection, was discreetly shelved. He arrived ninety minutes late for a dinner at the Chilean embassy and with a half-dozen unexpected guests in tow, but Tacho put the guests at ease by adapting the old American jukebox tune "Managua, Nicaragua, is a beautiful town."

At the press conferences customary on such state visits, he parried all the questions, recited two verses by the great Nicaraguan poet Rubén Darío and when Brazilian reporters queried him about the future, Tacho gave them one of his folksy replies. "I can lasso a horse, plow a field, milk a cow and ride in the open. I am just a *campesino* [peasant] who became president of the republic." He ended his eleven-day visit to Brazil and traveled to Argentina, Peru, Ecuador, Colombia, Venezuela and Panama.

In Panama he helped his old friend President José Antonio (Chichi) Remon celebrate the fiftieth anniversary of Panama's independence by attending every party during the week. One day he drove into the Canal Zone to the United States Air Force's Albrook Air Base and invaded its post exchange. As a visiting foreign army officer, one whose son had attended West Point and whose soldiers were enrolled in Canal Zone schools, Tacho was considered technically eligible for PX privileges —cut-rate prices and no tax. Somoza paid a thousand dollars cash for perfumes, toys and gadgets, which he handed out to Panamanian friends saying, "Now I know the PXes are unfair competition with Panama merchants."

On his return from his 17,000-mile fun trip, Tacho remained in Managua only a day, to inspect the twenty-seven race horses he had purchased in Argentina and shipped home by air. Then he was off again; this time in a new Swedish-built freighter he had purchased for his family shipping line. In neighboring El Salvador, Somoza gave the honor of christening the 4,000-ton vessel to Doña Leticia de Osorio, the wife of the president. Finally back home again, Tacho congratulated both Luis and Tachito. (Son Luis had been left in charge of the government, while Tachito had the National Guard.) They had served their apprenticeship well, he said, which would stand them in good stead at some future date. That date was closer than he surmised.

In 1954 the Eisenhower administration decided to do something about

Guatemala, from where, according to Washington, cancerous communism might spread to the rest of Central America. The CIA was put in charge of the operation, with adequate funds that totaled over a million dollars. Tacho quickly offered the CIA his territory for logistic support or for whatever reason they might want to use his country and its good offices. He would have liked to have done more, but Nicaragua's border didn't reach Guatemala and the CIA was counting on the support of Honduras. Somoza was particularly upset by the reformists in Guatemala, whom he considered more dangerous than communists. But like Washington, Tacho branded them communists.

Since the revolution of 1944, Juan José Arévalo and his successor, Jacobo Arbenz, had launched a series of broad reforms in Guatemala that included a social security program, the encouraging of labor unions, the expansion of rural education, agricultural extension, public health and the promotion of cooperatives. The university was granted autonomy, an industrial development law was passed, as well as a law forcing the rental of farmlands to peasants, which, in effect, prohibited share-cropping and profiteering by landowners. The range of legislation and decrees was extremely broad, too much so to implement fully.

Because of a shortage of trained local personnel, Arévalo and Arbenz had invited other Latins to Guatemala. Many of them were liberals and socialists, but some were from the outlawed Communist party of Chile and the Aprista party of Peru. Many Guatemalans who returned from exile after the revolution had socialist or communist convictions, but above all they were strongly nationalistic.

The most controversial step under Arbenz was agrarian reform—the title alone was anathema to the Latin American oligarchy. It spelled communism for them. When strikes hit the American United Fruit Company, the largest single landowner in Guatemala, and some of its lands were expropriated, the United States saw red and accused Arbenz of offering insufficient indemnification to the Boston-based company. Arbenz, not a communist himself, did in fact count on the support of the communists, and many were involved in the planning and implementation of agrarian reform. This was too much for Washington. Arbenz's days were numbered from then on. The CIA found Colonel Carlos Castillo Armas to lead a liberation army. The intelligence agency's involvement was covered up for several years, but Tacho immediately boasted privately about his "vital" role in ousting the "communists in Guatemala."

Somoza allowed Managua's Las Mercedes airport to be used by CIA aircraft. Six P-47s, piloted by Americans, were used in the attack on Guatemala. Two of the planes were shot down and another returned to Managua ripped by gunfire. One of the planes, piloted by American William "Rip" Robertson sank a British freighter ship instead of a Russian ship supposedly carrying arms to Guatemala. Lloyds of London, the insurers, were furious. It cost the CIA $1.4 million in damages. Robertson, suddenly unpopular with his CIA bosses, transferred his allegiance to the Somozas and became a business partner in a gold mine. After the operation Tacho kept two planes and Castillo Armas ended up with another.

But plotters were still active against Tacho in 1954. A group of rebel Nicaraguans slipped back into the country in two trucks with a plan to ambush Somoza. Nearly one thousand guns were shipped from Costa Rica by launch over Lake Nicaragua and kept near Managua. The head of the plot was Colonel Manuel Gómez, the first Nicaraguan enlisted in the guard by the United States Marines in the 1930s and considered numero uno. The conspirators lay in wait for Tacho, who was expected to pass down the highway en route to Montelimar. But the Spanish ambassador had called Somoza to show him some horses. And next to bulls, Tacho's passion was horses.

Somoza only heard about the plot when one plotter surrendered himself to the police. Said Tacho, "I never thought of that. I was thinking about the cotton crop." However, he took measures to punish the rebels. They were pursued by the guard and many of them were killed.

The following year, Tacho bolstered his personal security after his friend President Chichi Remon of Panama was assassinated at a racetrack. This assassination, coupled with the previously aborted plan to ambush him and end his rule, gave Tacho ample reason to be nervous. The fact that the rebels themselves had been ambushed before they reached Tacho didn't reassure him.

It was no secret that Somoza was again helping a group seeking to overthrow his bitter enemy, José Pepe Figueres of Costa Rica. Figueres, who had attended MIT in the United States and was now president of his country, was everything Tacho was not. Don Pepe, pint-size, was a democrat who hated armies and detested Tacho. Although he loved the land, he didn't want to own all of it like Somoza.

In January 1955, Figueres accused Tacho of fomenting an uprising against his government. Somoza's reply characterized the Costa Rican as a "damned liar," and challenged him to a duel with pistols on their common border. Both men considered themselves excellent shots with pistols. But the duel never took place.

In April 1955, Tacho ordered the constitution amended to permit his re-election. The election was scheduled for February 1957. His six-year term ended May 1, 1957, and he intended to rule until 1963, or even longer.

In early April Tacho, now greatly overweight and with a large double chin, came close to accidental death. Entertaining the American Legion national commander, J. Addington Wagner, who was on a tour of Caribbean countries with his wife, Tacho suggested a little deep-sea fishing. After a swim and a hefty meal at Tacho's Montelimar villa, the party, including Luis and several aides, boarded a bargelike eighteen-foot rubber boat propelled by an outboard motor. The boat ran into a squall about a half-mile offshore. As Somoza later told it, the waves suddenly rose to twenty feet and one washed Mrs. Wagner overboard. Her husband, a former Washington and Lee swimming star, retrieved her from the churning sea. Somoza said that he and Luis also went to her rescue, but it appeared that they had little choice but to join the Wagners in the water. The rubber boat capsized. The entire party had to cling to the buoyant boat until it finally washed ashore over an hour later.

The Wagners were representative of a general American attitude toward Somoza—that he constituted a strong defense against communist penetration of

Central America. Richard Nixon, who toured Latin America as vice-president of the United States in 1955, endorsed strongman rule there for the same reason. American participation in the Guatemalan coup and Nixon's statements showed where official priorities lay, but there may have been some twinges of conscience.

When President Eisenhower, who had been delayed by illness, finally met with most of the hemisphere's presidents and strongmen in July 1956 in Panama, the conference produced a curiously rhetorical declaration: "In a world in which the dignity of the individual, his fundamental rights and the spiritual values of mankind are seriously threatened by totalitarian forces alien to the traditions of our people and their institutions, America holds steadfastly to its historic mission—to be the bulwark of human liberty and national independence." The reference is probably more to a defense against communism than dictatorship in general, but its vague wording may have been intended to put some pressure on regional despots. This historic meeting also proposed, as so many before and after it, "inter-American cooperative efforts to seek the solution of economic problems and to raise the living standards of the continent."

Time was running out for most of the eighteen presidents at the Panama conference, many of whom, like Somoza, had raised their own living standards at the expense of their impoverished people. General Paul Magloire of Haiti, who sat next to Somoza at the conference table, was ousted in December. Carlos Castillo Armas of Guatemala was assassinated the following year. General Gustavo Rojas Pinilla of Colombia, who didn't attend, was driven from power in 1957, as was General Fulgencio Batista y Zaldivar of Cuba in January 1959. General Pérez Jiménez of Venezuela was ousted in 1958. Generalissimo Trujillo of the Dominican Republic was gunned down in 1961. The only remaining dictator still in power who attended that conference is Paraguay's Alfredo Stroessner. As for Tacho, two months later he was dead from an assassin's bullet.

On the night of September 21, 1956, Tacho was in rare form. He relaxed after dancing a cha-cha at a reception in his honor in the Casa del Obrero, a workers' club he had founded in León, his sons' birthplace. Somoza had gone through the motions of receiving the nomination from his Nationalist Liberal party for next February's election. The nomination had been made in the stronghold of the old Liberal party, which he had converted into his personal election vehicle.

Just after 11:00 P.M. a young man with a pencil-thin moustache approached him. Despite Tacho's concern for protection, his 220-pound bulk offered an easy target. Rigoberto López Pérez, a poet, whipped out a snub-nosed Smith and Wesson .38 revolver and, from fifteen feet, managed to fire four quick successive shots into Tacho before Arnoldo Ramírez Eva, chief of the government's National Construction Agency, grabbed him by the hair and pulled him backwards. The ballroom became a madhouse. Colonel Camilio González Cervantes, the president's aide and former counterfeiting partner, was one of those who shot and beat the assassin to death on the dance floor.

Rigoberto was shot thirty-five times by different caliber pistols. After he was dead, he was kicked and spat upon; then his body was taken to the González theater and left on the sidewalk until the next day. No one knows what happened to his body after that.

American Ambassador Thomas Whelan, a close friend and one of Tacho's favorite poker partners, alerted Washington upon hearing the news. President Eisenhower, who was later to decide that Fidel Castro of Cuba and Rafael Trujillo of the Dominican Republic should be gotten rid of, went to extraordinary lengths to save Somoza's life. The White House ordered a helicopter from the Canal Zone to move the wounded dictator from León to Managua, and then sent the commander of Washington's Walter Reed Army Hospital to Nicaragua to save him. Eisenhower was said to be acting on the suggestion of Ambassador Whelan, who urged that special medical aid of the type only the United States could provide was needed. Major General Dr. Leonard D. Heaton, accompanied by two surgeons, left by midafternoon for the seven-and-a-half-hour flight to Managua. Meanwhile, a medical team headed by Colonel Charles O. Bruce had flown in early on September 22 from the Canal Zone to attend to Somoza's wounds. Bruce, the Canal Zone health director, was accompanied by members of the staff of Gorgas Hospital, including the chiefs of surgery and orthopedics and an anesthetist. Tacho, as one eminent Nicaraguan doctor observed later, hadn't put his money into hospitals.

Four hours after arrival in Managua that Sunday morning, Heaton and the task force of doctors were en route to the Canal Zone with the wounded Somoza and his wife. All four bullets had scored. One struck Tacho in the right shoulder, another in the right thigh; one broke his right forearm. The fourth was the most dangerous. It had entered the upper right thigh and had lodged at the base of the spine. At Gorgas, four surgeons, including Heaton, worked for four hours and twenty minutes removing the bullets in the thigh and near the spine.

"I'm a goner," Tacho reportedly told his friend Whelan in his typically colloquial English the night he was shot. Despite the long operation and a windpipe incision to ease his labored breathing, Tacho never regained consciousness in the American hospital. He expired at 5:05 A.M., September 28, seven days after he was shot. Death was pronounced a result of bullet wounds and general organic fatigue.

Those seven days gave his heirs time to secure the realm. They clamped the country under a state of siege, jailed oppositionists, halted the departure of Nicaraguans from the country, and put the nation under curfew, all to give the impression that Tacho would be back to continue his rule.

The day before he died, Tacho received a cable of best wishes for a speedy recovery and an apostolic benediction from Pope Pius XII. Somoza, who had never been a practicing Catholic, was given a requiem high mass at the Sacred Heart Chapel at Ancon Hill in the Canal Zone. Following mass the body was escorted to Albrook Air Base, the site of his raid on the PX, by an honor guard. He was given a twenty-one-gun military send-off and a United States military escort back to Managua in an air force C-54. The escort was headed by the chief of staff of the Caribbean command.

President Eisenhower, in his expression of regret the day of Tacho's death, said, "The nation and I personally regret the death of President Somoza of Nicaragua as a result of the dastardly attack made upon him several days ago by an assassin."

Secretary of State John Foster Dulles, in his message of condolence, said, "His constantly demonstrated friendship for the U.S. will never be forgotten."

Ambassador Whelan said, "The United States has lost a good friend, I lost a good friend."

As a gesture of respect for his fallen fellow dictator, Rafael Trujillo sent a total of 118 persons in four aircraft, including a military band and honor guard, to the funeral. Ironically the Dominican dictator died himself five years later, a victim of assassins who this time counted on the complicity of the Eisenhower and Kennedy administrations and the CIA.[7]

While official regrets poured in, in San Francisco—the traditional American stronghold of Nicaraguan Conservative exiles in the United States—Tacho's death was applauded, as was the deed of tyrannicide committed by the twenty-seven-year-old poet. Some thirty automobiles paraded in the streets carrying signs: "Somoza's Heirs Should Not Be Recognized."

There were celebrations to mark the end of Tacho's dictatorship in many Latin American capitals. A Panama newspaper carried a photo of Tacho's assassin with the caption: "One may give a life for an ideal and thus fill the vacuum which he left." In Canada, the *Montreal Star* editorialized: "Retributive Justice Overtakes Somoza."

Hope had been trying to induce Tachito to run the family shipping line from New York. They had even gone to Manhattan, where she was happily enjoying the arts and social whirl. But any hopes she had to induce Tachito to become a Manhattan executive, or any hopes he had for a career there, quickly ended when his father was assassinated.

Almost at once, Nicaragua had a new Tacho, as Tachito dropped the diminutive form of his name. But it was the less arrogant, quiet Luis who had been chosen to take over in case of Somoza's death. Days before riderless Cashbox, Tacho's favorite horse, led his funeral procession to the crypt, the sons had taken command —Somoza style.

On September 28, Luis, president of the Congress, called an evening session and had himself elected acting president by acclamation. He would serve either during the period of his father's incapacitation or until the end of Somoza's term on May 1, 1957. At the same time Luis declared himself a candidate for the February elections, just in case some of the old man's buddies decided they should try for the post. Luis took the oath to support the constitution before Congress, then he thanked the United States for having "lent inestimable aid to save the life which guides our destiny."

Meanwhile, tough, quick-tempered Tachito, thirty-two, commander of 4,100 guardsmen, arrested hundreds of "suspects," as the constitutional guarantee of habeas corpus had been suspended. The new Tacho immediately branded his father's attacker a communist who had connections with exiled Nicaraguans in El Salvador. The poet had lived there in exile since 1951, working as a phonograph salesman until returning to his native León earlier in the month. An essay on poetry he had written had appeared September 12 in *El Cronista* in León. In it he wrote:

"The devil is the greatest poet who is not recognized by humanity." And, "Immortality is the aim of life and of glorious death."

Despite Tacho II's declaration, for many Nicaraguans the assassin was a martyr-hero in the same class as Sandino. He only wanted to free his country.

Captain Adolfo Alfaro, whose brother had been killed by the guard in the aftermath of the 1954 plot, had taught the poet to fire a revolver. Even though Alfaro was married to a Somoza relative, he had fled to El Salvador. It appeared that López Pérez had acted on his own, but this did not deter Tacho II from rounding up all the old foes, including the by now eighty-four-year-old Emiliano Chamorro. Also interned were Dr. Enoc Aguado and Pedro Joaquín Chamorro, the latter for intensifying his campaign against Somoza's re-election and protesting the tightening of presidential security. However, Tacho always insisted that Chamorro knew about the assassination before it happened.

Less than eight hours after his father's death, Luis was unanimously elected by Congress to succeed him. He became the thirty-first president of Nicaragua. Although violence had characterized much of the country's history, his father was the first president ever to be assassinated. Luis received fifty-three standing votes of senators and deputies, including a dozen from members of the opposition Conservative party.

Tacho II used a lie detector to establish the guilt or innocence of those he arrested. He said it had been "proved" that the assassin was a communist. He said López Pérez's longtime teacher quoted the killer as having asserted that "the people will be better off when the Russian system is established here."

By January 29, 1957, Tacho II had completed his investigation. Among those he implicated in the assassination of his father were student Tomás Borge Martínez and his brother, Emilio, whose family name was misspelled as Borje in court. Tomás was a student at the law faculty of the university in León. It was in the university, he recalled later, "that my political consciousness was aroused." He spent two and one-half years of his term in prison; then was taken from jail and put under house arrest. He later managed to escape to Honduras dressed as a woman.

Pedro Joaquín Chamorro was also found guilty. The Chamorros and Tomás Borge added their weight to the ghost of Sandino. Despite decrees and prison terms, or maybe because of them, they would chip away at the Somoza dynasty until eventually it crumbled.

Anastasio Somoza García died the richest and most powerful man in the country. He became wealthy by sapping the lifeblood of his people. He became powerful by stripping them of their freedom. With that wealth and with that power, Anastasio Somoza García, Tacho I, founded a dynasty so strong and personal that, in Panama, calypso king Rupert (Kontiki) Allen found that nightclub customers wouldn't let one of his popular songs die. Woven around Somoza's assassination, it began:

> *A guy asked de dictator if he 'ad any farms*
> *'E said 'e 'ad on'y one—*
> *It was Nicaragua.*

CHAPTER 4

The Boys in Power

Neither son was like old Tacho, who used to complain that they had inherited neither his brain nor his cunning. It was his daughter Lilian whom he considered most like him. At the time of Somoza's death Lilian was thirty-five and busy raising a brood of children in Washington. Her crafty husband, Guillermo Sevilla-Sacasa, had received the ambassador's job at the Washington embassy as a wedding gift in 1943. Lilian, who had attended Gunston Hall School for Girls, in 1940 had been crowned queen of the Apple Blossom Festival in Winchester, Virginia. This distinction pleased the old man, especially since neither of his sons had won any kind of honor at school, despite the money he spent on them.

In 1947 Sevilla-Sacasa, former speaker of the Nicaraguan House of Representatives, displayed his shrewdness when the United States withheld recognition from Tacho's stooge president, Uncle Víctor. He sent flowers to President Truman's mother who was ill in Missouri. Back came a note from Truman addressed to "Mr. Ambassador." This note he used later to prove his authority to the State Department, and he remained to become dean of the diplomatic corps in Washington. He used his position as much to forward the United States' interests as those of his own country.

When the Somoza sons inherited power, the opposition predicted that the day of reckoning had arrived. Even friends of the Somoza family wondered if the boys could hold power for as long as six months. Some believed that guard officers would revolt because Tachito was far too abrasive and arrogant to hold them together. Luis was soft and flabby in character. But the boys proved them wrong. It seemed that the boys, so different in temperament, provided just the right kind of chemistry to keep the dynasty afloat.

Of all the Somozas, Luis was the closest to being a real farmer. Instead of going from La Salle Military Academy on Long Island to West Point, Luis attended a series of universities devoted to other than military interests. He went to schools in California and Maryland and finally to Louisiana State University and returned home an agronomist. His easygoing manner was suited to the drawn-out playacting of congressional politics. His father, recognizing these traits, placed Luis in charge of Congress and of the subservient, well-disciplined Nationalist Liberal party as well.

Both sons understood that the smooth transition of power after their father's assassination was necessary to ensure the family's survival. Luis, then thirty-four and heir apparent, turned his energies to arranging the February 3, 1957, elections in which he would be candidate in his father's place. He wisely left the work of extracting vengeance to Tachito. The guard colonel needed no prodding; he rounded up everyone who might ever have been suspected of anti-Somoza thoughts, words or deeds.

The division of labor reflected the character of the two boys. Tachito, who had been a darkly handsome boy of ten when he left home to attend the Christian Brothers' Military Academy on Long Island in 1936, quickly fattened, as did Luis. But unlike his brother, he had gained, along with the added weight, a reputation as a bully. He was in addition a confirmed "gringophile" from the time of his enrollment in American schools.

It was not until July 28, 1956, however, that Papa, in order to be able to run for re-election, had relinquished the post he treasured most. Son Tachito became the de facto head of the National Guard. Two years earlier Tachito had received his pilot's license in the United States. Recalling the impact of American air power during the 1920s campaign against Sandino, Tachito believed that his country needed a good air force. He became commander of the air force on July 2, 1956.

Luis was a hypocrite. Tachito was vain and showed his anger easily. Luis was an introvert and a smooth operator. Tachito was inclined to be frank; Luis wasn't.

During the fading months of 1956 Tachito went about the job of avenging his father with fanatic zeal. He felt that all of his father's foes should suffer. Many had, of course, wished for Tacho's murder—although they had nothing to do with the assassination. Tachito was even suspicious of Colonel Francisco Gaitán, who had taught Tacho I to march and who was, in 1956, chief of staff of the guard. But Luis saved Gaitán, sending him to Argentina as ambassador. Tachito later said, "I didn't shoot Gaitán because my mother pleaded with me not to do it."

More than three thousand persons were rounded up and imprisoned. There was fear that Tachito's vengeance might cause a bloodbath. Certainly his actions served to throw the opposition into complete disarray, and any thought of presenting a candidate to oppose Luis in the election was unthinkable. By January the number of those detained in connection with the tyrannicide was reduced to three hundred, then eventually to twenty-one. Finally only five of the prisoners were accused of direct involvement in the act.

The locker room of Campo de Marte was the scene of the trial, actually conducted as a court-martial. A seven-officer court tried twenty-one Nicaraguans for complicity in the assassination.

The list of charges against the five primary defendants that the prosecuting officers read to the court sounded like a Hollywood script. One prisoner was accused of hollowing out the bullets provided for the assassin and injecting poison. Another was supposed to have doused León in darkness by pulling the master electric switch, to allow the assassin time to escape. The third was accused of firing a rocket into the night to signal the man who would cause the blackout. The fourth prisoner was allegedly in charge of driving the getaway jeep. The fifth prisoner had cast suspicion on himself by going into hiding after he learned his friend had killed Somoza. He was singled out as the financial backer of the plot.

The first five defendants were found guilty as charged, but in keeping with Luis's campaign pledge, the sentences were light. He had told a pre-election rally in Managua's Republican Plaza that "the sentences will be on the mild side" for the crime committed against his father. There was no death penalty in Nicaragua, and, besides, the assassin had been killed on the spot.

Of the first five defendants, three drew fifteen-year prison terms and the other two were sentenced to nine years. The three most closely associated with the assassination remained in prison for four years. Then they were killed, supposedly while trying to escape.

Six of the remaining prisoners were acquitted by the court and eight were sentenced to nine-year terms. Dr. Enoc Aguado, unsuccessful Independent Liberal-Conservative coalition candidate for president in 1947, and Dr. Enrique Lacayo Farfán, leader of the Independent Liberal party, were among those who received nine-year terms. Pedro Joaquín Chamorro, editor of the opposition *La Prensa* and childhood school rival of Tachito, received the lightest sentence: he was ordered to stay at least sixty miles away from Managua and León for the next forty months.

Just prior to the 1957 election, four years were lopped off the sentences of Aguado and Lacayo. Luis reasoned that a strong arm had, in the end, shortened his father's life-span. So Luis quietly launched what he called a liberalization of the dictatorship. Cabinet ministers were permitted more authority and made responsible to Congress.

Tachito moved into La Curva with Hope and the children when Luis moved into the Casa Presidencial.

Both sons had been exposed to the American media during their decade in the United States. They also remembered their father's explanation of the power of advertising, which he had learned in Philadelphia. They began to open up somewhat to the local and foreign press. Luis held regular press conferences during which he encouraged critical questions and even Tachito began talking to reporters at his guard headquarters. As a result, despite the fact that there were some twenty-five known political prisoners, the boys gained favorable press coverage abroad.

In February 1957 Tachito's military training and Luis's restraint were put to the test when trouble broke out with neighboring Honduras. The cause of the trouble was the disputed 7,000-square-mile district along the Coco River, claimed both by Honduras and Nicaragua. In 1906 King Alfonso XIII of Spain had awarded the area to Honduras in a royal arbitration decision, but Nicaragua refused to accept his verdict. When word reached Managua that the government in Tegucigalpa had carved a new state out of most of the disputed land and named it "Gracias a Dios," Tachito shrugged off the report. In answer to reporters' questions about Honduras violating Nicaraguan territory, Tachito acted nonchalant. "If our frontier were in danger, we would not be here enjoying the agreeable companionship which unites the soldiers of the guard." Then he tossed off another toast at a banquet offered in his honor by the enlisted men of the guard.

Newly elected President Luis Somoza was not so tranquil. He immediately called an emergency cabinet meeting to consider the border situation. Oil companies were said to be interested in the area, so it was now worth fighting over.

By the time of his May 1 inauguration, Luis found that relations with his northern neighbor had degenerated. Tachito had moved troops, usually stationed fifteen miles inside the zone along the Cruta River, deeper into the interior of the disputed area to the little village of Mocorón. The guard plowed up the little dirt airfield next to the village.

The Hondurans felt that Tachito's action was provocative retaliation. Instead of sending the fourteen-member delegation that had been invited to Luis's inauguration, they simply instructed their ambassador to attend the ceremony—a diplomatic slight. General Roque Rodríguez, fifty-nine, the head of a three-man Honduran military junta, waited until Luis's big day before replying to Tachito's action. On inauguration day he sent five hundred troops to retake Mocorón. The outnumbered Nicaraguans fled, leaving two dead on the battlefield. The news reached Managua just before the inauguration ball. The three orchestras were dismissed; no one danced on Luis's inauguration day—an ominous sign, some said.

Tachito ordered his P-51s to strike back at dawn. The clashes continued until little remained of the village of Mocorón, its cluster of thatch huts razed by air strikes. Spokesmen for the Organization of American States arrived in Tegucigalpa to settle the dispute and both sides broke off hostilities. Meanwhile Tachito, his chubby face a full moon under a steel helmet, toured the front where his troops had suffered their first defeat just eight months after he took full command. With an automatic rifle over his shoulder and a .45 pistol at his waist, he struck a warlike pose. Even though the five-man OAS truce team won assurances from both sides to observe a ceasefire, Tachito's troops, smarting from the Mocorón defeat, made a sneak attack on the towns of Cifuentes and Las Manos.

The Nicaraguans then complained that Honduran paramilitary groups were looting ranches in an undisputed part of Nicaraguan territory. Both sides finally agreed to an accord drawn up by ex-President Ricardo Arias of Panama and withdrew their troops. The dispute was submitted to the International Court of Justice at The Hague for arbitration.

Later in the year Nicaraguans had a good laugh at the expense of the Somoza newspaper *Novedades*. The daily offered a $140 prize for the best verse of homage to old Tacho. The winning entry was a flowery fourteen lines, titled: "Renowned Paladin and Cavalier Glory of America." The newspaper ran the poem, which was signed with a pen name. It was not until several days later that a bright reader noted that the first letters of the fourteen lines spelled the name of the man who had slain old Tacho: Rigoberto López.

Tacho Somoza left over a $100 million fortune including real estate consisting of at least 10 percent of all arable farmland in Nicaragua. Under the brothers, Luis wearing the silk gloves and Tachito providing the strong arm, the family—and the guard—became even more powerful and increasingly corrupt. As the guard prospered, their loyalty to the family grew proportionately.

At the beginning of 1958 Guillermo Sevilla-Sacasa, then forty-nine, stepped into the coveted post of dean of the Washington diplomatic corps. The Nicaraguan now spoke for eighty-two mission heads on matters of protocol and diplomatic prerogative. While his English left much to be desired, he was an excellent orator in his native Spanish. The fourteen-year veteran delighted the Eisenhower administration with his accommodating style. Four years earlier when John Foster Dulles needed a helping hand in pushing through an OAS resolution at a meeting in Caracas, he had come to his aid. The resolution, calling for the collective action of the OAS if communists infiltrated any nation in the Americas, was designed especially with Guatemala in mind. As chairman, Sevilla-Sacasa put on a convincing performance to get the resolution approved. Dulles stayed at the Caracas meeting only long enough to get the anticommunist motion passed. Later that year the CIA, with Tacho's help, intervened to end the leftist regime in Guatemala.

One of the many congratulatory letters the new dean received was from Dr. Milton Eisenhower, the president's brother, who had been designated as troubleshooter for Latin America. Nicaragua was now in a special position in Washington. Not only did Sevilla-Sacasa have the ear of the administration, but favors were a two-way street.

To improve the family image at home, in late April Luis gave the Congress a constitutional amendment to study. It appeared designed to end the dynasty. Not only would Luis be barred from succeeding himself, but anyone related to him by blood, "up to the fourth degree," would be prohibited from becoming president. The amendment would not only keep Luis and Tachito out of the Presidential Palace, but also their half-brother José, whom Tacho Somoza, before his assassination, had recognized as his natural son. (José was forty when his father died, and held the rank of major in the guard which he had joined as an enlisted man. Joe, or Papa Chepe as the family called him, also managed Tacho's sugar and cattle interests. But the boys bought José off by giving him ten million córdobas and twenty thousand acres along the Tipitapa River.)

Luis told allies and a skeptical opposition that "it is my firm intention to retire at the end of my elected term and to deliver my robe of office to the man who wins the majority of votes in the election of 1963." He explained that one of the motives behind this decision was to strengthen the popularity of the family's Nationalist Liberal party so that it could win elections on its own.[1]

Luis believed that the family, with its large fortune and business empire inside Nicaragua, could survive only if it didn't control the country politically as a dynasty. Diehard rebels, he decided, would never give up plotting and attempting to overthrow the regime. The name Somoza was anathema to the opposition. A loyal member of the Nationalist Liberal party could be front man and reduce the pressure on the family. In an emergency, amendments could be repealed; meanwhile the opposition could rejoice in the fact that after 1963 no Somoza would rule—at least in name. Old Tacho had repealed a similar constitutional provision in 1955, when he decided that his country needed him for yet another term as president. It was the mistake that led to his assassination. Tachito agreed to the amendment that would rob him of his chance of being president. But as head of the guard, he could read his future more clearly than others.

While Managua was busy discussing Luis's amendment, a trio of rebels, two of them former pilots of the Somoza airline Lanica (Lineas Aereas de Nicaragua) hijacked a Lanica C-47 cargo plane from a Miami airfield and flew to Honduras for a rendezvous with Nicaraguan exile Colonel Manuel Gómez. Their plan, according to Tachito's intelligence network, was to fly to Puerto Cabezas and either assassinate or kidnap Luis during a visit to that Pacific coast port. But the Hondurans located the plane and arrested the Nicaraguan rebels before they could activate whatever plan they had in mind.

As for United States relations with Latin America, 1958 became known as the year Latin Americans spat upon Vice-President Richard Nixon. Nixon got a hint of how his eighteen-day tour of Latin America might turn out on his first stop in Peru. He was greeted at Lima's University of San Marcos by signs saying "Nixon is a viper" and other less complimentary accusations. His next stop was Argentina for the swearing-in of President Arturo Frondizi. Here the students were less personal in their criticism. A student leader merely said to the vice-president: "We reproach the U.S. for its passive policy toward dictators."

Paraguay was a haven in a storm to Nixon. Here he was greeted warmly by the populace and received a big *abrazo* from dictator General Alfredo Stroessner. It was the same when he and Pat visited Nicaragua. In later years he demonstrated that he hadn't forgotten the friendly reception from those Somoza boys who could communicate so well in English.

A less cordial reception awaited Nixon in Caracas. Thousands of students rioted in the streets and showered his motorcade with rotten eggs and spittle. So recently freed from the dictatorship of Marcos Pérez Jiménez, Venezuelans, now under the rule of a military junta, wondered why Eisenhower had given Pérez Jiménez the Legion of Merit and why the United States had granted him asylum after his ten-year reign of terror had ended.

Nixon's turbulent visit soured him on Latin America permanently. Years later when, as president, Nixon was posing for the usual photo with an ambassador he had appointed to one of the Latin American nations, his bitterness welled up. Slightly tipsy, he told the new envoy, "Don't trust them, you can't trust them. They're all a bunch of kooks."

Although Nixon had been received warmly by the dictators of the Caribbean area during a tour there in 1955, in 1958 he seemingly turned against them also. He suggested that the United States espouse a policy of coolness toward them. But this was mostly political rhetoric and not followed up by any action. Nixon, of course, excluded the Somoza boys from any criticism. The statement Nixon made in May 1958 at Washington's National Press Club was in direct conflict with Dulles's policy of coddling dictators. "What we must do is to show that when private enterprise and the U.S. come into Latin America, we do not do so for the purpose of simply keeping the elite in power." He struck out at diplomats who spent their time at "white tie dinners," noting that the "universities and labor movements [are] the wave of the future." "Do we leave the field to the communists? If we do," Nixon said, "we are going to lose the battle."

Dr. Milton Eisenhower planned to make a tour of Central America beginning June 15, 1958, but the trip was delayed a month for fear of more violence. There was no violence.

In Nicaragua when Dr. Eisenhower met with the opposition he seemed to be acting almost as a second for Luis Somoza. After lunch with Luis, Dr. Eisenhower sat down with a group of intellectuals and professionals for an exchange of views. Dr. Juan Zelaya, president of a university graduates' club, made the usual charges against the United States: protecting dictators, using political intervention to protect its investments, and buying raw materials at rock-bottom prices and selling back the expensive manufactured products. Eisenhower countered that Luis could not be classified a dictator like his father, because now the opposition could speak out, whereas two years earlier they were not free to do so.

The discussions did have some effect, for on his return to the United States Dr. Eisenhower recommended a response "to the appeal of Latin American nations for more stable relationships between raw-commodity prices and the prices of manufactured products." Summing up his trip he said, "The vast majority of the leaders and people of Latin America are firm friends of the U.S. They do not intend to permit a tiny minority of conspirators to confuse and divide us."

When Tacho Somoza had Sandino killed and most of his followers wiped out, one of those who escaped was a lieutenant named Ramón Raudales. In September 1958, inspired by the progress of Fidel Castro against the Fulgencio Batista dictatorship in Cuba, the sixty-two-year-old guerrilla, his hair and moustache now white, slipped into Nueva Segovia. Raudales led forty men, carrying extra arms for recruits, into his sparsely populated native province. The intention was a Cuban-style revolutionary campaign, but they found the going rough and failed to capture the guard garrison at the little sawmill village of El Corozo. However, this attack brought them to the attention of Tachito. Using aircraft, he transported his best antiguerrilla troops into the area. Despite the rugged terrain one of his patrols caught up with the guerrillas. A clash on a pine-clad hill resulted in the end of the career of Raudales, who died with a bullet in his head.

"We have finished with this group of bandits," Tachito announced proudly to the press, and he praised the guard as being among the finest antiguerrilla troops on the continent. But to a new generation of Nicaraguans, Raudales was no bandit. The old general who had fought with Sandino a quarter-century earlier didn't die in vain. ("Raudales," explained Sandinista leader Tomás Borge years later, "is a kind of bridge between the fight directed by Sandino and the struggle of new generations of Sandinistas. Because after Raudales, other guerrilla movements arose until the need for a synthesis, a historical reply, was imperative. Thus rose the Sandinista Front."[2]) When students shortly after this staged a nationwide school strike demanding the release of two professors and a student from jail, Luis decided against force. He let the strike and demonstrations run their course.

On January 1, 1959, General Fulgencio Batista was forced to flee Cuba and take refuge with Generalissimo Rafael Trujillo in the Dominican Republic. Fidel Castro Ruz, thirty-two, who had launched his fight against Batista in 1953 with an abortive attack on the Moncada barracks in Santiago de Cuba, succeeded in showing the world that a guerrilla movement could oust a well-entrenched military dictatorship. Liberation groups throughout Latin America took heart from Castro's victory. The victory in Cuba overshadowed a ten-thousand-word report on Latin America by Milton Eisenhower. He recommended that from then on the United States "refrain from granting special recognition to a Latin American dictator, regardless of the temporary advantage that might seem to be promised by such an act."

Dr. Eisenhower conceded that the United States had made some "honest mistakes" and urged the adoption of Nixon's suggestion that the United States "have an *abrazo* for democratic leaders and a formal handshake for dictators." Ironically many dictators had felt Nixon's warm embrace.

One of the first attempts to emulate Castro's success occurred in Nicaragua on May 30, 1959. Three months earlier, gynecologist Enrique Lacayo Farfán and Pedro Joaquín Chamorro had begun marshaling forces in Costa Rica. The leaders instructed their men in the same guerrilla tactics that Spanish Loyalist Alberto Bayo had taught Fidel Castro in Mexico. The all-Nicaraguan strike force, consisting of only 112 men, hoped to gain support from their countrymen and quickly topple the Somoza regime. Some of the rebels trickled back into Nicaragua to set up training camps in the hills. The rest waited until the time seemed ripe for an invasion. When Conservative party businessmen, allies of Chamorro, called a general strike to protest the Somozas' commercial domination, the rebel leaders decided that their moment had come.

On the thirtieth, a chartered C-46 transport plane bounced to a shaky stop in a Nicaraguan pasture near Santo Tomás. Four men in olive drab, carrying 7-mm Mauser rifles and automatic weapons sprang down. As the plane rumbled back into the sky, sixty more men leading horses and mules loaded with food and supplies straggled onto the field; then the combined force melted into the trees and headed east toward the jungle between Santo Tomás and Bluefields.

The next day another C-46 set down in a boggy field near the town of Tierra Azul, thirty-five miles southeast of Matagalpa. Because the plane's landing gear was damaged on landing, its thirty-five olive-clad passengers hurriedly stripped it of usable contents and set it on fire. But even before the rebels could leave the area, an air force P-51 swooped from the sky and blasted the smoldering wreckage with rockets.

At this point the rebel forces made their first mistake. Instead of fading into the hills while they had time, they elected to lie in ambush for the foot patrol they knew would come to investigate the plane's remains. They succeeded in taking the twelve-man National Guard patrol by surprise, killing three guardsmen with their opening barrage. The rest of the patrol took cover and the two groups battled for four hours until dusk. When the invaders finally broke off contact and pulled back into the foothills of the Cordillera Dariense, they were carrying two wounded and had left behind three dead. These were the first casualties in the well-coordinated attempt to topple the Somozas. Not only had their first taste of action cost them the lives of three men, but carrying the wounded slowed the small troop down. Their betrayal of their position and loss of mobility changed them from a compact strike unit into a group of harried soldiers fleeing just one step ahead of Tacho's task force. The rebels soon encountered another major setback. The support that they had been counting on from the people of the countryside was not forthcoming. The peasants were either too poor to share their food or simply were not interested in another revolution. The leaders of this particular uprising had none of the qualities of an Emiliano Chamorro or a Sandino. The people couldn't or wouldn't identify with these bearded men from the city.

Chamorro and Lacayo, who had organized the invasion from Costa Rica, had planned to have food and arms dropped into the jungle by air. For this purpose they maintained close radio communication with their field unit. But this plan was foiled, first by Tachito's air force, then completely nullified when one radio was lost and the other broke down.

Tachito Somoza had learned his lessons well at West Point. Even more importantly, he had also studied the tactics used in Cuba and profited greatly by the mistakes made by Batista. Tachito sent only eight hundred men of the total guard force to subdue the rebels—and he split his forces into units large enough to overpower the rebels, but small enough so as not to stir up sympathy for his foes as the underdogs. His troops were under strict instructions that none but the rebels were to be molested. In another shrewd move, Tachito called up his reserves in the disputed area, giving them more incentive to fight against the rebels than with them. And then to ensure that world opinion would be on his side, or at least not on the rebels' side, Tachito invited the foreign press, giving them all aid possible for their coverage of the war.

In fact, the war was so well covered that it was to *Time* magazine's Mexico bureau chief Harvey Rosenhouse that the first groups of rebels made known their desire to surrender. Rosenhouse was returning from a National Guard outpost in the small town of Santo Domingo when he encountered a peasant who told him that rebels were on the trail up ahead. Instead of turning back, Rosenhouse went ahead to investigate. He found forty-five rebels, led by thirty-year-old commandant K. José Medina Cuadra, holed up in and around a large house. Medina, who had been a Managua lawyer until three months earlier, told Rosenhouse that he and his men wished to surrender. "Our radio went dead. We were always short of food and the peasants in these mountains do not have enough to spare." He and his men, mostly bearded and between eighteen and thirty, had been part of a force personally headed by Chamorro, who had taken two lieutenants and thirteen men farther back into the jungle to continue the fight.

Rosenhouse sent a message to the guard post written on one of his business cards. The message said simply: "Forty-five rebels want to surrender. They have laid down their guns. Please don't come in shooting." Later that afternoon a guard patrol surrounded the house. The guard commander stepped out and asked Medina to come forward and surrender. They shook hands. Medina said lamely: "I guess this had to turn out this way."

Chamorro and his holdouts surrendered three days later, ending the first airborne rebellion in Nicaraguan history. The entire operation from start to finish lasted only fifteen days. It was much later, however, before the captured rebels learned what was to be their fate.

The guerrillas were taken to Managua to stand trial. All 103 men were charged as traitors to their country. The trial turned out to be lengthy, beginning September 12, 1959, and ending November 21. The defendants were all found guilty as charged and sentenced to eight years in prison. But on December 21 Luis Somoza, acting through Congress, granted all of them pardons.

Despite Luis's kid glove treatment, the cry for freedom grew louder. In July 1960 students of the National University of León were granted permission for their annual student parade. When they took to the streets they let their emotions explode. Marching past the local guard post, twice they hurled insults; the third time they hurled stones. What happened next is open to speculation. The guard said a pistol was fired from the ranks of the students, wounding a guardsman, and that only then did they reply by opening fire on the crowd. But the consequences were clear. Five students were killed, and thirty were wounded. Tachito's guard had suddenly shifted from Luis's policy of tolerance to their own more natural policy of violence. Even though Luis rushed blood plasma and medicines to León the damage had been done. For Nicaraguans, the true face of the dictatorship loomed behind the gunsights of the guard on that July afternoon in León.

The León student massacre roused a rallying cry against the regime in the months that followed. Students in Managua demonstrated against guard "assassins" and there was more violence. Luis, forced to declare a state of siege and suspend civil liberties, saw his attempts to liberalize the dictatorship flow fruitlessly down the gutters of León with the blood of students.

There were attempts to organize a general strike, and another rebellion materialized as former guard lieutenant Julio Alonso Leclair crossed the northern border from Honduras with thirty-one men to raise the standard of revolt against the dynasty. He too failed.

Meanwhile the debate over whether the Somozas should remain in power was echoed in the church. Managua's aging Archbishop Vicente Alejandro González y Roberto, the country's Roman Catholic primate, came out in support of Somoza, citing Pope Gregory XVI's encyclical *Mirari Vos:* "All authority comes from God, and all things are ordered by that same God. Therefore he who resists authority resists God." While agreeing that rulers often abuse this power, the archbishop said the remedy was Christian patience.

Bishop Octavio José Calderón y Padilla replied from the little coffee town of Matagalpa, quoting Pope Leo XIII, "If laws of the state are in open opposition to divine right, resistance is a duty, obedience a crime." The bishop added, "However, one must forget the appearance of veracity of the communists' slogan that religion is the opiate of the people."

But the hemisphere forgot Nicaragua. Castro took the limelight. By late October 1960 there were invasion jitters in Havana. A fleet of anti-Castro exiles was expected to land momentarily from Guatemala. Then in November John Fitzgerald Kennedy was elected thirty-fifth president of the United States.

By mid-November there was another anti-Somoza flareup. A group of Nicaraguans on the Costa Rican border, waiting for a chance to invade, were surprised at their hideout by Costa Rican civil guard commander Alfonso Monge. Monge was shot to death when he opened the door of the old wooden shack where the rebels were holed up. Conservative President Mario Echandi, who had succeeded Pépe Figueres in a free democratic election, declared flatly that the rebels included Cubans. Guatemala's president Miguel Ydigoras Fuentes, who was at the time allowing the CIA to train recruits in his country for an invasion of Cuba, joined Luis Somoza in protesting to the OAS and to Washington. They suggested that the United States Navy patrol the area to prevent a Cuban invasion of Central America, which was only part of the camouflage for the coming American invasion of Cuba, in which both Nicaragua and Guatemala were deeply involved.

Around the same time, fourteen of Somoza's oldest enemies, all members of the Conservative party, seized the towns of Jinotepe and Diriamba, some thirty miles south of the capital. Tachito sent troops backed by tanks to retake Jinotepe, which was no problem since the rebels vanished before the troops arrived. Diriamba was a different story. Rebel leaders seized the Christian Brothers Boys' School and held 250 students and their teachers hostage for sixty-six hours before they finally surrendered.

At the end of 1960, the International Court of Justice in The Hague handed down its long-awaited decision on the disputed territory along the Mosquito Coast. The court upheld the arbitration award of the king of Spain. The territory was declared Honduran. Luis, weary from his internal wars, decided not to contest the decision.

Tachito was promoted to brigadier general in 1957, then to major general and finally to division general in 1964. The battle for land along the Mosquito Coast had been his first defeat. However, by February 1961, Tachito had forgotten the word defeat. He bragged that he was the victor in at least twenty-six attempted revolts and was just reporting success in his twenty-seventh encounter with various rebel forces.

"Peasants reported that twenty-two armed men crossed the Honduras border," a satisfied General Somoza told a reporter in his paneled office in the National Guard headquarters when giving a briefing on the Leclair invasion. "Within minutes, headquarters was alerted and P-51 Mustangs took off to strafe them. Inside a few hours, mobile ground patrols set an ambush. In three clashes six invaders were killed, including their leader, Julio Alonso Leclair, ex-guard officer, and nine were captured. The rest fled back into Honduras two days later after they were unable to shake patrols pursuing them," Tachito explained in a businesslike tone.

Old Tacho had made a wise choice in turning his younger son into a soldier. Modernization of the National Guard had begun in 1939 with the creation of a military academy in Managua, which gave the equivalent of a junior college education along with military instruction. When Tachito took charge in 1946, he ruthlessly weeded out disloyal and unfit cadets, often graduating classes of as few as six second-lieutenants. Although the course was four years long, each cadet spent at least one year studying abroad, usually at the United States Army's Fort Gulick in the Panama Canal Zone. The most promising cadets were sent to Saint Cyr in France or to West Point, or to other military academies in Italy, Spain, Mexico, Peru, Argentina and Chile.

Tachito replaced most of his father's fat old army buddies with young officers who were well trained. Their pay, which ranged from a lieutenant's $100 a month to Tachito's $700 a month as head of the guard, was not lavish, but officers had the run of cut-rate commissaries and were provided with better than average housing.

Guardsmen were recruited through voluntary three-year enlistments. Most joined as illiterates and were taught to read and write. Base pay was $20 a month —high for peasants—plus food, medical care and four uniforms a year. Most important was the gun, which gave them status and authority.

The backbone of the guard was a solid core of noncommissioned officers. In 1961 no one had less than five years of service and many were career noncoms, working toward retirement after thirty years. Noncoms earned from $25 to $50 per month, with 5 percent increases every three years. This group didn't share officers' privileges, but could hope for other benefits. All aspired to become police chiefs in small towns. Since the National Guard had been created as an internal law enforcement organization as well as a defense force, this was feasible. Police chiefs were allowed to take graft.

Old Tacho relied chiefly on the loyalty of noncoms to keep him in power. He once told a reporter: "My officers are disloyal as hell, but my sergeants won't let them pull anything on me." But Tachito concentrated more on officers, eliminating those prone to politics and intrigue.

Tachito attributed the National Guard's efficiency to its "good morale, superior communication," and his own ability to "estimate a situation." Good morale was fostered through rewarding merit. An eye was kept out for men showing ability. The deserving got promotions and were sent to technicians' school in Nicaragua or in the Canal Zone. While his men were required to be loyal to superiors, Tachito also insisted that officers be loyal to their men. He himself was accessible to any officer, and he received at least ten enlisted men a day to hear complaints and to solve problems. Most soldiers came to him because of family problems; often they wanted transfers to areas where they could be near their families. Several times, on complaints of soldiers' girlfriends, Tachito arranged shotgun weddings.

A key factor in the efficiency of the guard was Tachito's pet radio communications system. Every unit, even ten-man border patrols, was equipped with "angry nights," AGR-9 portable two-way radios able to contact headquarters in Managua from any point in the republic. Within minutes of receiving a message reporting an invasion or uprising, Tachito had his forces in action.

The National Guard was not a large force in 1961. It totaled only 3,369 officers and men, of whom 2,000 were assigned to police duty. About 500 were service troops. The strike force was called "General Somoza's Battalion." The guard was equipped with M-1 rifles, machine guns and mortars, but no artillery. Tachito, realistically, regarded artillery as "expensive and unsuited for our needs," although he did have a few antiaircraft guns. He also purchased three Sherman tanks and forty British-made World War II Staghound armored cars from Israel to complement his infantry. The air force consisted of twenty-five Mustang fighters, piloted by men who had been trained in the United States.

Although evidently a man of capacity, because of his abrasive, imperious attitude toward Nicaraguans, Tachito was hated by them. "If I had been soft, the Somoza clan would have been in exile instead of ruling Nicaragua," he said defensively when the subject of popularity came up. Luis, on the other hand, was never personally disliked. But it was Tachito who set his stamp on the government of Nicaragua in the 1960s and 1970s.

CHAPTER 5

Tacho II Takes Command

On March 13, 1961, President John F. Kennedy unveiled his Alliance for Progress for Latin America with the motto: Progress, *Sí*, Tyranny, *No!*

Addressing the assembled Latin American ambassadors in Washington, the young American president declared, "With steps such as these, we propose to complete the revolution of the Americas. . . . To achieve this goal, political freedom must accompany material progress. Let us express our special friendship to the people of Cuba and the Dominican Republic in the hope that they will soon rejoin the society of free men."

Listening to the president in rapt attention was Tachito Somoza's brother-in-law, Guillermo Sevilla-Sacasa, who sat in the front row between Jackie Kennedy and Vice-President Lyndon Johnson. Kennedy continued, "I have just signed a request to Congress for five hundred million dollars as the first step in fulfilling the Act of Bogotá—the first large-scale inter-American effort to attack the social barriers which block economic progress."

Kennedy had good reason to single out the people of Cuba and the Dominican Republic for special mention. The leaders of those two Caribbean nations were targets of the United States, or more precisely, targets of the Central Intelligence Agency. President Dwight Eisenhower had initiated CIA plans for the overthrow of leftist Fidel Castro as well as for putting an end to the long dictatorship of rightist Rafael Trujillo Molina. Kennedy had sanctioned the operations. However, while still campaigning in 1960, he had criticized the Eisenhower administration for decorating Tacho with a medal. Kennedy referred to Tacho as that "codictator of Nicaragua."

Sevilla-Sacasa also knew of the operation against Fidel Castro because the Somozas had been enlisted to aid in what was to become, a month later, the Bay of Pigs invasion of Cuba. The CIA had organized, trained, armed and now commanded the 1,300 troops of the Cuban exile army. And Nicaragua was integral to the plan of the attack. Ironically many of the same CIA planners who had worked to topple Arbenz in Guatemala in 1954 were once again employed in the business of wrecking a government.

CIA operatives were surprised at the willingness of the Somozas to cooperate in the Bay of Pigs. They asked nothing in return. However, they expected the Somozas would demand a fair slice of the Alliance for Progress funds and would take advantage of having an American president in their debt. They were sure the invasion would be successful and they wanted to get rid of Castro.

Years later Tacho II would tell American visitors stories about how he had suffered discrimination during his early years in the United States, and had been called a "spic," which he saw on the same level as a dog. But then he would elaborate to prove his pro-Americanism nevertheless. He would tell how in January 1961 he had attended the inauguration of John F. Kennedy as a cover for a meeting with Allen Dulles, then head of the CIA, to discuss whether in fact the new president would continue with plans to overthrow Castro. The Somozas had been enlisted more than a year earlier and had willingly agreed to provide a base and jumping-off point on Nicaraguan territory to invade Cuba. During the hour-long meeting with Dulles, Tacho recalled that the old spy chief had looked quizzically at him and asked, "Now, General, what do you want in return?" "Dulles pulled harder on his pipe and let out a cloud of tobacco smoke when I told him, 'Not a damned thing, Mr. Dulles.' He was very cordial and assured me that the project would continue. Reassuring him, I said, 'We are brother officers.' Then because of the enormous push Dulles had with the new administration I did say it would be a good thing if someone kept the liberals around Washington from poking at Luis and me."

The Somozas handed over the old airfield in Puerto Cabezas, one of those the United States had constructed, at their father's invitation, during World War II. On the Atlantic coast near the Honduran border, the little fishing and lumber port was an ideal staging area for an invasion flotilla and air strikes against Cuba. The brothers had no trouble keeping from the media all the warlike activity that was springing up in Puerto Cabezas. The port was isolated except by air and sea. Tacho assigned one of his toughest and most controversial officers, Colonel José Iván Alegrett, to be in charge of the Nicaraguan side of the operation. He quickly sealed off the port. The old airfield was repaired and given the code name "Happy Valley."

The initial base for the anti-Castro operation had been in Guatemala. But despite the efforts of old President Miguel Ydigoras Fuentes, it wasn't long before the world knew that Thompson-Cornwall, Inc., had carved a multimillion-dollar airstrip out of the Guatemalan jungle. On October 14, 1960, in Guatemala City congressional opponents of Ydigoras Fuentes complained that hundreds of Cuban exiles were being given commando training by United States instructors. In its January 6, 1961, issue, three months before the invasion, *Time* asked, "Could it be the base for a cooperative U.S.-Guatemalan-Cuban exile airborne military operation against Fidel Castro?"

So the invasion takeoff site was moved to Nicaragua. The equivalent of fifty freight-car loads of aerial bombs, rockets, ammunition and firearms was airlifted into Puerto Cabezas in unmarked C-54s, C-46s and C-47s "in such quantities that, on some days in March, planes required momentary stacking."

William (Rip) Robertson, a tough Texan, was one of two Americans who played a leading role in the actual Bay of Pigs landing. "Rip revered nobody. To him headquarters was 'city hall'; its functionaries were 'feather merchants.'"[1] After World War II, in which he served in the Pacific theater as a Marine captain, he entered the CIA as an aviator and participated in the 1954 CIA coup against Arbenz in Guatemala. Robertson fell out of grace with the CIA's Western Hemisphere division head, J. C. King, after the Guatemalan episode, because he sank a British freighter by mistake. He moved to Nicaragua and became very close to old man Tacho with whom he went into business mining gold. "When the CIA needed a staging base in that country for the Bay of Pigs, Rip was smuggled back onto the agency's payroll behind King's back."[2]

Members of the guard worked for the CIA in preparing the base, guarding it and doing odd jobs, even arming some of the troop-carrying vessels of the little invasion fleet. And they helped keep some of the Americans entertained.

American C-54 pilot Buck Persons, bored with confinement at the "Happy Valley" air base during preparations for the invasion of Cuba, was grateful when the Nicaraguan camp commander, Captain Cardona, flew him and three other American pilots to Managua for a weekend and checked them into a hotel. On Sunday, Cardona vanished. The Americans did not have enough cash to pay the hotel bill. They sat around the lobby for hours in T-shirts and work pants, knives stuck in their belts, feeling all too conspicuous among the tourists. Finally one of them decided to try a telephone number that they had been given for emergencies. It turned out to be President Somoza's palace. The American hung up, embarrassed. Persons thought it hilarious—like being unable to pay the bill at the Mayflower Hotel in Washington and calling the White House to be bailed out. Eventually Cardona reappeared and settled the bill.[3]

Finally the invasion brigade began to move by truck from the Guatemalan base to the point of embarkation at Puerto Cabezas. By April 13, men were beginning to board the seven ships in the small flotilla waiting off Puerto Cabezas. "In the late afternoon of April 14, Luis Somoza, the dictator of Nicaragua, appeared at the dock, his face powdered, bodyguards in his wake. He shouted boldly, 'Bring me a couple of hairs from Castro's beard,' and waved the patriots farewell."[4]

A field hospital with 120 beds that was brought to "Happy Valley" was loaded aboard the U.S.S. *Houston* for the invasion.

On the day before D-Day, Monday, April 17, 1961, Cuban exiles piloting B-26s took off from Nicaragua to Cuba, nine hundred miles away, to destroy Castro's airfields and air force. Air operations sent planes carrying paratroopers and even a PBY sea rescue plane from Puerto Cabezas. Then word was received from Washington to cancel the D-Day strike, even though forces were already on their way to fight without the benefit of the air cover. Finally Kennedy authorized a flight of six unmarked jets to fly cover for a B-26 attack from Nicaragua. The planes did little more than execute some strafing exercises. Kennedy had lived up to the doubts of mission planners who were afraid he would "turn chicken." "It was Kennedy's first major presidential decision. . . . There was no way to predict how an inexperienced leader might react to pressure when the stakes were higher than he had ever dealt with."[5] Kennedy's decision to call off the D-Day air attacks became a controversial issue and Somoza and his top lieutenant in charge at Puerto Cabezas, Colonel Alegrett, never forgave the American president, blaming him for the invasion's failure.

But the Bay of Pigs invasion, named after the landing site in Cuba, was ill conceived. It depended on a spontaneous internal uprising in Cuba that proved just wishful thinking on the part of the CIA. Castro had no trouble defeating the little invasion force. United States credibility throughout Latin America was damaged severely and the failure provided Kennedy with his darkest hours.

Until then, he had been looked upon by progressives throughout Latin America as a new hope for enlightened leadership in the Western Hemisphere. Afterward, it seemed like another case of "business as usual," with the United States flexing its muscles rather than following up on initiatives.

Tacho considered himself part of the anti-Castro operation and enjoyed visiting "Happy Valley" to confer with the Americans in command and members of the exile invasion force. But Tacho did not witness the launching of the invasion. The day the exile force left Nicaragua he was off on an official visit to Taiwan and India. Years later Tacho recounted that when he learned of the invasion's failure he fired off a cable to Allen Dulles warning him that Castro may have won a battle but there was still a war to win against "the communist upstart." The CIA chief, he said, thanked him for his concern but was not optimistic. Tacho later disclosed that Nicaragua was prepared to send its air force to relieve the trapped exile force at the Bay of Pigs, but the United States had refused to allow its P-51s to refuel on American territory, the distance being too great for the aircraft to fly direct to the beachhead.

On a visit to Mexico City a decade later, Tacho held a press conference at the Camino Real Hotel. Enjoying parrying questions, he admitted what everyone had known for a long time: that Nicaragua had provided the key staging area for the invasion and that its "Happy Valley" airfield was the point of origin for the bombing of Cuba. Said Tacho, "Dr. Castro was fiercely opposed to the Somoza family. He sent us twenty-two invasions so in the end we decided to send him one."

When the Cuban operation failed, orders were sent to halt the Dominican operation or to withdraw CIA support for the assassination of Trujillo. But it was too late. The assassins didn't fail. The Dominican dictator was killed on May 30, 1961.

In the United States young Tacho was always playing conservative Republican politics, except for one occasion when his chief aide, Colonel Roger Bermúdez, gave Lyndon Johnson $200,000 from the Somozas for his primary campaign against John Kennedy. Tacho, who knew American politics well and had close friends in Congress, decided it was going to be a Democratic year and he didn't like the liberal hue of the young Kennedy. However, to keep all bases covered, he also contributed $10,000 to the Kennedy campaign, apparently without Kennedy's knowledge.

There is some suggestion that Kennedy, when he became president, remembered the contribution to Johnson. He sent Ambassador Aaron S. Brown to Tacho's court. Brown was unlike Thomas E. Whelan, who had helped the boys consolidate their power over the country in the crucial days after Tacho's assassination. Ambassador Brown is said to have leaned on the Somozas to prevent Tacho II from succeeding Luis in the presidency, obliging them to put in the puppet René Schick.

The Somozas spent a lot of time trying to make the people forget and forgive the dynasty. They even allowed them to be anti-Somoza to an extent. A Nicaraguan was safe until he acted against the family; then he could be killed or at least thrown into jail. But by 1961 the caliber of their opposition was changing.

On July 23, 1961, in a poor barrio of Tegucigalpa in neighboring Honduras a trio of Nicaraguans argued for hours over what to christen their national liberation movement, which was to take up the armed struggle against the Somoza dictatorship. Twenty-six-year-old Carlos Fonseca Amador, a student of the career of Augusto César Sandino, prevailed and had "Sandinista" included in the title Frente Sandinista de Liberación Nacional (FSLN). For many Nicaraguans, Sandino's reputation remained in such eclipse during the Somoza family's rule that not until 1963 was the name adopted for the whole resistance movement. But the FSLN was born and the old anarchist red and black colors, which also made up the flag of the triumphant "26 of July Movement" of Fidel Castro, were accepted as the battle colors. The other two founders were Silvio Mayorga, twenty-five, and Tomás Borge, thirty.

While stimulated by the success of the Cuban rebellion in January 1959, as were other national liberation movements throughout Latin America, the trio had already spent most of their youth in clandestine leftist movements. They sought not only to overthrow the Somozas, but to change the entire politico-socioeconomic system. They wanted radical change, based on Marxist-Leninist ideas.

Of the trio, Carlos Fonseca, a bespectacled, tall, slim man with dark, close-cropped curly hair and a moustache (he later grew a goatee and let his hair grow longer), had the most impressive credentials. Born in the pleasant little coffee town of Matagalpa, the illegitimate son of an administrator of Somoza's vast commercial enterprises in the department of Matagalpa, Fonseca had been disturbed by the inequity of a society that responded to the whim of one man. Despite his father's post, the family was always poor. Young Carlos helped out by selling his mother's homemade candy in front of the local cinemas. While he despised his father he felt a great deal of love and compassion for his mother.

As a youth he studied in the same primary and secondary schools as Borge before leaving for Managua, where he finished his secondary education. He enrolled in the University of Managua law school, but suffered financial hardship. His political interests developed apace. He was active in revolutionary circles led by Marxist-Leninists and read any books which he thought might help him battle the Somozas. In 1955 he joined the Nicaraguan Socialist party.

Borge attended the university in León, where in 1954 he joined a Marxist cell that published *El Universitario*. When Tacho Somoza was assassinated in 1956 Borge and Fonseca were both jailed. Fonseca, who was released from prison after a few months, went to the Soviet Union and the Democratic Republic of (East) Germany in 1957 as a delegate to the sixth World Youth and Student Festival.

The year 1959 had marked a resurgence of the Nicaraguan guerrilla movement. Small bands carried out forays into the country from the Honduran and Costa Rican borders. Carlos was with a group named "La Guerrilla del Chaparral," after one of their battles. It was based across the border in Honduras and made incursions into northern Nicaragua. In June 1959 Carlos had been gravely wounded in a skirmish, receiving two bullets in the chest. He traveled to Havana, where he stayed in the home of Pedro Monett, member of the Cuban Communist party's central committee, and fully recovered.

Fonseca returned to Nicaragua in 1960 but was again taken prisoner. When released, he returned to Cuba, this time with Silvio Mayorga, where the two attended revolutionary meetings and mapped out their initial anti-Somoza campaign, launched in 1961 from Tegucigalpa.

Upon his return from his first visit to Cuba, Fonseca quit the Socialist party. He created a group which in 1960 called itself the Patriotic Nicaraguan Youth Group (JNP). That year provided euphoric months for the young revolutionaries. The Cuban revolution had succeeded; Fidel Castro still had an ambassador in Managua. But the United States, which had foreseen the rise of national liberation movements throughout Latin America, as well as anticipated an intensification of guerrilla wars, changed the curriculum at its training school for Latin American troops from classical textbook military tactics to counterinsurgency. In 1961 at the United States Army antiguerrilla school at Fort Gulick on the eastern shores of Gatún Lake, in what was then the United States Canal Zone, Nicaragua had seventy-four officers in training—almost two to three times as many as the other countries.

The Sandinistas went into the mountains along the Honduran border to fight the Somozas. In 1961 the guerrillas chose Colonel Santos López, who had fought with Sandino, to be their leader. They had no problems with president Villeda Morales of Honduras, a liberal who turned a blind eye to their activities. In the mountains near the Patuca River, the Sandinistas spent the next eighteen months training sixty-three guerrillas. Their base camp was in dense jungle in mountainous Honduran territory about thirty miles from the border, near the Coco River which flows parallel to the Patuca River on its journey to the Atlantic Ocean.

Once the guerrillas decided they were prepared, they chose as their first military objective Wiwilí, where they had already done some political proselytizing. Rainy season mud and lack of knowledge of the terrain prevented them from reaching their objective so they decided to seek one closer to the Patuca and Coco rivers.

"We made the mistake of attacking Raiti," Tomás Borge related to an interviewer seventeen years later, "without knowledge of the land or doing any proselytizing and without securing our supply lines. This was a backward area, not only politically but culturally. Many of the inhabitants didn't know Spanish and spoke an Indian dialect or pidgin English—the area had once been under the British— so we had a communication problem."[6]

The guerrillas attacked and occupied the towns of Raiti and Walaquistán. Colonel Santos López and a second group were to attack the town of Bocay, then send a small motorboat to Borge and the others. However, the guard had reinforced their positions at Bocay and also had airplanes in the area. Since gas was unavailable the boat could not make it back up the river. As a result the guerrillas broke into three groups—one directed by the colonel, another by Modesto Duarte (this group was eventually wiped out) and the third led by Borge. Borge's group remained downriver near Walaquistán. After realizing that their mission was impossible because of the long distances and the fact that reinforcements had to be sent by boat, they decided to attack San Carlos downriver. One group remained on the Honduras bank of the river with a wounded companion while the others crossed the river into Nicaragua.

"But instead of following the river we tried to take a shortcut and got lost in the mountains. We carried on for sixteen days, lost in the jungle. We were dying of hunger and did not know where the enemy was," Borge said.[7]

The group began following a small creek which turned out to flow into the navigable Zanzán River. They built small rafts but lost most of their weapons, including Borge's submachine gun. Though far from the Coco, they found a small town where they could eat for the first time in weeks. An Italian who had a small ranch was living in the village. Borge described him as not more than thirty years old, white, tall, well dressed. They never knew his name so they called him "The Italian."[8] He became their guide and took the group through the thick jungle to the Indian village of Zanzán. "The Italian" was later captured and killed by the guard.

About forty guardsmen were waiting in Zanzán, a village of only a few hundred inhabitants. "The confrontation was difficult," Borge said, "because the few arms that remained did not work [the bullets were wet] and a guard officer shot Silvio Mayorga in the leg with a semiautomatic M-2 carbine."[9] The guerrillas, about seventeen in all, retreated with Mayorga wounded and regrouped with the other fifteen men on the Honduran side. In a subsequent encounter with the guard, two more guerrillas, Raustino Ruiz and Boanerjes Santamaría, were killed.

"Then we had a meeting," Borge testifies, "in which we decided to retreat, abandoning the fight because under those conditions we could not continue. We retreated, and it was really a very difficult, very grueling retreat. We had eaten very little. And now the Sandinistas were stuck in the jungle because the government of Villeda Morales had fallen and those of the military who replaced him in Tegucigalpa did not demonstrate the same tolerance towards the 'anti-Somocistas.'"[10]

Marching on to the Patuca River, Borge's rear group encountered an American gold miner. They captured his motorboat, food and weapons. Borge called the seizure "a miracle because we did not have strength enough to swing a machete."[11]

The first episode of the FSLN guerrillas drew to a close with the greater part of the guerrilla soldiers actually captured by the Honduran military and deported to Mexico. Borge remained hidden in Honduras for a time, then returned to Nicaragua clandestinely to devise a "fallback strategy" deemphasizing armed struggle and directing the Sandinista militants toward political activity.

The Sandinistas struck an alliance with the traditional left, the Socialist party, and the Republican Mobilization party (the Socialist party connected with the Communist movement in Nicaragua). Although organizational efforts began in the countryside, the main thrust of the work was in organizing barrio committees in the cities to demand better living conditions, including paved streets and running water.

But the time came, Borge said, when "the contradiction between the traditional left and ourselves became abruptly and distinctly an issue as far as the electoral process was concerned."

In July 1962 Nicaragua's Congress experienced a ruckus that did nothing to help Luis in his image-building and so-called liberalizing of the regime. The Somozas had encouraged Milton Eisenhower to talk with the opposition during his visit in 1958. They permitted the opposition to publish almost anything it pleased in the newspapers, a favor they used as evidence of democracy. As 80 percent of the Nicaraguans were illiterate, the newspapers were not damaging.

The Somozas were less liberal with radio stations. Any radio program judged "of a subversive character" or likely to "undermine public order" was forbidden, under penalty of a $150 fine against the station owners, directors and program authors, when such programs were aired. In early July the Somozas' handpicked Congress passed a new law extending the penalties to all associated with a "subversive" broadcast, to even the technicians, advertising sponsors and announcers.

When the legislators relaxed for the usual routine vote, an anti-Somoza crowd entered the Congress Building to protest the law. They were expected. Waiting for them was a gang of eighty government thugs headed by Nicolasa Sevilla, a tough-looking woman who commanded the Somoza male street gangs in Managua. When the demonstrators cried, "Liberty" and "The Somozas must go," they were met with knives and sticks. Some of Nicolasa's boys even drew pistols and fired into the crowd. When the half-hour melée ended and the demonstrators had retreated, there were no dead, but there were thirty-five wounded, including "La Nicolasa" who had been hit on the head by a chair. The congressmen continued their session and passed the new broadcast law in the presence of the National Guard, guns drawn.

Nobody believed the Somozas would hold free elections in February 1963 and hand over the power to the winner, even under pressure from Kennedy. Although Congress had passed a law in 1959 barring the family from the ballot, the Somozas seemed very certain to hold on to their power, and this suggested keeping the presidency.

The Somozas made much of their promise to quit office. They wanted the Alliance for Progress funds, and liberalizing the regime was good for business.

Three months before the elections, the traditional Conservative party voted to withdraw from the campaign and boycott the elections. Conservative leader Dr. Fernando Agüero Rochas, told delegates to the Conservatives' convention in Managua, "We won't participate in a fraud rigged by the Somozas."

Agüero charged that Nicaragua's election machinery had been stacked in favor of the Somozas' Nationalist Liberal party. The regime controlled four of the five seats of the supreme electoral tribunal, which policed voting and the ballot count. Of the tribunal's five judges: one was chosen by Congress, where the Somozas had their majority party; the second by the handpicked Supreme Court; the third by the government party; the fourth by the official opposition (a weak splinter group of the Conservatives which often supported the government); and the fifth by the minority party receiving the greatest number of registrations, meaning the traditional Conservative party. The Somozas rejected a more equal distribution. And Dr. Agüero noted that the regime still refused to permit the United Nations or the OAS to observe the elections.

Agüero, a Managuan oculist and an outstanding orator, traced his opposition to the Somozas back to 1954 when he was a member of a band of revolutionaries who sneaked in from Costa Rica to ambush the Somozas and end their regime. Like so many such attempts, it backfired, but Agüero, disguised as a priest, managed to reach the Honduran embassy, where he was granted asylum. He went to Honduras and returned a year later to begin the revival of the old Conservatives. In 1960 he became party leader. His platform wasn't merely anti-Somoza but also a call for "democratic revolution" and for desperately needed social and economic reforms. Agüero argued that the continuation of the Somoza regime could pave the way for a Communist takeover in Nicaragua.

Luis was unimpressed by the Conservative boycott; "a sign of weakness. They know that we have 70 percent of the country with us," he exclaimed.

The government's candidate was former minister of education and foreign affairs René Schick, who based his campaign on the Somozas' "record." He had agreed to keep Tacho II on as commander of the National Guard. It was Luis who proposed Schick's candidacy. The United States supported him.

In public, the two brothers affected unity and agreement on most subjects, but in private, they often argued bitterly. Luis didn't want Tacho to be president. Tacho was too military. Luis knew it would be easy to put Tacho in, but difficult to take him out. Therefore he insisted that Tacho not take his turn, but let Schick become president. The brothers saw eye-to-eye on retaining power, but they differed as to the method. To Tacho, the key to power was his guard, whereas Luis, more of a visionary, felt that if a Mexican-type, basically one-party system was organized, they could retain power through "changing the monkey" (puppet president) every five years. He wanted a dictatorship of the party which would be more palatable internationally.

Luis had instituted a certain amount of social reform: social security, thirty-day paid vacations and other benefits—if one was lucky enough to have a qualifying job. There was also some increase in salaries and beneficent paternalism. As a result, the young Somozas of the early sixties were considered more enlightened than their father—or at least more alert.

Luis had all kinds of idiosyncrasies. He was careless about or indifferent to personal debts. He owed money for years to a man in Rivas for the tortillas supplied to his workers at his Dolores sugar mill and plantation. He had never paid a man for a kerosene stove he had bought in Managua. He had an engaging personality, but some considered him a petty thief. Others described him as a hypocrite. Still he was the more popular of the two brothers.

Tacho, besides running the now 4,500-man National Guard, operated most of the family enterprises. The family wealth was estimated at 10 percent of the country's gross national product ($300 million in 1961). They had control of a four-vessel shipping company, the Lanica airline, 50 percent of the country's cement production, 40 percent of its sugar and alcohol output, and 10 percent of its coffee crop.[12]

The boys revamped the electoral law under which only the ineffectual faction of the traditional Conservatives was permitted to run as opposition. Luis sent to Congress in the summer of 1962 a reform bill to legalize any party that could muster fifteen thousand members. This opened the way for the Independent Liberal party, the part of the old Liberal party opposed to the Somozas' Nationalist Liberal party. The other party permitted to run was the Republican Mobilization party, composed of communists, fellow travelers, "Fidelistas," labor unions and student groups.

While the elections were no bother to the Somozas, they did have to contend with internal bickering. The minister of the interior and police chief, Julio Quintana, had made up his mind he should be the presidential candidate. But this self-made man was far too dangerous for the Somozas to place even in a puppet's seat, so his candidacy was pushed aside in favor of the more docile Schick.

Although the Somozas kept their promise not to appear on the ballot on election day in February 1963, the people had no real alternative. René Schick, the Somozas' handpicked man, represented the Somozas' Nationalist Liberal party. Diego Manuel Chamorro, head of the Somoza-aligned splinter of the Conservative party, was the other candidate. This faction of the Conservative party was known as the Zancudo party, named after a type of mosquito found in Nicaragua.

Fernando Agüero angrily withdrew, calling the election a farce, and supporters of his traditionalist Conservative party gathered in Managua's Plaza de la República shouting "Viva Agüero" and "Down with the Somozas." The guard first tried to disperse the crowd by spraying it with blue-dyed water from a city water truck. But soon they were swinging billy clubs and firing bullets and tear gas into the crowd, killing two and wounding seven. Agüero was quickly placed under house arrest. The results were announced early that election day. With only three of the country's 1,388 precincts in, Schick claimed a ten-to-one victory over Chamorro, who quickly conceded defeat.

The United States decided this was a step in the right direction and let Schick know that he would be welcome to pay an informal visit to Washington before his May inauguration. For Washington, the dilemma over giving special consideration to the Somozas, at least in name, had been solved.

Agüero said, "I will not be a party to fraud. There will be trouble. We don't recognize Schick as president." On radio, Schick promised, "I will not be a puppet to anyone." No one, certainly not the Somozas, took him seriously.

As former president, Luis automatically took his seat in the twenty-member Senate. Said Luis, "Nicaragua is my home and I intend to live and work in it." He also stated that when he left office he would be free to join the anti-Castro fight. Many Cuban exiles then in Nicaragua kept promising that "something big" was being planned. But any planning for a new exile invasion of Cuba sponsored by the Somozas got no further than the publicity stage. Luis remarked, "I myself am willing to lead the invasion of Cuba by going into the front lines with the volunteers." But he was a most unlikely soldier and this bellicose statement reflecting continued enmity toward Castro's Cuba didn't fit his character.

During the 1963 elections, the guard also reported, for the first of numerous times to come, that the fledging FSLN had been annihilated.

President Kennedy met with seven Central American presidents in San José, Costa Rica in March 1963. The seven presidents agreed to send top representatives to an April meeting in Nicaragua. The aim: "To develop and put into immediate effect common measures to restrict the movement of subversive nationals to and from Cuba, and the flow of materials, propaganda and funds from that country."

In closed-door sessions, Kennedy said that the United States was keeping close watch on vessels outbound from Cuba to other Latin American ports, and would interfere with ships carrying arms or troops. Also, the United States would send to any Central American nation that requested it enough military force to combat communist subversion. The Somozas were gratified by Kennedy's performance. Luis said, "We hope and expect the U.S. will solve our problems." In 1963 alone, military aid from the United States to Nicaragua's National Guard was valued at $1,600,000, the eleventh highest grant in Latin America.

In the years following the Bay of Pigs fiasco, Cuban exiles discovered the Somozas to be sympathetic anticommunists. Manuel Artime, the civilian head of the Bay of Pigs landing, developed a close friendship with Tacho after finally being released by Castro in December 1963. Artime and some Bay of Pigs veterans formed the "Movement for Revolutionary Recuperation" in Miami and the secret war against Castro intensified.

Artime counted on material and financial support from the CIA. He could count on safe haven in Nicaragua for his attack craft. His movement organized secret camps in Costa Rica and Nicaragua, where the training of Cuban exile guerrillas continued. The Somozas openly supported the anti-Castro movement. Luis told foreign reporters that Cubans were being trained in "two or three Central American countries and in the U.S. but unfortunately none in Nicaragua." However, Nicaraguan newspapers reported that Cubans were training in their jungle along the coast. Artime's camp in Costa Rica was found to be involved in a $50,000 smuggling scandal. The privacy provided by the government was also an excellent cover for contraband liquor operations. Artime's little CIA-supported fleet—torpedo boats armed with 57-mm guns, recoilless rifles and other weapons—in addition to blowing up a sugar mill in southern Cuba—hit a Spanish freighter heading for Cuba, killing the captain. It was a mistake, they said. They thought it was the Cuban ship *Sierra Maestra,* not the Spanish *Sierra Aranzazo.* President Lyndon Johnson cut off United States support for Artime's commandos and in early 1965 the training camps had to be closed, but by then Artime and Tacho had become such close friends that the Cuban exile began to represent Tacho in Miami in business deals.

At first, President Schick managed to restrain the heavy hand of Tacho in the guard. (The younger Somoza brother was in early 1964 already laying plans to take his turn as president.) With help from Luis, Schick court-martialed Colonel Juan López, the guard commander in Chinandega, for murder—hitherto unheard of for a guard officer who, unless in disgrace with the Somozas, was invariably considered above the law. López was convicted and jailed for the January 1964 murder of three so-called "agitators" accused of trying to indoctrinate the peasants.

In 1965 Tacho, attending a wake for an air force captain killed in an air crash, was suddenly taken by one of the mourners—a luscious, bold and beautiful girl with skin the color of cinnamon. She was Dinorah Sampson, only seventeen years old and a telephone receptionist at Radio Mundial. Dinorah's facial bone structure was somewhat like Tacho's wife Hope's, but any resemblance ended there. Dinorah couldn't claim any aristocratic ancestry. Her parents, who were from León, had separated, and her mother had had an affair with a Cuban baseball star who ended up as radio announcer in Managua. Nor could Dinorah claim Hope's scholastic achievement and years at some of the best finishing schools in the United States.

Dinorah had begun work as a poor fifteen-year-old servant-receptionist in the office of lawyer José Antonio Mejía Robleto. From the thin hungry girl who became the friend and lover of newsmen who worked at the radio station, Dinorah blossomed into a beautiful young woman. Tacho found her an uninhibited mistress who didn't mind if their rendezvous was the old Somozas' Las Mercedes farmhouse or even a warehouse. In those early days of their affair the contrast between wife and mistress could not have been greater. Hope loved Tacho but spent much of her time trying to smooth his rough edges and make him into a gentleman. "She wanted to make Tacho into something he wasn't," said a friend. "She wanted him to mix in Newport society, eat caviar and drink champagne and watch his language and manners." Tired of Hope's constant correction of his barracks mannerisms, Tacho found release in the arms of the warm teenaged beauty.

Even before meeting Tacho, "La Dinorah," as she became known to Managuans, had friends in the guard and enjoyed the company of soldiers as much as Tacho did. Her first cousin Ronald Sampson had entered the guard and quickly became distinguished for his hot temper and bullying manner, even though he was of small physique.

The aloof and sophisticated Hope said of Tacho, "There is nothing gypsy or aristocratic about him. I have all that in the family, but he does have gypsy ideas."[13] From 1965 on, Tacho was no longer satisfied by periodic gypsy flings with girls at home and on his frequent trips abroad. He now had two women at home. It tended to complicate his life but he quickly drowned any tension with scotch whiskey, the drink of the times.

When President Johnson, unilaterally and in violation of the OAS charter, decided on April 24, 1965, to land United States Marines and the Eighty-second Airborne Division in the Dominican Republic (eventually 22,000 troops) to protect "American lives" and to prevent "another Cuba," Nicaragua was one of the first countries to agree to join in an OAS-sponsored peacekeeping force. The Somozas gave full support to this first action of President Johnson in Latin America. Tacho dispatched 1,200 of his National Guard to Santo Domingo under the command of Colonel Julio Gutiérrez, the popular commander of its armored battalion. Gutiérrez held a high post in the inter-American peacekeeping force in Santo Domingo. Because of his popularity Tacho saw to it that he didn't subsequently return to active duty within Nicaragua.

During the first half of the 1960s, Nicaragua's gross national product increased 40 percent, the highest rate of growth in Central America. During those years, the Alliance for Progress provided $30 million for the construction of 350 miles of roads to facilitate dairy and beef production and reduce the economy's dependence on cotton, a crop in which the Somozas weren't as heavily invested as in cattle. A new young group of entrepreneurs was appearing on the scene.

The guerrilla movement against the dynasty seemed stalled. Carlos Fonseca, who had been moving between Cuba, Honduras and Nicaragua winning converts abroad in support of the New Nicaragua Movement, returned in 1963 clandestinely, a wanted man. A year later in June, he was captured on a Managua street. President Schick, wanting him out of the way but not killed, changed his sentence from imprisonment to exile in Mexico in 1965. There Fonseca often lamented to other Caribbean revolutionaries that the "Frente Sandinista" was not further along the road to revolt. In 1966 he returned secretly to Nicaragua to prepare for Pancasán, the site chosen for a major battle effort, in order to establish the front as the major rural guerrilla force.

In early 1966 Tacho was asked about communism in Nicaragua. "It doesn't matter if it's homegrown or if it comes from Cuba, we can keep it under control." He estimated that "about 10,000 people in Nicaragua could be considered communists or at least sympathizers." He added that only 300 of them were "hard-core communists—the leaders." At the time, the population in Nicaragua was 1.6 million.

In March 1966, the press reported that even though guerrillas were very active in Guatemala, they were nonexistent in Nicaragua. It was also in March that Tacho said he would accept the presidential nomination of the Liberal party if it was offered to him.

Dr. Fernando Agüero Rocha of the Conservative party was the opposition's candidate. He had spent four years in exile for having plotted against the Somozas. Now he was back in Nicaragua. In one of his first campaign speeches he attacked United States support for the Somozas. He said, "The U.S. insists on its policy of supporting governments imposed by the military boot."

While campaigning for Dr. Agüero, Pedro Joaquín Chamorro claimed that if Somoza were elected, "then political tensions will continue until a crisis is reached. One day, our society, under continual pressures from all sides, will have to explode." He admitted, however, that freedom of the press did exist in Nicaragua.

There were anti-Somoza activities inside and outside the country. In mid 1966, Costa Rican students protested the Somozas' estimated 223,000-acre landholdings in their country. But due to poor economic conditions at the time, no effort was made to nationalize the Somozas' land because Costa Rica would have to pay for the land seizure. Domestically, the week before the Nationalist Liberal party's convention in León, there was a student strike against the government. A few days before the convention, three bombs believed to have been set by anti-Somoza forces exploded in the building where the party had scheduled its meetings.

Tacho was, automatically, nominated for the presidency. He immediately agreed to give up his title as head of the guard—the constitution stipulated that no military officer on active duty could be candidate for the country's highest civil office. But from his father's palace, La Curva, he retained control over the guard as completely as he had before he shed his title.

Tacho, a hefty 225 pounds, dressed in his military uniform to accept the nomination for president in August 1966. He was not in the best of health. While in the United States some months earlier he had checked into Johns Hopkins Hospital where he learned that he was having a calcium reaction in his kidneys. The doctors said he must lose fifty pounds. After losing some weight he noticed the effects—during the campaign all the women screamed for him, he averred.

In Nicaragua four Sundays were set aside for voters' registration. Although Tacho remarked, "In some ways, we have purer democracy and human rights than in the U.S.," the registration centers were set up in the homes of guard officers or known Somoza supporters.

President Schick, in reaction to Tacho's increasing arrogance and imperious behavior—especially toward loyal family retainers—took to drink. His health collapsed and he died on August 3, 1966, only two days after the loyal Somoza Nationalist Liberal party duly nominated Tacho. Schick had never been able to shake his image as a Somoza puppet. And due to his strong anti-Castro ideas, he had been very popular with the Cuban exiles, who tended to support the Somozas vocally.

But Schick had generally been considered an honest, friendly and capable person. The last Thursday of every month he habitually held a public audience, putting aside affairs of state. He gave petitioners money from his pocket. That could not solve major problems but it had provided brief relief for a few of his fellowmen.

When Schick died, Tacho's aide Lorenzo Guerrero Gutiérrez, former chief of police, minister of the interior and vice-president, was given the job and the title of president until elections were held. Meanwhile brother Luis ran the election campaign.

In August and October of 1966, Sandinista guerrilla forces were tracked down in the mountains of Matagalpa near where Fonseca and other guerrillas had been born. They had launched a rural guerrilla movement with funds from bank holdups in Managua. But because of the new emphasis on counterinsurgency and difficulty in winning over a poor and apathetic peasantry, this movement also failed. The guerrillas were not annihilated as Tacho once again claimed. Still, Tacho was in a jubilant mood. To show what a good anticommunist friend of America he was, he offered to send some of the guard to fight for the Americans in Vietnam. The United States quietly declined the offer.

Tacho was very much still in control of the guard. He juggled some of the guard command posts to ensure that the guard played its usual role in getting out the vote. He chose his half-brother José to command the guard's elite combat battalion, the mobile fighting unit. In 1966 this unit, along with other guard groups, participated in two counterinsurgency exercises with the armed forces of sister Central American countries also concerned about the leftist guerrilla threat.

In an effort most of them recognized was futile, the Conservatives, Independent Liberals and the new Christian Democrats formed a united front known as UNO, the National Opposition Union. The UNO put up Conservative Dr. Fernando Agüero Rochas as their candidate.

Despite the odds in Tacho's favor the UNO went out and campaigned, attracting large crowds. There was a noticeable difference between the crowds attracted by the two sides. Tacho had the state organization at his disposal and also the aid of the guard and a paramilitary organization known as AMOROCS *(Asociación Militar de Oficiales Retirados, Obreros y Campesinos Somocistas)*. Government bureaucrats, if they valued their jobs, had to attend a Somoza rally. UNO crowds included the most vocal elements of the general population opposed to Somoza rule, as well as influential figures whose fortunes had suffered under the dynasty.

It was a bloody campaign.

CHAPTER 6

Beginning in Blood

On January 22, 1967, electoral violence reached its peak. Dr. Agüero, Pedro Joaquín Chamorro, and other opposition leaders, decided that Somoza's grip on the electoral levers made it impossible for anyone else to win an election. A Somoza victory was a foregone conclusion.

For days they appealed to their partisans to converge on Managua for a demonstration of support and each call carried a reminder not to forget to bring "the little package of food." This was not in itself a suspicious request because the Somoza machine always provided its voters with little packages of food and containers of rum on election day. But to some members of the opposition, little packages meant "arms."

The opposition planned to use the crowd to try to tip a revolt, hoping the guard might come out against Tacho. It was a wild, totally desperate plan, given the guard's record of loyalty to the family.

On January 22, some sixty thousand opposition members gathered in Managua to hear Dr. Agüero speak at a rally. The demonstrators carried signs saying: "No more Somozas. No more assassinations." Agüero called for a general national strike to "demand electoral guarantees." He had already appealed to acting President Guerrero to postpone the elections in order to make sure they would be "free." He announced that he had received no answer. Then the demonstrators began shouting at the guard to rise up and overthrow the Somoza dynasty. The guard ignored the plea. Instead, when the crowd began to march on the National Palace, the home of the Congress, the guard opened fire.

In the shooting and street fighting, approximately forty members of the opposition were killed and more than a hundred wounded. The dead included one guard officer and two soldiers. Then, in a move which brought the foreign press streaming into Managua, a large group of the opposition seized the Gran Hotel on downtown Roosevelt Avenue, across the street from the National Palace. There they held 117 foreign guests and the management hostage.

Within a short time a Sherman tank appeared on the narrow avenue facing the Gran Hotel, occasionally firing a round. The major physical damage to the hotel was a soccerball-size hole on the southern exterior. A few shots went astray—one destroyed a small barber shop next door. Miraculously the tank caused no casualties. The rebels who immediately surrendered their arms were allowed to go free. (Some who were arrested on Sunday and Monday said they were beaten upon arriving at the prison.)

Acting President Lorenzo Guerrero was reportedly in León, some sixty miles away. Negotiations didn't get off to a quick start. The standoff lasted twenty-four hours. A reporter who was being held hostage said he thought that was because of lack of communication between the guard and the 897 civilians, many armed, in the hotel. During the night, the papal nuncio and other representatives of the Catholic church were mainly responsible for negotiating a truce. When it was learned that eighty-nine Americans were being held hostage, United States embassy officials James Engle and Edward Cheney also took part. The standoff ended peacefully the next day when the occupiers were allowed to go free in exchange for leaving their arms behind. The hotel was looted, its storerooms ransacked; many of the rooms suffered minor damage. The opposition won its only demand—to be able to leave the hotel peacefully.

Agüero and Chamorro remained free, but their telephones were cut off. The office of Chamorro's newspaper, *La Prensa*, was occupied by guardsmen and it remained closed until February 3. The newspaper claimed it suffered 100,000 córdobas worth of damage and that the National Guard took two typewriters, an eighteen-inch Japanese saber and a portrait of Sandino from the premises. Three opposition radio stations were also closed.

"An almost eerie situation has resulted. Bitterness and hatred are apparent on both sides, yet the campaign for the presidential election on February 5 is continuing as if nothing had happened," wrote the observer for *The New York Times*. [1]

The city returned to a semblance of normality for a couple of days. Tacho continued to campaign but he was careful always to be surrounded by bodyguards. Practically everyone in a Somoza rally crowd was known as a loyal government employee, but nevertheless all were watched carefully by Somoza guns.

Hope stood at her husband's side during the rallies, but in the first row, in the place of honor, was Dinorah. An aide later explained, "Dinorah's presence improved his performance."

Wednesday, January 25, was a tense day. Mothers and wives of missing antigovernment demonstrators gathered before the block-long El Hormiguero (Ant Hole) Prison. Then late in the afternoon, as offices were emptying on Roosevelt Avenue and shops were closing for the day, the guard appeared to break up small groups of people, mostly youths, on street corners. The street-corner demonstrations were actually a daily event in which students—sometimes three hundred or four hundred strong—gathered on Roosevelt Avenue with placards in silent and pacific protest. They had taken place as usual on January 23 and 24 without interference.

The guard opened fire on agitators and workers alike—they made no distinction. They shouted obscenities as they shot into the evening crowds, including many women on their way home. Some people backed into doorways to hide; others formed additional groups at the end of the block, further angering the guard. These small groups of people were not all demonstrating. Despite the danger of such incidents, Latin Americans have the habit of staying around to watch police confrontations from a distance. Protest demonstrations where police interference is expected are popular spectator sports.

As the crowd dispersed, running down side streets and into homes, offices and shops for protection, guardsmen flitted from doorway to doorway prepared to open fire on the unseen enemy. Foreign newsmen, including American TV network reporters, followed in their wake, filming the scene.

This was the first of a long series of almost random acts of violence by the guard that I was to witness over a period of more than a dozen years. As I took photographs of the scene, a guard captain who showed evident distaste for the anticitizen terrorism before us, approached me and tapped me on the shoulder. "Just like Santo Domingo," he said. He had been a member of the Nicaraguan peacekeeping contingent in the Dominican civil strife. He was a rare humane guard officer who was later promoted to a desk job and then sent abroad.

Tacho held a press conference at El Retiro, his Spanish-style ranch house built in 1964, two and one-half miles from La Loma on a hundred acres of rolling grassland. He did not give the performance of a Latin American strongman. Seated at the head of a long table, ordering drinks for foreign newsmen and taking a bloody mary for himself, he acted as though he were conducting a business board meeting. There was no speaking in Spanish, the official language. Somoza appeared more at ease in English. Gregarious, he warmed to the company of newsmen and took all their questions. He dismissed his opponents as a bunch of malcontents, stressing that constitutionality was his byword, and, to prove how magnanimous he was, waxed expansive on how the arrested opposition leaders would be released. He wanted to be thought of as a regular guy. "Right out of the American comic books," joked one of the newsmen later.

When beginning his campaign for the presidency in 1966, Tacho was at first afraid of journalists and they of him. One Nicaraguan newsman recalled having treaded softly at the first conference. Then Tacho was well prepared and it went very well. "But the next time we newsmen were bolder and asked some really tough questions. Tachito was not prepared and he got mad at three of us and later reprimanded us." He soon learned how to handle the press, and Nicaraguan newsmen learned to be careful with their questions.

He shrugged when foreign newsmen noted that his boys had torn down all the opposition electoral posters. "It was tough luck," was his uncharacteristically mild-mannered reply.

Opposition spokesman Pedro Joaquín Chamorro was arrested at 9:30 A.M. on January 24, the day before the downtown guard melée. Although constitutional guarantees were then officially still in effect, he was taken without a warrant from his home where he was meeting with his family. Earlier in the day Pedro Joaquín had told newsmen that after the guard searched La Prensa they would "plant something and say they have found arms in the place. They are not difficult to predict, they always play the same simple games." And indeed the arrest came after the government claimed it had found a cache of weapons at *La Prensa*. But a guard lieutenant admitted privately that they had only found a "few small-caliber shells."

Chamorro was taken to El Hormiguero and kept in a cell known as "La Leona." In later testimony he said he was kept in a cold bath for the first twenty-four hours and had a gun held to his temple several times. He added that one soldier grabbed his testicles on one occasion saying he wanted "to find out what size they were."

On Saturday, January 28, General Gustavo Montiel, National Guard chief of staff, charged that the opposition, which included the communists, planned to burn down the city in an attempt to overthrow the government. He said the plotters were armed with rifles, submachine guns and explosives and hoped to "create chaos" that would bring about armed intervention. In fact, the Frente did not participate in the 1967 election protest. Recalled Sandinista Tomás Borge, "The contradiction between the traditional left and ourselves became abruptly and distinctly an issue as far as the electoral process was concerned." By that time the Frente was already back in the mountains organizing the Pancasán attack.

The intervention would come as it had two years earlier in the Dominican Republic, by means of a hemispheric force that would see to it that Somoza's regime was replaced by a provisional government that would supervise elections. As proof of the plot, Montiel exhibited a sheet of paper on which were written the names of several buildings in Managua and of leading opposition leaders, including some known communists. The general said they intended to launch urban guerrilla warfare and had the weapons to do so. The plan was purportedly seized from a columnist for *La Prensa* who had been arrested Sunday morning before the anti-Somoza demonstration. Montiel also declared that a complementary plan was found in the *La Prensa* offices and charged Chamorro with inciting terrorist acts and disturbing the peace. The charges against Chamorro were not officially announced until Saturday.

Agüero went into hiding but declared he was still a candidate in the February 5 election. Somoza, in an act designed to show who was boss, called his last political rally of the campaign in a little tree-shaded square almost on the doorstep of the Chamorro house. The usual group of obedient bureaucrats and bodyguards turned out and applauded both Tacho and Hope. There were no incidents. In the front row was Dinorah Sampson.

Hope had never given up her American citizenship, and she had seen to it that her children were all born in the United States. She checked with the American embassy whenever she believed her role as Nicaragua's first lady might jeopardize her citizenship. The embassy advised her that as an American citizen, she could campaign for her husband but not vote for him.

On February 5, 1967, Somoza was elected president. After only one-third of the districts reported, Somoza claimed 176,633 votes with Dr. Agüero trailing with 67,868. When all the tallies were in, Somoza declared he had received 480,162 of the reportedly 652,244 votes cast. The majority of votes were cast by women.

Somoza thinks the Conservative Party opposition criticized him during his campaign for speaking too simply to the Indians and farmers, but the opposition, in the form of Pedro Joaquín Chamorro, publisher of Managua's *La Prensa,* says the president read wrong. " 'Too stupidly' is what we said," Chamorro gladly clarified. "You can talk simply and speak Spanish very well, but Somoza thinks in English and translates into Spanish. When he talks in Spanish, he has pretty bad grammatical construction. He makes bad translations."

If Somoza is more fluent in English than his native Spanish, it should be no surprise. He left Nicaragua when he was almost 10 and spent the next 10 years studying at La Salle Military Academy in New York and at West Point. He is a product of a North American education system in both language and thought, which can be some-thing of a political liability in Latin America, where nationalism is a rising force.[2]

Somoza and his wife went to the States for a few weeks in late March and early April. He planned to accompany President Guerrero as an "observer" to the presi-dential summit in Uruguay in mid-April. In New York Tacho was asked about the fiasco at the Bay of Pigs. He replied that the operation could have "had all the probabilities of success if it had been implemented as it was supposed to go. Unfortunately they didn't." He quickly added, "Castro is a cancer that is going to get them sooner or later," and it is necessary "to clean up our continent of commu-nists."

Overweight and unhappy with his brother's taking over as president, Luis Somoza suffered a massive coronary on April 8. He was forty-four. The chest massage administered to restart his heart was so violent that it cracked a rib. Tacho inter-rupted his stateside visit to fly home to be with his brother. President Johnson sent a doctor but Luis died on April 13.

Tacho was alone now. He no longer had Luis's restraining hand or political savvy to aid him. Luis's last contribution had been managing Tacho's 1966 cam-paign. One of Tacho's first moves after Luis's funeral was to take his half-brother, Joe, as he always called him, out of obscurity. Somoza made Joe a general.

The decorum of the inauguration ceremonies for the twenty-seventh National Congress in April was shattered with charges by Fernando Agüero that the February elections were fraudulent. The fraud charges included the alleged seizure by Somoza forces of a third of the ballot boxes in Granada, an opposition stronghold. The ballots in those boxes had then been counted in the city's military barracks. Intimidation at the polls and the exclusion of some poll watchers were accompanying charges, along with the violation of voting secrecy and the illegal use of propaganda.

Agüero, sworn in as a senator, blamed Lorenzo Guerrero's puppet government for the January 22 riot and its forty deaths. He made his ringing charges before the assembled diplomatic corps and the cabinet. One faithful deputy retorted that Agüero was using this solemn occasion for "political brawling."

Tacho began a five-year term as Nicaragua's thirty-fifth president on May 1, 1967. The Somozas arranged the term of office to suit themselves through constitu-tional amendments (Luis had served a six-year term; Schick was allowed only four years in office). They were specialists in constitutional hanky-panky. Once in office, he took back his title of head of the guard and gave himself a new rank: *jefe supremo,* commander in chief of Nicaragua's armed forces.

He preferred not to think of his position as an inheritance and rejected any suggestion of a dynasty. "Dynasty hell, we're a family which likes politics and knows its job," he said.

The guard won back its right to immunity when he assumed the presidency. Instead of receiving a presidential pardon, Colonel López was absolved of any guilt in the murder of the three "agitators" and freed.

Tacho learned in 1967 that the price he had to pay for being president and *jefe supremo* was allowing anyone to ask him anything. He learned to keep his cool. The local press exercised caution, however. One Nicaraguan newsman would begin his interview with Tacho by saying, "What can I ask you?" Another decided to stick to economic questions to avert trouble, but he soon learned not to include questions about the Somozas' industrial empire. Tacho commented to one friend in the press, "It's difficult to make people believe that we're not ogres."

In the Cordillera Dariense mountain range north of Matagalpa is the 1,090-foot humpbacked peak called Pancasán, the site of another FSLN defeat in August 1967. However, the Sandinistas considered Pancasán the most important step to date in the revolutionary struggle against the Somoza dictatorship. Pancasán caused a lot of reflection and self-criticism within the ranks of the Sandinistas and the tragic episode led many to reconsider future strategy.

The Pancasán campaign, which took place five years after Río Coco and a long history of retreats, failed because the Sandinistas still lacked military experience. The campaign provided that experience. It was a tough lesson. "Among those who died were Silvio Mayorga, Rigoberto Cruz, Francísco Moreno, Dr. Danilo Rosales . . . and many others—a total of twenty of the thirty-five who took part. Many deserted, given that difficult situation. In the end, those few of us who were left returned to the city," Tomás Borge recounted.

"Pancasán lasted nine months, from December to August. Our work was slow: organizing the farmers, establishing conduits. We set up a good communications and intelligence network. We gained political control of the area; we had a lot of support. But we had a lot of firefights [with the guard] and our military capability was limited.

"Furthermore, we made tactical errors that were of a strategic nature: We divided into three groups. One led by Carlos Fonseca, who was the guerrilla leader. Another was led by Silvio Mayorga, who was to make incursions into the mountainside. I was in charge of the third group near Matagalpa to open conduits. The guard came between us like a wedge. When I found out what was happening, I moved towards Carlos's position. I arrived but Silvio could not—he and his whole group died. Rigoberto Cruz also died there—a heroic death, really: even the guardsmen recall that Rigoberto, horribly wounded, held his intestines with one hand and fought with the other. . . ."[3]

Another oppositionist recalled, "Pancasán opened a new chapter in the annals of guerrilla warfare in our nation, turning the tide against the bourgeoisie and underlining the need for a well-oiled revolutionary machine to throw against their institutions. While the struggle at Pancasán worked the turning point for the Sandinista National Liberation Front, it also represented the culmination of a continuous effort since 1963, at the battle of Boray, conserving as it did the continuity of our struggle for liberation in the mountains, villages and cities—a continuity highlighted by the guerrillas of Zinica (1969–70) and by all the battles we have won and will continue to win in our country."[4]

A jubilant Tacho traveled to the town of Jinotega, north of Pancasán, and declared: "I want to announce to all the north that the guerrillas no longer exist. I want to announce that the National Guard exterminated them. I want to announce to the people of Nicaragua and the world that our country is at peace."

Wounded, but not defeated, the active FSLN members at the end of 1967 numbered approximately fifty men and women willing to give their lives for their cause.

One of seven Frente activists in prison was twenty-three-year-old Daniel Ortega Saavedra who had been arrested that year in Managua. Ortega was an example of the youth being radicalized by Somoza's rule. Born in Libertad, Chontales, a mining area in the central Atlantic region of the country, Daniel was the third child of Daniel Ortega Serda and Lidia Saavedra de Ortega; of the two older children, only a sister, Germania, lived past infancy. Daniel's father was the son of the rector of the Pedagogic Institute in Granada. Born out of wedlock, he grew up to fight with Sandino in Nueva Segovia, where he was captured and spent three months in prison. He was an accountant when he met Daniel's mother, who was a cashier in the mines. Soon after Daniel's birth, the family moved to Juigalpa, also in the department of Chontales, where his brother Humberto was born in 1946. The family then moved to Managua where another child, Camilo, was born in 1950. The children were pumped full of pills and cod liver oil to protect them from the diseases of the mine region.

A quiet, disciplined child, Daniel became a catechist and from an early age began to give Bible lessons in the poor barrios of Managua, as did his brother Humberto. Gradually he was drawn into student protest movements and his first arrest came during a protest meeting when he was sixteen. He studied for a time at the Instituto Pedagógico in Managua and then at the Salesian Fathers school in Masaya. For a brief period he attended the Salesian school in San Salvador in neighboring El Salvador, and finally Maestro Gabriel's School in Managua. His father's small import-export business fell on hard times and they could no longer afford to keep him in boarding school; but some of the changes in school were designed to keep him from becoming involved in the student movement. His grades were good. He was a good orator and was thought by many to be destined for the priesthood because of his serious character and devotion to the Bible. By the time he entered the Jesuit-run Central American University in Managua to study law for a year he was already a member of the FSLN.

Daniel was to spend seven years in jail. In the first days after his arrest he was severely tortured, an experience which left him with a scar on his forehead and almost cost him the sight in one eye. But as the days in prison turned to weeks, months and then years, Daniel and his six companions organized their activities down to minute detail, from early morning running exercises around the patio to intense study. Daniel continually asked for law, history and geography books. But like so many revolutionaries, especially Nicaraguans, who consider their country the land of poets, Daniel continually wrote poetry which he sent to family members and friends as well as to Monsignor Miguel Obando y Bravo, later the Archbishop of Managua, whom he had met at the seminary in San Salvador. Ortega and his companions were continually active politically even during their confinement. When Somoza refused to release Francisco Ramirez, a National Guardsman jailed for giving a rifle to the Sandinistas, upon completion of his jail sentence, Daniel organized a month-long hunger strike. While many of his poems written while in prison were political, some were not. One poem comments on his long time in jail. It is entitled: "I Never Saw Managua When Miniskirts Were in Fashion."

These were happy times for Tacho, who was enjoying being president. He decided that his eldest son, Anastasio III (the new Tachito), would go into business, and that his second son, Julio, would go to West Point. He felt that a Harvard business education would serve Tachito better for his role as heir to the family empire. The entire family, including pretty Caroline and Carla and little Roberto, was treated by their father as a guard unit. But there was nothing disciplined about his own personal life. He spent more and more time with Dinorah and less with Hope. His cronies liked to say that the fact that the aloof Hope refused to have any more children had helped sour their marriage, while others speculated that he was truly in love with the sexy Dinorah. The triangle Tacho conducted on two sides of town became the talk of Managua. As Dinorah grew in stature, having "won the right to his pillow," society snickered at Hope's predicament. The latest Tacho-Hope-Dinorah news was always prime gossip at Managua cocktail parties.

While Tacho, drinking heavily, battled at home, he appeared to be losing touch with both government and his guard as his term progressed.

Some guard officers were causing a scandal by openly enriching themselves through graft. José Iván "Pepe" Alegrett, an engineer and the director of immigration, was one official not to be crossed. It was rumored he was involved in drugs. But it was the violent executive officer of the Third Company, Major Oscar Morales, known as "Moralitos," who gave Tacho a full-scale scandal that began in April of 1968 and lasted for two years. Moralitos interrogated a former guard lieutenant, David Tejeda, and his brother René, young men accused of "subversive activities." Moralitos beat David to death and threw the body into the Santiago volcano crater, situated between Managua and the city of Masaya, some twenty miles away. (One can still see red molten lava in the middle of the volcano's large crater and its white vapor joins the clouds.) So many people went to the rim of the volcano to look for the ex-lieutenant's body that the Red Cross director warned the search could cause landslides and further deaths. Tacho had no alternative but to allow Morales, identified as his protegé, to be tried. *La Prensa* carried a headline accusing Major Morales of making human sacrifices to the volcano.

The guard was divided on the issue and Major José Ramón Silva Reyes, who was appointed prosecutor, did a surprisingly good job of handling the case. Captain Fernando Cedeño, the medical officer of the Third Company, supplied damaging evidence that helped bring about Morales's conviction, not for murder, but for neglect of duty and discrediting the guard. Given an eight-year sentence, Major Morales was a hero to some guardsmen and detested by others, a few of whom just blamed him for getting caught. But Major Morales was not jailed and he remained free, under escort, still dressed in his uniform. It was common talk that he had vowed to "get" both Major Silva Reyes and Captain Fernando Cedeño to avenge his conviction.

On the first anniversary of his conviction, Morales was riding in a jeep when he spotted Captain Cedeño in the traffic. Taking a revolver from one of his escorts, he shot Cedeño to death. An attempt had already been made against Major Silva Reyes. Even the guard didn't approve of one officer killing another. Somoza was obliged to have Morales jailed. During the confusion over the 1972 earthquake, he was allowed to escape to Honduras where he lived in comfort and received a regular guard pension.

Morales had a lot of friends in the guard. One, a close aide to Tacho, Air Force (FAN) Commander Colonel Orlando Villalta, was annoyed at his boss for allowing Major Morales to be judged in the first place. Villalta came close to shooting Silva Reyes when he met him at Campo de Marte one day in September 1970. The meeting ended in hot words and a lot of pistol waving.

Even his Nationalist Liberal party was unhappy with the way Tacho was running the country and the fact he intended to continue the same way after his re-election to another five-year term when this one expired on May 1, 1972. There were malcontents who had not landed lucrative jobs or enough graft. Tacho practiced nepotism, as had all Somozas, and his relatives were sprinkled throughout the best jobs. Even half-brother Joe's growing influence in the guard was causing problems throughout the officer corps.

Business was good, however. Benefiting from the high prices caused by the Vietnam war, Nicaragua's traditional exports were bringing in good prices and business and small industries were expanding. From 1968 to 1971 the gross national product was reported to have increased nearly 8 percent annually.

The Frente Sandinista, which was rekindled in 1969—and which Tacho continued to report as "killed off"—began concentrating on building up its war chest with attacks on banks and commercial enterprises. The fact that they netted over half a million didn't concern Tacho. His director of internal security, Colonel Samuel Genie, demonstrated the guard's future tactics when he attacked an urban guerrilla unit of the Frente discovered hiding in a house in the Delicias section of Managua.

Using Staghound armored cars, Genie surrounded the little house and opened up with heavy weapons and tear gas, killing five of the guerrillas and capturing two.

The guerrillas fought back and killed two of his soldiers. Among the dead Sandinistas was Julio César Buitrago, head of the Frente's urban guerrillas, and the FSLN delegate to the meeting of the Organization of Latin American Solidarity in Cuba in 1967.

Once again, Tacho declared the Frente finished. The Frente moved to Costa Rica. In August 1969, FSLN secretary-general Carlos Fonseca was arrested and jailed on bank robbery charges there, though it was known that Somoza's security agents had notified Costa Rican police of his presence in their country. A group of Sandinistas attempted a jailbreak at Alajuela, Costa Rica, to free Fonseca, but the plan failed. Guerrilla Humberto Ortega was hit about an inch away from the heart and in the shoulder during the shootout that followed the jail raid. He spent ten months in the Costa Rican capital, being shuttled from the hospital to jail. He was operated on many times but he never regained the use of his arms. Fonseca was held fourteen months longer until, on October 21, 1970, an FSLN commando unit hijacked a Costa Rican Lacsa airliner and took four American officials of the United Fruit Company hostage, demanding safe passage for Fonseca to Cuba. That provided the necessary leverage to get Fonseca freed. Also released were Humberto Ortega and fellow guerrillas Rufo Marín and Plutarco Hernández.

In December 1969 there was a gala inauguration of the Rubén Darío Theater, named after the native son who had become one of the world's foremost Spanish-language poets (1867–1916). Construction on the large, columned edifice on the shores of Lake Managua, a short distance from the National Palace, was begun by a nonpartisan group during President Schick's term. It was a considerable effort to add a touch of culture to a city not known for its charm. Tacho personally found the arts a bore, and apart from war movies, he had little interest in the stage or screen. For cultured Hope the opening night was to be the high point of her reign as the first lady of Nicaragua. Instead it was a night fraught with tension and embarrassment. Tacho was the star of the show. Throughout the performance of the famous Mexican Ballet Folklórico, Tacho, fueled with his favorite drinks—switching from bloody marys to whiskey—which an aide dutifully refilled from the bar in a small room built behind his mezzanine seat, spent his time looking adoringly, not at his chic wife, but at his comely mistress in the audience. The audience, in turn, spent much of the evening watching all three and snickering throughout the performance. Few felt any compassion or sympathy for Hope, whom they considered an interloper, too aloof and sophisticated for their tastes.

Though Tacho's domestic problems were mounting, internationally speaking he was feeling secure. Richard Nixon was president of the United States, and he looked with favor on Tacho, whom he recalled as a staunch supporter during his ill-fated Latin American tour in 1958. To fill the post of ambassador, Nixon sent Turner B. Shelton. The rotund Shelton soon outshone the memory of Thomas E. Whelan, Tacho I's poker-playing buddy, as a Somoza lackey.

Shelton had a special way of bowing when he clasped Tacho's outstretched hand. He became Somoza's confidant to the point that many at the time joked that a cabinet meeting was when Tacho met Shelton.

In early April 1971, Tacho went to Washington for a private dinner with Nixon. Concerned about the reaction to offering a formal dinner for a dictator, Nixon chief of staff Alexander Haig, a West Pointer, decided to call the dinner a West Point Class of 1946 reunion. While both presidents were staunchly anticommunist, the two leaders also had other ties. Tacho contributed a million dollars to the Nixon campaign in 1972, according to a Central American foreign minister who traveled to Washington, D.C., with Tacho's mother. She had asked the minister what his country was contributing to the campaign. When the foreign minister said "Nothing," Salvadora rebuked him, "You people are so hopeless, we are giving a million and, as head of the family, I'm taking it up to him."

Tacho was also granted a public meeting with U Thant, the United Nations secretary general, during his trip.

With Nixon and Shelton in his corner, tedious, complicated arrangements were made to ensure that Tacho could retain power and be re-elected. The farce began in 1971.

Like his father, Somoza went in for election gymnastics. Somoza was barred by the constitution from running for reelection in 1972, but a pact was hammered out between the Liberal party and the opposition Conservative party. Somoza would have to step down as president, leaving a three-man junta (two Liberals and one Conservative) ruling until a constituent assembly studied electoral reforms—a process some said would take as little as one year, while others guessed it would last five. The final agreement was reached on March 29, 1971. The constitution had been rewritten twice during Tacho I's regime so that he could retain the presidency for twenty years, until his assassination. The 1972 to 1974 constitutional rewriting would be the nation's sixteenth since independence. It would ensure *continuismo*, an unpopular term for presidential self-succession.

The plan drew immediate criticism. Pedro Joaquín Chamorro called the pact between Liberals and Conservatives a "political farce" while Dr. Fernando Agüero, the former Somoza foe who had expelled Chamorro from the Conservative party, referred to it as a "national solution." Agüero insisted his opposition to Somoza was still strong but that he was indifferent about the possibility that Somoza would be able to seek re-election—"That would be entirely up to him." The speculation ran the gamut, from those saying Somoza, then forty-five years old, would surely seek to regain the presidency to others who surmised a figurehead president would be selected after the transition period and Tacho would continue to rule the country through the National Guard.

Chamorro and Agüero took their debate to Managua's Hall of Justice, where they squared off over mutual charges of defamation, Chamorro even accusing Agüero of taking money from Somoza before he accepted the pact. But the real fight came outside. Several hundred members of the Conservative party battled with police, leaving one dead and one wounded during the armed clash.

Somoza himself remained noncommittal for a time. A month after the Liberal-Conservative pact was agreed upon he announced he would not seek re-election in May 1972, when his term expired. However he said he "could be a candidate when the presidential elections were held in 1974. There's no way of telling right now."

In August 1971 the House and Senate each voted to dissolve themselves with Somoza assuming all functions until a new Congress was installed April 15, 1972. When the February 6, 1972, elections did roll around, the Liberals defeated the Conservatives by a 534,171 to 174,897 margin for a new national constituent assembly. The victory gave the Liberals 60 of the assembly seats and 278 mayorships and the Conservatives were apportioned the remaining 40 seats in the 100-seat assembly—in other words, exactly as had been prearranged when the pact was signed eleven months earlier. Agüero, who had negotiated the deal with Somoza, assumed the position of the Conservative junta member.

Many Nicaraguans were angry that Agüero had accepted Tacho's plan, yelling "traitor" as he met with Somoza to sign the agreement. The junta was referred to as "The Three Little Pigs." It was the first time the opposition party had been involved in the country's ruling body and Somoza liked to refer to the pact and the junta as "the debut of a democratic revolution in Nicaragua." He bragged that the nation would have a strong two-party electoral system after the constituent assembly and added he would favor OAS observers in all future elections.

The church did not think so highly of Somoza's plans. Managua Archbishop Miguel Obando y Bravo, in a lengthy statement which had widespread impact in predominately Catholic Nicaragua, called the country's political situation "muddled" and said he would like to see "rulers who know how to rule and who are interested in their people." The archbishop's statement was seen as marking the end of cordial relations between Somoza and the church. It defined the principles the church would like to see implemented in Nicaraguan politics and added that the church was seeking a whole new system. "The old system has too many faults," the statement said. Bishops did not attend the inaugural session of the new national assembly, claiming it would only reinforce Somoza's hold on the country and manipulation of the system. Chamorro's *La Prensa* greeted the document with the hope that political apathy was coming to an end.

On February 20, 1972, Nicaragua made headlines when recluse billionaire Howard Hughes suddenly chose the eighth floor of the Managua Intercontinental as his home. United States newsmen who descended on the scene to stalk the mysterious Hughes also witnessed a performance by American Ambassador Shelton and Tacho, who was returning from a four-day trip to Panama. The diplomatic corps was assembled at Las Mercedes airport to greet Tacho. A Pan American Airways flight arrived from Panama minutes before Tacho's personal jet. Wife Hope, seated in a Mercedes, suddenly ordered her chauffeur to leave the scene with tires squealing when she noticed that Tacho's mistress, Dinorah, was the first person to alight that plane.

Tacho stepped confidently off his plane, acknowledged the newsmen and cameras of the United States networks, and casually saluted the diplomatic corps. Then he halted and chatted with Shelton, who seemed to grovel before Tacho. Shelton had been instrumental in arranging for Hughes to take up residence in friendly Nicaragua.

Robert E. White, deputy chief of mission at the embassy, wrote to the State

Department reporting on Shelton's bizarre behavior which he described years later as verging on that of a courtier to Somoza. White was to fall out with Shelton when he objected to the ambassador turning out all the embassy vehicles to bring Howard Hughes and his entourage into Managua. "The embassy was placed at the entire disposal of Howard Hughes, a private citizen, which was not the embassy function," White complained.

Tacho was relaxed under the glare of TV lights at the airport press conference. He appeared more like a seasoned American politician than a Latin American strongman. In fact, this was the beginning of a period in which he liked to portray himself as a sort of American proconsul in Central America—an unofficial Washington emissary. At least that is the impression he made upon some other contemporary Central American chiefs of state.

When a reporter at the news conference asked if Hughes was indeed in Managua and, if so, where, Tacho replied:

"As far as I know, he is staying at the Intercontinental Hotel. We have talked with some of his men about the purchase and sale of airplanes, mergers of airlines, about meeting with him . . . it's a matter that I'll have to look into a little later, because I left when he came in; I can't answer that question. Anyhow, this country . . . he's invited personally by me, not officially. So as two persons who are in business, each of us has to look to our conveniences. I know he was delighted to accept my invitation because Nicaragua represented to him a country which was at peace, that could give him all the guarantees he needed, and that he would be welcome. So it all depends on him." Tacho didn't mention the polio and dysentery that constantly plagued the country, things that certainly would not have been appealing to the bacteriophobic Hughes.

Tacho then showed the newsmen a letter he had received from Hughes. Tacho read, " 'His excellency, Anastasio Somoza Debayle, President, Casa Presidencial, Managua, Nicaragua: Dear Mr. President, Please accept my heartfelt greetings, appreciation for your cordial invitation to visit beautiful Nicaragua. Your efficient aides have been most gracious and helpful beyond expectation to me and my staff. Please convey my sincere thanks and good wishes to all. I look forward with pleasure to our future contacts. Sincerely yours, Howard R. Hughes.' The letter was brought to me today." It was typed on the Intercontinental Hotel's stationery.

When asked why he personally invited Hughes, Tacho replied, "Well, it's very simple. I have my personal business. We are talking about personal business, and he has Western Airlines. [He had said this also in Panama and was finally corrected on the name: Hughes Airwest.] We operate and run Lanica Airlines, and when we talked to his vice-presidents and delegates, I said to him, 'Why don't you invite Mr. Hughes to come down?'

"We are gonna try and see if we make a merger, if he sells me some airplanes, and I buy some airplanes from him. So I always invite people to Nicaragua who might do business with me. Mr. Hughes is not the only one." When asked who the others were, Tacho responded, "Nelson Rockefeller. Nelson and I are very good friends and I have invited him a few instances. We've had D. K. Ludwig and a couple of millionaire Texans that I can't remember their names."

Tacho was then asked if Hughes might be staying in one of Somoza's many private residences. He replied, "Mr. Hughes can stay in Nicaragua any place he wants to because property here is respected, privacy is respected. He doesn't really have to go any place that we own to be private and respected . . . if he wishes to become a guest in one of our private places, he, like any other man who has a lot of money in the United States, is welcome to it.

"Let me say this to you gentlemen. I have talked to many powerful corporations and not one man represents it. This time Mr. Hughes represents the majority of the corporations which he runs, so let's not make so much fanfare about the man. If he wants to be respected and be let alone, that's his business. If he wants to do business in Nicaragua I don't have to see him. My lawyers can see his lawyers. My managers can see his managers . . . come on now, I was brought up in the U.S. and I don't believe in all of this egotism that they're trying to create on this gentleman. If he wants to do business he'll do it through his bank account and his lawyers. I'm sorry, maybe I'm a sour apple for you guys, but I believe that every man has a right to decide his own future. Have you been treated well here? Good, I hope [some newspapers] treat me that way. Let me say this to you gentlemen. I have my friends in the U.S. who are very, very wealthy. They come in and go out of this country, they call me by telephone, I say hello to them and then they are off on the errands they are going to do. Undoubtedly, Mr. Hughes is a personality who has the possibility of fixing his attitudes which in reality creates the interest of a great deal of people. But as a human being I respect his right to keep his privacy. If he comes to my country he has the right like any other citizen to do as the law of Nicaragua allows him to do and to take advantage of the law of Nicaragua. My belief is he came to Nicaragua because he believes that in this country there is security, there is peace —there is social peace—and he feels, perhaps he can find peace here."

While in Nicaragua, Hughes made a deal to buy 25 percent of Lanica.

Hughes spent almost three weeks in the Intercontinental. As quickly as he came, he left. Just before flying out of Managua, Somoza and Ambassador Shelton had an interview with Hughes. He told them he was off on a "business trip." He left Nicaragua for the exclusive Bayshore Inn in Vancouver, British Columbia, to return later in the year to Managua.

A swing through the Caribbean in March showed Somoza was not really so well liked abroad. He was forced to employ strict security precautions in the Dominican Republic where student protests threatened to disrupt his visit. The mood was friendlier in Haiti where bands and three thousand Haitians greeted him at the airport. As a result, Tacho extended his two-day visit to three and thoroughly embarrassed his host, President-for-Life Jean-Claude Duvalier, who neither smoked nor drank. Haitian officials were disgusted with the Nicaraguan's carousing. During a day at the beach in Haiti, he was such a compulsive eater that he insisted on being fed Haitian delicacies from a boat while he floated in the sea. But the consumption of food and drink proved too much for him and he collapsed and passed out. He had to be carried to his room where he slept off the drunkenness.

CHAPTER 7

The Earthquake

The city of Managua sits on the shores of Lake Managua, once only a dead sea, now also a great open sewer. It is built over not one, but three faults, and sits on volcanic ash and lava. The most important avenues lie below La Loma de Tiscapa, with the exception of Roosevelt Avenue which gradually climbs to the foot of this stubby volcano. Unlike pretty Granada and León, the capital has little in the way of saving grace. It is a hodgepodge of hybrid American architecture, with adobe often covered with plaster.

On December 23, 1972, a series of earthquakes convulsed Managua. The old clock on the cathedral stopped at 12:27 A.M., as did most clocks in the hot, unattractive city. Rubble filled the narrow streets. Although no one was ever sure just how many people lost their lives, the official death toll was set at 10,000. More than 20,000 were injured and 300,000 of the city's population of 400,000 were left homeless. Damage was listed at $1 billion with a $1.5-billion price tag for reconstruction. Registering only 6.3 on the Richter scale, the heaviest tremor was a shallow quake with its epicenter almost directly under Roosevelt Avenue, in the downtown shopping and commercial area. It was like Hiroshima. Only about 20 percent of the structures remained intact. The death, devastation and misery in a city festooned for Christmas but suddenly turned into hell covered 589 city blocks, a 1,500-acre area. Ruptured gas lines in the ruins set off fires that blazed and lit the skies at night and there was no choice but to let them burn.

Earthquakes were nothing new to this city. At 10:10 on the morning of March 31, 1931, a six-second tremor had devastated Managua. There had been another previously in 1885, just a few years after Managua had become the capital.

After the 1972 earthquake only a few well-built structures remained standing. One was the National Palace. Others included the twin skyscrapers Banco de America and Banco Central de Nicaragua. Tacho's La Curva Palace on La Loma de Tiscapa was cracked open. Part of the Casa Presidencial hung on to the hill, the rest slid from its perch on the rim of the Tiscapa volcano into the crater below. The military hospital also on Tiscapa's rim was undamaged. The National Guard headquarters at Campo de Marte and its jail fell into ruins. The nearby American embassy collapsed. Ambassador Shelton's secretary, Rose Marie Orlich, of Philadelphia, died when the staff apartments behind the embassy were partially destroyed. (Shelton later moved the embassy to a country club.)

Tacho's suburban hundred-acre El Retiro estate southwest of the city, with its sprawling Spanish ranch-style house with reinforced concrete walls and tiled wood roof, away from the epicenter, proved a safe place to be that night of terror. The house wall nevertheless suffered a crack. Tacho and Hope had returned from a wedding in Masaya and were up talking. He was having a nightcap when the first tremor was felt shortly after 11:00 P.M. "We got up and ran to an alley. Something knocked against Hope and bruised her arm and ankle. Then came another tremor and another. The first oscillated horizontally and that gave some people time to get out of their homes. The second and third oscillated up and down. That third one was the killer. We thought we were pieces of ice in a cocktail shaker." He continued, "I saw the city had suffered major damage. The lights were out. We used the radios in the cars to contact the guard and the police. When I learned of the casualties suffered by the guard I realized how grave the situation was."[1] He ordered the three-man junta to declare martial law. It lasted for the next eighteen months.

President Nixon, Tacho said later, called from Key Biscayne. "He expressed condolences for the people of Nicaragua through me. He asked how my family was. He offered aid."[2]

Anarchy prevailed for the first seventy-two hours. The guard disintegrated— its members disappeared, leaving their posts and barracks to find their families. Shelton called the United States Southern Command in Panama, which immediately dispatched a force of some five hundred American soldiers who bivouacked by the garden of El Retiro to help in the emergency. They also afforded Tacho protection as even his security guard had disappeared. An American hospital was set up between the ranch and the road. All medical supplies were distributed through Somoza's headquarters. An American army captain who discovered tons of medical supplies stacked in the back of an old warehouse had them sent to the command post. The move was highly criticized because the needy were on the immediate outskirts of the city and nothing was transported from the more removed El Retiro *casa presidencial* and operations center until a destination had been determined by Tacho and his cohorts.

The guard had gone into a panic right after the earthquake, as had much of the population. The guardsmen were more concerned with finding their families than worrying about their duty to Somoza. Finally, Somoza sent his defense minister General Heberto Sanchez Barquero to collect what troops he could from the department commanders. Some guardsmen were among the looters roaming the streets. Scores of citizens were treated for gunshot wounds and Tacho said in a radio broadcast that the most immediate problem was the "abominable beings" who were seeking loot in the city. He didn't mention that some guard officers were indulging in looting but they were seen looting automobile dealerships and appliance shops, while spurning pleas for help. These actions by uniformed soldiers were explained by one United States embassy official, who told a reporter, "Salaries are low and the people were scared. You can't really compare them with the U.S. Army." It was said that a member of the United States Army caught guard lieutenant Roland Sampson in the act of blowing up the Bank of Nicaragua vault. Lieutenant Sampson, the cousin of Dinorah, was then reportedly taken to Tacho who laughed and told them to let him go. Both the lieutenant and Tacho's mistress denied the charges.

Just as Ambassador Whelan had played a crucial role in helping the boys in that critical transition period after their father's assassination, so Ambassador Shelton played an important role in the early postearthquake hours. The guard had its defenses down, although no one really contemplated a blow against Somoza, at least in Managua. Everyone was in the state of shock and inertia that follows such natural disasters.

Shelton had been in his spacious hilltop embassy residence, tuning in the news when the earthquake hit. "Chairs, pictures, everything that was movable was flying around. The lights went out," he told reporters. As soon as the emergency generator was turned on Shelton contacted Washington. "That was my first duty," he recalled later in the week. After the earthquake, Shelton was the most frequent visitor to the ranch. His car was always swinging into the driveway and parking next to the two Somoza black Cadillacs with license plates GN-1 (National Guard One). Scuttling back and forth to El Retiro made Shelton appear more like Somoza's top aide than ambassador. He seldom delegated contacts to staff members—he preferred to deal directly with Somoza, with whom he sometimes spent much of the day. Few people were witnesses to what went on during the frequent daily meetings.

Nixon, who considered Somoza the type of friend the United States needed south of Key Biscayne, ordered an "all-out effort" to aid Nicaragua after receiving detailed reports from Shelton, whose casualty figures were initially even higher than those of Tacho. *Time* noted that United States Air Force C-141 and C-5A transports shuttled in with medical supplies, bulldozers and other items at a tonnage rate that exceeded the first days of the Berlin airlift in 1948.

Tachito, a senior at Harvard, was at a debutante ball in New York when ordered home by his father. Julio, the eldest, who admitted, "I guess I'm just as much an American as anything else," was preparing to enter West Point in 1973. He remained in the United States with his two sisters who were attending Wellesley and Foxcroft.

At home, the tall extremely pale Tachito, who never seemed to tan in the tropical sun, donned a uniform and, like a good Somoza, began to shout orders. The earthquake transformed him into a soldier.

Time's David DeVoss reported that young Tachito's first command was in dispatching supplies from the airport. But the Somoza heir apparent was too absorbed with personal preoccupations to be at all effective.

"God damn it," shouted a handsome twenty-two-year-old man in tailored army fatigues on one occasion, "What I need is some concertina wire. The U.S. gives me everything but concertina wire." Indeed, he spoke the truth. From his perch atop a stack of Sears chalet camping tents, he had an excellent view of the fine fruits of capitalism. Crates of Canada Dry, boxes of baby food and a seemingly inexhaustible supply of Kellogg's corn flakes closed in from every side. The problem was that the goods were gathered in a decrepit airport, far away from the hungry and homeless masses of Managua. A bevy of Red Cross volunteers and unctuous army officers awaited to do his bidding, but "Tachito Tres," as he was called by those who anticipated his eventual succession to power, had other things on his mind, namely his misplaced automobile. "Where is my car?" he screamed. "I want the person who took it arrested immediately," he said and ran off in search of the culprit. Silence. Since nothing could be done without a Somoza signature, all activity stopped. As for keeping any record of relief shipments, Tachito's position was "You can't keep books in a situation like this. What comes in, goes out."[3]

There were a lot of complaints about where it was or was not going out to. When Granada, the old Conservative stronghold, saw that supplies from its nineteen relief points were not being properly distributed, it began its own effort. An appeal for assistance was made by ham radio—the city was overcrowded with refugees from Managua. In response a plane loaded with medical supplies and beans was sent from Houston. When the plane put down at Las Mercedes the supplies' destination was indicated as Granada. At first a furious Tacho blocked the supplies and then ordered the ham to halt operating. But the Granadans established their own relief effort. Ration cards were issued to more than 30,000 refugees, food distribution centers were set up and medical and job replacement files were begun. Fernando Sequeira, former dean of the school of engineering at the University of Central America and a leader of the Granada relief effort, said, "We got some of the food from the government, but everything else was done through private initiative. Somoza was in control of the government. He staged a coup d'état with no effort. The mask is off and the powerless junta has been cast aside."

It was not until four days after the earthquake that food began to be distributed. Even the 324,000 gallons of water airlifted to Managua by the United States Air Force was difficult to find. Soft drinks were selling for two dollars a bottle—Lake Managua was so polluted that it could not be used as a source of drinking water. "We determined that a human can live seven days without food," Somoza later told David DeVoss, who covered the aftermath of the disaster. "So we tried to get water distributed first. The fact that people are peaceful shows that they are satisfied. The Nicaraguan people believe in me."

But contrary to Somoza's claim to being loved by the people, there were a lot of disgruntled Managuans who soon began to direct their anger against Somoza. In an effort to force out some 150,000 persons who refused to leave the devastated city, the government had held up food supplies pouring into Las Mercedes airport from donors and relief agencies from around the world. The hardship for these people was compounded by heat, the stench of death, and red dust that seemed to get into everything. The red flag indicating refugees' presence began to make its appearance on homes outside the city and in the towns of Masaya and Granada. But in the countryside around the capital, in a country which had suffered eight months of drought, there was as much hunger as in the devastated city.

There were reports that when the Managua jail collapsed, some prisoners managed to escape but that others were shot down by the guard.

The scene at El Retiro grew into a major sideshow. The 185-man United States Army medical team from the Twenty-first Evacuation Hospital, based in Fort Hood, Texas, operated behind a barbed-wire camp on the field in front of the ranch. Tacho, his fat frame stuffed into a khaki uniform adorned with his five commander-in-chief stars, seemed to be the only totally self-assured person around. "He runs his family like an army base: children are assigned tasks and expected to do them. Like Nixon, he has a deep respect for business, social stability and education," noted DeVoss. "Somoza," he added, "is disliked more for his style or lack of it than anything else."

The postearthquake days also gave newsmen an opportunity to view Tacho at close range. Marlise Simmons, a reporter for *The Washington Post*, watched in disgust one day when members of Tacho's emergency relief team, in hard hats and covered with the inevitable red dust, arrived to talk with Tacho. They were seated at the end of the swimming pool. The obviously hungry, thirsty and tired officers had to sit there while Tacho, tying a napkin around his neck like a bib, ate a three-course meal, offering them nothing, not even a glass of water. "He looked like a gargantua stuffing himself," she recalled.

The elegant Hope seemed completely out of her element. Reporter Pat Alisau, at El Retiro after the earthquake, said the first lady's bedroom was littered with fashion magazines from Neiman-Marcus and other such stores and that she looked the smart American woman she was. "Next to Tacho's vulgarity she was a refined lady." At the ranch she was often followed around by a Yorkshire terrier while attending to Red Cross relief work for quake victims. She proved to be an independent woman with no qualms about standing up to Tacho. During committee meetings she constantly harangued Tacho for the shortage of trucks. When asked by Alisau what it was like to be married to a dictator, she gave an annoyed look and replied, "Benevolent dictator."

Nicaraguans who knew her felt she was only trying to play the first-lady role and that her contribution was more cosmetic than substantial. Her major concern was her children. She had lost Tachito to her husband who had taken over his upbringing and this along with the competition from Dinorah caused her more anguish than the plight of the Nicaraguan people, whom she knew despised her.

The earthquake demonstrated to the commander in chief that the opposition was divided and weak. The government soon became the amorphous "national emergency committee" to which the three-man junta ceded power. Martial law had been declared the morning of December 23 right after the quake. Every Monday thereafter the national emergency committee, composed of wealthy industrialists and politicians who were under Tacho's full control, met on the tarpaulin-covered tennis courts at the rear of El Retiro. Somoza, presiding from a yellow rocking chair, had to review every single piece of government business, no matter how small. If he did not give his consent no action was taken.

Tacho II, who had once believed that a government that governed least governed best, began to decide on the smallest, most mundane business of state. By June, the government had spent less than it had collected in taxes. And reconstruction required active government support.

The business class was unhappy. Even though merchants had lost everything, they were required to pay customs duties on all goods previously ordered that were now entering the country. Unable to pay, they saw their merchandise, which had been held by customs, sold at bargain prices by wives of favored guard officers who were planning to build their own stores in the "new Managua." While Somoza repeatedly said the city would be reconstructed—Mexico even furnished a plan for a new earthquakeproof Managua—nothing was done.

Not waiting for the government to decide what to do, many merchants in suburban areas, which were relatively untouched by the quake, converted their homes and garages into new stores. Suddenly these residential areas sprouted signs advertising old businesses in new, small locales. Street lights and telephone poles were festooned with signs announcing minipharmacies, supermarkets, office furniture stores and business offices. Wealthy businessmen, who'd joked about the much-delayed master plan for the new Managua, began planning a series of commercial centers in those same suburban areas outside downtown Managua. Overnight, the city's commerce was resurrected in residential Managua. If business entrepreneurs had waited for Tacho to keep his promise to rebuild the city, they would still be waiting. Managua has yet to be rebuilt.

Those who believed the Conservatives might take advantage of the situation to pick up votes for the 1974 election or force Tacho to moderate his rule were sadly disappointed. Dr. Fernando Agüero Rocha, who had lost the popular backing of students and other groups by joining Tacho in his junta scheme, was replaced on March 3, 1973, by Edmundo Paguaga Irías. Agüero opposed Tacho's appointing himself president of the national emergency commission with special powers. So the Conservative leader resigned from the triumvirate. He was fired as Conservative party leader and went on to form the "Movimiento Popular Conservador" and took many of the Conservatives with him. Tacho charged that Agüero's resignation was a betrayal of Nicaragua. After two months of being almost completely ignored, the "regular" Conservatives compounded their disaster by again switching alliances. Now they were backing Paguaga's lieutenant José Joaquín Cuadra in the 1974 elections.

The rubber stamp opposition always seemed more interested in patronage than in political service. Although a March 1971 agreement increased their power in the National Constituent Assembly from thirty to forty seats, they did little to oppose Somoza. They provided him with the democratic facade he needed, and they were content to receive their $715 monthly congressional salary. During its first nine months, the newly reconstituted assembly was in session in the old National Palace for a total of only twenty-one half-day sessions.

In the sprawling shantytowns that grew up outside the capital the seeds of discontent germinated. Somoza now openly ruled as president of the national emergency committee and commander in chief of the guard—no one dared to contradict him. Even the longtime, servile oligarchy was not happy with the state of affairs. The multitude of poor citizens who had lost everything in the quake, who had no credit or means of rebuilding the little commerce they had had, suppressed their anger. As a result, depression was one of the most common diseases in the postearthquake months and at least one suicide was registered daily for many months. Most poor Managuans had lost all hope of recovering their precarious little livings.

But Tacho thought differently. "The earthquake has given a lot of people opportunities for a new life," he told a reporter in June. "Many debts were wiped out and a new generation with a lot of 'umph' has a great chance to break into the business cycle. This, in itself, is a revolution." In a way he was prophetic but the revolution to come was not the one he was thinking about.

One person who did not break into the earthquake recovery business was Nicaragua's number one guest, Howard Hughes, the recluse billionaire industrialist, who was shaken out of his eighth-floor hideaway and was the first American to leave, taking off in the early hours in his personal jet. (Four other Americans were among the casualties.) The great investments Tacho had sought never materialized.

Even the rumor of such investments brought a spate of denials. When the *London Observer* implied partnership in an undersea mining deal, Somoza's information and press secretary Efraím Huezo fired off a letter to the *Miami Herald* (November 11, 1973) calling the report "a lie. . . . I have no contact with Mr. Hughes. . . . I want to deny the fact that the state of Nicaragua and I have anything to do with this fantastic tale. There is no contact, nor does a license exist, and I never have spoken with Mr. Hughes over such a matter. . . . When Mr. Hughes was in Nicaragua he was my guest. Then I sent him the persons necessary to communicate with him."

Billboards were placed on the highway into Managua announcing, "1973— Year of Hope and Construction." But as Marvine Howe of *The New York Times* pointed out during a visit to Managua on April 23, four months after the earthquake, people were losing all hope. Only some had any optimism. On the side of a battered two-story building that remained standing on what was Avenida Bolivia the owner had handwritten in crude letters: "With faith and hope in the reconstruction— Managua sleeps but it is not dead."

Howe noted remarks by some observers who stated, "The whole nation is traumatized. They are angry; they don't blame the government for the earthquake, but they do blame it for not providing relief for their losses." At times the mood became rebellious and the Marxist-Leninist groups increased their agitation against Somoza.

The United States Agency for International Development (AID) moved quicker than the Nicaraguan government and used American funds to build four "Las Americas" temporary housing areas astride the Pan American highway, miles from the city. The homes were wooden one-room shacks with tin roofs. When I visited them in the early months after the quake they had no drainage and no streets, which the Nicaraguan government was supposedly to provide later. When the eight-month drought finally broke in June 1973, the torrential downpour made life for the refugees—many of whom were still homeless—even more wretched. Though the dust settled, the red earth turned into mud. And residents complained about the continued lack of law and order and how they were preyed upon by thieves who stole everything they could find. Eleven thousand of these so-called temporary houses were built from salvage material. They housed some 55,000 refugees and they rented for six dollars a month. The rent and other expenses added up. For example, because of the additional cost of bus fare and the fifteen-cent tribute each child had to give the underpaid government teacher every week, many children didn't go to school.

The only housing built by the Nicaraguan government was via Somoza and his cronies: they decided where new roads would be built with concrete paving blocks (from Somoza's factory). A series of real-estate killings was in the making. Somoza immediately went into the construction business, starting up a company and calling its success a credit to "my business ability." Congress President Cornelio Hueck must have had some of Somoza's Midas touch rub off on him. A headline in *La Prensa* on June 6, 1973, summarized Hueck's real-estate savvy: "Land bought for 120,000 córdobas [$20,000] sold for 8 million [$1.2 million] two days later." The buyer was the National Housing Bank.

The Sandinistas were also doing a little construction work of their own with an eye to the future. In León, the three BeRais brothers put the finishing touches to a new room they had added to their little home on a corner of a dirt road leading to the *fortín*. Under the new room was a large cellar reached through a false bottom in an old wooden wardrobe. This large arms depot, within sight of the old fortress a half-mile away, was so carefully concealed that it was to escape detection even though the National Guard was to search the house nine times in the next eight years.

Other income opportunities were exploited as well. In the first six months after the quake the national emergency committee received $24,853,000 in cash. The United States had sent $32 million in government funds, plus an additional $112,181 from private sources. But the Nicaraguan treasury listed the United States as providing only $16.22 million. No one seemed concerned to explain the discrepancy.

There were growing signs of hostility from refugees whenever they saw guard and other official vehicles they suspected were carrying off relief supplies. Somoza's Nationalist Liberal party and the guard were known to be misappropriating the relief and reconstruction aid but no one could prove it. Already people were predicting there would be trouble for Somoza if any evidence of massive theft were found.

Bishop Obando y Bravo sought to distribute relief supplies at his churches but Somoza insisted they be distributed through his party's precincts. More bad blood developed between the church and Somoza.

It was not long before people were saying that the best-kept secret in Nicaragua was the so-called reconstruction program. In the end it was clear that Somoza had benefited handsomely from the earthquake. The profiteering went on. Somoza, gearing up to have himself reelected president, found it a simple way of paying off some political debts.

Martial law continued throughout the summer and citizens became even more upset with Somoza. Meanwhile, despite a ban on political activity, the FSLN became more active as the lower and middle classes rapidly lost faith in the entire political system. When Tacho ventured forth from El Retiro, he was jeered by vendors and pedestrians behind his back whenever they spotted his black Cadillac, always well protected by bodyguards, many of them in an accompanying big white Airporter limousine.

In June 1973, Tacho, accompanied by Hope, made his first trip out of Nicaragua since the quake. The occasion was Tacho III's graduation from Harvard. Tachito announced he was prepared to spend two years in the guard but that he hoped to get a master's degree from Harvard and maybe enroll after that at Cambridge University in England. Afterwards, he planned to go into business. "I don't see the army or politics in my future," the twenty-two-year-old graduate told reporters.

After that trip Somoza began to travel more often. He made another foray to the United States in November 1973. In a speech at the Commonwealth Club in San Francisco, he praised Nixon and dismissed Watergate. Then adding an extra stop to his itinerary, he and his entourage left the plush Commonwealth for a trek to the Condo nightclub in North Beach, California. There they stayed for an entire show featuring a nude Carol Doda, whose forty-four-inch bust after extensive silicone implants had gained her notoriety. Always making a play for the ladies, Tacho sent her a note calling her show "most outstanding." The management, in return for a presidential visit, paid the party's tab. Tacho left no tip and American taxpayers had to pick up the tab for some two dozen Secret Service agents who had to stand guard at the club's doors.

In preparation for the September 1, 1974, election, Tacho made a great show throughout the year of campaigning. The cosmetics of the election, which he was assured of winning, were important to Somoza. He could parlay the fact of the election into a public relations campaign to show that the political system, as well as the city itself, was being reconstructed in the aftermath of the earthquake. Finding a believable opponent was the first problem. In the end, the only other candidate was Dr. Edmundo Paguaga Irías, who offered only token opposition. The new constitution allowed the Conservatives 40 percent of the seats in the House of Deputies while Tacho's party was to be allotted 60 percent.

Widespread apathy persisted. In Managua people a year later were still suffering the trauma of the earthquake. Tacho began to be known as the "man in the ticket booth." The booth was a cubicle of bulletproof glass that Somoza had custom-made in the United States and tested prior to launching his campaign. The glass tended to emphasize his fatness and distorted his face when he spoke. People remarked most on the distortion evident when he was pronouncing the words "democracy," "liberty" and "progress" as they were piped out through a microphone to the bureaucrats and peasants who were trucked in for the occasion. Tacho was characteristically confident and arrogant. He began his campaign prematurely, forgetting to wait until his Nationalist Liberal party had formally nominated him.

Paguaga, who had been a member of the triumvirate, had the reputation of being pro-Somoza. There was no question of anyone really backing his pro forma candidacy, which only provided Tacho with the facade he needed. But then a coalition consisting mostly of lawyers, opposition politicians, and two labor unions formed. Known as "The Twenty-seven," the group included rightists and leftists as well as moderates, all bound together by their aversion to Somoza. Among "The Twenty-seven" was Pedro Joaquín Chamorro. They campaigned for electoral abstention. As declared Chamorro's La Prensa on June 24, 1974, "There is no one to vote for."

"The Twenty-seven" were taken to court by Tacho. They were cited for "inciting to abstain," illegal according to the constitution, and found guilty but no specific criminal penalties were assessed. Their civil rights were suspended for six months, though they were not prohibited from voting. All of them were barred from traveling. By then Somoza's "ticket booth" sideshow had become a real production.

The union's presence in "The Twenty-seven" demonstrated growing labor unrest. In August 1973, some 2,000 textile workers had in fact gone out on strike, demanding higher wages. They were followed by some construction and metal workers. The following month there were street protests over a hike in bus fares. (Transportation fares in an underdeveloped country like Nicaragua can hurt a worker and his family if they are hiked even a few cents.) When, in October, following reports in *La Prensa* about public officials making fortunes, a law was passed that could subject newsmen to fines for "defaming" government officials, there were protests from journalists throughout the hemisphere. These were not happy months for Tacho, despite his confidence.

The strikes continued into 1974 and included hospital workers and universities and even Standard Fruit Company workers. On April 25 Tacho, concerned because the strikes were snowballing, declared press censorship which was to last one month. *La Prensa* had two guard officers assigned to its offices to check and approve all copy.

In January 1974, students in León demonstrated in support of eight political prisoners who had declared a hunger strike. The prisoners included members of the FSLN. The guard used tear gas to disperse students who had occupied the university and the city's churches.

The disturbances in León were based on demands not only for better wages for teachers but for a study program free of control by the United States universities. The strikes and evident general malaise were interpreted as indicating an awakening of new forces. But with his wealth and power to back him, Tacho went to the polls on Sunday, September 1, 1974, exuding supreme assurance and confidence.

The results were a foregone conclusion. To point up the charade, on Saturday *La Prensa* ran the headline: "Candidates who won tomorrow's elections."

Although 40 percent of the electorate did abstain, Tacho's vote counters declared he had received 748,985 of the 815,758 votes cast. There was no secret ballot. When a ballot was marked, the mark could be clearly seen through the thin paper. It was imperative for almost everyone to be recorded as having voted "Nationalist Liberal," because only those who voted for Somoza were given the ID card called a *magnífica*, required for all government employees.

The government claimed that 70 percent of the electorate had voted of the 1,150,000 that were registered. "It's hard to believe that in a country of two million, that many were inscribed," a United States embassy official commented privately after the election. Besides those who were coerced into voting—and some had no choice—children were allowed to vote. Many twelve-year-olds were seen showing off fingers red with the ink from polling station controllers.

In a country where hunger and poverty remain rampant, the inducement to get out the vote was a meal of rice, yucca and meat, plus a two-córdoba note (twenty-eight cents). In some areas the electorate received ten córdobas ($1.40) with a small plastic container of fiery white rum. No one received the food, drink and money until after voting for Somoza, which led the opposition to refer to them as the "guaro and nacatamale" elections.

While the overall illiteracy rate in the nation was 80 percent, it was closer to 100 percent in the rural areas. In 1974, according to a United Nations survey, only 84,000 of the 350,000 children of school age were attending primary school. Some 31,500 youths were attending secondary school with only 7,400 of them graduating that same year. The 6,000 total enrollment in the universities was Central America's lowest. But Somoza's priorities, like his father's, included neither education nor public health. Members of the oligarchy sent their children to schools abroad and went abroad for health care. The Somozas had no faith or interest in local scholastic pursuits or health services and sent their children to the United States for both. At home the children all spoke English and the library at El Retiro was made up entirely of books in English. Nor did the Somozas suffer any twinge of conscience over running the country as a business enterprise, taking advantage of their position to make innumerable deals for personal profit. "Conflict of interest" was not in their vocabulary. In such a society the Frente Sandinista had fertile ground in which to sow the seeds for change.

A new constitution gave Somoza a hold on the presidency until May 1981, but it stipulated that he could not succeed himself following his new six-year term. Nor could anyone within the fourth degree of family relationship follow him into the presidency. However, since the Somoza family had seemingly forever broken the constitution or bent it to suit themselves, no one gave the limitation the least credence.

Just prior to the election, the Nicaraguan bishops had issued a pastoral letter highly critical of Somoza politics, saying that no one could rightly be compelled to vote to benefit a particular group. The church refused to sanction Tacho's re-election and boycotted the inauguration ceremonies. The talk among the clergy and the newly formed Union Democrática de Liberación (UDEL)—composed of Pedro Joaquín Chamorro, the Christian Democrats, the labor unions and the Nicaraguan Communist party—was that Somoza would certainly not step down after his term. Their conviction was that the family clan had no intention of giving up the reins of power. Meanwhile the FSLN was stepping up its guerrilla attacks in the mountains around Matagalpa.

Although the church and others were absent from the inauguration, it was well attended by delegates from forty-three countries, including the presidents of Honduras, El Salvador, Guatemala and Costa Rica. The event served a dual purpose, doubling as a summit to seek the normalization of relations between El Salvador and Honduras that had been strained following the 1969 "soccer war."

At a cocktail party, Tacho, with a straight face and holding a drink in one hand, told interviewers, "I'm especially proud that the same number of people in Managua who voted for me in 1967 voted for me again this year." And then he went on to discuss his government's plans to rebuild Managua and how private investment and tax collections had increased since the earthquake. Asked about outside aid he beamed and replied, "This is another example of how the Western world can do things the Communists can't." Reminded that the Cubans had also come to the rescue, he became furious. A *Time* report noted: "In some cases, the U.S. effort has not been as effective or as widely noticed as it might be. While a 185-man Army medical team from the 21st Evacuation Hospital based in Fort Hood, Texas, operated in a barbed-wire enclosed compound in a meadow in front of Somoza's El Retiro residence, a team of 50 Cuban doctors and paramedics worked in the densely populated Managua barrio of Máximo Jerez. The result was that while U.S. medics were seeing 250 patients per day the Cubans were treating 1,000."[4]

Since the Casa Presidencial and La Curva, both on the edge of the extinct volcano, had been leveled, Tacho moved his new command post into the military compound that became known as "the Bunker." The Bunker was a long reinforced-concrete structure built after the earthquake with precast aluminum forms and shaded by leafy laurel trees. Except for two windows on each side of the doorway, its yellowish walls were blank. Somoza later had the roof topped at both ends by huge steel screens meant to deflect rockets and mortar shells. Within a warren of waiting and conference rooms were the surprisingly spartan chambers where Somoza eventually came to live, making much of the fact that he lived there rather than in some lavish residence. The truth was that, because of the earth's upheaval and his own increasingly urgent need for security, he ultimately had little choice.

On the ruins of his father's La Curva palace with its splendid view of the city Tacho built a modern, California-style bungalow he christened La Curvita, the diminutive for La Curva. Tacho spent more time sleeping and exercising with his mistress at La Curvita than he did at El Retiro, which became Hope's domain. He ran the affairs of state from the Bunker, a short ride down the hill.

Next to the Roosevelt monument, at the foot of the volcano, a small tank was positioned as sentinel at the entrance to two roads—one leading to La Curvita, the other winding up to the rim of the Tiscapa volcano, where munition warehouses and the offices of the security force had been moved. The dreaded security apparatus occupied the now vacant sheds, garages and servants' quarters once attached to the Presidential Palace which had been leveled. The famous dungeon and cages in which the Somozas were charged with having held prisoners over the years disappeared along with the palace.

On Roosevelt Avenue, across from the Bunker, the pyramid-shaped Intercontinental Managua Hotel remained standing—a palace of luxury in a sea of misery. Above a scrubby, crabgrass-infested square of balding lawn called Esplanade Park, its better rooms gazed out on the ruins of Managua. Next to the Bunker, separated by a street called the Esplanada de Tiscapa, was the military casino. This formidable three-story white structure was turned from an officers' club into the executive office building of the Somoza regime. General headquarters of the National Guard spread out below the Esplanada de Tiscapa.

The military complex was scraggly in the best of times, a chicken-wire compound, its sagging gates watched over by near-illiterate National Guardsmen. The sheds, offices and barracks were prefabricated structures put up after the earthquake.

They gave the Somoza guard a transient, makeshift appearance. To a very real extent they mirrored the nature of the regime. Somoza's dictatorship was becoming increasingly sloppy and ad hoc. If dictatorships were rated for organization and efficiency on any scale, his would barely make the scale.

In Tacho's Bunker, American Ambassador Shelton continued playing the role of courtesan, providing all the support he could squeeze out of the United States. But Shelton's unswerving loyalty and continued efforts on behalf of Somoza's causes finally became suspect in Washington, especially as President Nixon sank into the mire of Watergate. The State Department even awarded Managua embassy political officer James Richard Cheek the department's Rivkin award in recognition of his detailed reports on Nicaragua, which contradicted those filed by Shelton. The citation said, "Cheek was the first to recognize, seek out and report on the new sociopolitical forces in Nicaragua. . . . In the process, he differed strongly with his superiors and others on the country team. He persevered, challenging the conventional wisdom . . . [and] submitted through the Dissent Channel, critical, but balanced analysis of the issues." But Shelton was decorated by Secretary of State William Rogers for his earthquake effort in 1973 when he visited Managua to lay the cornerstone for a hospital to be built with United States aid funds and a matching contribution from Nicaragua.

After September 1974, Somoza, once again president and spokesman for "all Nicaraguans," renewed with vigor his attacks on Castro and other opponents. Cuba was definitely linked with the Latin American guerrilla movements, he charged, and was lending both strategic and tactical aid. "We are seeing a new stage of Fidel Castro demonstrating his open willingness to interfere in internal affairs of other countries and overthrow governments. . . . International Communists are trying to organize cell groups in remote parts of Nicaragua," he maintained. The object was installing a Communist regime. He estimated their strength at at least twenty guerrillas, including one Mexican.[5]

Any criticism fired at Somoza by the opposition parties he shrugged off.

"Somoza," said forty-year-old architect and aspiring Conservative party leader Eduardo Chamorro, "is obsolete. He is using all the obsolete measures to try and solve new problems and he's not delivering."

Somoza responded with a typical salvo. "The trouble with him is that time has passed him by. . . . This has been a very liberal and nationalistic government where we mix socialism and free enterprise. What's happening today in the rest of Latin America and is shaking some people in the United States happened in Nicaragua thirty or more years ago." As evidence, Somoza cited the nationalization of the port of Corinto, the railroads, the power and light and telephone companies, and major waterworks, as well as a dispute with the United Fruit Company that eventually led to the banana company's withdrawal from Nicaragua.[6] Of course, as leader of the nation, Somoza had a slice of all the pies, but that was something he discreetly omitted mentioning.

CHAPTER 8

The Party's Over

A series of explosions caused a sudden halt in the cocktail chatter in the suburban Managua home of wealthy businessman José María Castillo Quant shortly before 11:00 P.M. on December 27, 1974. Conversation resumed shortly, the guests assuming that the commotion had been caused by festive fireworks. To their shock, a group of strangely dressed individuals, their appearances made hideous by nylon-stocking masks over their faces, burst into the chic party yelling: "This is a political operation. Hands on your heads. To the wall. We are the Frente Sandinista de Liberación Nacional. Viva Sandino!"

Most of the guests stood petrified, drinks in hand. The host, forty-eight-year-old Castillo, former minister of agriculture and a close associate and friend of Tacho, was quick to react. A gun buff, he managed to slip away, open his gun cabinet in his bedroom and distribute his collection of hunting rifles and automatic weapons to the stupefied musicians who had backed into his bedroom clutching their instruments. They quickly dropped both weapons and instruments and fled into a bathroom. Unseen by Castillo, two Sandinistas had also entered the bedroom. As the businessman turned with a machine gun in hand he was shot dead. He collapsed into the gun cabinet still gripping the unfired weapon.

The action of the commando Juan José Quezada that balmy Managua night echoed throughout the world. The audacious raiders, ten men and three women, waving the red and black Sandinista colors under Somoza's very nose, reaped dividends far greater than the release of leading guerrillas from Somoza's prisons and the million dollars for their war chest. The raid brought them publicity, recruits and credibility.

Ambassador Shelton, along with his wife and mother-in-law, had left the cocktail party, given in his honor, a half-hour before. The remaining guests, held captive, comprised a who's who of Somoza intimates. Included was Tacho's brother-in-law, Guillermo Sevilla-Sacasa, who managed to slip into the garden and hide his rotund form temporarily among the hibiscus until he was discovered in the morning. Among the other notables were Dr. Alejandro Montiel Argüello, foreign minister; Dr. Luis Valle Olivares, minister of the national district and mayor of Managua; Guillermo Lang, Nicaragua's alternate ambassador to the United Nations and consul general in New York; Chilean ambassador Alfonso Denecken-die, and their wives.

Besides Castillo, three guards posted outside the house also died, and three more were wounded. A Sandinista was wounded in the chest.

Tacho had left the day before to vacation on Corn Island in the Nicaraguan Caribbean. General José Somoza was in charge during his absence. When word reached guard headquarters and the general was informed, he ordered some troops supported by a Staghound armored car to surround the house. One of the first to arrive at the scene to help direct a counterattack was Gunther Wagner, a German-born United States citizen serving as a police adviser to Somoza under a private agreement. He had come to Nicaragua in 1970 under a United States Agency for International Development public safety program and stayed on in the pay of the Nicaraguan government.

Around midnight the soldiers launched an attack on the Castillo home and managed to smash the garage door. During the attack the terrified hostages had been grouped in a corridor between the living room and the garden for their own protection. Esso oil refinery manager Danilo Lacayo Rappacciolli, hiding in the garden, was wounded during the firefight. One of the hostages, Castillo's daughter Irene, served as a go-between to warn Police Chief Colonel Agustín Bodán, who was in command, that if his troops renewed their attack, the hostages' lives would be in jeopardy.

At 1:30 A.M. the telephone at the Castillo home rang. "What's going on there?" asked General José Somoza.

"We are the Sandinista Front, we have seized the house and have taken several prisoners."

"Who?" he said, trying to decide if it was worthwhile negotiating.

"Several—you know who. We have concrete demands."

"All right, what are your demands?" he asked brusquely.

"The immediate freedom of some political prisoners."

"What are their names?"

"Jaime Cuadra, Carlos Argüello Pravia, David, Adolfo and Ariel Nuñez Rodríguez, Manuel Rivas, Jacinto Suárez, José Benito Escobar, Julián Roque, Lenin Cerna, Daniel Ortega, Carlos José Guadámuz, Oscar Benavides and Adrián Molina."

"And what else?" José Somoza replied. "We can reach an agreement through dialogue. Why do we have to be so violent?"

"We have a written communiqué that must be given full coverage in the mass media."

"All right, what is it you want?" Somoza said, trying to sound conciliatory.

"First, we want Archbishop [Miguel] Obando y Bravo as mediator."[1]

José, after this brief telephone conversation with a man who had identified himself only as Zero, contacted Tacho and informed him of the situation.

The guerrillas had confused their illustrious captives by identifying each other by numbers, a system used by prisoners in some penal institutions. The commando chief was known as Zero; his nom de guerre was Marcos. His real name was Eduardo

Contreras Escobar. Born in the little town of Ticuantepe, September 4, 1945, he was the fourth of five children. As a boy he had befriended a German woman he met while selling milk from door to door. The woman suffered from elephantiasis. When her husband died, Contreras, then only fourteen, took care of all the funeral arrangements. Recognizing the quick intelligence of the boy, she taught him German and when he was seventeen, the year after he graduated from high school, scraped together enough money to send him to Germany to study. He spent six years studying in Berlin and returned to Nicaragua with degrees in both engineering and economics. At fifteen, he had tried to join the Socialist Youth but was rejected. In 1960, he did manage to join the little guerrilla group that invaded Ocotal from Honduras, but he was quickly caught and jailed. A friend of the family arranged his release from prison. On his return to Nicaragua in 1970 he joined the FSLN and spent two years in Mexico setting up the first solidarity committee there. He did the same thing later in Honduras. In Honduras he also established a pipeline for arms to the FSLN cadre in Nicaragua. A month after his return home two members of the directorate, Ricardo Morales and Oscar Turcio, were killed and he stepped into the directorate and began to clean up what he found to be a "sloppy organization," bringing to bear his German training for methodology and precision. It was he who recruited the famous Nicaraguan musician Carlos Mejia Godoy to the cause.

Contreras's mania for precision was displayed in the now famous "Christmas party" raid. His military commander for the raid was Germán Pomares, thirty-nine, "El Dante," an arms expert, and one of the Frente's toughest fighters. The dark stocky Pomares had become literate only after joining the ranks of the Frente. He had worked the Chinandega cotton fields in his youth and later moved into the Frente from a trade union. Another of the commandos, identified by a hostage as a "chico bien" because of the fine quality of his imported clothes, was Joaquín Cuadra Lacayo, son of one of Nicaragua's richest corporation lawyers. Four months earlier, when the youth disappeared, he'd left a letter in his parent's villa informing them that he was going to Cuba. Now Somoza was to pay for his ticket there.

The raid was a shock both to Somoza and to his not always well informed intelligence service. Tacho actually believed that the Frente was no threat. He was convinced that the antiguerrilla unit of the guard was the best in Latin America. But in Managua's most elegant suburb the guard was rendered helpless because only through negotiations could the lives of Tacho's relatives and friends be guaranteed. Hardliners in the guard saw it as a first test for Tacho and afterwards they noted how he had failed it. One of them, Lieutenant Colonel José Iván Alegrett, who had quickly flown home from a brief trip abroad, stalked outside the house like a hungry tiger. He protested that any deal with the guerrillas would only furnish them with funds to fight the guard in the future. The guerrillas made no secret of this and said in their communiqué they needed the funds for their war. Alegrett wanted no deal with the guerrillas.

However Somoza, whose sister, Lilian, was demanding from Washington that he make a deal in order to assure her husband's release, decided to negotiate a settlement. He played the few cards he could. Between 2:00 and 3:00 A.M. on

December 28 he convened his cabinet and imposed martial law, suspending all individual rights. Anyone suspected of harboring strong anti-Somoza sentiments was rounded up. A number of students and university professors had been jailed by the end of the day. The Sandinistas later alleged that Dr. René Nuñez, ex-vice-president of the University Federation (CUUN), was savagely tortured on this occasion, his arms, legs and spinal column broken.[2]

These detentions reached massive proportions in the cities of León, Matagalpa, Chinandega and Managua.

By early that morning the shaken hostages had yet to hear of or see what had happened to their host, Castillo. They first thought he was hiding somewhere but, as the tension grew in the rooms into which the guerrillas had divided the guests, constantly under gunpoint, they began to suspect the worst. But it wasn't until the following day, December 29, when they saw a body being removed from the house, that they realized that their host, popularly known as Chema, had been among the first casualties.

Foreign newsmen who arrived in the vicinity of the besieged Castillo residence began using the wealthy neighbors' telephones to file their stories. It was then they learned, for the first time, that Somoza was not particularly loved by Nicaragua's upper class. Even the wealthy spoke disparagingly of Tacho and of the Somozas' corruption, especially of the post-1972 earthquake relief efforts and the unknown destination of millions of dollars in aid.

"Many were happy when they heard that the list of hostages included Tacho's brother-in-law," one lady told a newsmen. "The Somozas are so unreasonable that you can hardly blame the leftists," a middle-aged doctor said. He added, "I can understand the frustration of these young people, but I fear this may bring on a wave of similar kidnappings. The perpetuation of the Somoza regime had already increased class consciousness here and I'm worried that there will be even more polarization now."[3]

As guard reinforcements began to arrive in the exclusive Los Robles suburb of Managua, the commando unit inside the Castillo home used Castillo's personal arsenal to bolster their small supply of single-shot rifles, handguns and six hand grenades. They were now prepared either to fight or to withstand a long siege. There was enough food in the house to last weeks. Besides what had been displayed for the ambassador, they found two hundred turkeys, as well as other provisions. One of the Sandinistas, a veteran sugarcane cutter, remarked, "Never in my life have I seen, or tasted, such food."

Although the captives, many of whom were suffering from hypertension, were treated well, some panicked. One of the women, afraid that the Sandinistas might take her seven-carat diamond ring, valued at some $15,000, swallowed it. After being freed, doctors informed her that the cost of an operation to remove it from her stomach would probably exceed the value of the ring. But nature took its course and the ring was finally recovered with a new historical value.[4]

One of the less affluent guests, Colonel Pataky, a foreigner residing in Nicaragua, had his wallet taken away by the guerrillas. "Commander, please, there are more than a thousand córdobas [$200] in my wallet which were to be used to buy food for my family. Please don't take the money." His wife was in Costa Rica and his young children were alone with the maid. In a display of compassion the guerrilla said, "There's no problem," and ordered the wallet be returned. All the money was still there and the colonel asked how he could send it to his home. Zero replied, "When the archbishop comes, he will see to it that it is delivered to your family." The guest thanked him—a tremendous burden had been removed from his shoulders. Although he remained a captive in the residence, held at gunpoint, this gesture on the part of the Sandinistas left him relaxed to a certain extent.[5]

Archbishop Obando y Bravo, in his white cassock, arrived at the house at 6:15 A.M. on the twenty-eighth to begin the negotiations. This meant that Somoza had satisfied the first of the guerrillas' demands. When the archbishop left, the guerrillas, in a preliminary gesture, released thirteen persons, all politically uninvolved, including waiters, Castillo's servants, the musicians and the wives of some of the prisoners.

The electricity in Los Robles was cut off, and without air conditioning the house became unbearable. Somoza maintained constant contact with the United States ambassador and his own ministers and guard commanders. Meanwhile the guerrillas made their demands known: 1) Freedom for all political prisoners. 2) Five million dollars in bills of small denominations and with different serial numbers. 3) An immediate increase in the minimum wages of exploited Nicaraguan workers, as well as fringe benefits such as bonuses, loans, etc. (ironically, members of the National Guard were to benefit as well when this concession was granted). 4) The suspension of all repressive measures. 5) The immediate and complete publication of the FSLN's communiqués in all the mass media. 6) Absolute freedom of information. 7) A deadline of thirty-six hours to comply with the demands.

Somoza stalled by claiming he couldn't find that amount of money in Nicaragua in dollars and would have to wait until the banks opened Monday in the United States. The day drew to a close. A decision to impose an overnight curfew was reversed minutes before it was to go into effect at 10:00 P.M. The opposition newspaper *La Prensa,* heavily censored, appeared without reference to the hostages held by the guerrillas.

With less than $200,000 dollars in the Central Bank in Managua Tacho dispatched an aide to New York in his personal aircraft to pick up five million dollars in cash from the Federal Reserve Bank.

December 29 dawned with one of Somoza's hostage ministers, Dr. Luis Valle Olivares, telling an Associated Press reporter by telephone that "some of us slept well last night: the prisoners have been well treated." The Sandinista deadline was to expire at 11:00 A.M., some four hours later.

The remaining women were set free at 9:35 A.M. Upon release, one of them, the former Lois Nash, an American married to Nicaragua's foreign minister, told reporters that the guerrillas had treated their hostages "magnificently. It is incredible the treatment they have given us."

At 11:00 A.M. the negotiations were stalemated, the deadline had expired and the archbishop, meeting with Somoza, failed to keep his appointment with the

Sandinistas. Tension in Los Robles mounted. Some felt an attack was imminent with the arrival of heavily armed troops. Journalists and photographers were forced to leave the area. Traffic was detoured away from the scene.

During the archbishop's meeting with Somoza, Tacho told him: "Archbishop, these kids are wrong. This problem can be solved today."[6] But for the time being, negotiations were his only recourse. When the archbishop approached Zero for extension of their deadline, the latter recited a Sandinista phrase that was to become famous in the years that followed: "We are fierce and unrelenting in combat, but generous in victory." Zero added, "If he [Somoza] asks us for forty-eight hours instead of thirty-six to further the negotiations . . . we will accept."[7]

The government then announced that the deadline had been extended to forty-eight hours. A Lanica Convair aircraft was kept on standby at Las Mercedes airport. At Los Robles, a fleet of Mercedes Benz arrived, filled with high military officials and aides; again an attack appeared imminent.

Later that afternoon the ambassadors of Spain and Mexico agreed to fly to Cuba with the archbishop, the Sandinista commandos and the political prisoners who were to be exchanged for the hostages at the airport.

At 7:15 P.M. Radio Difusora Nacional began to transmit a 12,000-word Sandinista communiqué. The document, which depicted the day-to-day violence experienced by those who made up the lower strata of Nicaraguan society, was divided into two sections. The first dealt with the oppression which the FSLN claimed the people suffered and named capitalist landowners, the National Guard and the *jueces de mesta* (local sheriffs) as the three groups responsible for this oppression. The second section described the past battles which the FSLN had fought against the regime and reported alleged atrocities committed by the guard.

Nicaraguans were told that the FSLN was winning its battle against "the most despicable dictatorship in Latin America." "The people's patience is reaching its limit," the communiqué declared. "At present, the daily plight of the peasantry can be summarized as misery, hunger, malnutrition, fear, night blindness, premature death and illiteracy."[8]

In describing the working conditions which the landowners forced on the poor peasants, the document charged, "Subsistence wages are—literally—policies that, if they were not so inhuman, would be curious. . . . The landowners seek to reduce even further the dollar a day received by workers for ten to twelve hours work. . . . These subsistence wages, together with the hopelessness of the peasant's lot . . . has led him to reject the economic system in which he was born. He has lost the incentive to work. . . . The peasant in the Northern, Atlantic and Pacific zones of Nicaragua works all his life and dies indebted to his employer." A statistical table was also included which described what portion of the peasant's wages went to support his family, which the document said, had an average of eight children. The statistical table read: "Salary—$1.00 U.S. a day. Price of salt—20 cents U.S. per bag; price of soap—30 cents per bag; price of gas—30 cents per liter; price of medicine for amoebic dysentery—40 cents per dosage (intestinal illnesses caused by amoebic infections are endemic); price of mejoral (a type of aspirin)—4 cents per dosage (the average peasant is always in pain); *cususa* (an alcoholic mixture)—$1.60 a bottle; the average fine from the *juez de mesta*—$10.00; the average fine from the guard —$16.00."

The *juez de mesta* was described as the scourge of the peasant, a servant of the landowners and agent of Somoza as well as the embodiment of political repression. The communiqué charged that the guard's tactics were not only physical but psychological repression and that its forty-five year reign of terror was "such that it is equal to how a commercial slogan conditions the mentality of a consumer. . . . The guard, its name, weapons and uniform have conditioned the mind of the peasant with terror, rape and crime." It followed to say that "the weight of the Sandinista resistance falls fundamentally upon the peasants in the mountains. This is an important historical precedent."

A new phase in the "fight for national liberation" had begun with the taking of the hostages, the communiqué said. This initial step was designed to free imprisoned Sandinistas and acquire funds needed for "prolonged war." As to the 1967 Pancasán fight, the guerrillas had taken their quota of blood but the GPP (*guerra popular prolongada*—prolonged popular war) lost by failing to consolidate the peasants in the mountains. "Such a limitation forced our organization to make a strategic retreat in order to recuperate and regroup for new confrontations with the enemy." The defeat was followed by a new phenomenon in Nicaragua, the focus of three Sandinista groups in the political and labor arenas in addition to organizing peasants to fight abuse with arms.

This was the first indication that the FSLN had split into three groups or tendencies. Contreras was now a leader of the new third force, the Tercerista tendency, and he was about to win the funds and release of fellow Sandinistas to press acceptance of his faction. But it was to be a bitter internal struggle that would continue for the next five years.

The document said "revolutionary violence" was "indispensable" in reaching "popular victory." "We will go to war to kill or be killed but only so that our people have a real opportunity to live." The kidnapping, it said, was an "obligatory response to the repressive politics of the regime," instigated by "profoundly humanitarian reasons." In contrast with the repressive forces, it added, "We take prisoners, a group of diplomats, so that they respond to the liberty of our brother prisoners."

The Sandinistas ended by saying that if their demands were not met the first prisoner would be executed, followed by another execution every twelve hours. Somoza, while capitulating to their demands, displayed a certain business acumen in negotiating reduction of their ransom demand from five to one million dollars.

At 8:00 A.M., December 30, the fourteen political prisoners, among them Daniel Ortega, were transferred from the prison to the airport. Like Ortega, most of them had been in prison for seven years. At 9:00 A.M., preparations began to transfer the hostages and commandos to the airport. At 10:50 A.M., the archbishop left the Castillo home. Behind him was a man in civilian dress. Immediately following, was a Sandinista commando, masked and carrying one of Castillo's submachine guns. Following him was another priest, then the Mexican and Spanish ambassadors, and finally the hostages and the rest of the commandos. They boarded a yellow bus. The hostages were forced to sit on the flanks of the bus as security to the Sandinistas. Along the road to the airport they were subjected to cheers for the Sandinistas and jeers for their own predicament.

That morning the nation's daily papers had printed the Sandinista communiqué as part of a government decree. Along the route to the airport, taxis and motorists honked their horns at the bus and groups of people quickly gathered and gave the victory sign to its occupants. Clamors and shouts of *Viva el Frente* and *Viva Sandino* were heard clearly and spontaneously in the streets of Managua as the yellow bus passed. The bus arrived at the airport at 11:45. Samuel Genie, chief of the office of security, was next to the plane, his head in his hands, an expression of impotence on his face.

Hundreds of young Nicaraguans cheered wildly as the plane left the runway at 12:20 P.M. for Havana, and emotion ran high inside the terminal building. With the thirteen guerrillas and fourteen political prisoners were Archbishop Obando y Bravo; the papal nuncio, Monsignor Gabriel Montalveo; Mexican Ambassador Joaquín Mercado Flores; Spanish Ambassador José García Banón; and an estimated one million dollars. Most of the guerrillas, including Joaquín Cuadra Lacayo, went on to spend nine months of military training in Cuba.

One exhilarated man waxed poetic and said, "This is a new dawn, a beautiful dawn after forty years of night."

In contrast Tacho, in an ugly mood, spat out his words. "They are cowards, blackmailers, psychopaths and fools," he said, referring to the Sandinistas. "This is the work of communism equal to the assassination of my father." In private, Tacho's anger was described as apoplectic. He tried not to reflect his rage in his New Year's message to the nation, which he said he was obliged to make in order to explain the details "that culminated with the tragic deaths of a group of citizens who were peacefully gathered at an honorable home and who were violently assaulted." Somoza tried to justify his actions to critics in the guard—he had acted to avoid unnecessary bloodshed. He also attacked the Sandinista communiqué on an almost paragraph by paragraph basis.

"Sirs," Somoza said, "if in Nicaragua we have had a history of revolutions and of disorder, among other things we have had a history of nobility, of frankness, of truth." He then charged that the communists had showed their first intent to bloody the nation when they assassinated his father and that "they calculated that a young man like I was then, was going to take massive reprisals and this would commence the crossroads for Niacaragua so that later they could seize the nation."

The National Guard he characterized as an organization sworn to enforce the law, to guard the peace and respect a prisoner when he is captured. He went on, "It is a disciplined institution, an institution which has not committed the atrocities that they claim. . . ."

Sandinista communiqués in general were attacked as "filthy manifestos." "I'm happy the documents went on the radio and were published in the papers. I'm glad they [the Sandinistas] are in Cuba as these were part of the demands and I want to demonstrate to them and those who stay here that I am a man who keeps his word. It did not hurt me to publish these documents, because I know that the Nicaraguan people, above all things, love peace, above all things love liberty, the security of their family and no piece of paper of this class is going to make anybody believe that these Sandinistas have the political force to make changes."

The demands, growled Somoza, were interesting in that the only two points on which the lives of the hostages depended were the quantity of money and the "divulging of these filthy manifestos that I ordered published in the nation . . . they were not philosophical points, they were not points that could be really constructive to our country."

The most disgusting episode of the entire event, the president went on, "was the blackmail and the barbarity of wanting to keep Castillo's body for thirty-six hours in an air-conditioned room so that they could present him as the first prisoner executed. God is very great, but He did not make Castillo of stone, He made him of flesh and bones like us and his body was already in the state of decomposition." At this time, Somoza claimed, the guerrillas began to discover they would have to kill somebody else in cold blood. "Because of this, sirs, I want us this night to remember this act as the biggest disgrace that has occurred in this nation, a disgrace that will remain recorded in the history of all of the peaceful citizens of Nicaragua."

In his speech to the nation Somoza said, "The business of this government is to guard against the killing of innocent people who are in the hands of psychopaths and fools, like those who took the house. The business of this government is to maintain human life and human rights. Because of this we demonstrated an enormous amount of patience and, up to a point, weakness. And I'm not afraid to say that I demonstrated weakness because these riffraff demanded I give them money when they know all the banks in the world are closed on Saturday and Sunday, and I thought they would kill the first hostage if this demand wasn't met in thirty-six hours. So I had to ask for an extension and take all the means I could take, to have all the instruments in my hands for the negotiations so that it would not remain on my conscience that I did not do everything possible to save these human beings. . . . It gives me pride to say that by my actions and that of the diplomatic corps and of my ministers that Nicaragua avoided a bloodbath."

Somoza ended by saying, "The form in which the problem planted by the assailants was resolved does not in any manner constitute a precedent for establishing a future norm of action on the government. The rule of the law will continue firm in Nicaragua, the state of siege will continue until we terminate the investigation and we establish who was responsible for this hideous crime."

But before ending his dialogue with the people, Somoza took time to attack *La Prensa* publisher Pedro Joaquín Chamorro, whose paper, he said, created the climate for the terrorism. He not only ordered Interior Minister José Mora Rostrán to make *La Prensa* publish his accusation on the paper's front page for three consecutive days, he attached the rider that his picture accompany the speech. Chamorro was forbidden to publish an editorial reply. *La Prensa* normally never published a picture of Somoza.

However, Somoza's problems with the left and the conservative opposition, whose charges were labeled "reactionary bellyaching," did not become so serious that he could not continue to devote his time to being Somoza the businessman ruling over his family's vast empire. Unlike his father, Tacho was not satisfied with just the family empire in Nicaragua. In the late sixties and early seventies he became interested in investments abroad. In addition to his aborted attempts to become a business associate of Howard Hughes, he amassed large stock portfolios and shares in United States companies as he began moving some of the family capital into what he considered more lucrative businesses abroad. Congressman Charles Wilson, a Texas Democrat, recalled that when he visited Somoza in Managua, Tacho was continually interrupted by telephone calls from American brokers to whom he would give terse orders to "buy" or "sell."

But even the periods of martial law, higher oil bills and the Managuan reconstruction costs did not keep the Nicaraguan free-enterprise economy from growing steadily. Many businessmen felt that under the Somoza family the nation was a safe place for investment. Good prices for the nation's traditional agricultural exports led to a certain economic prosperity. Nicaragua had a $46 million trade surplus in 1976 due to high cotton prices and record coffee prices—the nation's first trade surplus since 1972. While coffee sales in 1974 tallied $46 million, that figure doubled in 1976 and reached more than $150 million in 1977, when coffee surpassed cotton as the nation's prime export. Inflation was down to 3 percent in 1976 from a high of 17 percent in 1974 and that year the country's gross national product grew by 8 percent.

In spite of this, few Nicaraguans received any direct benefits from the nation's growing prosperity. As in the rest of Central America, with the exception of democratic little Costa Rica, disease, malnutrition and illiteracy were endemic in Somoza's Nicaragua. The infant mortality rate was 130 per 1,000 live births but because of rampant intestinal infections, as well as the other common diseases and a lack of medical assistance, the death rate among the undernourished youth was even higher. The average daily calorie intake was only 1,800 compared with a recommended minimum of 3,000. The best-fed members of the lower classes were the members of the guard. Often an inducement for poor peasants to join the service was the promise of three meals a day—and a gun. Guardsmen were also taught to read and write, rare skills among their fellow countrymen.

In the summer of 1975 opposition groups began pressing for the withdrawal of the American ambassador, which would mark the end of the total identification of the United States with the regime.

However, Somoza campaigned in Washington to have Ambassador Shelton's assignment extended and even tried to influence Capitol Hill to offer the ambassador a prestigious new assignment on the grounds that his abrupt demotion or dismissal would otherwise imply censure of his close ties with the Nicaraguan president.

The criticism of Shelton grew from the fact he spoke no Spanish, and, more importantly, that he cultivated his relations with Somoza to the exclusion of all other political figures, particularly well-known opponents of the regime. When in commemoration of the abrogation of the 1914 Chamorro-Bryan treaty, a twenty-córdoba note was minted, Shelton was even depicted on the note—perhaps the first time a current ambassador in any country in the world had been so depicted—his head bowed to Tacho and the minister of finance.

While Shelton had a falling out with the State Department and several senior members of the United States mission in Managua, he defended himself by saying, "It's the job of an ambassador to establish the best possible relationship with the president of a friendly country. I don't think of it in terms of a personal relationship, but I think President Somoza is a very nice man. He is friendly to the United States, he does a good job and he's a hard-working leader who has done a lot to improve things in this country. I'm sure if there were elections supervised by the United Nations, General Somoza would win."[9] Ironically, because Shelton was so subservient, in time of crisis even Tacho preferred to deal with the deputy chief of mission or a political officer of the embassy. He realized full well that Shelton had lost all credibility in Washington.

Newspaper publisher Chamorro expressed the hope that Shelton's replacement, James D. Theberge, would be "an honest person who does not interfere in the struggle of Nicaraguans to obtain their liberation and who reverses the policy of supporting corrupt dictatorships like that of the Somozas." But American embassy personnel noted that Theberge "may have a different personal style but will probably have the same politics."[10] He was rabidly anticommunist and suspicious of local reformist movements. Theberge's studies prior to his appointment included *The Soviet Presence in Latin America* and *Russia in the Caribbean.* In August 1980, he toured much of Latin America as the representative of candidate Ronald Reagan.

Somoza's health and his wife afforded him problems. Reports had it that he suffered from kidney failure, was seriously ill, and flew once a month to the States for treatment. Hope and Tacho began to grow more distant and they agreed to separate. Rumors were rife that she had taken a lover. Tacho continued to drink heavily. Dinorah was still at his side, a kind of first lady by proxy, even to the point of accompanying him on that embarrassing (to the Dominican people) trip to the Dominican Republic in 1972.

Hope in 1976 decided to move to London and purchased a house there. She also commuted to Miami. Most of her friends in London were from the Latin American diplomatic corps. Her son Tachito lived there for the short time he studied at Britain's Royal Military College of Sandhurst.

Any pretense of respect for human rights Somoza may have shown now vanished. He began 1975 in an angry mood, determined to purge the country of the "communists," as he referred to the Sandinistas. "We are masters in the art of antiguerrilla warfare in the countryside," he bragged. Martial law continued, the media were heavily censored, and Nicaragua continued to be, as it had been for forty-two years, a leading violator of human rights in Central America. And still, as for four decades, the Somozas had the support of the United States as an "anticommunist bastion."

But in the United States the winds of change were blowing. Congress began seriously to question military and political alliances that entangled the United States with unpopular, repressive governments. Even the State Department began to be nervous about the United States' relations with Nicaragua. Somoza's hard-hitting crackdown on political activity and dissent in the cities and harsh repression in the countryside could not have come at a more inopportune time for his relations with the United States. Although Jimmy Carter would later receive most of the credit for the United States' tough human rights policy, it was the 1973–74 Congress which acted first to prohibit military and developmental assistance to consistent gross violators of human rights, unless there were extraordinary circumstances justifying such assistance.

Tacho was still very much the man in charge, but there were increasing signs that the urban population was awakening from years of apathetic resignation to the family dynasty. The cocktail party raid served to point out the vulnerability of even Tacho Somoza but no one yet maintained that he was in serious trouble, at least not in 1975. However, in unleashing his guard he was responding in the only manner he knew how—militarily—and the guard's excesses proved to be what eroded the foundations of the dynasty.

Despite denials that there was danger to his government, Somoza's mood changed. He began traveling outside his well-guarded home only when surrounded by heavily armed soldiers. He continued to speak, but always separated from his people by his bulletproof glass cage.

Government officials expected the guerrillas to strike again soon after the year's end triumph, but little action developed in 1975. General Samuel Genie had claimed before the party raid that the Sandinistas were completely under control. To be doubly sure of holding control, Somoza created a new special counterinsurgency unit within the 8,000-man guard to concentrate on guerrilla fighting.

Among the few guard-Sandinista confrontations, one came in August in El Sauce where four guerrillas were killed in a raid on an FSLN training camp, including pretty Arlene Siu, a Chinese-Nicaraguan student. But the guerrillas, mostly from middle-class urban families, were successfully recruiting growing numbers of peasants to their cause. Most of the forty or so rebels who in March briefly occupied the town of Río Blanco in the hills above Matagalpa were peasants. The government responded by transferring its crack 400-man "General Somoza García" combat battalion to the village under a Colonel Gonzalo Evertsz. The unit was equipped with four twelve-soldier secondhand Huey helicopters purchased from the United States.

The guard ignored the peasants' social problems and guard tactics increased the hostility of the peasantry. There were indiscriminate arrests of those suspected of collaborating with the guerrillas, and there were summary executions.

Sandinista activities spread from the Matagalpa area. A clash occurred in Ocotal, ninety miles north of Managua. Suspected Sandinistas were arrested in Chinandega and Jinotepe. Some citizens took their complaints of guard brutality directly to Somoza. One, the widowed María Magdalena Rugama de Ochoa, whose son had been captured and beaten by the guard until one arm was broken and the youth urinated blood, wrote an open letter to Somoza which was widely circulated in mimeographed form in Managua. A more organized appeal came from people who "had always been Liberals [party members] . . . a party which we have served faithfully. We profoundly lament that the National Guard proceeds to capture and torture honorable citizens without an investigation. . . ." Tacho ignored the complaints.

Meanwhile the guerrillas were having internal problems. Differences within the leadership over tactics and methods of struggle against the dictatorship had caused the Frente to split into three groups by 1974. It was not an ideological split. Most of the leadership had at least adopted Marxist-Leninist terminology even if they didn't completely adhere to Marxist-Leninist ideology. They all fought for a socialist Nicaragua. Most of them had received their indoctrination while attending the universities of León and Managua. Carlos Fonseca, who wrote the book *A Nicaraguan in Moscow* in the late 1950s, believed in the "prolonged popular war" and sought to emulate Sandino and Fidel Castro by fighting that war in the far-off mountains. Fonseca believed the war would be long and drawn-out. He confided to fellow Latin American revolutionaries in Mexico in the late 1960s that the Frente was far from reaching its goal. In early 1975 he was again pessimistic.

Borge years later reflected that the growth of the Frente was considerable at the time. "There were entire regions with us." But he lamented, "An error was involved because we sacrificed the quality to the quantity." New middle-class recruits had the "characteristic training of a small bourgeoisie." This created problems the FSLN directorate did not know how to handle.[11]

Borge and Fonseca backed the GPP faction, whose motto was the words of Henry Ruiz, known as Comandante Modesto and later GPP leader: "In the mountains we will bury the heart of the enemy."

Sanctions and expulsion of the opposition called the Proletarian tendency *(tendencia proletaria)* were devised. "We said that all this could be discussed," Borge said, "but at the same time there were disciplinary faults. We took measures, sanctions. And these sanctions were interpreted as reprisals for the political statements that were being made." Borge said that the Sandinistas operating within Nicaragua applied sanctions against the *tendencia proletaria* while those outside of Nicaragua resisted them.[12]

The rural and urban factions numbered only approximately sixty and forty members each. The split was noticeable enough to allow Somoza's agents to infiltrate the movement. Castro was providing some training in Cuba for exiled FSLN leaders but supplied neither arms nor money. The GPP strategy for a drawn-out war was questionable in the face of high guerrilla and peasant casualties. Proletarians stayed loyal to socialist goals but differed as to the method. The third force known as the Tercerista tendency, which advocated insurrection, was less dogmatic than either of the other two tendencies.

Recruitment was likewise divided. The GPP sought university students and workers while the very poor sectors of the barrios were worked by the proletarians. The GPP favored a decade-long revolt while the proletarians sought to raise the consciousness among the people for an eventual popular uprising. Finally, the Terceristas recruited widely among Catholic militants and social democrats, and rebels without any particular ideology. The FSLN splintering became disastrous, and even a bit ridiculous—sometimes more than one group chose to rob the same bank on the same day.

The Sandinistas estimated their strength at two hundred guerrillas while others placed the number closer to one hundred men. The Sandinista leadership, when not squabbling among themselves, saw their ranks decimated by the guard. Arrests and killings ravaged the guerrilla cells and the remnants were forced to flee deeper into the hills or to neighboring countries. Another two hundred suspected guerrillas were behind bars, including Borge.

The first serious blow to the leadership came on November 7, 1976, when Eduardo Contreras Escobar, the handsome Zero, was killed with two others in a shootout with a *Becat*, Somoza's special antiterrorist patrol, in suburban Managua. Becat is the acronym for Brigada Especial Contra La Acción Terrorista (Special Brigade Against Terrorist Action). But a more severe shock came the next day when FSLN Secretary-General Carlos Fonseca Amador, who some saw as a reincarnation of Sandino, was killed with two companions. The most important leaders of the Frente Sandinista were dead, and Somoza rejoiced that the FSLN threat had been eliminated. He had made them pay for his losing face at the 1974 Christmas party.

There were no witnesses to Fonseca's death in the northern mountains. Some said he fell in combat while others maintained the trio had been captured and executed. Borge, writing about Fonseca from his jail cell after receiving reports about his death, said that Fonseca and an eight-man squad (including Carlos Agüero and his beautiful companion Claudia) were walking to an encampment in the mountainous region of Zinica in the rain, the tranquillity seemingly suspicious, when they heard three shots and found a *juez de mesta*, drunk on *cususa* (an alcoholic concoction of beer, wine, whiskey or whatever is available). Carlos decided the group should wait twenty-four hours before resuming their march. When they left the next day they heard a Garand rifle. At about the same time a machine gun lit up the darkness; Carlos fired off a shot. He told the rest of the group to retreat. The group heard several grenades a few minutes later; then there was silence. Fonseca had been killed. In the morning helicopters arrived carrying high-ranking officials who had Carlos's head cut off to give Somoza irrefutable proof that the legend he hated so much had indeed died. (Three years earlier Somoza had claimed that Fonseca had been killed and that even his aged father had identified the body.)

"The commandant of the Tipitapa jail came to our small cell, jubilant, with *Novedades* in his hand to give us the news: 'Carlos Fonseca is dead,' he told us. We responded after a few seconds of silence: 'You are wrong, Colonel. Carlos Fonseca is one of the dead who never dies.' The colonel told us: 'All of you are really unbelievable.' "[13]

Between 1970 and 1975 Fonseca had traveled widely abroad promoting the FSLN and the fight against Somoza. His trips took him to Cuba, Allende's Chile, and other socialist nations where his political beliefs had been strengthened. Fonseca had returned to Nicaragua in 1975. He grew a beard in later life. Inside, like most revolutionaries, he was a poet. He once said, "Nicaragua, despite the terrible ignorance in which they've kept us, probably has more poets per capita than any other country in the world."

Following Fonseca's death Somoza persuaded the Central American Defense Council or CONDECA *(Consejo de Defensa Centro-americano)* to hold its "Aguila Six" military maneuvers with three thousand troops in the area where Fonseca was killed. The plan for the maneuvers was discreet—the Sandinistas' *foco* (headquarters) was there in the Cordillera Isabelia. The dictator also considered the nearby Mosquito Coast the likely spot for a potential Cuban landing. This was also the region where Sandino himself had carried out his struggle against the United States Marines, and the area had maintained its reputation as a center of opposition. Participating in the exercises were the military of Nicaragua, Guatemala and El Salvador with Panama, Costa Rica and Honduras sending only observers. The exercise received moral and material assistance from the United States Southern Command. The United States Senate approved the American army's participation in the maneuvers, but the army opted to send only fourteen observers.

Somoza continued, at the people's expense, to solidify his standing as the richest man in Nicaragua. He was seriously overweight, reflecting his partiality for food, drink and fun. And he was rarely without one of the huge cigars made for him by Cuban exiles residing in Nicaragua. There was no sign that he would take his health into consideration, even though his brother Luis had died of a heart attack.

Tacho's 1976 Bicentennial gift to the United States backfired. He liked to boast he was one of three West Point graduates to become president. To celebrate the United States' two hundredth birthday he ceremoniously presented West Point a painting, in May 1976, of George Washington, U. S. Grant and Dwight Eisenhower, the angle being that it presented for the first time, on a single canvas, all the nation's generals who went on to become presidents. Somoza stood to be corrected, however. It was pointed out to him that William Henry Harrison, Andrew Jackson and Zachary Taylor were all generals too. As one newspaper writer put it, "This being the case, it appears now that Somoza's gift may be one of the more useless things ever painted."

In the meantime, following the death of Fonseca and Contreras, the Terceristas or *insurreccionales,* who rejected the GPP and proletarian plan to accumulate their forces slowly and selectively, was in the ascendency. Correctly gauging that anti-Somoza sentiment was growing rapidly, they advocated popular insurrection and joining forces with non-Marxist groups, even nationalist elements of the bourgeois and private sector. Many of the Terceristas were non-Marxist and some were the sons of wealthy businessmen.

The Terceristas pushed for a series of spectacular military strikes to grab headlines. They saw spectacular guerrilla attacks and raids in the cities as the quickest way to build popular support and rout Somoza. Their leaders, former GPP members Daniel and Humberto Ortega and Mexican Victor Manuel Tirado, disagreed with the GPP theory of organizing forces primarily in the mountains.[16]

"To make war in order to organize, to organize in order to make war until victory" was their motto. They tempered their revolutionary rhetoric; socialism would not come "overnight," but in stages. Their program demanded the overthrow of Somoza followed by free elections, the disbanding of the National Guard, the nationalization of all Somoza's holdings and of all private banks. Until that was achieved, they pledged never to lay down their arms. Their actions soon made them the best known and most publicized of the three factions.[14]

CHAPTER 9

A Victim of Human Rights ?

The United States began taking measures to demonstrate its worldwide commitment to human rights. The United States Congress's ban on military and development aid during 1973–74 to those countries that were notorious violators of human rights was a promising step. But an escape clause was introduced that made exceptions in special cases where American assistance was "justified." This rendered the policy toothless. The pre-Carter Ninety-fourth Congress put the bite back into it in 1976. Seeking to return "moral purpose and traditional values" to America's foreign policy, it not only ruled that gross violators of human rights throughout the world should be punished for their acts, but that the United States would seek to disassociate itself from repressive regimes, no matter what the price. To monitor human rights violators, Congress called upon the secretary of state to name a coordinator for human rights and humanitarian affairs who would submit to Congress an annual report on the status of human rights in all nations that were recipients of United States aid.

Somoza was begining to feel a slight chill in his close relations with the State Department in 1975, and he found himself brushing away icicles when he met with an old family foe, President Carlos Andrés Peréz of Venezuela. The reason the Somozas had hated Andrés Peréz was the fact that he had been President Romulo Betancourt's private secretary and later interior minister. Betancourt was far too democratic and reformist for the old Caribbean dictators, who labeled him a communist and tried to kill him. He had been a threat to their old dictatorial rule.

When Andrés Peréz invited the five Central American presidents and General Omar Torrijos of Panama to Venezuela to discuss and sign a loan which would help them in the oil price squeeze, Tacho had arrived in a Sabre-60 on loan from the Rockwell aircraft builders. The trip only served to confirm Andrés Peréz's low opinion of Somoza. Somoza returned to Managua and fired off a confidential memo to the United States State Department, as was his habit, detailing what he believed were dangerous weaknesses of the Venezuelan president, who saw no reason for not having close diplomatic relations with Communist Cuba. Tacho also felt Andrés Peréz was exploiting his position as the major petroleum supplier to the area and "not doing us any favors." To an aide Tacho later explained, "The son-of-a-bitch wasted my time talking about Pedro Joaquín Chamorro, his good friend whom he was in exile with in Costa Rica. He was worried about Chamorro's health. I told him he [Chamorro] was the healthiest man in Nicaragua because I needed him to give us a clean slate for freedom of the press."

Somoza at first believed that his credentials as the most pro-American leader in the hemisphere, with influential friends in the United States Congress, would enable him to weather what he perceived as a backlash in the wake of Watergate and Vietnam and a policy originally aimed at Soviet treatment of political dissidents such as Solzhenitsyn, Ginzburg and others. But toward the end of 1975 Somoza was worrying aloud to his friends about "leftists in the State Department ganging up on me." At times he wondered whether he had been singled out by anti-Nixon forces in Washington because of his closeness to the President. The arrival of Ambassador James Theberge, he noted, had signaled a real change in years of close, accommodating relations with the State Department. Theberge had told him that his instructions were to "keep his distance from me." And Theberge was mixing with the opposition, which came as a shock after Shelton who drew the line and enjoyed only the company of loyal Somoza people.

The 1976 election campaign in the United States between Gerald R. Ford and James Earl Carter became a burning issue in the Somoza household in Managua. Carter's victory was both a surprise and a shock to Tacho, who soon realized that his unswerving loyalty to the United States and all things American would be put to the test. "Procommunist Jesuit priests," he said, were out to undermine that long and firm relationship. And the clergy took the cue.

It was the clergy who brought world attention to violations of human rights in Nicaragua. They were appalled by the repression in the countryside, where the National Guard systematically went about stamping out the opposition and any suspected guerrilla sympathizers. The priests, nuns and lay people were often the only witnesses to guard brutality in far-off isolated regions.

One of the first Nicaraguans to testify before the United States Congress was Rev. Father Fernando Cardenal, a radical Trappist priest and philosophy professor at the National University who was incensed at the abuses of the Somoza regime. Father Cardenal's brother, Ernesto, a Jesuit and a poet also opposed to the dictatorship, became well known for his *Gospel in Solentiname* (named after the Solentiname archipelago in Lake Nicaragua where he organized a peasant community). Father Cardenal appeared on June 8, 1976, before the House subcommittee on foreign affairs, where he outlined a series of atrocities ranging from assassinations, torture, rape and arbitrary arrest to the complete lack of freedom and the general climate of repression. He also charged that the guard had set up concentration camps in rural areas, where peasants were held illegally. Father Cardenal explained that many of the charges were already documented by the Inter-American Commission on Human Rights of the Organization of American States, the International Federation of Human Rights and the International Catholic Jurists Federation.

Among the priest's demands were the immediate withdrawal of all United States military personnel and the suspension of all aid and military assistance; also the denial of financial credits or donations, along with pressure for the OAS Human Rights Commission's right to demand jail visits and take prisoners' testimony.[1]

Cardenal said he went to Washington representing "the peasants and poor laborers of Nicaragua, 'to be the voice of those who have no voice,' and to bring the abuses to Congress' attention." He said he was not afraid to return to Nicaragua after testifying because "I have the assurance that Somoza will not do anything to me, because, on the contrary, it would be like endorsing the document I presented in Washington. To Congressman [Donald] Fraser I then said that one thing was sure, that the government newspaper [*Novedades*] was going to immediately call me a communist. And that has occurred."[2] *Novedades* called him, among other things, a pervert, and mentally unbalanced. Nicaragua's congressional president Cornelio Hueck labeled him a traitor and demanded he be tried for treason. That Cardenal survived is credited to Donald Fraser, chairman of the House subcommittee on foreign affairs, who sent word through the State Department warning Somoza that the United States Congress would hold him personally responsible for Father Cardenal's well-being. Somoza also received a hint from his friends in Congress to limit attacks on Cardenal to name-calling.

Cardenal's visit was followed on June 13 by devastating testimony. Thirty-five American Capuchin priests in the diocese of Estelí and the apostolic vicarate of Bluefields wrote a letter to Somoza complaining of human rights violations and listing cases of torture by National Guard patrols. Their letter, made public, dramatized the oppression.

"The American Capuchins serving the local church of Nicaragua in the diocese of Estelí and in the Apostolic vicarate of Bluefields cannot under any circumstances remain passive" to the tense situation all over Nicaragua and particularly in the mountain region of Siuna and Matagalpa. The priests granted that Somoza's position was difficult: "We know that the threat of communism exists as well as that of increasing militarism." The Capuchins said they "unite their voice to that of the poor people of the mountain regions who are looking for their relatives who were found missing after the National Guard operations against subversive elements."

The letter listed cases of torture by patrols and included beating, extraction of teeth, electrical shock, rape of women, cutting faces with knives and making a person swallow a button with a string on it while the accuser violently tugged at it. The guard was also accused of dressing as guerrillas and going to the homes of farmers and burning them. They said repeated protests to the guard achieved nothing.

The priests traveled from village to village on foot and by donkey. Their journeys into the countryside and mountains sometimes took as long as two to three months before return to Bluefields on the Atlantic coast. Therefore there was sometimes a long delay before reports of murders, kidnappings and torture could be made public.

One priest said that "the repression and reprisals continued unabated in the mountains. They [the guard] are preparing the terrain for the next guerrilla movement, although there will probably be few peasants left there to have a choice in the future."

"We received numerous complaints from peasants," said Father Patrick Forton of Detroit, Michigan. "We saw several peasants with signs of torture on their arms and on their feet. They had scars from electric shocks applied to make them talk. Many have also disappeared. Many women were killed when they resisted arrest for questioning." His report said that among those killed "were infants and old people; their houses were burned to the ground and their land, livestock, pigs, chickens and crops distributed among officers of the guard."[3]

The new wave of criticism in 1976 infuriated Somoza. The attacks from the church mounted. Reports of new, stepped-up atrocities by the National Guardsmen against the peasants were released. While the guard was told on the one hand to clean up their act, in hopes of appeasing the United States Congress, one National Guard source candidly explained to me that in reality they had been ordered to "clean up the hills": "This time we want to be sure no new guerrilla focal point will rise in those hills with the aid of peasants. We intend to eliminate the contaminated peasants," he said.

Almost three weeks before the inauguration of Jimmy Carter, the bishops of Nicaragua for the first time spoke out unequivocally on human rights in Nicaragua and the state of terror in which much of the rural population was living. The message of the Nicaraguan Episcopal Conference, signed by seven bishops and delivered on New Year's Day 1977, was a challenge to the new Carter administration.

The pastoral letter, read from the pulpits of churches throughout Nicaragua and distributed in a mimeographed form because of the censorship of the Nicaraguan press, was designed to awaken the consciousness of all Nicaraguans. Specifically it called for: (1) The right to live and work and a return of civil rights. (2) Due process of law for criminal and political offenders. (3) Freedom, justice and equality. "All this cannot be achieved without freedom of expression and without religious freedom," declared the bishops.

This and other church documents drew Washington's attention to the situation in Nicaragua. In response to them, both United States Ambassador Theberge and the State Department were forced to concede that human rights were being violated in Nicaragua, although the American officials hid behind legalisms by speculating whether there was sufficient evidence of "a consistent pattern of systematic violation of human rights," the key condition for the suspension of economic aid.[4]

The pastoral letter did not mention any specific incidents but was directed against the general acts of repression committed by the National Guard. "Investigations go on against suspects using humiliating and inhuman methods, ranging from torture and rape to executions without benefit of trial, civilian or military." While the letter from the bishops of Nicaragua was considered a conservative document in the Latin American sense, it gave an idea of just how serious the situation in Nicaragua was. And it was eloquent:

> We are anguished by the suffering of our people, urban and rural, rich or poor, civil or military, who cry out to God in search of the protection of the right to live and enjoy the fruits of their labor. . . .
> Unfortunately, many of the sufferings are caused and inflicted by many of our own

Nicaraguan brothers. . . . The state of terror forces many of our peasants to flee in desperation away from their own homes and farmlands in the mountains of Zelaya, Matagalpa and Las Segovias. The arbitrary accusations and subsequent detentions because of old quarrels and personal envy still continue to disturb the peace. . . . It has been verified that many villages have been virtually abandoned: houses and personal property have been burned and the people, desperate and without help, have fled.

These actions, far from bringing justice, rather inflame passions and disturb the peace. They even put government officials beyond the jurisdiction of the institutional laws of the nation and of all sane principles of public order, and similarly, the so-called freedom movements that call themselves liberated but that actually favor libertinism, lead to personal vendettas and end up as "new lords" who take charge of governments with no regard for the right to enjoy the exercise of human liberties.

As an actual consequence of these events, the confusion and ills of the nation are growing: On the one hand the accumulation of land and wealth in the hands of a few is growing. On the other hand, the powerless peasants are deprived of their farmlands through threats and are taken advantage of because of the state of emergency. Many crimes are ignored without the corresponding legal sanctions which diminishes respect for fundamental rights. The number of prisoners who have not had due process and who do not have legal recourse is increasing.

Another area touched by the letter was interference in the religious realm: "In the mountains of Zelaya and Matagalpa the [National Guard] patrols have occupied the Catholic chapels, using them as barracks. . . . There are cases in which Delegates of the Word [laymen] have been taken prisoners by the army and have been tortured, while others have disappeared." There was also the issue of human dignity: "Let us reflect: Who is profiting from this situation of terror and extermination? . . . To violate rights and the constitutional laws of the nation is to provoke institutional disorder."

While the peasants died, so did the sons and daughters of some of Nicaragua's more prominent citizens. Claudia Chamorro was killed on January 9, 1977, and the announcement sent shock waves through Managua society. The tall, beautiful Claudia, a guerrilla, was eight months pregnant when she was stopped by the National Guard en route to a safe place to give birth to her child. Claudia was the daughter of a well-known Nicaraguan family. Another of the Sandinista martyrs was Carlos Agüero Echavarría, a nephew of Dr. Fernando Agüero Rocha, president of the opposition Conservative party and a member of the ill-fated triumvirate.

Besides the deaths of Fonseca and Contreras a year earlier, the toll on the Sandinista leadership grew, with the detention of some thirty to forty suspected guerrillas in Managua. Among those awaiting trial was Tomás Borge Martínez, whose fate received widespread attention.

Borge was held incommunicado for seven months and his attorney, Dr. Rafael Córdova Rivas, complained that the charges, ranging from homicide to assault, kidnapping and robbery were trumped up. He also alleged that Borge had been tortured all during the time he was awaiting trial. In one document detailing the abuses, Córdova Rivas alleged that "for the first fifteen days of detention [Borge] was beaten twenty-four hours a day, except for the times when he passed out, but the minute he regained consciousness the inhuman beating continued." The document also alleged that Borge went through two months on his feet with guard henchmen at his sides to keep him from changing position. Borge calculated that during another two-month period he was fed only every four days and could not remember what kind of food it was because he ate it "like an animal."

University groups rallied behind Borge's cause as well as that of the other Sandinista prisoners. One communiqué signed by seven university groups called for the authorities to: (1) End the isolation and confinement of Borge and Marcio Jaen Serrano. (2) Transfer women prisoners from the central police station to the Modelo prison. (3) Allow the prisoners to read newspapers and listen to the radio and television news, establish ample visiting rights and decree daily freedom to exercise in the sun in the Modelo prison yards. The communiqué also drew attention to a forty-three-day hunger strike the Sandinista prisoners were staging. It complained that the National Guard was taking up combat positions around the university to intimidate students, and this violated the school's autonomy. The protest went on to denounce the dismissal and deportation, in some cases, of various professors.

Imprisoned Sandinista inmates themselves released a communiqué from the Modelo prison complaining they were jailed without due process of law, waiting months before being taken before a judge; that they suffered beatings after capture; were left nude in dark cells, only seeing daylight months later when taken to court; and were victims of psychological and physical torture and lack of legal representation when finally brought to trial. They protested the solitary confinement of Tomás Borge as well as an alleged massacre and disappearance of peasants throughout the country—a list of names was added at the end of the document. Although demands for better treatment had been delivered to the warden, the Sandinistas claimed that the lack of a response was to be expected from the dictatorship.

Other citizens filed petitions directly with the Supreme Court asking for investigations into human rights violations. A petition filed on January 16, 1977, asked the court to explain the numerous disappearances during 1976 of peasants in Zelaya, Matagalpa and Estelí. (Names were taken from lists supplied by the Capuchin priests.) The petition asked the government to explain how the National Guard operated in the various departments and why martial law was still in force, with the consequent suspension of constitutional rights and habeas corpus. Two-thirds of the six-page document carried names, hometowns and, when possible, the age and number of children of the missing persons. Allegations at the end of the document charged that in Waslala the guard had forced men to build an airport. In Cubali, the document said, the Guard entered the town, took over the church and used religious books for toilet paper. In Zapote the villagers were forced to leave their small farming plots and move nearer to the chapel where they felt safer. The town of Bilwas, it charged, was bombed by planes.

On Friday, February 25, 1977, a military court in Campo de Marte convicted 110 Nicaraguans of crimes ranging from plotting against the Somoza dictatorship to killing four sheriffs, kidnapping and robbing banks. Tomás Borge was among the defendants.

Attempts by attorneys to keep the trials from being "kangaroo courts" went unheeded. Among the motions denied was that, under a 1911 law, the military did not have the right to try civilians. Private contact between defense attorney and client was restricted, as well as defense access to witness lists. Limited press coverage was permitted and show trials began in small, cramped quarters called "the justice chamber."

"What a laugh, we have not had justice in this country for four decades," a tall, distinguished-looking Nicaraguan lawyer said with bitterness in his voice.

The 111 Nicaraguan defendants—one person, living in Switzerland, was found not guilty because of a lack of evidence—were tried in different groups until the trials ended in September. More than half of the defendants were tried in absentia. Among the thirty-six accused who were present in the National Guard courtroom —and the last one to receive his sentence—was Tomás Borge. He had denied murder charges but not crimes committed as a guerrilla during his life's devotion to fighting Somoza. He was sentenced to a total of 129 years and eight months in prison and fined approximately $4,200.

The day after the trial ended the newspapers, under strict censorship, published the military communiqué covering the sentences of the guilty 110. For most Nicaraguans whose sons and daughters were not guerrillas or university students, the sentencing of the 110 was of little interest. A sample of opinion at the time showed that many of the Nicaraguan middle class believed that those under arrest "are probably communists . . . and we don't like communism or the idea of living under a communist regime." There was a feeling that, having lived with the status quo for forty-two years, "Why rock the boat? It can only bring repression."

Many Nicaraguans knew about the guerrilla war that had been going on in the hills eighty and a hundred miles north of Managua, and they had also heard about the atrocities committed by the guard, but they preferred to ignore it.

While it is one of the largest of the Central American republics, and the most sparsely populated, Nicaragua in the mid-1970s was a study in contrasts. It is a country of natural beauty, with fertile valleys spread alongside lakes below smoking volcanoes. Excellent coffee country in cool high altitudes contrasts with the hot lowlands. The land was not farmed anywhere near its potential. Sixty percent of the nation's 2.2 million population lived in the countryside but, in spite of a much-heralded Somoza agrarian reform, 0.6 percent of the farmers owned 30.5 percent of the arable land while 50.8 percent of the farmers had just 3.4 percent. Seventy-seven percent of the rural population earned less than $120 annually, although the nation's per capita income was $600.

Because the Sandinista forces were keeping to the mountains with only sporadic forays into the cities in 1977, the National Guard continued an attempt to ferret them out of the countryside, punishing the peasants in their wake though some of them might not have seen a guerrilla in a year or more. Although some peasants did sell food to the guerrillas during this time, they sold food to any stranger who entered their isolated and remote areas.

Many felt that only Washington's much heralded human rights policy could end the wave of terror and scare Somoza into compliance. While the United States embassy claimed that the violation of human rights was diminishing and that the National Guard had been told to be more humane, the peasants felt no change.

When the bishops' New Year's message was only three weeks old "a fifteen-man patrol of the crack 'General Somoza' battalion surrounded Varilla, a cluster of homes in Nicaragua's Zelaya province. With the troops were several *jueces de mesta*. The official charge that brought them there: five of Varilla's peasant families had aided anti-government guerrillas. The soldiers shot, bayoneted or strangled four men, eleven women and twenty-nine children. After dumping the bodies in an unmarked pit, the sheriffs divided the villagers' land among themselves."[5]

The fourty-four deaths at Varilla had come about because two camps of guerrillas were reported in the area. The evidence was a piece of tenting found by the guard and said to belong to the guerrillas' camp.

For days after the incident, the region of sparsely populated wilderness was closed off. American Capuchin priests and refugees from the area brought the story out. The graphic description of the massacre came from a conscience-stricken rural sheriff, a participant who later confessed.

Two months later the church released documents giving the names of hundreds of peasants killed or captured by the guard over a two-year period in Matagalpa and Zelaya, claiming two mass executions of eighty-six civilians, of whom approximately twenty-nine were children, had taken place since the pastoral letter had been released. Even as the bishops had been laboring over the choice of words for their New Year's pastoral message, National Guardsmen were slaughtering forty-two peasants—men, women and children—in a little place in the hills called Kaskita. Light planes were reported to have bombed some areas. It was impossible to compile a list of victims' names because of delays in travel and the time lapse between hearing of the atrocities and being able to document them. Torture for those captured was considered the norm. Mass graves were not uncommon, though at times they were difficult to locate because of guard-imposed travel restrictions in some areas.

The *Time* article mentioning the Varilla massacre brought more than the denial published in the same story that "spokesmen for Somoza insist that the bishops' charges are grossly exaggerated. Many *campesinos* [peasants], they explain, have not been killed, but simply fled their homes to avoid the fighting."[6]

Somoza was furious. He ordered his press chief, General Roger Bermúdez, to send off a denial to *Time*. Then he ordered his United States public relations representative and Guillermo Lang, his United Nations representative and New York consul, to deny the *Time* story.

Ian R. MacKenzie, director of the Washington-based Nicaragua Government Information Service, immediately fired off complaints to the National News Council and *Time* for "unfairness and inaccuracy." MacKenzie, an Argentine citizen, took exception to a quote stating, "The massacre at Varilla, two months ago, was not unique, according to a pastoral letter by Nicaragua's Roman Catholic bishops," and to other passages. He complained during congressional hearings on aid packages to Nicaragua that the article would have "an effect on the lives and well-being of 2.3 million people." The National News Council was asked to substantiate the allegations against *Time*. The Accuracy in Media, Inc., publication, *AIM Report*, subsequently criticized the council's mostly favorable report on *Time*. AIM, a conservative, Washington-based group, was continuously to defend Somoza against what it claimed were biased attacks by the media.

According to AIM, "MacKenzie has expressed shock at th⌐ degree to which the National News Council bent over backwards to justify this story by *Time*. . . . We believe that the Council was guilty of sloppy research in this case, and its standard of accuracy implied in its findings leaves much to be desired."[7]

The *Time* article was also attacked in Somoza's *Novedades* on March 13, 1977. It cited the Liberal Somocista Association as saying that it was "conscious of the moment we are living, in that a group of professional agitators reveal false news articles and tendencies before international public opinion in a deliberate campaign to cause a loss of prestige concerning the armed forces of the Republic and the Government of Nicaragua, such as that done by *Time Magazine* correspondent Bernard Diederich. We consider it essential that all Liberals close ranks and that we present a single front to defend our democratic institutions. . . ." *Novedades* then went on to attack Castro and how he had duped the United States. The article cited the lack of bread, soap, rice, electricity and independence in Cuba and the nationalization of United States companies. The Nicaraguan army was hailed as "glorious" and praised for the spilling of "young and generous blood of the fallen on the fields of battle fighting the communists who were trained in Cuba."

Though worried about how far the Carter administration would go in its human rights campaign to limit assistance to Nicaragua, Somoza had friends in the United States Congress he could count on. In fact, he appeared to have more congressional muscle than the president of the United States. Somoza's cronies came to the fore during the debate on his $3.1 million in military assistance. The aid package had been defeated initially in the House appropriations committee, with Representative Edward Koch, the New York Democrat, heading the Somoza opposition. Another New York Democrat came to the rescue however. Representative John Murphy's friendship with Somoza had begun when they were classmates at La Salle Military Academy in Oakdale, Long Island. Murphy had kept in close touch with Tacho over the years and, according to Tacho's press secretary, General Bermúdez, "Murphy has been to Nicaragua at least 100 times and stays at Somoza's house. So what's wrong with friends helping him?" Bermúdez asked.[8] Prominent on Tacho's desk was a file of names of West Point's Class of 1946, used, Bermúdez said, "so that the president can keep track." Somoza often invited his entire West Point class to an anniversary bash, sending out airline tickets and footing the bill for the party, usually held in the United States.

Somoza did not really need the aid for his army, called one of the best in Latin America but never really tested. Nevertheless he launched a costly campaign to overturn the Koch vote. Murphy led Somoza's fight in Washington and at the same time Somoza hired ex-Florida congressman William Cramer, a Republican and at the time the legal counsel of the Republican party. Cramer received $50,000 from the Nicaraguan government as a six-month retainer—his law firm had previously received $57,000. On June 10 Cramer registered as a foreign agent (entitled to lobby for a foreign government). Before that, on June 3, the American Nicaraguan Council had registered as a lobby with the House of Representatives, citing Cramer as its legal counsel. This led the Justice Department to launch an investigation into Cramer's dual registration. In Cramer's registration statement he indicated that, among other things, his services to the Nicaraguan government would relate to earthquake reconstruction, and that he would be lobbying for "economic and military assistance." One Justice Department official commented: "It is peculiar they would need military assistance to help in earthquake reconstruction."[9]

Ambassador Theberge had already assured some United States congressmen that human rights violations were not part of Nicaragua's domestic policies. Murphy, leading a floor debate on the matter, went even further. In what Koch described as "a vitriolic attack upon the opponents of the Somoza regime," Murphy testified in Congress that priests, missionaries and American academics had lied about the political arrests, torture and suppression of political expression in Nicaragua. He managed to save the military assistance program for Nicaragua by a vote of 225–180 that went against the wishes of the appropriations committee and the White House.

Playing an important role was another Somoza crony, Texas Democratic Congressman Charles Wilson, a member of Koch's subcommittee, who drafted what was known as the Wilson amendment to restore the aid in the House. Assisting him free of charge was Fred Korth, a close friend from the Texas law firm Korth and Korth and onetime secretary of the navy under the Kennedy administration. Korth had been registered as a lobbyist with the Justice Department but not with Congress.[10] Senator Edward Kennedy had to watch in dismay as his attempt to lead a Senate fight over the money was shot down in flames by the powerful Nicaraguan lobby.

Novedades hailed the aid approval as a great victory for Somoza's diplomacy. However, an American State Department spokesman said later that despite the House approval "no specific agreement will be signed . . . unless the situation of human rights in Nicaragua improves." Aides to Somoza called the statement, which was distributed locally by the United States embassy in Managua, "an affront to the traditional friendship between the two countries."[11]

It was a typical Murphy act to help out an old friend. According to New York lawyer Francis J. Purcell, "Mr. Murphy has long been one of the Somoza family's most vigorous defenders in Congress and, in the last two years, in particular, he has fought for continued American military and economic assistance to the country. Such aid has come under attack on the grounds that it reinforces an arbitrary and corrupt regime that has persistently violated human rights. . . . He has also acted in other fields on behalf of the Nicaraguan head of state."[12]

The congressman became implicated by reports surfacing in 1977 linking him to an oil refinery proposal for Nicaragua during the 1973–74 Arab oil embargo. Controversy arose after documents were released showing Murphy had attempted to arrange financing and crude oil shipments from Iran to a proposed refinery on Nicaragua's Atlantic coast on a site named Monkey Point. While the refinery was never built, the local partner in Nicaragua was to be a company 98 percent owned by Somoza. Among Murphy's attempts to win the 250,000-barrel-a-day refinery for Somoza was the arrangement of a meeting between Somoza and the late shah of Iran (which failed to materialize) and agreements between American oil companies and the shah's Pahlevi Foundation to commit $40 million backing. The Iranians backed out of the deal because of more lucrative offers and the American oil companies eventually lost interest. Representative Murphy was finally indicted June 18, 1980, on conspiracy and bribery charges resulting from the FBI's ABSCAM investigation.

Some guard officers were beginning to feel that Somoza was running the nation too much like the chairman of a family corporation. They also wanted him to shift his dependence for military aid away from the United States, which was now dependent on the human rights policy of the former "peanut farmer"—they used the title disparagingly. They wanted Tacho to open up new avenues for arms purchases, but Somoza held on, not believing that the United States policy or his congressional clout would desert him.

Tacho was upset by the loss of projected profits from the abortive Howard Hughes deal, from which he said he had reaped only unwanted publicity, and the abortive oil refinery deal at Monkey Point. But at home the family fortune was spread ever more diversely. By 1977 Somozas were in everything from sugar and coffee to rice and cement, alcohol and Lanica Airlines and the Mamenic steamship line. Tacho owned the Caribe Motors Company, representatives of Mercedes Benz. The police and traffic cops used Mercedes, as did most Somoza politicians and the National Guard brass. Even the city's garbage disposal trucks were Mercedes Benz. Somoza coffee interests included plantations in the departments of Managua, Jinotega, Matagalpa, Nueva Segovia, Madriz, Estelí, Carazo and Masaya. The amount of choice real estate they owned was vast. They were the proprietors of the Carnica slaughterhouse, and the national cement company, Canal, was founded in 1945 as the family cement monopoly for Nicaragua. All paving blocks were made by a Somoza company. The Somoza farms raised pigs and cattle which went to the export market. On at least one occasion the United States rejected Somoza beef because it did not meet import health restrictions but Tacho, ever the businessman, reportedly took it back and put it on sale in his own country. The family held controlling stock in the local cigarette and cigar business, the latter established with the assistance of Cuban exiles. Hope's family owned the construction firm Panelfab, established in 1973 to take advantage of the postearthquake building boom. Hope was also president of the Junta Nacional de Asistencia y Previsión Social (JNAPS) and IMSS, the national social security institute.

Despite the mounting criticism, Tacho felt sure he could weather the storm. He even had time to advise others. The military regimes of Guatemala and El Salvador, which had owed their very existence in part to past United States military aid, learned in 1977 that future aid would be conditional on their human rights performance. They haughtily declared this to constitute interference in their internal affairs and rejected further United States aid despite advice from Somoza that they make no such hasty decision. The Carter administration, he reasoned, would find it difficult to sever a special relationship with Nicaragua that had lasted more than sixty years. He insisted that Nicaragua was the United States' most dependable Central American ally, and bragged that during the Nixon years he had acted as proconsul in the area, serving United States interests as much as his own. No country had received—on a per capita basis—as much United States development and military aid as had Nicaragua over so long a period. The American-trained National Guard was the bulwark against communism in the region, Somoza claimed. In the first six years of the 1970s his praetorian guard had received more than $32 million in United States military assistance.

The cutting of the umbilical cord that had tied the United States to Somoza for so long was not swift. Rather, it was a long and painful process that was to continue up to the bitter end.

During the summer of 1977 Tacho's American friends, especially Congressman John Murphy, were concerned about his eroding image in the United States. At home Tacho surrounded himself with doting admirers. The friends he relaxed with had to be the kind of people who would laugh at his jokes and never forget who was *el jefe*. Almost without exception they were court jesters who squabbled among themselves to be the first to concur with or to applaud his ideas or utterances.

A rare exception in this clutch of sycophants was Raymond Molina, who seldom was kept waiting for anything. Molina was no crony. Somoza didn't like him but he respected him. He was one of the few voices Somoza heeded.

Molina was among the few men Somoza never had to fear. Tall and lanky, Ray Molina was a Georgia-born Cuban who had fought in the Bay of Pigs and, returning to Nicaragua, battered his way into Somoza's confidence through sheer brass. A vice-president of Peterson Enterprises, he had once gotten a $2.5 million contract from the Somoza government.[13] He was cordially hated by the Bunker society. (Molina was just one of many Cuban exiles in business with Tacho. There was also Manuel Artime. He had given up his war with Castro and was Tacho's agent in Miami running his meat export business to the United States as well as being a practicing physician and psychiatrist.) Somoza took Molina seriously. It was on his advice that he hired former Florida congressman William Cramer to lobby the Somoza cause in the halls of Congress.

Somoza's influential American friends suggested a public relations campaign to counter what they considered the Carter administration's efforts to turn Nicaragua into a human rights cause. To help groom Somoza's image with the American media they also called in the New York public relations firm Norman, Lawrence, Patterson and Farrell.

Norman Wolfson, the firm's chairman, made his first visit to Managua in July 1977 to review Tacho's problems with the media at the request of Jack Calkins, former White House aide to President Gerald Ford, and Bill Cramer, Somoza's lobbyist, who went along on the trip.

"Somoza cut me off before I was finished," Wolfson recalled. "He told me I had walked into his office 'with shit on my feet,' that I had 'a hell of a nerve' trying to tell him how to handle his relations with the press. 'Who are you to tell me I have to kiss Sulzberger's ass?' (I didn't tell him that. I explained that he had to explain his side of the story to the Sulzbergers of this world if he ever expected to be understood.) 'You Americans sure give me a pain in the ass,' were the last words I heard as I left. The man acted like a spoiled brat who had evolved into middle age, a know-it-all who asked for advice and couldn't take it, a boor, a rude, overbearing bully. I left impressed with his height, all six-feet-plus of him, the more than 250 pounds of heft, and the booming voice that pounded me as I sat in his presence. Yet, as I crossed the street to return to the Intercontinental Hotel, headquarters for most foreign visitors to dirty, paper-strewn Managua, I wished there had been a different outcome. He did fascinate me."

Somoza had reason to be displeased with the flamboyant Wolfson. Tacho, like his father before him, believed the regime's finest public relations representative was Tacho Somoza.

During brother Luis's reign in the late 1950s, a reporter wrote, "Somoza confronted some of those North American liberals in their own lair by visiting *The New York Times*, which had attacked the Somozas editorially. He wanted to make perfectly clear that neither Luis nor himself was a carbon copy of their father. 'I showed them that I had a different attitude, philosophy, education and decade than my father. They were surprised that I was so articulate,' Somoza recalled."[14]

But Tacho had a strange manner of keeping abreast of changing trends even in public relations. He was an addict of fad books about health, wealth and sex. For years he used to swear by Gayelord Hauser's *Treasury of Secrets* which rewarded the reader with tips on how to "protect yourself against poor skin . . . falling hair . . . sexual apathy . . . failing potency . . . and depression."

"I had mixed emotions a few weeks later when the telephone rang at home and I was told, '*El Jefe* wants to see you, there's plenty of work to be done so get to Managua fast—say tomorrow,' "[15] Wolfson reported. He began a series of vain attempts to line up reporters and top media management persons to meet personally with Somoza, hear and print his side of the story. Maybe, just maybe, Tacho's personality would win them over. Though Wolfson later wrote about Tacho's meetings with the press and was just as biased in his reports as he alleged the press was concerning Somoza, his efforts to sell Tacho the man and the Somoza personality were most interesting. When Wolfson began trying to sell Somoza in Washington, D.C., he ran into immediate difficulty.

"Desperate to get some facts about Somoza in the Oval Office, I phoned long-time friend Theodore C. Sorensen [former aide to John F. Kennedy]. After I told Ted why I wanted to see him, he refused the luncheon invitation. I baited him about being open minded and said that he should hear Somoza's side of the story from me. Finally, and only after stressing that he was joining me as a friend, he agreed to the lunch.

"As a rule, any time spent with Sorensen—who has to be one of the brightest, most attractive men I know—is a pleasure for me. This lunch wasn't enjoyable; Ted was skeptical about everything I said. He advised me to drop Somoza. He claimed that Somoza was ruining my reputation. And, obviously, he flatly refused to have anything to do with Nicaragua at any price. At one point I said, 'Look, I don't believe half of what is printed about Somoza.' Sorensen snapped back, 'If 10 percent of what is said about him is true, I want no part of the man.'

"Somoza still wanted to get his side of the story into the White House, so he called on an old retainer, Clark Clifford. Unlike Sorensen, Clifford had been a Somoza lawyer for many years and earned plenty for his service. The Somoza-Clifford meeting took place at the Waldorf Towers in New York. Now, however, Clifford viewed Somoza as a hot potato and he, not too gracefully as I saw it, bowed out. He explained in about ten thousand words that 'regretfully' he would 'not really be able to make a contribution at this time.' Somoza has to be a bit naive. He accepted the excuse and said to me, 'What an impressive man!'

"Sorensen is to be respected for sticking by his convictions when he was in a position to earn a boxcar full of money for his counsel.

"Clifford, since he had accepted money from Somoza before, cannot be accorded the same regard as Sorensen. Put simply, I thought Old Silver Tongue proved himself to be a two-faced son-of-a-bitch."[16]

Wolfson saw Tacho's business side while on a shopping expedition in New York.

"One day in New York Somoza invited me to join him while he shopped for a special massage machine. We went into a store on Fifty-eighth Street, near the Plaza Hotel. The retail price of the machine was $3,000. Somoza haggled with the store owner. Finally, there was a handshake and Somoza nodded to me that it was time to go. He told me on the way out, victory spilling all over his face, that he had gotten the machine for $1,500. I laughed. He laughed too, but for a different reason. Then he snapped, 'What are you laughing about? Think of the promotional value —he can say the president of Nicaragua bought one of those. Shit, that's worth a lot more than $1,500 to the guy. I maybe should have charged him.' "[17]

Tacho and Hope continued to have their problems. By the summer of 1977 no one knew why the two were still together.

"One night in New York, Somoza and his wife were joining friends for dinner at '21.' She looked stunning. But his day had been a tedious one and his beard, never light, looked especially heavy when he stood next to Hope. 'Tacho, you should shave before we go,' she admonished him. 'Fuck you,' he said, gently turned her around, and steered her out the door for the dinner party.

"His religion, Catholicism, is important to him, at least in a modern way. The day after the incident with Hope, I remarked that she certainly was beautiful. Pleased, he agreed, but added that she could be a 'royal pain in the ass. Just too damned bossy, picks at me about everything.' It being general knowledge that this was no longer a working marriage, I asked why he didn't divorce her. 'Because of my religion and because of my position,' were the answers. I asked the next question, 'Which is the most important, religion or politics?' His answer—'religion'—was emphatic."[18]

So detached was Tacho from Hope that in 1977, when she returned from London to Managua, she met Tacho at a party and he simply said with genuine surprise, "Oh, you are back."

CHAPTER 10

The Heart Attack

At the end of the 1960s, Tacho, tired of clandestine rendezvous with Dinorah, built her a mansion that soon outstripped El Retiro in size and splendor. The dream house was built on land that had belonged to Luis Manuel Debayle, on a lush green hillside overlooking the southern highway leading to Diriamba at kilometer ten. Despite the deceptive gray exterior the mansion was gay within. There was a large swimming pool and every modern convenience and gadget that wealth and privilege—including the right to import goods without paying import duties—could afford. A high wall surrounding the well-guarded villa was watched over by closed-circuit television, something Tacho himself didn't have at El Retiro or even at the Bunker.

Dinorah lacked education but she had cunning and a keen sense of commercial enterprise that rivaled that of the Somozas. For years she flew on Somoza's airline to Miami, always returning with contraband with which she breezed through customs before being welcomed by her ever-vigilant bodyguards and a chauffeur-driven Mercedes Benz. As Dinorah's influence over Tacho grew, so did her power. Hope received her state income and had agents who collected regular revenues from a variety of state sources for her. Dinorah soon rivaled Hope with her own agents providing her revenue from state rackets. She dispensed favors like the godfather of a gang who expected the favor to be reimbursed and anyone seeking a favor from Tacho found it more expedient to seek out Dinorah first.

When wife and mistress attended the same party in the early 1970s, the crowd around Hope gradually thinned and gravitated to the circle around Dinorah. Invitations to a private party at Dinorah's villa were sought after by politicos and favor-seekers. Whenever a foreign musical group, such as Mexican mariachi bands, visited Nicaragua they would give a command performance at Dinorah's home. There she would often sit in the center of the patio, her beautiful white teeth flashing pleasure at being serenaded. The invited guests applauded the performance of both musicians and courtesan.

In the end it was Hope who surrendered Tacho. But first she went to see Dinorah to have it out woman to woman. However, there was no confrontation. Instead of a fight, Hope was so overcome by emotion that as she arrived at Dinorah's home she fainted.

Hope gradually separated from Tacho. She made rare trips home from London, where she had set up housekeeping, for board meetings of the Social Security Institute and other groups she headed. There were also occasional meetings in Managua for her favorite charity, the building of a children's hospital for which she appeared as sponsor on 1.50-córdoba stamps. There were rumors that Hope had received a sizable cash settlement from Tacho and freedom to do as she pleased. She acquired considerable real estate in Miami and investments with an eye to the future. The smartly dressed Hope was well known in the best Miami shoe stores. An attendant in one recalled, "She always wanted no-color shoes. I don't know how many times I said, 'Sorry, Mrs. Somoza, we have no no-color shoes.' " A close friend admitted, "She couldn't reform a man with an ego the size of Tacho's."

Somoza continued to travel the fourteen miles from *El Retiro* to Dinorah's villa incognito in his curtained recreational mobile home. There he satisfied the passionate side of his character. Yet the scenes at his mistress's love nest were not always idyllic. He was insanely jealous. On several occasions he changed her bodyguards, sensing she had grown too fond of the men. Sometimes he even had her followed in Miami.

In the summer of 1977 it was Tacho's personal life, more than the growing problem with the Carter administration's human rights policy, that was weighing heavily on his 267-pound frame. He was worried about his eldest son, Julio, who had dropped out of West Point, mainly because of an uncontrollable aggressiveness that occasionally gripped him. Julio began taking up hippie ways in Miami and reports reached his father that he was going around barefoot and sporting long hair. The huge youth was also involved in the drug culture. He was finally taken off the streets and committed to Topeka's Menninger Clinic, to treat his psychotic outbreaks of uncontrollable aggression.

On July 26, 1977, Tacho was stricken by a heart attack at Dinorah's villa. His condition was kept secret. For twenty-four hours he lay in the villa while medical help was being arranged. He was moved in a caravan of military and hospital vehicles to the old military hospital, a modest institution on the back side of the rim of the Tiscapa volcano that provided safety and privacy but little in the way of modern medical facilities. A pair of heart specialists were flown in from the United States and, upon their advice, he was flown from the hospital to the Miami Heart Institute aboard a United States Air Force medical jet. One of the heart specialists was Dr. William C. Phillips, chief of medical staff at the institute and a veteran cardiologist who had flown to Managua ten years earlier at the request of Lyndon Johnson to treat Tacho's brother Luis, who did not survive. An institute spokesman said of the moving of Tacho to Miami, "It was a hell of a decision."[1]

Accompanying Phillips were heart surgeon Dr. Ernest A. Traad, two Miami nurses, Hope, and Tachito. Tight security followed the flight to Miami, and when they arrived, the hospital had little news to release about the patient. "This is the first time we've ever had the president of a country as a patient," spokeswoman Kathleen Rank said.[2]

Somoza's chest pains were diagnosed as angina, a primary symptom of irreversible coronary artery disease that signals the heart is receiving too little blood. Nitro-glycerin and other drugs were administered to prevent additional angina or heart rhythm disturbances and to decrease the heart's oxygen requirements or increase the blood flow or both.[3]

A catheterization, an invasive X-ray exam of the heart chambers, showed that Somoza's main anterior descending artery, one of the heart's two major arteries, was closed off by arteriosclerosis, causing the heart attack.[4] The fifty-two-year-old ruler was faced with two choices: a drug regimen with careful eating or an open-heart operation to construct a bypass. Doctors were wary that if they had to resort to surgery Somoza might die on the operating table. Phillips and a team of cardiologists finally decided to treat Somoza conservatively—with drugs, diet and, eventually, exercise.[5]

Despite the tense political atmosphere in Nicaragua at the time, a national joke began circulating concerning Somoza's possibility of undergoing an operation. Its humor was in the Somozas' ownership of the cement and paving block factory which supplied the materials to build two bypasses around Nicaragua after the earthquake. *Miami Herald* editor Don Shoemaker wrote, "It seems that Somoza . . . was lying on the operating table when surgeons recommended a heart bypass. 'Bypass!' the dictator cried, wide awake, 'then they must use my bricks.' "[6]

In the hospital Tacho had time to reflect on the fact that his "American connection" now appeared about as strong as his heart. He was both "shocked and bitter" at the slow United States response in the emergency when it was decided he should go to Miami after his heart attack. "We called Washington for an air force plane and their response was, 'It'll cost thirty-thousand,' and goddammit we paid it and the plane took longer than a kite to reach Miami," he told an aide. There had been no such delay when his father was shot or Luis had his heart attack, he noted.

Somoza's stay at the hospital was marked by extraordinary security precautions. He and his entourage took up the third floor of the Storer Pavilion wing of the institute, a total of ten rooms, one paid for by the United States government to house Secret Service agents who patrolled the floor and were stationed on the roof. Some fourteen of the institute's 258 beds were occupied by Somoza, family and bodyguards.

Nicaraguan consul general Luis Debayle handled Somoza's public relations work from the hospital. He would not initially admit Tacho had had a heart attack, classifying it only as "a kind of coronary insufficiency of some kind."

Debayle announced upon Somoza's arrival at the hospital that he would not be allowed visitors, not even Hope or his children. At visiting time Tachito, who was running back and forth between Miami and Managua, stuck close to his father. He used all the force he could muster to have his mother barred from visiting Tacho. However, one guest who was always welcome was Dinorah, and Tachito never shut the door on her. Another exception was his friend Congressman John Murphy. The break with Hope was to become final in Miami.

The doctors told Tacho that his complicated living arrangement had contributed to his heart attack. When the doctor told him, "You have to straighten out your private life," he followed the orders perfectly. He turned completely to Dinorah.

Tacho's health remained delicate but his condition was apparently stable as long as no other attack occurred.

In Managua news concerning Somoza's health could not be published. Most Nicaraguans lived on *bolas* (rumors) in the absence of any real news in the heavily censored press. Many believed Tacho was already dead. General Roger Bermúdez, Somoza's pressman, continued to announce that his boss was well on the road to recovery and needed only a couple more weeks of rest in Florida. *Novedades* began publishing pictures on a nearly daily basis of Tacho smiling from his sickbed. More than one news service, however, began preparing the strongman's obituary and analysts were quick to begin speculating what would happen in the event of Tacho's demise.

Suddenly in Nicaragua there was a power vacuum to fill. Those who didn't already think Tacho was dead waited for him to die. A struggle surfaced between the Liberal party and the National Guard—politicians and army officers began battling over who would succeed him.

Despite the uncertainty of the time, the opposition groups, be they the Sandinistas or the traditional opponents, were powerless to seize the opportunity to tilt the balance of power one way or another. Opposition to the Somoza regime was widespread but in a state of confusion. The Conservative party was split into several factions, including followers of Agüero Rocha; the so-called "auténticos" opposed to Agüero; the "Zancudos" who collaborated with Somoza and were awarded with legislative seats; and lastly, but not forgotten, the Nicaraguan Tories who had stuck with Pedro Joaquín Chamorro when he organized the *Union Democrática de Liberación* (UDEL) in 1974. UDEL, organized mainly to boycott the 1974 elections, was unified only on paper. In addition to Conservative members, it included the Partido Social Cristiano, the Partido Socialista (Moscow-line communists) and two major labor organizations. It was difficult to imagine UDEL working cohesively except as an electoral boycott vehicle. The Sandinistas were primarily on the defensive against the guard. The "Group of Six" played on middle-class fears of communism in an effort to muster loyalty to the regime. But there was no guarantee that the cronies wouldn't break up into feuding Somocista factions if Tacho disappeared.

In the event of the president's incapacitation, the Nicaraguan constitution provided that the minister of the interior would take over administration. Congress, a bicameral institution in Nicaragua, was then to choose one from among its hundred members to finish the president's term—in this case, until 1981—or until his incapacity ended. But the government refused to recognize Tacho's incapacity.

Instead, an ad hoc shadow government of family and cronies arose. Known variously as "the Committee" or "the Group of Six," the group consisted of General Herberto Sanchez, the defense minister and ex-director of Lanica Airlines; Tacho's son Tachito; General Sam Genie, chief of the security service; National Guard Director José Somoza; Pablo Renner, the corpulent president of the Senate; and

Luis Debayle, the vice-president of the Chamber of Deputies. Another person who was near and sometimes a part of the elite group was Cornelio Hueck, speaker of the Chamber of Deputies, the lower house, but his star, once high, was falling.

While the jockeying for position went on, Tachito suddenly moved into the breach as messenger boy between the Miami medical institute and Managua, delivering his father's orders. Somoza still made his presence felt. Even so, many thought they were witnessing the end of an era and believed that even if Somoza survived, he would have to dilute his regime and divest himself of some of his awesome political and economic power. There was a lot of expectation, much speculation and considerable uncertainty. No one thought things would remain the same as before.

Knowledgeable observers agreed that if anything happened to Somoza, long-time crony Pablo Renner would be named to finish out Tacho's term even though the constitution would then disqualify him from running for a full term in 1980. Also disqualified would be any Somoza next of kin. The door would be open for Tachito in 1986, but the likelihood of Tachito ever making it as president was slim. His succession would immediately invite a power struggle that would be counterproductive for all. Even though the politicos and the armed forces were fighting among themselves for power, all agreed that Tachito was not the one to take over if Somoza died.

As Somoza had his own father, Tachito idolized his dad and remained completely loyal to him, as demonstrated in the hospital when he sided with Dinorah against his own mother. Born on December 18, 1951, the tall, stocky Tachito was already fighting a receding hairline. Like his father he barked and screamed orders at his men, belittling them at times, as when he cut his first teeth as an officer immediately following the earthquake. But despite Somoza's wish for Tachito to take over the reins of government in the future, nobody thought he had enough ability. His prime interest appeared to be girls and he was viewed as neither brainy nor of strong character. One observer told me, "There is no viable heir. Tachito is an inept nincompoop. Sickness and U.S. opposition may oblige Somoza at last to leave office." Other Nicaraguans called Tachito "the little boy" or "the Dauphin" and *La Prensa* nicknamed him "the apprentice dictator." No one doubted that he was being groomed to follow his father, grandfather and uncle.

Major Somoza said it was natural for others to think he was being groomed to succeed his father. "I can honestly tell you that I was born into a family that has political prestige, political pull and power," he said, "but I've also seen the ravages that it does to a family as human beings. I'd have to think about it twice."[7] Despite the denials, his errand-boy missions for his father brought Tachito out of the woodwork and gave him more confidence, power and ambition. As a member of the "Group of Six" he was increasingly active in the political and economic dealings of the family empire.

Like his mother, he was born in Tampa, Florida. His military training took him from Harvard Business School to the Royal Military Academy at Sandhurst in England, to training courses with the United States Army in the United States before receiving his first assignment after the earthquake. At the age of twenty-one he opted for Nicaraguan citizenship. He would have forfeited his American citizenship anyway by joining a foreign army—the National Guard. He then began to rise rapidly, was promoted to major in May 1976, and became director of the Basic Infantry Training School, EEBI, in June 1977.

At the time of the heart attack, "They had this big rumor in Managua that my father didn't quit because I didn't let him quit," Tachito said. "But that's ridiculous, because you don't tell dad anything once he's made up his mind. Some people may have got the wrong ideas because I was called upon to explain to the ministers the exact state of dad's health."[8]

Tachito did not sit on his haunches as a guard commanding officer. Opponents charged him with leading attacks on student and women demonstrators. Other allegations were of huge commissions made from business deals with the government for his own businesses in fishing, tobacco, timber and heavy-vehicle distribution. He denied them all. "I'm purported to be lots of things," he said, "among which I'm a sort of economic monster gobbling up every contract that the government can let loose, which is false." He said that he had won some contracts, but only after open bidding.[9]

While Somoza was recuperating, Amnesty International released a report on August 15, 1977, covering the martial law period between the end of 1974 and January 1977, blasting the extensive "political imprisonment, denial of due process of law, use of torture and summary executions" of peasants by the National Guard. Other charges included the imprisonment without trial of a dozen political prisoners and the disappearance of three hundred peasants in 1975 as well as relocation of many peasant families and the theft of food and animals from the campesinos' small farms. The Amnesty International representatives sent to Managua in May 1976, had been denied access to Somoza and military officials as well as denied interviews with the alleged political prisoners.

When the report was released, many in the church and the United States announced that the human rights issue had been heeded by Somoza—conditions had improved greatly since the beginning of 1977 and the killings of campesinos had been brought to a halt. "All last year and until February this year, we were getting regular reports of mass executions or disappearances of peasants," one well-placed source told The New York Times. "Since March, we haven't received any reliable report of a massacre. The National Guard has definitely been told to clean up its act."[10]

According to both the church and diplomats, the repression under martial law had begun to ease, and as part of the reason for the more peaceful atmosphere they pointed to the relative inactivity of the Sandinistas and the relaxing of a government campaign to wipe out the insurgents. "I'd estimate there are probably only about twenty or so guerrillas left in the hills and they have only been sporadically active in urban areas," one person said.[11]

The demise of the FSLN was also reported by a United States Foreign Service publication, "Foreign Economic Trends and the Implication for the United States," which in March of 1977 claimed, "Nicaragua should continue to enjoy political stability for some time to come. . . . During 1976, the government inflicted heavy blows on the local guerrilla organization and now faces no serious threat from that quarter."

While the Amnesty International report may have angered Somoza, the good word from the church and others may have helped speed up his recovery. Tacho ended his six-week stay at the medical institute on September 7. His stay cost him an estimated $1,500 a day for the hospital rooms he and his entourage had occupied. In addition, there were political scores to settle when he arrived in Managua.

Once home Somoza quickly moved against the centers of power that had emerged in his absence, dumping Hueck after twenty years as secretary-general of the Liberal party and even arresting Colonel Alegrett after the latter refused assignment as garrison commander in remote Bluefields. Tacho was angered by the evident ambition of cronies who had sought to take advantage of his illness to assert themselves.

Tacho did not stay in Managua. He retreated to the old family plantation mansion at Montelimar which he said was a better place for his government anyhow —just as his father once said before him. He was accompanied by an American nurse who kept him on a strict diet and exercise regimen, and he began living a healthy life unknown since his West Point days. Despondent and depressed after his close shave with death, he obeyed his doctors' orders. Tacho himself admitted the heart attack had frightened him badly. "It is a very sobering experience to meet death on the highway and get away from it. I don't look forward to another such encounter." He told visiting newsmen late in 1977 that Montelimar was healthier than Managua and it kept him away from parties and his active social life. Exercise machines were installed and he used them religiously.

Rising at 5:00 A.M. every day he walked six miles along the beach accompanied by his nurse. Next followed a workout at his gym, a routine he carried on for six months and which he claimed helped him shed sixty-seven pounds. Though still hefty, he was considerably slimmer. His target was 166 pounds. Doctors placed him on a low-fat breakfast and for lunch he substituted lean beef for venison or wild boar. Though they were not very substantial, Tacho made a ceremony of his meals, bedecking the table with fine silver and lace tablecloths and filling the old mansion with doting servants. He followed a rigid diet using the menus in the *Live Longer Cookbook* by Jon N. Leonard and Elaine A. Taylor.

His appearance began to change as well as his outlook on health. In the morning he dressed like a jogger in the tropics in tennis shoes, white shorts and a polo shirt. His military uniform stayed in the closet. He even grew a moustache. The "new" Somoza looked like a Central American Babbitt rather than how one might picture a president or even a dictator. He might have been boss of an Ohio insurance agency, a self-important buffoon who tried to terrorize his staff. He also could have been a Rotary Club president pretending to be a big shot—pretending because Tacho lacked the aura of leadership. He seemed an ordinary person trying to impress others with a greatness that he was not convinced of himself.

In the old days before the heart attack, things had been different. Most government offices had pictures of a heavyset, cigar-smoking *vividor,* a hard-living general—Somoza as he had been.

Somoza was disturbed about the prospect of obituaries abroad describing him as a reactionary tyrant. "It's the damnedest contradiction I've ever seen in my life," he snapped. "Here my opponents claim I'm a flaming Marxist." Although Somoza had little patience with local critics, he seemed to prefer their description of him. He claimed that his Liberal party was indeed liberal and that he himself was a socialist. Statistics, however, made it evident that he was one of the most powerful capitalists in Latin America.

Despite his doctors' orders to take it easy, Somoza kept very active. As Montelimar was now the seat of government, Tacho had built, at government expense, a beautiful jet runway at the plantation so he would not have to go to Managua's airport. He continued doing what he enjoyed most—being president, meeting with a few cronies, being with other men, usually the men he worked with. He enjoyed weekends with his buddies at the plantation, maybe watching a movie together. "I like war movies best," he said, "I'm a military man." He acquired a video-cassette player to watch American television programs taped especially for him. He claimed to read when he could, usually books dealing with current affairs.

Tacho liked his business deals most of all. One of his new investments in 1977 was reviving the fishing industry at San Juan de Sur, near the Costa Rican border. "The port was dying when we went in there," he bragged. Admitting at the time that he owned a "few boats," Somoza claimed to have created three hundred new jobs, while boats bought by others in response to Somoza's initiative supposedly created work for six hundred more families. In 1977, the general boasted, four million tons of shrimp and lobster were exported from San Juan de Sur to the United States whereas a few years earlier there had been no exports at all.

As a businessman, Tacho was remarkably disinclined to talk about business, the one subject he dodged in most of his press interviews. It was said that the key to operating a successful business was having Somoza as a partner. He had a pat answer to that. "I go abroad seeking investors to come into this country," he said. "Getting foreign investment in Nicaragua is a big part of my job. Often that isn't easy. So, to convince potential investors that Nicaragua is sound and has a future, I offer to take a piece of the action myself. I put my money where my mouth is."

He was also fond of stressing that while other Latin American leaders squirreled away funds in Switzerland, "Everything I have is right here in Nicaragua." Apparently, that was not entirely true. Sources indicated that most of his holdings were used as security for loans from foreign banks, that his properties were mortgaged to the hilt.

His family life was nonexistent at best. Hope remained estranged from him in London where daughter Caroline joined her, accompanied by her new husband, Nicaraguan lawyer Victor Urcuyo, nephew of Tacho II's former vice-president. Urcuyo didn't seem to enjoy the same diversions as his wife. They failed to arrive at dinner parties to which they were invited and before long Caroline told friends her marriage was just not working. She divorced him and moved into a small apartment with another woman, cooking her own meals and living like any other working woman. She landed a job as secretary with the Merrill Lynch stockbrokerage firm in London. The news concerning Tacho's son Julio remained discouraging. His only semblance of an immediate family was Tachito, who remained completely loyal to him. Tachito was evidently the only hope for Somoza "continuismo."

The political atmosphere in Nicaragua was relaxed for the first time in as long as anyone could remember. In a concession to Washington and on the advice of his American friends, on September 19, Somoza lifted martial law for the first time in thirty-three months. He also allowed the opposition newspaper to resume its daily blasts against the regime. The opposition was fragmented and disorganized "with little self-confidence in its power to negotiate with Somoza any plan to democratize Nicaragua," Ambassador Solaun later recalled. (He arrived to take his post in Nicaragua that month.) As far as the United States diplomatic corps knew, the guard had eliminated the Sandinista threat and "the civic opposition was mesmerized by Somoza—to many of them he seemed unbeatable without the help of the U.S. government."[12]

Mauricio Solaun was a former political science professor from the University of Illinois at Champaign-Urbana. A short, intense man who had been born in Cuba but who had moved to the United States long before the Cuban revolution, the forty-year-old Solaun made up for his lack of diplomatic experience with a keen understanding of Latin America and how he was to handle Somoza.

"When President Carter appointed me to go to Managua in the summer of 1977, my mission was plain," Solaun recalled in a speech at his university in April 1979. "I had to implement our human rights policy. This initially implied a need to maintain proper relations with the Somoza government, while, at the same time, opening broad contacts to the opposition and encouraging respect for human rights and the democratization of Nicaragua.

"This policy became known among some of its supporters in the State Department and the National Security Council as a policy of 'neutrality.' It was 'neutral' in that, following the described interventionist constraints of our human rights policy, we were not to place ourselves entirely within either the camp of the government of Nicaragua or the opposition. In effect, Washington was periodically critical in public of the Somoza regime but the embassy was not to side with opposition to the extent of organizing the overthrow of the government, nor was it to help organize the opposition or finance any of its factions.

"Objectively, really, our policy within Nicaragua was to avoid any commitment to either side. This is not to say that our policy was one of indifference to the situation; hardly so, inasmuch as we were critical of the status quo, and privately and publicly favored a change in Nicaragua. As we were not committed to the overthrow of the government of Nicaragua, the embassy was restricted from direct or indirect contact with virtually all groups."[13]

Solaun noted that until recently "Nicaragua was a client-state of the United States. This term refers to an alliance between states that have vastly different resources and power. The dominant power provides its client with protection from external and internal enemies; in synthesis, it supports the local government. In exchanges the client provides special services to its patron, such as economic privileges and political and military services.

"Nicaragua was a faithful client of the United States. The Somozas were our friends. To this date it is rare that top Nicaraguan officials do not proclaim their allegiance to the U.S.—'somos americanistas, we love your country' are expressions often heard, delivered with the sincere and strong emotivity so common to many Nicaraguans. This sense of fealty and of an alleged betrayal by the U.S. because of our human rights policy is a frequent claim made nowadays by the highest officials of the government of Nicaragua: 'When you needed us—Guatemala, 1954; Cuba, 1961; the Dominican Republic, 1965—we gave you our support, why do you betray us now withholding your support from us? You are leaving us alone to face the hatred of our common enemies' were statements often repeated by Somoza himself to me as President Carter's envoy to Nicaragua. In fact, it was not so long ago that the American ambassador was militarily saluted by Nicaraguan National Guards in public buildings, as if he were one of the highest officials of the land, a 'proconsul' of sorts to paraphrase President Somoza. It seems only yesterday that the progovernment press wasted no opportunity to publish photographs symbolizing the warm relations between our two countries."[14]

Solaun had little notion of whether the human rights message Carter told him to deliver would be accepted by Somoza. "Although the task seemed formidable, I proceeded to carry out my instructions, keeping in the back of my mind that perhaps it [was] necessary to hope in order to undertake but it is not necessary to hope in order to persevere."

Solaun's first contact with Somoza came on September 23. Since just a few officials and some of Somoza's business partners were the only ones to have seen the *jefe* since his return from Miami this had an important psychological impact. Rumors made the rounds that Somoza had had a relapse or was on his deathbed. "The president's image as an omnipresent, omniscient, ruthless leader began to evaporate—he was seen as highly vulnerable."

On October 13 the FSLN Terceristas launched a new offensive with an opening ambush on a National Guard patrol in Ocotal in the north and, a few hours later, a hit-and-run attack on a guard barracks in San Carlos near the Costa Rican border. In accord with the Terceristas' advocacy of a broad political front aimed mainly at overthrowing Somoza quickly and setting up a national election, as opposed to the popular prolonged war strategy of the GPP, they had decided to launch a large-scale military offensive.

Alvaro Baltodano, the son of wealthy businessman Emilio Baltodano Pallais, was a surviving commander of the October offensive. In a speech commemorating it two years later, he explained that it was not a spontaneous action. "October permitted the beginning of an insurrectional offensive. It permitted the armed fight to extend to all parts of Nicaragua so that the genocidal National Guard could not concentrate its forces in a single area. The guard had to disperse throughout national territory, losing in this way its offensive capacity and marking the beginning of a defensive posture until July 1979." Baltodano said that in October 1977, the military objective was the taking of different *cuartels* (barracks) in the country, but the objective could not be realized because of many intervening factors, including lack of experience, arms limitations and unforeseen difficulties in the political infrastructure. But the attacks had reaffirmed "that the nation was on its way to an armed fight and that the people could not return to the democratic-pacifist view."[15]

What was very significant was that the Sandinistas had for the first time shown themselves capable of launching coordinated attacks in diverse parts of the country and of achieving brief occupations of small towns from north to south. A few more hit-and-run assaults were carried out, including two surprise raids in the capital that led the government to position troops throughout the city. The Sandinistas were poorly armed, most with M-1 rifles and .22-caliber guns. Their assault in San Carlos was launched from passenger cars.

The San Carlos attack had other implications for the Nicaraguan government. Costa Rica approached the Organization of American States with charges its frontiers had been violated and that its minister of public security, Mario Charpentier Gamboa, had nearly been killed when Nicaraguan planes fired on three boats in the Frio and San Juan rivers. Nicaragua responded by alleging that the FSLN was being permitted by Costa Rica to use its territory in launching its attacks. Furthermore, said the Nicaraguan response, the planes had fired only warning shots.

The guerrilla attacks achieved one of their objectives by drawing troops out of Managua. On October 17 a dozen guerrillas attacked the guard post at Masaya, twenty miles south of the capital. They were repelled by a garrison of seventy guardsmen in a daylong campaign that included a three-hour gun battle on the Tipitapa-Masaya highway. Commander Pedro Arauz Palacios, in the FSLN since 1973, was killed along with four other Sandinistas in the attack. The death toll for the week climbed to nearly two dozen guardsmen killed and approximately ten guerrillas. One of the wounded Sandinistas was the nephew of Foreign Minister Alejandro Montiel Argüello. The Sandinistas suffered another casualty when a guerrilla was killed while firing on the National Guard police headquarters in Managua; two others were arrested in the act of holding up the Bank of Nicaragua in the capital. One was identified as Yadira Baltodano Gutierrez, the daughter of a rich and prominent provincial family. All around the country there was a flurry of skirmishes, bombings and ambushes.

The strange assortment of weapons used indicated that the guerrillas were not armed by Cuba as popularly alleged. Their arms appeared to have been purchased on the local black market. Many of the Sandinista leaders had received some training in Cuba but most realized the need for "on-the-job training"—in guerrilla warfare only practice makes perfect soldiers. The Castro regime was giving only moral support, providing asylum for those on the run and allowing them some use of Radio Havana airtime. United States military sources in Managua confirmed that there was no evidence that the Sandinistas were receiving Cuban arms and pointed out that if any communist weapons had been found, the Somoza government would have been sure to have put on a huge propaganda show.

"If we had received more effective support from Cuba or from any other country, we'd have been in power a long time ago," one Sandinista leader said a week after the Ocotal raid. "Our problem is that we've had to fight entirely alone. But it also means that when we achieve victory we will owe nothing to any outsiders." He claimed that the Sandinistas had one thousand armed guerrillas throughout Nicaragua though the group did not have sufficient money to buy modern arms.[16]

The raid on Masaya proved to be most disastrous for the members of the GPP meeting near the town at the time. They had had no warning of the attack plan and were captured. This demonstrated to the FSLN that the division was dangerous to all. The Terceristas, by aligning themselves with non-Marxist elements and announcing opposition to a communist regime, had clearly broken with the FSLN's original goal. They soon ruled a broad coalition of opposition groups and individuals ranging from Marxists and radical Christians to Conservative lawyers and businessmen and dissidents from Somoza's Liberal party. The GPP had been continuing its part of the struggle by trying to organize students and by robbing banks.

The Terceristas forced the issue of how opposition was to be carried forth with their attacks. As one of the planners, Humberto Ortega Saavedra recalled later, it not only signaled the beginning of organized military offenses, but it established the participation of the people in the popular insurrection. He noted that October 1977 brought the war to the cities, to combine with increased guerrilla action in the mountains. "It accelerated the forces of the masses to be what they were, the fundamental protagonists of the war."[17] The three Ortega brothers had emerged as leaders of the moderate Tercerista tendency.

A week after the Ocotal and San Carlos attacks a Sandinista leader described what the month, later known as "Sandinista October," signified. "Our call now is for the population to prepare for the future insurrection," he said. "These new actions are trumpet calls so the people can get ready. So far, we've disproved the government's claim that we've been liquidated. We're stronger than ever."[18]

Also in the month of October they announced as their objective the overthrow of the regime and the institution of democracy, not the inauguration of a Marxist-Leninist state. The Terceristas were aware of the impossibility of establishing a Marxist regime in a region dominated by United States–backed right-wing military regimes.

"We are only concerned with attacking the seventy-five hundred men of the National Guard," a Sandinista spokesman explained to me. "We want to make clear that at no moment will our military forces use their arms against the civilian populace . . . on the contrary, one of our objectives is the creation of a Sandinista army recruited from the people."

"After the insurrection, we will hold the first free elections in Nicaragua's history," said Plutarco Elias Hernández, one of six members of the front's national directorate. "We must pass through the stage of democracy because socialism cannot be built overnight. Those who think we'll be going straight to communism are wrong. Our basic program is not communist. It is a threat to no one who favors a just society. . . ."[19]

The groups of non-Marxists joining the ranks of the rebels were of great concern to Somoza. Coinciding with the October 13 offensive an anti-Somoza group that became known as "Los Doce" (The Twelve) was formed in exile in Costa Rica. The Twelve—including an aristocratic corporation lawyer, the millionaire owner of a chain of supermarkets, a teacher, Catholic priests, a writer, an economist, an agronomist, a dentist and an architect—met on October 17 in Costa Rica to issue *El Documento de Los Doce,* which called for popular insurrection to overthrow the dictatorship and demanded that any political solution should include the Sandinistas. The statement praised the Sandinistas' "political maturity" and warned the Sandinista Front that they must participate in any "national solution" of Nicaragua's problems.[20] The Catholic priests who were members of Los Doce included Father Miguel d'Escoto, a Maryknoll priest, and Fernando Cardenal, who had testified before House committees concerning foreign aid to Nicaragua. His brother, Ernesto, had seen his small community on the Solentiname Islands, near the southern end of Lake Nicaragua, destroyed by the guard. This included destruction of his valuable library and museum of pre-Columbian and peasant art. Ernesto Cardenal went on to join the Sandinistas. As their spokesman he made eloquent appeals for help throughout the world saying that although "every authentic revolution prefers nonviolence to violence, one doesn't always have the freedom to choose."

Somoza did not return to martial law during the tumultuous week beginning October 13, but common sights around the country included young guardsmen crouched behind sandbags and security forces searching cars. Somoza's press secretary, General Roger Bermúdez, tried to play down the situation. He issued press statements saying the situation was under control and that a guard "cleanup" operation would soon halt guerrilla activity. "Everything is normal and calm," Bermúdez assured Nicaraguans.

Bermúdez's words were of little avail. The guerrilla attacks set off an avalanche of opposition party protest. Communiqués and manifestos issued from both inside and outside Nicaragua clamored for an end to the forty-one-year-old Somoza dynasty, or at least for a genuine democratic opening. There was a sense of urgency. Many, even the wealthy families, feared that sons and daughters might also join the ranks of the Sandinistas. In fact, the sons of aristocratic families were well represented. Good, solid bourgeois names like Cardenal and Cuadra were represented in the rebel leadership. Brought up in a Conservative party, anti-Somoza tradition, the children of the Nicaraguan Tories had become radicalized. "The discontent is so high that the children of the monied and privileged elite are putting their lives on the line against Somoza," one businessman said.[21] Said an opposition politician, "The attacks have produced as a corollary the realization by the country that if we don't repair the situation, our sons are going to try to repair it. And, most likely, they will die in the attempt when they clash with the National Guard. That gives urgency to the political process. It has become a national clamor: remove the Somoza family from power once and for all."

One of the most outspoken critics of the Somoza regime was the UDEL, the

Democratic Union for Liberation, a group that encompassed the Independent Liberal party which had splintered off Somoza's Nationalist Liberal party.

"In this country there is a legalistic fiction of democracy and a dictatorship in fact," a UDEL spokesman told me. "Young people resort to violence because they have no democratic access to national life, which has been monopolized for forty-one years by the Somozas. If the action of the Sandinistas continues, the demand for a political solution is going to have more force. The political temperature may drop a little if the attacks do not continue. Not that it will disappear," he added, "because there are much more profound causes behind the questioning of the government."

A UDEL communiqué went further and stated, "The present violence is a result of the institutionalized violence in the country, particularly in the long years of dictatorship which had blocked all possible civic and democratic avenues towards resolving the acute economic and social problems suffered by Nicaraguans."

The guerrilla attacks stimulated formation of another civic-religious group which added its voice to the call for a dialogue in an effort to "eliminate the causes of the violence." This committee included Archbishop Obando y Bravo, two other bishops, a leading lawyer and the president of the Nicaraguan Institute for Economic Development (INDE), Alfonso Robelo. The plea of the group was endorsed by the Nicaraguan Chamber of Commerce which gave full support for an open dialogue that would permit Nicaraguans to express their thoughts and actions in a civilized manner, rare in a nation where disagreement was equated with subversion. The idea of a dialogue with the opposition first came after the October 1977 offensive by the Frente, when Somoza felt threatened enough by their strength to acquiesce. The meeting, arranged by Ambassador Solaun in December, was set to take place on February 5.

Hopes had never been higher for a major change. Some observers even foresaw a final end to Somoza rule. Though the streets of Managua were calm, beneath the surface the capital was brittle with tension. Fearing a period of economic uncertainty, Somoza supporters as well as opposition businessmen transferred close to forty million dollars in capital to foreign banks, a sign of a breakdown in confidence. Businessmen said the only reason Tacho didn't establish currency controls was for fear it might spark a wholesale panic of Nicaraguan bank accounts abroad. Rolando Ruiz, executive secretary of the national Chamber of Commerce, said a survey showed that a week after the guerrilla attacks retail sales dropped 43 percent.

With the government demonstrating its control over the country, sales began a slow recovery. But businessmen were uneasy at increases in the public debt from $680 million at the end of 1976 to a projected $825 million by the end of 1977. They feared a financial squeeze would develop in 1978–79, when interest and principal payments would reach a cumbersome level. An electricity shortage and increased prices of imported petroleum raised the possibility of an energy bottleneck; there was persistent stagnation in the construction industry since a tapering off of the building boom following the 1972 earthquake; world prices for coffee and cotton, Nicaragua's two biggest foreign exchange earners, were dropping. Inflation in 1977 was at least double the 1976 rate of less than 5 percent. But the currency appeared stable and the country had a trade surplus. However, there was no significant private investment in the nation, despite the availability of business loans from the banking system.[22]

Ruiz said that businessmen in Nicaragua wanted Somoza to remove his half-brother, José, from the post of National Guard inspector general and replace him with someone from outside the Somoza family; they wanted him to change the government cabinet "to eliminate corruption"; they wanted a guarantee of freedom in the presidential elections scheduled for 1980 and guaranteed respect for human rights. "Every day there are a number of arbitrary arrests," Ruiz said. "We believe that with this, a climate of tranquility and real peace would be created. . . . With a climate of tranquility, business is better."[23]

By November opponents and businessmen were speaking of the October offensive as the beginning of the end. "There is a horizon now that did not exist before, even if he lives," Xavier Chamorro Cardenal, co-owner of *La Prensa*, said. "People have arrived at a consensus. Somoza must go and this time Washington will not come to his rescue."

The Nicaraguan Institute for Economic Development (INDE), which represented a broad segment of the private sector, attributed the new situation to important changes in Somoza's power bases. An INDE document noted that "the church, one of the early pillars of Somoza power, has abandoned him and has joined INDE in demanding a dialogue of all political elements, including the Sandinistas, with a view of democratizing Nicaragua. The private sector has also turned against the regime and more importantly, the United States under President Carter's human rights program has removed American support. A third factor, of course, is Somoza's health. A relapse or new attack could remove him from the scene without any further moves by the opposition or the guerrillas." INDE ruled out a business strike or boycott at that time.

Tacho's health remained the subject of gossip and government efforts to portray him as well on the way to recovery were widely disbelieved. The man in the street had given him, in addition to heart ailment, a whole gamut of afflictions. "He is doomed," a taxi driver told me. "Cancer of the rectum. He's had five operations on his ass. If his heart won't get him, his ass will." Somoza was also believed by many, including doctors, to have suffered a stroke due to an embolism, and was said to be recovering from partial paralysis. Supposedly he had grown his new moustache to disguise partial paralysis of his face, particularly his upper lip. Others contended he could barely move his left arm.

People in Managua, formerly reserved and guarded on the subject of politics, were now speaking up defiantly, even to strangers. The Sandinistas had become heroes to many Managuans, including opposition business elements as well as urban workers. An outspoken minitaxi driver put it simply, "We're not afraid of him anymore. The events two weeks ago are only the beginning. There will be more fireworks, and serious ones, later. The boys out there are our heroes."

The pampered National Guard, the foremost prop of the Somoza empire, thought to be personally loyal to Tacho, had become an unknown factor as a result of the president's illness. The guard's loyalty did not extend beyond Tacho and his illness had reportedly aroused ambitions in the higher ranks of the officer corps.

"The Sandinista rebellion is being used by many sectors," one diplomat observed. "It could be used by elements of the National Guard for a preventive coup. The perceived withdrawal of U.S. support for Somoza has stunned the guard."

There were fears that the Sandinistas would try to disrupt the November 10 opening of the Superbowl Baseball Tournament in Managua, a major distraction for Nicaraguans. Baseball is the country's most popular sport, a heritage of the United States Marine occupation days. The best teams in the Caribbean were on hand to thrill Managua's fans, including a squad from Cuba. Somoza made a major festival of the event, even to the point of suppressing anti-Castro cartoons in *Novedades* so as not to offend the visiting team from Havana. Although increasingly bold, the guerrillas decided not to disrupt the tournament.

After the guerrilla attacks, Tacho still spent most of his time at his seaside sugar plantation. But the atmosphere of relaxation found there in September was gone, as was evidenced by the number of guards posted in trees during newsmen's visits. Besides newsmen, another visitor that November was Ambassador Solaun, who had orders from Washington to tell Somoza that the Carter administration was opposed to developmental loans for Nicaragua. "This information was leaked to the embarrassment of Somoza and to the opposition's delight. By politicizing our assistance programs or applying the carrot-and-stick policy Washington had created a serious problem for the embassy's management of our policy of neutrality, since Washington, itself, had proclaimed in effect that development loans had political implications, i.e., support or condemnation of the regime, as opposed to the exclusive goal of satisfying the basic human needs of the poor. Naturally, when loans were subsequently approved because of congressional and bureaucratic political considerations made in Washington, the opposition raged with anger."[24]

But Somoza got the carrot. His move to lift the three-year-old martial law after Solaun's arrival in September prompted the State Department to agree to a $2.5 million arms credit agreement, part of a larger agreement passed for fiscal 1978 in which the pro-Somoza forces led by Murphy and Wilson in Congress won $3.1 million in military aid and $15.1 million in "humanitarian" economic aid. The Nicaraguan opposition was quick to point out that Somoza in the past decade had received $20 million in military aid—the highest per capita allotment in the area.

The Carter human rights policy was faltering badly in December 1977, as demonstrated by Congress's reluctance to deny aid to nations such as Somoza's Nicaragua. The policy in Central America began to come across as vacillating and opportunistic. Law and order people hated the American president's human rights preachings, and trade unionists and liberals did not see much consistency between Carter's words and deeds. The initial stance on human rights was watered down considerably; the policy's selectiveness in application made it suspect to many. Nevertheless, the policy heartened opposition groups in Nicaragua and El Salvador. Pedro Joaquín Chamorro attributed the new situation in Nicaragua to Carter's policy.

But much to the opposition's regret, Somoza was cheating those who had forecast his death. And it still wasn't clear that the United States felt his position was in danger. There was acknowledgment of the possibility of a successor government. An American embassy official in Managua said, "We are prepared to deal with the next Nicaraguan government. Our relations are with the country—not a particular regime." But the *Intelligence Fact Book,* prepared by United States government intelligence agencies in January 1978, minimized the hard-core opposition to Somoza. It put communist strength in Nicaragua at sixty members for the hard-line Nicaragua Socialist party (PSN) founded in 1944, and forty members for the soft-line Nicaraguan Communist party. It also placed the FSLN under the communist heading, describing it as a "small pro-Castro" group numbering between 50 and 150 members.

CHAPTER 11

Pedro Joaquín Chamorro

To some he was garrulous. He was anticommunist even though he made an alliance with communists. He had dedicated his life to fighting the Somozas with gun, pen and from the political podium but when he failed to end the dynasty his opponents blamed his lack of success on his inability to unite the opposition. However, what he failed to accomplish in life was accomplished by his death.

Pedro Joaquín Chamorro tended to dominate the opposition, often fighting for its leadership. He was always outspoken and was the source of many stories distributed abroad—he gave information about the Somoza regime to columnist Jack Anderson. But he was never really the main source for anti-Somoza news in the foreign press, although Tacho claimed he was. Somoza felt that Pedro Joaquín, as he was called, had organized a news campaign against him abroad. He was paranoid about Pedro Joaquín, vehemently denouncing him privately, but at the same time he often contended that Pedro Joaquín helped keep the opposition divided because he wanted to monopolize its leadership, an old Chamorro trait.

A leading member and onetime president of the Inter-American Press Association (IAPA), Pedro Joaquín traditionally used their annual meetings to denounce the Somozas' infringements on press freedom. Generally Tacho would shrug off the IAPA condemnations, but by 1977 Pedro Joaquín had become an encyclopedia of Somoza sins. In January 1978 he was a serious threat to Tacho. There was real danger that in the White House President Carter was listening to dissidents like Pedro Joaquín.

Pedro Joaquín Chamorro Cardenal and Tacho had known each other since both were eight years old. They were enemies even then, fighting constantly because, according to Tacho, Chamorro's family newspaper "kept attacking my dad, and I couldn't stand for that." The fights in the schoolyard marked only the beginning of Chamorro's lifelong crusade to unseat a dynasty he later described to me as "permanent parasites, stealing and corrupting everything in sight."[1]

In pre-Somoza Nicaragua, the name Chamorro was associated with the presidency from the very first—Fruto Chamorro was the first Nicaraguan president (1853–55). Three other Chamorros occupied the presidency four times: Pedro Joaquín Chamorro (1875–79), Emiliano Chamorro (1917–21), Diego Chamorro

(1921–23) and Emiliano again briefly in 1926. In his book *Our Neighbor Nicaragua,* published in New York in 1929, Floyd Cramer, describing the Conservatives of Granada, wrote: "The families of the Chamorros, Cuadros, Lacayos always have been looked upon as royal families."

The acid-tongued publisher Pedro Joaquín had not always confined his battle against the Somoza dynasty to his pen and to the seventy-thousand-circulation *La Prensa* which his father, Pedro Joaquín Chamorro Zelaya had purchased in 1933. A law school graduate from the National Autonomous University of Mexico, Chamorro was imprisoned for taking part in a rebellion against the elder Somoza in 1954, two years after succeeding his father as editor of *La Prensa.* In 1956 he was arrested for publishing a photo of Somoza's assassination and banished from Managua for forty months. In 1959 he led a small band of armed rebels into the hills but they were no match for the guard. Chamorro was captured and jailed for three months. During that time, he contended, he was beaten and kept in irons for long periods. He had been sentenced to twenty years in prison but was released in a general amnesty. After that he carried on attacks for nearly two decades in the outspoken *La Prensa,* at least when it was allowed to publish and was not censored. Its only serious competition was the smaller, Somoza-family-owned daily *Novedades.*

When the Sandinistas opened up their October 13, 1977, offensive, *La Prensa*'s sympathetic coverage of the attacks led Somoza to forbid Chamorro to leave the country. But a month later Somoza, anxious to appease critics in the United States and as always denying charges of tyranny, was forced to permit Chamorro to fly to New York City to receive the Maria Moors Cabot Prize from Columbia University for his "distinguished journalistic contribution to the advancement of inter-American understanding." Elie Abel, dean of the graduate school of journalism, said, "If there is a journalist in the hemisphere who has been more consistent in his opposition to dictatorial government than Dr. Chamorro, we have not been able to find him." He went on to call Chamorro and his paper "synonymous with the opposition to the Somoza family rule."

When asked once why he took the hard road of opposition Chamorro replied, "When I see what there is in the country—violence, immense poverty, and egotism on the part of people who want to perpetuate their wealth, I want to do something . . . as a free man, satisfied with my conscience and useful." As for the people Pedro Joaquín had to dethrone to obtain his goal, Chamorro wrote that "the consolidation of a dynasty in America is a phenomenon that profoundly damages the historical aspect of our continent. It is certain that the first guilty ones to permit it to happen were we Nicaraguans, but to our credit it can be said that the pages of our contemporary history are overflowing with struggle and heroism.

"The Somoza [dynasty] is an original and strange phenomenon, uprooted from past times . . . but facing them has been and always will be a distant shout and eternal rebellion."[2] He was Central America's most famous newspaper publisher, a man with many enemies but considered too prominent to kill.

"Somoza considered Chamorro to be a bumbler and no threat," his PR man Wolfson said, "so he was not about to make a martyr out of him."[3] He admitted however that "Somoza didn't like Chamorro. Anyone who was called names and insulted by Chamorro every day of the week and still liked the man would be a real freak. But, Somoza saw a value to him. In effect, Chamorro was crying wolf too often to be effective and Somoza recognized it."

On January 10, 1978, Chamorro began his usual drive, alone, through the deserted streets of the ghost town that had once been the heart of pre-earthquake Managua. Driving at a leisurely pace around 8:20 A.M. he suddenly found the path of his Saab blocked by a green Toyota pickup truck. As his car screeched to a halt, two men stepped out and fired three shotgun blasts through the driver's window at point-blank range. Chamorro slumped over the wheel with twenty-six pieces of buckshot in his body. The gunmen abandoned their vehicle and sped off in another car which had been trailing the victim. A passerby called an ambulance but Chamorro was pronounced dead on arrival at a nearby hospital.

A hemispherewide outcry immediately condemned the Somoza regime. "One of the world's most courageous newspapermen—he ran an opposition journal in one of the most sophisticated dictatorships in the hemisphere—was assassinated Tuesday morning in downtown Managua, Nicaragua," the *Mexico City News* said. "Whether Chamorro, director of *La Prensa*, was shot to death by supporters of the Somoza dictatorship or by extremists who wanted to make it look that way, the tragic result is the same, and the cause is the same—the venomous asphyxiating atmosphere of a dictatorship in which the exercise of freedom is almost tantamount to suicide."

The Chamorro family and public opinion blamed the regime for the murder although many believed that Somoza would not have ordered the assassination of his most prominent enemy at a time when his government's human rights violations were under close international scrutiny. But it was equally obvious that a person or persons close to the regime were responsible for the crime. As Wolfson pointed out, "There [were] many heads around the president of Nicaragua who [did] not think too clearly and [were] not capable of projecting very far into the future."[4]

The fifty-three-year-old Chamorro's death provoked a political earthquake that rocked Nicaragua. Rioters immediately took to the streets burning an American bank, factories, businesses and cars. The government labeled them "communist gangs" and pleaded with the family to bury Pedro Joaquín ahead of schedule. Assistant Secretary of State for Inter-American Affairs Viron P. Vaky described the mood: "The assassination . . . fanned tension into open conflagration. . . . This assassination, more than any other single factor, catalyzed opposition to the regime. It resurrected the ghost of the political assassination of Sandino in 1934—and with it the fears and outrage of a frustrated people. It led to an unprecedented outburst of popular revulsion."[5]

When Chamorro's body was removed from the hospital, an estimated forty thousand angry mourners accompanied it first to his house and later to his newspaper, where Chamorro's campaign against the Somoza monopoly and against corruption in high places had been carried out. Many felt that two of his last exposés of corrupt practices involving Somoza friends and cronies were what had cost him his life. One of these exposed favoritism and malfeasance in the government housing bank and forced its director, Fausto Zelaya, to resign. Earlier Chamorro's newspaper had conducted an investigation of a Cuban-exile-owned blood bank which, the newspaper contended, bought the blood of impoverished Nicaraguans for $5.25 per pint and sold it abroad at an enormous profit. Because the Somoza family had been known to share business ventures with Cubans, and the exiles were perceived as enjoying a place of privilege in Nicaragua, there was some speculation about Somoza's share of profits in this venture.

When the crowd behind Chamorro's casket approached the blood bank, it battered down the door and allegedly set the building on fire. The angry mourners later burned down El Porvenir, a Somoza-owned textile and yarn mill also on the procession route. The police did not intervene.

Other *La Prensa* articles had charged Tacho with mishandling foreign relief during the earthquake. Following his heart attack six months earlier, *La Prensa* had come out strongly for his retirement due to physical incapacity and demanded democratization of the country. And Chamorro had publicly defended the subsequent Sandinista rebellion against Somoza as a "movement to overthrow an illegitimate regime." Chamorro had acknowledged that "yes, the communists are against the Somozas, but so are the rest of the Nicaraguans." His printed opinions of Somoza and his cronies were often couched in sneering tones. When Luis Somoza, dressed in work clothes, addressed a submissive trade union meeting, Chamorro editorialized, "Look at this shirtless millionaire. Who does he think he is deceiving?" Chamorro was hopeful, however, telling one interviewer, "I am very optimistic. I see the end of the Somoza dynasty. The majority of the people are against Somoza, except for the government workers. Somoza's regime is near the end because he lost support of the U.S. administration and public opinion in America and Europe. The newspaper now gives the truth about Somoza. He is a thief. He doesn't distinguish between his own interest and the interest of the state. When the dynasty disappears it will happen in Nicaragua as it happened in Spain when Franco died."[6]

The chambers of commerce and industry declared three days of mourning— in effect a strike freeing employees to go to the funeral or demonstrate. One businessman commented, "This is a very ticklish situation. Any heavy-handed action at this time could touch off massive rioting. People are extremely angry."

Tacho himself proclaimed that the government would "do everything possible" to arrest the culprits, praised Chamorro as "a man faithful to his principles," and called the assassination a "tragedy for Nicaragua." The government denied any complicity in the murder and claimed it would soon arrest the guilty party. Somoza insisted he personally had nothing to do with the killing of his longtime adversary. "I am very chagrined at Pedro Joaquín's killing. He was in the opposition, but he was in the honest opposition."[7] Nevertheless the Somoza regime stood condemned in the eyes of many Nicaraguans and the fallout from the murder was more unsettling than hundreds of attacks by the Sandinistas.

When Chamorro was buried two days after his death, wreaths and flowers were stacked high on his grave. One of the floral wreaths sent to Violeta Barrios de

Chamorro, his widow, came from Tachito and indignant mourners destroyed it.[8]

The Nicaraguan public was convinced that a Somoza had killed Pedro Joaquín. Reports at the time implicated Tachito, "El Chigüín," directly in the crime. There was widespread speculation that Tachito, who had tasted power as his father's top aide during Tacho's ten-week illness, wanted Pedro Joaquín removed from the political scene in preparation for his own turn as *jefe supremo*. Others speculated that the CIA had masterminded the killing, and others that the extreme left had done it in hope of producing a popular uprising.

After the killing it became evident to all that Pedro Joaquín had won in death a seemingly impossible objective—the unity of the opposition, a unity rarely seen in Latin America, comprising an unlikely anti-Somoza coalition of both left and right, business and labor. However this unity didn't come overnight.

The day after Pedro Joaquín's assassination four men were arrested by the guard and charged with the killing. One of the accused, Silvio Peña Rivas, told a Managua judge that he had been paid 100,000 córdobas ($14,285 dollars) to kill the publisher. Later he said the killers were paid $100,000 by Dr. Pedro Ramos, the blood bank owner. Ramos, who was in Miami, termed the charge "a monstrosity."[9] Peña Rivas then said he would divulge more information but only to Somoza. A week later a total of six men, including Peña Rivas and Ramos, were charged with murder and association to commit a crime by District Criminal Judge Guillermo Rivas Cuadras. The four others were Silvio Vega, Harold Cedeno, Domingo Acevedo and his son, Juan Ramos Acevedo. All but Ramos were in custody. He had flown to Miami a day before the killing. He told reporters he had "absolutely nothing to do with this assassination nor with any other," adding, "Since I have been formally charged, I cannot tell you anything. I am in the process of naming a lawyer." Though Nicaraguan law stipulated that a person must be formally charged within twenty-four hours of arrest for an alleged crime, the suspects were not taken before the judge until six days later.

In an attempt to disassociate the government from the murder, Somoza had the suspects testify on radio and television, but Peña Rivas's brother and attorney, Ronaldo Peña Rivas, maintained that the confession was extracted through torture. He also complained that the eight detained men were being held incommunicado and that witnesses who could prove Silvio Peña Rivas's innocence had been silenced by death threats. The other seven suspects had no legal representation.[10]

The events surrounding the case were so suspicious that even Somoza's public relations man had his doubts. "I am not impressed that within hours . . . murder suspects were arrested and confessed. On the contrary, the very speed of their apprehension—when so many people get away with a rash of crime right under the nose of the National Guard, which also serves as the police force—is reason enough to question whether the jailed suspects are the real killers."[11]

The burning of the blood bank destroyed any evidence that might have linked Ramos with the crime. The government blamed the burning on the demonstrators, but others said the fire appeared to start inside the building and not as a result of the protesters' fire bombs. Then, two weeks after the murder, two witnesses appeared to support the government's version of the events. *Novedades* news editor Antonio Díaz Palacios said Peña Rivas had told him in December that the murder was being planned but that he had dismissed the information as braggadocio. He said Peña Rivas had come to the paper to seek protection from editor Luis Pallais Debayle, though Somoza's cousin was not called to give evidence. Ramos's secretary, Lucrecia del Carmen Castro Barahone, then testified that she delivered four thousand dollars to Peña Rivas on the doctor's behalf a few weeks before the murder. Many considered the secretary, whose stepfather also worked at *Novedades,* an unconvincing witness. She was not closely cross-examined.[12] While Somoza had said he would seek Ramos's extradition if the "judges deem it necessary," there were few who believed that he would be returned to face trial.

In addition to the accused, Peña Rivas testified, some prominent Nicaraguans were connected with the killing as well. He named House Speaker Cornelio Hueck and former government housing bank president Zelaya, in addition to Ramos. The charges were roundly denied. With rampant contradictions ignored and questions left unanswered, the Chamorro family attorney, Roberto Argüello Hurtado, promptly charged, "It's quite obvious there's a cover-up. There are many people involved and there must be big shots in this or else a cover-up wouldn't be necessary." Chamorro's widow also spoke out on the murder investigation. "There's never been a fair trial of a political case in Nicaragua. The government claims that the case has been solved, but I hold Somoza responsible because no one does anything without permission from above." And Xavier Chamorro, Pedro Joaquín's brother and his successor as editor of *La Prensa,* said, "The investigating judge also seems to be on strike. The judge is doing nothing. He isn't asking questions that should be asked, he is showing no interest in getting to the bottom of things. There's a cover-up in all areas."[13]

The nation in general was critical of the government and demanded a full investigation of the murder. On January 24, the day the formal charges were filed against the defendants, business and labor leaders claimed that more than half of the nation's labor force was out on strike to demand government action. The previous day some four thousand Managua construction workers had walked off the job. The strike spread like wildfire to León, Chinandega, Estelí, Masaya, Rivas, Matagalpa, Jinotega, Ichigalpa and Granada with about 80 percent of the stores and offices closed in those cities, along with half the businesses in Managua. The strikes and shutdowns were viewed as a spontaneous reaction that spread through the nation. The major banking group, Banic, one of the most powerful economic institutions in the country, also joined the strike and closed its banking and financial operations. It was the beginning of what Somoza soon referred to as "the most serious crisis of my political career."

The political opposition demanded Somoza's resignation. Benjamin Gallo, president of the Nicaraguan Chamber of Industries, said, "We are asking that the government intensify the investigation of Chamorro's assassination and reveal who was responsible." He added that the national strike was growing "because we want to find out the truth." Antonio Tefel, chairman of the executive committee of UDEL, alleged that "Somoza is responsible for the death of Pedro Joaquín Chamorro. He must resign." Nodding to friends gathered at a comfortable residence in Managua's southern outskirts, he remarked, "Never have we had a better chance to get rid of him."

Alejandro Solorzano, secretary-general of the Nicaraguan Workers Confederation, took credit for organizing the strike. He was disappointed when United States Assistant Secretary of State for Latin America Terrance Todman canceled his visit. The American embassy announced that "due to recent events it is considered more convenient that the visit take place at a later date." Solorzano said the strikers wanted Todman "to see for himself that the Somoza dictatorship has no support." Opponents of the regime had planned to demonstrate against Somoza at the airport during Todman's arrival; the government was readying a counterdemonstration.

When workers themselves didn't stay home, employers often sent them back. "Nobody is losing any pay," Rogelio Montenegro, a distributor of educational materials in Masaya, stressed. "Some of us paid our people through the end of the month, others to February fifteenth."

By the end of January the general strike was proving only partially successful. Most shopping centers and factories were closed, but smaller businesses continued to operate. Managua was far from shut down; traffic remained heavy on the avenues running through the outskirts where most of the capital's inhabitants lived and worked. Grocery stores, gas stations and bus service were all operating and relatively few people seemed affected by the strike.

Edmundo Jarquín Calderón, secretary of UDEL, and others thought the guard might move in and force businesses to open. "The regime has handled the situation intelligently," he commented. "Businessmen have folded their arms and said, 'We are closing our establishments.' The government has answered by folding its arms and letting them close." Jarquín Calderón said that the group's only complaint "is with Somoza. We have made it clear we are not opposed to the National Guard." The implication appeared to be that UDEL would not object if the guard staged a coup. It would have preferred, of course, that Somoza step down voluntarily. "We can't put up with three more years of this," he explained.

While UDEL demanded Somoza's resignation, Somoza's supporters replied that it may very well have been UDEL that was behind the murder. Somoza's people maintained that civil war would break out if Somoza resigned. They also argued that UDEL would inevitably fall apart because of tensions within the union's mixed membership—reactionaries, radicals, paternalistic businessmen, socialist labor leaders and Marxists. The latter would end up running Nicaragua. "They claim that everyone who doesn't agree with them is a communist," Amadeo Vanegas, of the Nicaraguan Workers Central, said. "If they are communists, Somoza has made them that way."

The strike continued. The Somozas, who worried little about public opinion at home, were becoming more desperate to receive the blessing of Washington. Former Florida congressman Bill Cramer—Somoza's lobbyist on Capitol Hill—was flown into Managua with a hard-sell public relations team to handle the foreign correspondents in town.

The strike committee announced businesses would remain closed until Somoza resigned. In response Tacho pulled out the bulletproof ticket booth to deliver a public forty-five-minute speech. The banner headline in *Novedades* earlier quoted *el jefe* as saying that "as my father said, I will not go, neither will they force me to go." Tacho, officially inaugurating a new office building in the Pacific port of Corinto, was in rare form. He claimed that the general strike was neither spontaneous nor touched off by the death of Pedro Joaquín. "It was planned to happen in December, and the opposition predicted all hell was going to break loose in Managua. They just used Pedro Joaquín's death as an excuse. They want to give the impression that the Somozas are losing their power base—at least they attempted to give that impression."

Before an audience of approximately two thousand supporters, Somoza claimed he was seeking to determine the intellectual authors of the killing of Chamorro. "I'm very interested in finding this out because my family has been the victim of an assassination. My father was assassinated, and we don't like that kind of stuff happening in Nicaragua."

As for the strike, Somoza charged that "a lot of people in Managua closed down because they were threatened by the opposition. The telephone has been a major weapon in the strike. Callers have told them they would be burned down, so they went on strike." He added that the strike was led by the owners because "the workers don't want to go on strike, but they have no choice."

Somoza followed his Corinto speech with a press conference, during which he smiled broadly and said, "They wouldn't dream I'd make a speech like I did today. They think I'm sick. But I am far from it. I'm in better shape than when I got sick.

"Some of these oppositionists think they are speculating with my health. You [the press] ought to put them straight. If I was sick, I would get out. All right. I've got enough brains for that. So I don't want them to make mistakes speculating on my health. You ought to let them know they are dealing with a guy who's completely back on his health. I may be in better shape than before. I knock off six miles a day Monday through Friday without panting. A year ago I couldn't walk an hour. I can pronounce myself very healthy."

In discussing government attitudes toward the strike, Tacho told the press that "when the strike becomes a jeopardy for the people, we have the means to take over those industries, but we are not going to unless it is necessary. When they can't pay their workers I think the government will have to intervene and run their business for them. This is the sorriest time that private enterprise should pull a strike like this because in the socialist world today private enterprise is not king anymore. I'm a capitalist and I am telling you." Earlier Somoza had told newsmen that the wealthy of Nicaragua had always opposed him because "I'm a socialist."

"Look," he said, "a guy decides to go on strike, that's his business. If he doesn't pay his workers, that's his business. But if he doesn't pay the workers, that's our business because he is violating the law. You have a good opportunity to see how civil liberties work in Nicaragua," he said with a wide smile. "So you have the farmers' strike in the States and I have the merchants. Ha ha ha."

Somoza then told newsmen he personally felt that the assassination of Chamorro was a mistake. "Playing politics tells you practical politics and it is best to know your enemy. We thought he was a good enemy. We thought he was a good enemy to have, even though he was very caustic in what he wrote and said." Tacho added that he was saddened by Chamorro's death. "I can be killed too, you know. I'm a human being too." He defended his family's rule. "We have a bad reputation outside that our people are violent. But the fact we are in power so long [proves] that we are not violent people. . . . We are taking a very passive attitude because these people are still utilizing their basic freedoms that there are in Nicaragua, and it's a good thing you are here to see how basic freedoms are in Nicaragua." As he spoke in the Pacific port, government troops were literally banging heads in dealing with an opposition attempt at a nonviolent demonstration a hundred miles away in Managua.

Later that day strike leaders meeting with foreign newsmen vowed to continue their protest "until the dictatorship falls." Once again charging that Somoza was responsible for the murder of Chamorro, Rafael Cordova Rivas, leader of UDEL, issued what many considered to be an invitation to Nicaragua's military men to oust the president. "We are hoping the leaders of the National Guard will observe the sentiments of the Nicaraguan people and do their duty."

Conservative party leader Fernando Agüero also admitted a military regime might be in the offing if Somoza stepped down. "Anything is better than what we have now," he said.

Conservative Congressman Alberto Saborio, noting that in the past the capitalist sector had always been behind Somoza, said that Pedro Joaquín's death had awakened those who had "ignored the dictator's crimes, paying no attention to them until now." Saborio charged Somoza with running a "corrupt government which stifles competition and destroys opportunities for honest men. . . . He is the most ruthless capitalist in Latin America," Saborio said. "Since his family came to power more than forty years ago they have amassed a fortune in excess of half-a-billion dollars. They own one-third of all the land in Nicaragua and in many cases they have killed the original owners and stolen their property."

The three men reaffirmed that the aim of the strike was to force the resignation of the president, but Agüero said he doubted that there would be any voluntary resignation and that if there was one, nothing would be solved. "The regime would continue. It has the machinery to keep power." They added that only the National Guard had the power to change the situation. "We have no weapons, we cannot fight except in a pacific way," Agüero said.

The speakers at the press conference accused the United States of supporting Somoza in the past, yet gave the United States credit for inspiring the strike. "We have heard President Carter's statements on human rights and we know that nowhere in the world are human rights violated more than in Nicaragua," Saborio proclaimed. "We cannot ask that Carter support us directly, but if the U.S. government ends its support of Somoza, that will be enough to assure our triumph." While the three men agreed that they hoped a democratic government would replace Somoza, they were unable to predict that the nation would be so fortunate. "With the end of the dictatorship, we will be faced with an economic crisis," Agüero forecast. "The extreme left is well organized. Whatever happens, any change will be for the better."

The following day, January 30, Somoza held another press conference in Managua.

"They want to make me out to be a very devilish man and I'm really just a simple farmer," Tacho said between mouthfuls of his diet food. The group was lunching at Los Gauchos, one of the few Managua restaurants not closed by the strike, now in its eighth day. The restaurant was owned by the Somoza family.

Tacho expressed some sympathy with the original aim of the strike. "If I was a merchant and was asked to join in a show of a demand for justice, I probably would. But think again about wanting the president to resign and upsetting the whole applecart." Twisting his West Point class ring with its huge diamond, Tacho explained that the strike was in its eighth day because "these guys are up in a coconut tree and don't know how to get down." A reporter asked if the strike was not an indication that many people, especially in private enterprise and labor, were opposed to his regime.

"I agree," he said. "I have opposition. I have never denied it. Many people dislike the longevity of the Liberal party's power and the longevity of the Somoza family's being in power. This is a democratic country and they have their right to oppose me. This has been a definite countdown to see if the Somozas are in or out. Well, in my view, the answer to that is that we're very much in."

What he disliked, he said, were what he considered the many unfair charges being hurled against him. He especially objected to being pictured as repressive and crushing all opposition. "Is there freedom in Nicaragua? I think there is. Anyone who reads La Prensa can see that. The fact that the opposition newspaper published all these charges against me shows that there is liberty in this country." He said that the public relations team flown in from the States and headed by ex-Congressman Cramer was in Managua because "I think any politician is always in the business of improving his image."

Tacho then encouraged his guests to keep on with their aggressive questioning. "If I were a journalist, those are the kinds of questions I would ask," he said.

Returning to strike questions, Tacho held his volatile temper in check until he was asked about the "brutality" in breaking up a peaceful demonstration of two hundred women—wives and daughters of the upper class—shortly before lunch. (Although it was not brought up during the meal, it was later reported that Tachito had led the attack.)

"The demonstrators were violating the law. They had no permit," Somoza said. "Tear gas is the most civilized way available to clear people away in an incident such as this." Nevertheless, someone observed, two women had been hospitalized because the gas was used incorrectly. "You want to give us lessons in how to use tear gas?" he snapped.

Lunch was over.

The incident referred to had been the worst so far in the unusually passive resistance action. The women had packed the front lawn of a United Nations office in a residential house when the National Guard moved in. The guard fired tear gas into their midst and ended the demonstration. Some of the women and their daughters in blue jeans had arrived in Mercedes Benz. Two priests had been called to say mass for them. The women had unfurled banners saying, "Where are our *campesino* brothers?" "Somoza is jail, torture, crime and exploitation, he must go." Inside the United Nations building at the time were a dozen wives of missing peasants believed jailed or killed by the guard during its antiguerrilla campaign in 1977.

Leaders of the private sector called a meeting at which they voted to continue the strike, but there was growing realization among the strikers that Somoza was not about to quit. INDE executive director William Baez admitted that the strike might be nearing the end of its course. "We have proved our point. We are fed up with corruption and injustice," he explained. "If Somoza has not got our message, too bad." He added, "We have also shown the world how labor and employers can unite against a dictatorship. Also important is the fact that for once the U.S. has kept its hands off. Tacho does not have Ambassador Mauricio Solaun in his pocket as he did many of the American ambassadors in the past."

Baez said he felt the American hands-off policy was very significant because before Carter, a strike such as the one being conducted would have brought in the United States Marines. "The U.S. policy is correct," he said.

Fears that the National Guard would step in and try to stifle the strike were not entirely groundless. Six persons were reported killed and sixteen injured when guardsmen fired on rioters in the city of Matagalpa. Guardsmen occupied the country's only oil refinery, owned by Esso, in Managua, to prevent its twelve thousand workers from joining the strike. Food and fuel scarcities were reported in many parts of the country and the government imposed total censorship on the nation's radio stations. Many of them temporarily went off the air. Five of the stations had been briefly silenced for ignoring government emergency orders and continuing to air news of the strike. Many businesses feared a repetition of the 1959 merchants' strike, when the stores were forcibly opened by the National Guard. Tacho, on the other hand, liked to make the claim that the strike would end because "this is a capitalists' strike. Sheer competition will end the strike. This is just a matter of time."

Members of the guard were on alert throughout the country as the popular outrage reached a peak. On the night of February 2, squads of FSLN Terceristas entered Nicaragua from sanctuaries in Costa Rica and launched hit-and-run attacks against Peñas Blancas and Rivas. In an attack on Granada the Sandinistas forced the guard to retreat to their barracks. The guerrillas held a popular assembly in the city. Meanwhile, the GPP sent units against guard posts along the northern border with Honduras.

Municipal elections were drawing near. Tacho, playing for time, announced he would wait until after the municipal elections before beginning the scheduled dialogue with the opposition. His method was to stall and hope the "guaro and nacatamale" elections would come off without a hitch. The Conservative party asked for a postponement of the nationwide municipal elections scheduled for February 5, the same day as the canceled dialogue. The Conservatives threatened to withdraw from the elections if they were not postponed.

Somoza and his cabinet decided not to cancel the February 5 municipal elections but they were boycotted by thousands of voters. Some 52 of the Conservative party's 132 candidates voluntarily withdrew and polling stations in León and Granada were virtually deserted three hours after the elections began.

On February 21, Monimbó, the little Indian enclave that begins where the asphalt streets of the city of Masaya end, honored Pedro Joaquín with a memorial mass. A shantytown barrio that had been neglected by the Somozas, Monimbó had no sanitation and residents suffered a high incidence of intestinal parasites. Nevertheless, the Indians of this ancient barrio are a proud and independent people, not at all the stereotyped Indians depicted half a century earlier in stories by the American writer O. Henry.

The guard, which had reinforced its small post in Monimbó, brutally dispersed the mourning mass celebrants with tear gas and rifle butts. But, unlike the crowds the guard attacked elsewhere, the people of Monimbó fought back. It was an uneven fight but overnight it caught the imagination of the rest of the country. With the type of homemade bombs later to become famous as "contact bombs," the Indians fought off guard tanks and helicopters. Small-caliber hunting rifles were pitted against powerful .50-caliber machine guns. Although the first revolt was quelled, Monimbó was not subdued. Each night the guard had to retreat to its post—the dark streets belonged to the anti-Somoza Indians. Scores were killed and wounded. The indomitable spirit of Monimbó was contagious. Other rebellions flared up in Subtiava, the Indian district of León, and in Jinotepe and Diriamba. There were peasant land seizures in the northwest. As a result, the guard could move in the countryside only in heavy detachments with air cover. A prerevolutionary situation had emerged and Monimbó became the center of the anti-Somoza revolt.

Killed in Los Sabogales in the heart of Monimbó was Camilo, the youngest and most outgoing and spontaneous of the three Ortega brothers. Camilo had been active in the Student Revolutionary Front (FER) and then began to work on the consolidation of small Sandinista commands. He participated in an attack on La Perfecta milk-processing plant in 1967, and in 1970, began work directly with José Benito Escobar, a Sandinista leader, in student organizations. Taken prisoner twice in 1970, he spent only a brief time in jail, and, in 1972, traveled to Cuba. In 1975 he took over responsibility for the western region of Nicaragua, including Masaya, Granada and Rivas. He organized and directed the brief takeover of Granada in 1977, and then, when Monimbó rose up against Somoza, he rushed in to help the spontaneous insurrection.

"The bourgeoisie had lost control of the anti-Somoza movement," wrote one commentator." Isolated uprisings had begun to coalesce in groups that identified themselves as Sandinistas. What was needed now was stronger organization to wage a unified military and political battle. It was up to the FSLN to transform prerevolutionary conditions into a revolutionary crisis."[14]

Somoza began to be convulsed by problems. The strike was drawing to a close but scandal within his business empire forced him to jail two partners and dismiss his principal financial adviser. Businessmen were approaching the American embassy to pressure for Somoza's resignation.

Solaun reported that businessmen were sure Somoza would respond if the United States asked him to resign. If not, the American mission should approach the guard to demand Tacho's resignation through a coup d'état, Somoza's opponents said. But, "our instructions were clear—follow the policy of neutrality," Solaun said. "The embassy was to continue encouraging all parties to dialogue in search of a peaceful solution, a made-in-Nicaragua formula; we were not to serve as messengers, mediators or guarantors of any solution."[15] The United States had admitted that it was waiting for the 1981 elections to roll around. It was hoped they'd provide an avenue to avoid bloodshed and provide Nicaraguans with a peaceful succession to the Somoza regime. "The United States wants to see a liberalization now to prepare the ground for free elections in 1981," diplomatic sources related.[16]

United States relations with Nicaragua were "all right," according to Somoza in a February interview with Karen DeYoung of *The Washington Post*."Why should I be disappointed? We haven't made a deal." All he wanted, Tacho said, was "that the U.S. cooperate for development of Nicaragua. But nowadays, I'm not surprised at anything." American aid was welcome and necessary, Somoza said. "When it comes to the last stand, I need the help for development, the same way your country did. I would be absurdly stupid to say no." Some United States congressmen didn't like him, he alleged, "maybe because I'm anticommunist." He was more critical of Carter's Latin American policy, however, and answered a question concerning it by asking, "What policy? Listen, it's good enough I told you 'what policy.' " He remarked that he was receiving support from other Latin American countries for the way he ran Nicaragua but refused to elaborate, calling it a "secret."

Tacho dismissed any idea of resigning. Somoza again claimed, "There is democracy in Nicaragua. They [the protesters] can blow their mouth like anybody else." Charges of fraud and corruption against him were shallow. "When you get down to the nitty-gritty, they don't stand up." He further stated that priests' allegations "were not in accord with the political establishment in Nicaragua. We'd like those priests to make a legal deposition. They're becoming activists. The church is highly politicized." As the discussion went on, Tacho pointed out that Nicaragua had an agrarian reform law "giving owners guarantees. Workers guarantees." Peasant complaints such as "They took my pig, my house" were false, he said, and designed to "work on your sentiments. We have got a human feeling." Tacho touched his heart. "We built public dorms in Chinandega. We give them rights. We are helping them. But they [the peasants] are trained, indoctrinated by activists. There is political freedom to indoctrinate them. One of the troubles with you," he told DeYoung, "is you don't want to realize that Nicaragua is an open society." Then, as if to defend himself, he told the reporter, "You're not the Virgin Mary, and I'm not Jesus Christ."

With all the problems facing Somoza, he returned the government to Managua from his retreat at Montelimar and set up housekeeping in La Curvita with Dinorah.

Like the Bunker, the predominant color of La Curvita's decor was light brown. One recent addition to the house was Tacho's exercise room. It had a large bay window offering him a splendid view of the city below while he worked out on a stationary bicycle, which he liked to point out checked his heartbeat as he cycled. There was a large screen on one wall to show his videotapes and war movies.

To emphasize he was in the best physical condition of his life, he sometimes permitted news photographers to record his daily exercise routine which ended with a massage by an American nurse. At 6:30 A.M. he would emerge from La Curvita in shorts and jogging shoes and begin forty-nine laps around the house. A soldier stationed on the Staghound armored car under a tree guarding the entrance would keep a record announcing each lap. Perhaps the most bizarre sight was a dwarfish aide, no more than a meter-and-a-half tall, jumping up to the general and dabbing the sweat off his forehead with a small towel.

On the rare occasions Tacho left La Curvita and the Bunker nearby he went around Managua in a black armored Cadillac Fleetwood, probably the only one in Nicaragua. The license plate bore five stars, the national escutcheon and the legend "Presidente de la República." Once, when asked what model year the Cadillac was, Somoza shot back, "How the hell should I know? I don't get my kicks by being the guy with the newest car on the block." But as for being president: "It's the best job in the world," he liked to say in late 1977. Then again Tacho regularly claimed that he was really a businessman taking a little time out to serve his country. He dressed in dark business suits, a rarity in stifling Managua but in his air-conditioned quarters of the Bunker, where he spent most of his day, heat was never a problem. The suits looked as if they had been bought off the rack at a Sears department store. More elegant were the *guayaberas* he occasionally wore. They bore his name embroidered above the left breast pocket—A. Somoza D.—and were of an expensive cut.

Visitors who got beyond the carved mahogany door of the Bunker were shown into a small waiting room where perhaps seven people could find a seat. It might have been a dentist's outer office, minus the old magazines. This was a man's world. There was not a female employee in the place. Only rarely did a woman visitor enter —usually Dinorah. The receptionist and clerks were soldiers of the National Guard although they were more likely to be dressed in sport shirts and slacks than uniform. Top aides—Colonel Porras, Max Kelly and some of the other most powerful men in the country—worked in cramped offices on one side of the reception room, but the dim, cold, quiet atmosphere gave no hint that anything important was going on.

No one got into the waiting room without an appointment to see Somoza, although appointments were often all but meaningless. *El jefe* himself would open the doors to his more private quarters and beckon whomever he might deign to see. Others, not quite so favored, perhaps would win a handshake and the assurance he would be right with them. Once through the door, an audience was not always forthcoming. Somoza might sit his visitors in any of three other small rooms, step out, promising to be right back, and return an hour or two later.

His office was the size of a living room, the furnishings of chrome, leather and mahogany. The walls were of two-foot padded leather squares. Pictures of Somoza's father, poster-size blowups of Somoza in action, even one of the old cigar-and-uniform official portraits leaned against the wall, unhung. A mahogany carving of the West Point seal lay on the brown carpeted floor. The presidential office looked as if the man had just moved in—or was about to move out.

Except for a bit of glass around the main front door there were no windows. Within, there was no telling anything about the world outside—whether the sun shone or rain fell, whether it was night or day.

Although his handshake was limp, Somoza would greet his visitors with a warm smile. But once the talk turned to business, he would glare. Everyone who came to see him was asking for something and the glare, no doubt a learned mannerism, must have kept the requests somewhat reasonable.

Somoza could be a bully, brutal to his underlings. "You shit-eating son of a whore, I want that data now!" I once heard him scream in Spanish at an aide who failed to act quickly enough.

Tacho's family life and personal problems continued to besiege him. Julio remained in the hospital because of drugs, Tachito was heavily suspected of involvement in Pedro Joaquín's murder, Caroline's divorce in London pained him as she was his favorite daughter. Even Dinorah was often angered with Tacho. He could no longer seek surcease in alcohol as the doctors had limited him to an ounce of wine a day.

On his own, he enjoyed relaxing with his friends—being the life of the party, the center of attention. He had grown up being important, but not important enough. As a boy, he rated attention because he was his father's son. At La Salle and West Point he was discriminated against and suffered when chided, "You may be hot stuff at home, but here you're just a piece of shit." In the United States they had called him a "spic" but when they wanted a place to launch the Bay of Pigs invasion, the Americans came to him with hat in hand, as an equal.

The Sandinistas, meanwhile, kept issuing demands to their friends and supporters for arms. In addition, the October and February attacks prompted new developments in the areas of leadership, organization and unity. The lines of demarcation among the factions were becoming less pronounced as each of the FSLN tendencies demonstrated a new strategic and tactical flexibility. The "Proletarians" focused on the urban proletariat but also began organizing rebellious farmworkers—it formed the Rural Workers' Association in March. New emphasis was placed on military organization, with the formation of grass roots militias called the Revolutionary People's Commandos.

The GPP emphasized organizational efforts among urban groups in the northern part of the country. The massive uprisings had convinced the GPP that popular sentiment existed for insurrection, but popular organization to that end was still judged inadequate. Nonetheless, as the insurrection had been set in motion, the FSLN had to provide it with revolutionary leadership.[17]

Previously the FSLN factions had figured that without strong mass organizations, the bourgeoisie and the United States would be the beneficiaries of a revolt. But now the bourgeoisie too was divided and unable to exploit the situation. These developments gave credence to the Tercerista position that the revolutionary forces would emerge as the strongest within a broad anti-Somoza coalition. Though the October and February attacks strained the guard, the Terceristas had nevertheless underestimated the fighting capacity of the guard and its loyalty to Somoza. They had also overestimated the strength of spontaneously arising insurrectionist groups. But FSLN actions had propelled the mass movement forward, held the initiative in revolutionary hands, and expanded the popular base of all three factions. By July the Proletarian, GPP and Tercerista groups arrived at a shaky agreement for tactical unity and established a general coordinating commission. Each one recognized that important ideological differences remained, that reunification would be long and difficult, but that the revolutionary process depended on the unity of *sandinismo*. Immediately thereafter, the United People's Movement (MPU) was formed. The three factions of the FSLN joined with the PSN (Nicaraguan Socialist party), the traditional left and more than twenty student, labor, women's and civic organizations to develop a concrete program for mass action and to forge unity in the revolutionary movement as a whole. The MPU organizers set up neighborhood committees to help direct the offensive against the dictatorship. Each of the factions accepted the MPU program for the post-Somoza period.

According to Solaun this period saw Washington walking a tightrope, "evinced by the mixed public signals that it was perceived to be sending. For instance, on the one hand, Somoza was periodically criticized in public for bad human rights performance and the government of Nicaragua was encouraged to seek an enduring democratic solution, but, on the other hand, despite acute local polarization two aid loans were approved and President Carter sent a highly misinterpreted letter praising President Somoza for his political concessions—the state of siege had not been reimposed despite the extensive disturbances . . . [and] Carter continued to encourage Somoza to further democratic progress in Nicaragua."[18]

Somoza went to the United States in June for a round of politicking, striving for a new human rights image on visits to New York and New Mexico. While spending time with his son Roberto, a recent prep school graduate, Somoza told the press that Carter's pressure for policies respecting human rights was an act of "moral imperialism." The Nicaraguan dictator indicated he disapproved "of the use of human rights to subvert public order." Among his charges was that the United States wanted "to sacrifice Nicaragua on the altar of human rights." He also launched a verbal attack on opposition leader Alfonso Robelo Callejas, who in an earlier visit to New York predicted the dictator would be out of office by the end of the year. "Robelo isn't even a deputy sheriff. He has no political mandate and I don't consider him an opposition leader."

Winging to New Mexico at the end of the month for a "nonpolitical and noncontroversial" visit to discuss "energy problems and geothermics" at the Los Alamos nuclear laboratory, Somoza and his official American public relations chief, Ian MacKenzie, launched a small PR drive among friendly members of the United States press.

On the trip, despite his past refusals, Somoza finally succumbed to appeals from Venezuela and the Carter administration to allow the Organization of American States' human rights commission and Amnesty International to conduct on-the-spot investigations in Nicaragua. Tacho came off as a reasonable, tolerant man, reiterating that accusations of human rights violations in Nicaragua were "inspired by communism."

During his visit he met with an Amnesty International representative in Albuquerque though he had previously denied them meetings in Managua. Somoza was reported by Amnesty delegate Dean Haggard as being receptive to a general amnesty to both sides in the recent civil clashes. Haggard presented him a list of twelve prisoners considered "prisoners of conscience," and called the meeting a victory for human rights. In fact it was a coup for Somoza.

In the meantime Venezuelan delegates to the OAS continued to blast Somoza's human rights record, prompting Somoza's brother-in-law, Guillermo Sevilla-Sacasa, who was also Nicaraguan OAS ambassador, to denounce Venezuelan allegations as "slanders and unjust accusations" that amounted to intervention in Nicaraguan internal affairs.

Upon his return to Nicaragua, Somoza faced new problems along with the old. Among the first was a direct attempt on his life. Two Sandinista guerrillas checked into Howard Hughes's former suite on the eighth floor of the Intercontinental Hotel, assembled an 81-mm rocket launcher, and took careful aim on the Bunker only fifty yards away, where Somoza was meeting with his cabinet. The two rockets went astray and hit twenty yards beyond their target, crashing into Tachito's conference room in the Basic Infantry Training Center. One rocket exploded, the other was a dud, but the single explosion caused more than 250 guardsmen to come running from their quarters, shooting wildly at the hotel. Curious guests poked their heads out of the windows. One passerby, the son of a prominent doctor, was running past the hotel when he was shot and killed by the guard. An estimated seventy thousand dollars' damage was caused to the hotel in the attack.

The guard seized Fernando Chamorro Rappacciolo, forty-two, an auto import executive, who allegedly admitted firing the rockets, though the FSLN later claimed the assault unit escaped.

Somoza himself would still not entertain the idea of resigning even when the Roman Catholic hierarchy asked for his resignation to make way for a "pluralist national government." The six-bishop, eleven-priest Nicaraguan Episcopal Conference also demanded the establishment of a new economic order; the right of free political association; reorganization of the armed forces based on national, rather than personal, interest; annulment of laws limiting freedom of expression and an end to violent repression. "With the retirement of Somoza a national government could be formed which would obtain the support of a majority of Nicaraguans and prevent the country from falling into anarchy."

Backing the church demand was the Nicaraguan Chamber of Commerce, the Chamber of Industry, the Broad Opposition Front (FAO), the Nicaraguan Institute for Economic Development, and Banking and Financial group (BANIC) owner

Alfredo Pellas, called the wealthiest man in Nicaragua after Somoza. Observers saw the move as a chance to avoid a Sandinista government and allow Tacho to slip out quietly with his money. His replacement would be a coalition of Nicaraguan groups working within a representative government stopping short of the far left and favoring a free enterprise economy. Some, such as INDE executive secretary William Baez, feared that "if Somoza remains in power, Nicaraguan society will disintegrate. Somoza foments communism solely by remaining in power." The groups were hoping the guard would step in and play a role in fulfilling their demands, but it became clear the guard continued to support its commander in chief.

Somoza answered all demands with an emphatic no. Following the Bunker rocket attack he told reporters he had twice considered stepping down, once after his heart attack and then following the riots succeeding Chamorro's assassination. But he decided to stay on. "Who is going to get the pie if I quit, I asked myself. The Conservatives or the Sandinistas? No way! I was elected to serve until 1981 and if I quit before then civil war will break out." Somoza publicly announced that he would not resign. He used the occasion to launch the Liberal party's 1981 election drive, telling a rally of Liberals that "we have the majority, a powerful party, a loyal army and a peace-loving people. Neither I, the president, nor the party intends to quit."

At the same time Somoza hit his enemies in the private sector by reimposing a profits tax on industry, raising the invoice tax from 6 to 8 percent, creating sales levies on 120 new products, and raising existing levies on 249 others. The money was needed to raise $43 million to meet a credit crisis. At the same time the government was taking out a $41 million loan to cover "budgetary deficiencies." Interest on the foreign debt was more than $52 million a year and the debt service was equal to 18 percent of the value of the nation's exports.

Nicaragua became even more of a tinderbox with the return in July of Los Doce, the group of respected intellectuals, wealthy businessmen, professionals and two priests who, during the October offensive, had gone into self-imposed exile in Costa Rica and signed a document in support of the Sandinistas. The government had tried the group in absentia in Masaya and issued an order for their arrest upon their return, even though the Masaya judges rejected government charges. The regime then told Taca Airlines to refuse to sell them tickets for their return but Somoza, trying to improve his image in the United States, had no alternative but to let them come back and try to weather the storm.

More than ten thousand people showed up at the airport, many walking the twelve-kilometer route after the guard closed down public transportation in that direction. Upon landing, the Group of Twelve, now dwindled to ten, told their cheering supporters they intended to fight Somoza "from our own soil." Among the exiles' first acts was to visit the antigovernment stronghold of Monimbó. The government overreacted, setting off new clashes when it arrested prominent journalist César Cortés Tellez in Masaya while he was en route to cover Los Doce.

Writer Sergio Ramírez Mercado served as spokesman for The Twelve and immediately told rallies that the group would work within the Broad Opposition

Front, (FAO) and urged all Nicaraguans who opposed Somoza to begin forming a single front. Ramírez, also a lawyer, was known throughout Latin America for his depiction of dictatorship in his novel *Do I Make You Afraid of Blood?* He had also published a book on Sandino. Joining him at the group's daily meetings and joining in the issuance of manifestos to "somehow save lives" were corporation lawyer Dr. Joaquín Cuadra Chamorro, whose son was an FSLN Tercerista leader; Emilio Baltodano Pallais, wealthy coffee planter and former chairman of the Nicaraguan Human Rights Commission; former rector of the National University Dr. Carlos Tunnermann; Ernesto Castillo, lawyer and professor and organizer of free legal services for the poor; Casimiro Sotelo, architect and urbanist; Dr. Carlos Gutierrez, a dentist active in professional circles; Ricardo Coronel Kautz, a prominent engineer; poet and priest Fernando Cardenal; and Miguel d'Escoto, a member of the Maryknoll order and witness before United States human rights panels.

Many of Somoza's advisers thought allowing the return of The Twelve a mistake, especially with the upcoming visit of the OAS human rights commission, an event they feared would set off riots and bloodshed. Two years later Somoza agreed that permitting the return of The Twelve was a mistake but complained that he had capitulated to American pressure at the time.

On July 18, 1978, the FAO called another strike, this one for twenty-four hours, to protest National Guard repression in which at least fourteen people in Jinotepe, Masaya and San Marcos had been killed. The FAO joined with the nation's labor unions to shut down some 80 percent of the nation, but business organizations did not take part in the action—a reversal from the January strike which had business support but little from the unions. Stores and factories closed and buses had but few riders. Demonstrations broke out in a half-dozen cities; most were broken up by guard tear gas. The strike, however, had little effect except to reiterate continued opposition to Somoza rule.

The FAO had gained considerable strength since its formation earlier in the year. It now numbered sixteen organizations comprised of moderate political groups, trade unions and student bodies. Among its supporters were the Group of Twelve, UDEL, Liberal Independent party, Nicaraguan Socialist party, Nicaraguan Christian Socialist party and others. Robelo served as a spokesman for the group which was by now prodding Washington toward a peaceful removal of Somoza.

When President Carter sent his letter of support to Somoza that same month, he was chastised by the foreign press, though Americans defended it by saying the message was a joint White House–State Department effort and that Somoza was worthy of support until the 1981 elections as no viable alternate leader was visible in the opposition. Many raised the specter of a second Cuba as the only likely immediate alternative. The rocket strike on the Bunker and the Sandinista attempts to gain legitimacy among the opposition did little to sway official American opinion at the time.

When Ambassador Solaun had delivered President Carter's letter, dated June 30, to Somoza, he had noted it was a private letter and not for publication. Ruling out the publication of the letter as ammunition to throw his opposition off balance,

Somoza saw another use for the communication. The letter was eventually leaked to the press, but in the meantime Somoza determined to use it to "cool off" President Andrés Pérez, who was among those who held Somoza responsible in the killing of Pedro Joaquín, a longtime friend. Somoza had sent several government officials to try to convince Andrés Pérez of his innocence, without much luck. But armed with Carter's letter Tacho flew one day in July to a secret rendezvous with Andrés Pérez on the island of Orchilla.

The Venezuelan president was "unyielding and hostile to me as if I had pulled the gun that had shot his friend," Tacho later recounted. "It didn't matter that Carter had complimented me and had said I was doing my best. Pérez didn't horse around and said flatly I would have to quit. I realized that Pérez had hated my guts since he shared exile with Pedro Joaquín, and worked for Betancourt when he was a communist. I knew now he was determined to overthrow me."

Returning to Managua after his unhappy encounter Somoza said he already knew Carter's letter by heart, having read it so many times, and it had begun to have a hollow ring. The letter complimented Somoza for "steps towards respecting human rights," citing his willingness to cooperate with the Interamerican Commission on Human Rights. The commission, it noted, would be favorably impressed that he had allowed the so-called Group of Twelve to return to "peaceful lives in Nicaragua."

"Tacho was so desperately searching for straws to hang on to, it was some time before he fully realized just how devious Carter's letter was," a close aide explained. For a while he actually thought the letter reinstated him as the "American he always thought he was," the aide added.

The letter in fact was a cautiously worded—except for the remarks on The Twelve—prodding Somoza along to elections. "I was also encouraged," the letter stated, "to hear your suggestion for a reform of the electoral system in order to ensure fair and free elections in which all political parties could compete fairly. This step is essential to the functioning of a democracy." "Carter," Somoza's aide noted, "was telling Tacho he ran a dictatorship." Carter ended, "I look forward to hearing of the implementation of your decisions (including amnesty for political prisoners) and appreciate very much your announcement of these constructive actions. I hope that you will continue to communicate fully with my Ambassador, Mauricio Solaun, who enjoys my complete confidence." The letter ultimately made Tacho realize, the aide explained, "just how far Washington was now from Managua."

Somoza continued to attack the unrest as the work of a minority and refused to admit there might be a threat to the stability of his government or that there was any likelihood of his leaving Managua before 1981. With *The Washington Post's* Karen DeYoung in July he discussed the situation at length. "I want you to know something, you are living a very interesting experience in Nicaragua. There's no other country that has been able to stand the publicity, the onslaught of subversion, of misguidance, etc. This is a tremendous society." Tacho told the *Post* he was farther away from a fall than in January 1978. He predicted less unrest in the last six months of the year. "I think the [unrest] is going to quiet down because we are going to move the Liberal party and when the Liberal party moves, it's a devastating machine. It's going to be quiet. I have identified my problem. A small minority that are handled by the leftists, and they are all the ones who are creating all the problem, the potential problem. I think the best way to handle it is to treat them politically, show them that there's a bigger force than them in the civilian population that will make them quiet down.

"They thought they could overthrow the government just by using Chamorro's assassination as a fuse," he told DeYoung. "But now that they've seen that the people who are the vanguard of [opposition] organization are the Sandinistas, they are now thinking twice because the Sandinistas represent the Marxists, which means they have to give away their property. There are a lot of people who say that all of this agitation is not in their interest. Businessmen and some of the labor groups. Who is doing the agitation? They are kids between fourteen and seventeen, and they're a very small minority. I'm not saying they have support." In reference to demands he get out of office Somoza said, "I would be crazy." He admitted they wanted him to leave but, "Yeah, well, that's their privilege."

Tacho continued to express the opinion that things were going to wind themselves down and problems would go away. "I think we're going through a process of mediating. People are seeing that one side offers them something that they don't know anything about. Confiscation of their property. Changing of the structures. And the other side is the one of the Liberal establishment. Ours. And that's permeating among the people." If the "kids" who were threatening the Somoza regime did not go away, Tacho said, "Well, we're going to have a cultural confrontation. You see, we have not moved our political people yet. Well, we have not moved the Liberal party in the sense that the Liberal party would take political activity and neutralize these people. This in many ways, including fighting in the streets."

The political campaign for the 1981 elections would actually begin as early as August 1978, Tacho said. "I wanted to save the country from that political campaign. You know, actually go out and get to the grass roots, and talk to them, indoctrinate them, and explain to them what these other guys are going to do. They are forcing me to do that, to turn on a switch and say okay, we're going to start working on the voters and the people for the campaign and we're going to see Nicaragua in a campaign that's going to take us two and a half years." The possibility of this causing more violence, however, was in Somoza's mind. "Oh yeah," he said to DeYoung concerning the possibility of violence. "And you see what these people don't understand is that we've had fifty years of constitutional government and people here believe that the government should not be changed violently, that it should go through an election. It's very simple to say let's break the law. That's a human right? Well . . ."

According to Somoza, nothing could prove to be the handwriting on the wall for his regime. "I don't think so. I'm a hard nut. You know why? Because I believe that things should be done orderly. I swear to you that I am not motivated by anything else but the best interest of the Nicaraguans."

And if the people didn't agree? "They elected me for a term and they've got to stand me. That's it. That's the essence of democracy. The answer is that you uphold the constitutional conventions. Otherwise, this country will go to hell."

Among his supporters, Somoza counted many. "I think you would find them on the farms, you will find them in the small shopkeepers, in the masses of the Nicaraguan people. Six months ago, we had an election [the widely boycotted municipal elections of February] where the Liberal party had the majority. That's the best contention I have. I don't remember the percentage, but well over 50 percent of those registered voted."

As for his enemies, Somoza said he could not dismiss communist influence among Los Doce. "I analyze all of them. I see what their background is, what they've done, what they've been trying to do, how they've motivated some of the people to do it. . . . We've had a very difficult situation here with the Conservative party. They have been prostituted by the prosperity and peace that this government has given the Conservatives. They have reaped the profits, and politically, they haven't done very much. And their sons, they don't want to be Conservatives like that, they want to be active politically. So they pose a problem. Some of those fathers for instance, Cuadra, Baltodano, they're both in a corner, put there by their children."

The huge welcome at the airport for the returning Los Doce was given "because a lot of those people have been freely working in the population of Nicaragua. There is political freedom in Nicaragua. Look, the way I've been brought up is that you have to respect your constitution, and that's where my game is. That's part of the great stability of the United States. There are a few things which are sacred to people. One of them is their stability. There are certain things that are untouchable, and that's the secret of a great democracy."

Somoza said that at the beginning of the turmoil in Nicaragua the international press had not been fair to him, but it had become more so toward summer. As for his personal wealth, "Well, with inflation and everything, I think maybe $100 million, but I wouldn't want you to put it in the paper because that wouldn't be cricket. There are certain things we keep by book value, acquisition cost. There's a lot of myths to how we handle our businesses, but I think we handle them properly. A lot of allegations they make are not true."

Somoza said the communist pressure in Nicaragua would never die down because of the Soviet Union and Cuba and "a sort of vendetta between Castro and the Somozas. From the time he was at the University of Havana, the fact that we were anticommunist, that we were a dictatorship, the Somozas got singled out. My father began the social revolution in this country, passing the most advanced labor code in Latin America. He made enemies of the communists. Somoza was a bad example [for the communists] in Latin America. The capitalists didn't like it. The right called my father a communist. Castro, before he got to be an activist, he got brainwashed by the activists. Castro had sent one man here to ask for training when he was in the Sierra Maestra. Instead, we sent munitions to Batista. My life association with democratic countries against the communists has brought me the ire of the communists. And my local boys here—most of the main leaders have committed this mistake of going out in the bush, fighting like guerrillas, and they got killed."

But at a Mexico City press conference on July 10, Plutarco Hernández Sancho, one of the six members of the Dirección Nacional del Frente Sandinista, told reporters the Frente was preparing "the general insurrection of the people." Plutarco clarified the statement by saying "all steps are being taken to prepare for this. The raising of the consciousness and the mobilization and arming of the masses. It is a difficult process which takes time," he said, "but its main objective is insurrection of the masses, to seize power. There is no other way in Nicaragua."

CHAPTER 12

The Palace Captured

The night of August 21, 1978, was hot and humid. Novelist Graham Greene and I were in Panama City visiting the small apartment of Dr. Ramiro Contreras in whose bedroom was a larger-than-life portrait of "Zero" Contreras, leader of the attack on the Castillo home, who had been killed nearly two years earlier in Managua. His lovely Panamanian wife had chosen to remarry. Her new husband was Contreras's brother, Ramiro.

She had made a cake, Nicaraguan music filled the apartment and some of the women, pregnant combatants of the FSLN, rocked to the beat. Latin American guerrillas can be deceptive-looking but there was nothing deceptive about the swarthy muscular man whose thirty-seventh birthday was being celebrated. He was German Pomares Ordoñez. Prior to the party he had been held captive in Tegucigalpa. The Honduran authorities had threatened to turn him over to Somoza who would have considered the stocky veteran fighter a prize. But student demonstrations in the streets of the Honduran capital finally persuaded the military authorities to acquiesce to the request of Panamanian leader Brigadier General Omar Torrijos that Pomares be handed over to Panama, where he was extended political asylum.

As the party wore on Pomares, never removing his black beret, talked quietly about the fight to come. He agreed that the FSLN now needed a spectacular success to take the initiative in the brewing war against Somoza. He voiced concern that the Sandinistas would be cheated by a coup d'état which would leave a system of *somocismo* even without Somoza. The Sandinistas wanted the whole system removed, not just the man. The FSLN wanted radical change, Pomares said. That could only come with war or revolution, or the people would remain subject to the corrupt system that had already "enslaved" Nicaragua for decades. Less than twelve hours later, at noon the next day, a new Zero led an act so audacious that Nicaragua was suddenly front-page news throughout the world: Guerrilla forces seized the National Palace.

The National Palace, a durable building almost fifty years old, still sits undamaged among the ruins and grassy vacant lots of what was busy downtown Managua prior to the 1972 earthquake. It faces Lake Managua on a plaza reaching over deserted potholed streets on which also face the damaged, empty national cathedral

176

and the undamaged national theater. The building was a beehive of activity at midday on Tuesday, August 22. On a lamppost on one corner of a nearby street hung a dried wreath in memory of Pedro Joaquín Chamorro. A strong wind blew off the lake, bringing some relief to the usual crush of citizens coming to pay taxes and more than a thousand others doing business or working in the building, which housed not only the Congress but the ministries of finance and the interior. Somoza had never bothered to occupy the presidential offices there, preferring the more secure Bunker quarters.

Plump Carmen Parrales Tellez, who maintained an improvised open-air restaurant on the corner of the palace next to the Central Plaza, was cooking fried pork and other luncheon dishes with her daughters for her noontime customers when she noticed two olive green trucks drive to the side door of the seat of government. Out jumped smartly uniformed cadets of the EEBI (the Basic Infantry Training School) with their distinctive black berets and well-polished boots. Another truck had unloaded a squad at the opposite side door. Carmen heard one of the men give the familiar command, "Viene El Hombre," as he opened a path through the crowd toward the building's entrance. Still frying a piece of pork, she looked around to see in what direction *El Hombre,* Somoza, was coming. Suddenly shooting rang out. Carmen, who had been operating her little kitchen-diner for twenty-five years, didn't wait to see what was happening. Grabbing her money, she fled for cover into the park with her daughters and customers.

Only two and one-half minutes after the soldiers had disembarked from their trucks in smart military fashion the entire Nicaraguan Congress had been captured intact. By disguising themselves as Somoza's elite, twenty-five members of the Terceristas Sandinista commando "Rigoberto López Pérez" captured to hold as hostage forty-nine deputies, two dozen palace reporters, and nearly 1,500 others present in the salmon-colored building. Most were hiding behind doors and couches or under desks, not knowing the origin or the meaning of the shots they heard.

Working expertly, the Sandinistas broke into groups of four inside the palace. Each member was assigned a number designating not only his name but also his group and function in the raid. They had fanned through the hallways of the blocklong building, yelling, "Out of the way, here comes *el jefe,* " disarming soldiers standing guard or loitering, who were used to such precautions when Tacho paid a visit.

Commanders "Cero" and "Dos" led their groups up the wide stairs toward the second floor Chamber of Deputies. Discussion had just opened to give approval to the signing of two new United States AID loans for nutrition and education. The Sandinistas moved quickly to chain doors and ferret out high officials in their offices, careful not to stretch their limited forces too thin. As commanders Cero and Dos reached the main hallway they encountered two guard officers, one of them a captain with a machine gun, guarding the doors.

"Here comes *el jefe,* " Cero shouted again in an authoritative voice. The guardsmen, not fooled, immediately opened fire. The guerrillas in Dos's group returned the shots, killing the captain and wounding the other soldier. The gun blasts were heard downstairs by comandante "Tres," whose group was entering the offices of the minister of the interior. A captain and lieutenant who served as bodyguards to the minister ran from the office to seek the origin of the gunfire but were cut down as they passed through the door.

The discussion in the Blue Room, as the Chamber of Deputies was called, continued despite the firing but was hushed when the short, handsome Cero stuck his G-3 rifle between the emerald green doors of the stately chamber and walked in giving the order, "The guard. Everyone to the floor."

"Without warning he fired into the ceiling and shouted, 'Everyone to the floor!' " *Novedades* reporter Luis Manuel Martínez recalled. "We all dived down. We could see there were eight other armed men and one woman who had come in after him and taken up positions."[1]

Although many of the congressmen—and bodyguards in the gallery—had pistols, they offered no resistance. Most stayed down under their desks; few dared move their heads while the guerrillas moved through the chamber to take up positions. The only man not down on the floor was Somoza's cousin, Luis Pallais Debayle, who remained frozen at the presidential table. The initial thought that ran through the minds of many was that the soldiers who had entered the chamber were indeed National Guardsmen, now staging the oft-rumored coup d'état and ready to begin eliminating what many called the "rubber stamp" congress. The internal and external strife developing over the last eight months had given them ample reason to believe anything was possible. The soldiers were wearing uniforms similar to those of the EEBI, Tachito's soldiers. Everyone knew how much the younger Somoza's lust for power had grown since his father's heart attack.

But the legislators' fear of a guard-inspired mass execution soon passed. The officer who leaped through the door to terrorize them was forty-two-year-old Eden Pastora, known to the other twenty-four members of the commando as Cero. A medical student in Nicaragua and Mexico between stints as a guerrilla, he was carrying out a daring act he had planned and fought to put into action for eight years. The FSLN had acceded to the plan—broadly called "Operation Death to Somocismo, 'Carlos Fonseca Amador' "—only fifteen days previously.

The Sandinistas had waited until August 22 to get the optimum gain from their risky operation—they knew the building would be filled with congressmen gathered to vote on the important economic aid package. The attack plan itself was named "Operacion Chanchera," or the assault against *la casa de los chanchos* ("the house of swine"). Cero's first in command was thirty-year-old Hugo Torres Jiménez, a seasoned guerrilla who had served as "Uno" once before—in the attack on the Castillo home. Along with Dos, twenty-two-year-old Dora María Tellez, a former medical student from León and the only woman in the group, they had recruited twenty-two other Sandinistas. The average age was twenty; three commando members were just eighteen years old. Most of them had never been in Managua before, meeting in a safe house in the capital only three days before the attack was to take place and willingly accepting the risk of death. Except for the three commanders, none of the others had ever seen each other or even knew the nature of the plan.

Cero was the only one who had ever been in the National Palace—when he was a small boy accompanying his mother, who went to pay taxes. Dos had never seen the Chamber of Deputies except on television news broadcasts. But with the help of others they had studied the layout of the building for weeks until they knew every door and portal.[2]

On the morning of the attack the twenty-two recruits were advised of the secret plan. They dressed in uniforms made by clandestine tailors and boots bought in three different stores. They were equipped with red and black handkerchiefs for identification, two more kerchiefs to tie possible wounds, a flashlight, gas masks, rope, bags to fill with emergency drinking water in the palace and bicarbonate for stomach problems in a gas attack. They were also given weapons taken in previous combat with guardsmen—two Uzi machine guns, a G-3, an M-3, an M-2, twenty Garand rifles, a Browning pistol and fifty grenades as well as three hundred rounds of ammunition apiece.[3] The trucks had been bought for 13,000 córdobas each and painted an off-color olive drab, a factor Cero was concerned would give them away. The deputies lay on the floor for twenty minutes after the attack, while guerrillas took their names, tied them up and began photographing them with a Polaroid camera. When Dos asked *Novedades* reporter Martínez his name, Dora María Tellez shouted, "Cero! Cero! Martínez is here!" Cero turned to Martínez, an official apologist for the government by virtue of his position, and said, "If the Somoza forces attack, you will be the first shot." Elsewhere in the building other commandos rounded up government employees and officials. Besides Pallais, among government officials caught were Interior Minister José Antonio Mora, his chief assistant, several other Somoza relatives including José Somoza's son, and Deputy Eduardo Chamorro. Not caught was General Alegrett, who was having a coffee break.

As the Sandinistas were taking inventory of their newly won prize, firing erupted outside the building. Cero ran from the chamber to discover a guard patrol attempting to break through the principal doorway. He took a grenade from the belts crisscrossing his chest and threw a perfect strike below, killing four soldiers on the red marble steps and dispersing the rest of the assault squad.

Somoza learned of the situation as he was sitting down to eat lunch. His immediate reaction was to order an indiscriminate attack against the palace. The guard squads, led by American mercenary and Somoza military adviser Michael Echanis, attempted assaults to take the building but could not get close enough—Sandinista sharpshooters held them at bay. A helicopter made passes over the building for fifteen minutes, strafing the windows where the gunmen were located and wounding one guerrilla in the leg. Tachito helped in the attack command, but he stayed behind the firing line as it was forced back by the Sandinistas. "It was evident that Echanis prepared the assault with all of the elements he had, so we gathered some of the most prized *Somocista* prisoners and placed them in front of the windows," Cero said. "They were trembling with fear and believed that the guardsmen were going to kill them without further thought. It was at this moment that Luis Pallais and José Abrego telephoned Somoza and asked him not to leave them to die."

Some twenty minutes after he had ordered the assault, Somoza received Pallais's phone call giving him the first Sandinista demand—cease fire or the guerrillas would begin executing the hostages, one every two hours, until he decided to discuss conditions for their release. Somoza ordered the guard to stop shooting. The decision left the soldiers furious, especially Echanis, who had a six-million-dollar budget to run all antiguerrilla warfare operations for the guard.

Echanis later reported he took seventy-eight of his black-bereted commandos to the palace in trucks when it was seized. "They shot up the lead truck and killed one of my captains. I dragged his body around the side of the building.

"We wanted to hit them right then, before they got organized, but they told us by radio to hold off," Echanis said he drew up plans to attack the palace for the chiefs of staff.

"We could have taken the building in eighteen minutes. I figured maybe two hundred to three hundred would be killed. The plan was to shock the building with tank fire and blow the doors with recoilless rifles. I was going to helicopter in with my commandos and drop down through the roof hatches. The old man wouldn't buy it and the only reason was they held Papa Chepe's [José Somoza's] son. My guys were unhappy."[4]

A little later Pallais called Somoza again to inform him that the Sandinistas had proposed that Archbishop Obando y Bravo and two other bishops then coincidentally meeting in Managua act as intermediaries. The ambassadors of Costa Rica and Panama also offered their services as mediators. The churchmen quickly reported back with the guerrillas' demands: (1) the release of fifty-nine political prisoners; (2) one million dollars; (3) repeated broadcasts over government radio of an almost two-hour-long Sandinista communiqué; and (4) Mexican, Panamanian or Venezuelan planes to escort them from the country. The Sandinistas also demanded the guard stay some four hundred yards from the building and that the government immediately accept the demands of striking hospital workers.[5]

The eyes of the world immediately focused on Managua. The Sandinistas' audacious raid was "the biggest thing to happen in years, anywhere. Where else could they ever capture a national palace, with the congress intact?" a Guatemalan newsman asked. There was undisguised admiration for the action throughout Latin America.

Envoys carrying demands back and forth between the palace and the Bunker worked throughout the night. The condition of the hostages was different from those that had existed in the Castillo home. The congressmen remained tied up, there was little if any food, and there were only four bathrooms in the building. Some hostages needing to relieve themselves did so in a wastepaper basket behind the chamber's speaker's lectern. They lived with the awareness that Somoza was not beyond calling on the guard to storm the palace, thus forfeiting their lives. They also knew failure to comply with the guerrillas' demands might spell death for any of them. As Dos told a United Press International reporter on the phone, the execution threat was "no joke, this is something very serious."

The bishops, acting as intermediaries in the negotiations, reported that Somoza would not deal with the Sandinistas if anybody was harmed. Soon after the church-men left that night, the guerrillas untied the legs of the legislator hostages in the large rectangular chamber and took them upstairs to an office on the third floor.

"At 1:20 on Wednesday morning they untied my legs and took me outside," reported Martínez, the Cuban exile now working for the Somoza newspaper. "Cero personally took me upstairs and put me on a steel office chair outside an office where about twenty-seven legislators were being held prisoners. I spoke to him for about fifteen minutes. He asked why I attacked the people who are making the revolution." Martínez said he could not remember what he replied. "Monsignor Obando y Bravo gave me absolution. He told me to pray and I prayed. I prayed the whole time. I was terrified the whole time. On one occasion they caught me trying to loosen the cord around my wrists and knocked me on the floor."

During the night three hundred people, including one hostage in a wheelchair, escaped by pushing out an air conditioner and climbing out a window. The guerrillas later released all children and most of the women but more than one thousand hostages remained in the building—more than the guerrillas seemed to have bar-gained for.

Wednesday dawned, a grueling day for all sides. The threat of execution of three of the hostages became stronger if the demands were not met. Early in the day Comandante Cero was overheard by a radio reporter as saying, "There will be a massacre here." The mediating team of the bishops was joined by Costa Rican Ambassador José María Echeverry and Carlos Boyd Arias of Panama. The five men entered the National Palace before 8:00 A.M. and then reported to Somoza. Tacho, hoping for support and tales of horror, was angered to learn that many of the hostages sympathized with the Sandinistas—some actually volunteered to remain prisoners in order for the Sandinistas to win their demands.

Newsmen on the inside managed at times to make calls to their newspapers on the outside. They reported that life inside the palace was becoming unbearable, the overcrowding in rooms making the heat rise despite the air conditioning. They described how the podium in the chamber was draped with a huge red and black Sandinista flag. Some of the guerrillas continued to hide their identity with red and black kerchiefs around their mouths. Among the captives there were those who expressed unabashed admiration for Dos, the petite, coolly efficient woman guerrilla. Others wrote that Cero was "impressive. As handsome as Che Guevara."

An agreement in principle was reached early Wednesday morning. Final ar-rangements took until late in the night to work out—the mediators left the palace at 10:00 P.M. Two planes had been prepared to fly to Managua from the Panama airport—one a Copa airliner and the other a Hercules C-130 air force plane from Venezuela. Though the evacuation details had been agreed upon around 4:00 P.M. Wednesday, Somoza tried a last-minute move to dislodge the Sandinistas—he gave them a three-hour ultimatum to leave the palace for the airport and exile. The guerrillas refused to move for the obvious reason that it would soon be dark.

Wednesday evening saw a more relaxed atmosphere after the long hours of tension. Soldiers lounged on leaking sandbags in front of the Telcor telecommunications building two blocks from the palace. Some talked freely about the daring raid; others were not so friendly. One group warned newsmen away, refusing them access to the Red Cross post with tents and a half-dozen ambulances on standby on the far side of the plaza next to the Rubén Darío Theater and the train tracks.

Many Nicaraguans stayed in their homes to listen to the Sandinista communiqué on the radio or watch it on television. It was clear that Somoza had had little choice but to negotiate and bend to the Sandinistas' demands. The FSLN was in control of events. The public image of the guerrillas was one of romantic freedom fighters.

"The war communiqué makes us believe Somoza has accepted the Sandinistas' demands," said one barrio resident Wednesday night, sitting around a radio in his clapboard house with his ten children. "Everyone in the world is talking about the Sandinistas," he said. There was no question as to where poor Nicaraguans' sympathies lay. They had heard every word of the Sandinista "War Communiqué Number One," read over a nationwide radio hookup at 6:00 that evening.

The communiqué was read three times a day for the next two days and published in the press the next morning. It took 105 minutes of radio and television time to read the political statement. Businessmen were unhappy because of what they considered the socialist tone, which took the wealthy classes and tame opposition to task. The message had a strong leftist tinge that made private entrepreneurs uneasy about what the future might hold.

The Sandinistas called the anti-Somoza struggle a war waged between two sides. The first was represented by the worker, the peasant, the exploited consumer and the student who were forced to "battle against miserable salaries and the *latifundista* and forced to earn their wages under the shadow of *somocismo*. They are the poor of our nation, the humble, those who have supported the entire weight of economic exploitation and political-military repression of the Somoza tyranny. And only these people, firmly supported by the workers and peasants, will be able to forge a society of free men."

On the other end of the economic ladder were the "rich Conservative party members who have continually sold out to Somoza; the new rich of the Christian Socialist party who have continuously begged Somoza to accept their legitimacy; and the old rich of the Liberal party who form the bulwark of Somoza's support. The other people with money, such as the trade people, industrialists and big financial capital, until a few months ago had no great participation in the anti-Somoza struggle. It was not until the offensive of October 1977 that all these forces, with the exception of the financiers, pronounced themselves to be in favor of a dialogue with the tyrant," the communiqué said. "These gentlemen want an escape in which the National Guard will participate as though it were a savior. To tell the truth they don't trust the people. . . .

"Now, to speak clearly, we want to affirm that we are not opposed to the fact that the financial capital, the commercial capital, the industrial capital and all the types of capital that can exist take part in the anti-Somoza fight. What we cannot accept is that it is they who try to make the conditions for Somoza to leave power.

For a long time they supported Somoza, silently complying with him and causing a sectarianism among them that even led them to deny support to Pedro Joaquín Chamorro.

"They can't try to impose formulas in which their personal interests come before those of the populace. . . ."

Other points included were charges that "in the military academy *somocismo* has deformed the minds of hundreds of young Nicaraguans. . . . We call on the young men who are in the National Guard to rebel against Somoza, against Somoza's son, against Somoza's brother, against the leaders of the National Guard. . . . Don't join the guard, don't sign new contracts, desert with your weapons, judge [those] who torture and murder the people."

The communiqué ended with a call for the "democratic and revolutionary forces to fight for the installation of a true and democratic and popular government in which the participation of all Nicaraguans is allowed without sectarianism of any kind." It was then generally the opinion of the Sandinistas that they would oppose any solution that did not provide for a complete change. Somoza himself was not unhappy with the communiqué. He told newsmen it would at last show the world whom he was fighting.

The communiqué had told the people to prepare for the final offensive, and the threat of *somocismo* without Somoza was reiterated to the people, as it had been by Cero in the Chamber of Deputies. There he had cursed the Conservatives as well as the Liberals, belittling the former and accusing them of complicity with the Somoza government and saying their turn was over as the "opposition" to the dictatorship. To drive home his point Cero gave each of the Conservative deputies a bullet, telling them they could show their opposition by using it against Somoza.

A few minutes after midnight on Thursday morning this newsman managed to reach Cero by telephone. A low voice answered the phone, *"Diga?"* His cool, calm voice confirmed that their demands had been met. They and the political prisoners would leave the airport that morning for Panama and Venezuela. The departure from the National Palace was set for 9:00 A.M. and they would release their hostages at the bus door. Cero refused to answer questions about the ten-million-dollar ransom, saying it was "a military secret" though it was known that Tacho, ever the shrewd businessman, had bargained the desired figure down to a twentieth. The Sandinistas were in no mood to argue. Cero said that the money was secondary and lack of sleep made them anxious to get on the road before fatigue worked in the government's favor.

Thursday dawned cloudy but it was soon sunny, clear and hot. Some of the guard were in an ugly mood. "We should not give in to their demands. They will only go off with the political prisoners and return with arms they are going to purchase with the money we pay them," said a guard officer as he sat in his jeep before the National Theater waiting the outcome of the 9:00 A.M. departure. He hissed out the words with anger but refused to discuss whether others in the guard shared his opinion. It appeared they did.

The tired-looking archbishop and his two bishops entered the palace at 8:15

A.M., soon followed by the Panamanian and Costa Rican ambassadors. A score of newsmen tried to press forward, but they were shut off from a view of the palace door by the elevated land and tree-shaded plaza in between them and the building.

"The people will obey or be shot," a young lieutenant ordered, waving his machine pistol in the air and ordering his soldiers not to be intimidated by the foreigners and their cameras.

The tops of the buses were barely visible before the ornate palace door, a tall ironwork affair. A few minutes after nine the National Guard suddenly came to life and began moving in on the palace. "They are gone." Elderly deputies and other hostages began to move slowly down the steps of the palace entrance.

With a lone motorcyclist in the lead and three ambulances following in their wake with the International Red Cross representatives, the bus loaded with Sandinista guerrillas took off for the airport. Accompanying them as security were Archbishop Obando y Bravo and the bishops of León and Granada, two diplomats and three government hostages, including Luis Pallais.

"We'll be back in two months," Cero promised as he waved his rifle to *Novedades* reporter Martínez, and he entered the bus last. With the black and red Sandinista flag flying and the guerrillas holding their guns aloft for all to see, the trip to the airport was a victory parade. Screaming, waving Nicaraguans jumped up and down on the dusty banks of the northern highway. For nine miles they cheered the guerrillas. The sympathetic outpouring of feelings for the Sandinistas was blatant —the people loved them.

There was no military or police escort, in compliance with the negotiated agreement. Hundreds of people tried to keep up with the Sandinistas, running for miles in their wake. Others tried to hitch rides or catch buses to the airport.

Las Mercedes was in an uproar as thousands poured into the terminal waiting rooms to catch a glimpse of their "heroes." "Yes, they are our heroes," said a youth taking my arm. "To hell with the Somozas."

The Venezuelan Air Force C-130 and Panamanian "Copa" prop aircraft were stationed at the end of the runway, out of sight of the terminal. The shops in the terminal were closed as were the offices. When the crush of people broke several windows on the second-floor observation deck, the National Guard cleared them off. One youth was beaten.

Thousands of youths chanted Sandinista and old leftist political slogans: "United, workers and peasants, with Sandinistas, we will win."

A young woman in a checked shirt climbed onto a seat and gave a Sandinista political pep talk to the crowd. It was like a rerun of the war communiqué. Nicaraguans were beginning to know it by heart—it had been published in the papers that morning and would be played again that evening after the guerrillas had gone. Other young Sandinista speakers had their say, even though under the guns of the guardsmen.

At the planes the guerrillas appeared to be in no hurry to take off. Newsmen managed to reach their aircraft and take pictures; there were no police or National Guard. The guerrillas handed arms to the newly released fifty-nine political prisoners. They had accumulated more than forty pistols just in disarming the deputies' bodyguards the day before.

The lone Sandinista casualty raised himself from the stretcher and saluted with his gun. Cero was the last to enter the plane. He turned slightly and saluted the distant crowd with his rifle. His pose captured by photographers became a popular FSLN poster.

As the Venezuelan plane took off, tailgated by the Panamanian craft, there was a tremendous roar from the crowd. His face alive with feeling, a tall youth, shaking his fist, said, "They'll be back, be sure of that."

Hundreds of youths who had been taunting the guardsmen at an airport gate now had to run from an elderly guard officer who came charging with a pack of guardsmen waving their guns and cursing loudly. They did not shoot, limiting themselves to swearing. An hour later people still stood in little clusters along the airport highway obviously discussing for the hundredth time the day's dramatic events and their possible consequences.

Somoza kept the international press waiting most of the afternoon near the Bunker as he held a "political prayer meeting" with members of the cabinet and some of the hostages. They could be heard applauding Somoza's statements, but it was not the emotional applause experienced on the airport highway.

Tacho was not his usual glib self when he faced the press. He appeared subdued, more drawn than usual and obviously under great strain. He confirmed that the guerrillas were paid a half-million dollars and said he "hoped the people of Nicaragua understand why I acted as I did. My intention was to save human lives." Referring to Comandante Cero he said, "There were pregnant women inside and he wouldn't let them out." At another point he said, "It's sad, but it's a reality that we must take all the precautions to avoid a repeat of this."

Somoza said he was "grateful to the representatives of the church and to the ambassadors for their cooperation," and when asked about the way he had handled the capture of the palace, he asked, "Let history judge me." When confirming he had released fifty-nine political prisoners, including leader Tomás Borge, he denied them the label political prisoner, calling the term "debatable. Most of them were in jail for assault and battery, murder, robbery, kidnapping and so on."

When asked whether he felt betrayed by the United States which had been watching the human rights developments in Nicaragua, he replied by saying, "I'm a politician and I recognize that every administration has different attitudes. Therefore a change of attitudes of the government in the United States . . . I don't consider it an act of betrayal. So therefore they and we have to adjust our new relations." He dismissed the previous forty-five-hour drama as "a continuation of a battle the government of Nicaragua started in 1959 when Castro came to power. It is something that has become popular in Latin America" and then avoided directly answering another question about the Nicaraguan discontent. "This particular act to regain their people who had been legally placed in jail [means] they can count on people who will be ready to take violent actions in Nicaragua. Therefore we must be prepared for an escalation of such acts."

Somoza charged that the Sandinista National Liberation Front had been liquidated and that the commando group involved "new leaders." Los Doce ordered the attack, Somoza alleged, and said, "We are going to have to spend more on security. . . . These people are trying to take the freedom away from the Nicaraguans in the same way it was done in Cuba." He warned that "Nicaraguans have to face up to the fact that ideologies other than traditional ones are on the ascent in Nicaragua and that someday the country will be divided into democratic and communist people." He placed blame on "complicity by Radio Havana and some Cuban officials."

Most of the press conference was taken up by pro-Somoza newsmen and officials making their own declarations of backing and congratulating him on saving lives.

Talk of a coup d'état continued. One officer who bragged as if he were supporting a coup was hard-liner Brigadier General José Iván Alegrett Pérez, the National Guard chief of operations, who took credit for having cleaned out the guerrillas in the mountains. But arrested in another plan, which never reached more than the talking stage, was its would-be instigator, Lieutenant Colonel Bernardino Larios, a forty-two-year-old electrical engineer assigned to ENALUF, the government electric utility. The attempt was detected as he sounded out other officers who had graduated with him from the Nicaraguan Military Academy.

Alegrett made no bones about his opposition to Somoza's new, light-handed policies. Tall, stocky, blondish, Alegrett was a hearty, bluff professional soldier whose cramped base quarters were crowded with captured weapons and bookshelves of pornography interspersed with such volumes as *How to Score with Single Girls, Getting Sex Through Hypnotism* and the like. As early as March 1978, Alegrett was urging to be allowed to go into towns like Masaya and clean out the rebels. He protested at being held back, warning that the longer Somoza waited, the greater the number of people who would die.

Somoza's virtual surrender when the National Palace was seized sent Alegrett into a rage. He drew up plans with mercenary Echanis to take the palace back by force, although he also admitted as many as three hundred hostages might be killed. "Somoza threw in the towel to save three hundred lives. It's going to cost three thousand lives before this is over," he fumed.

Alegrett's passionate dislike of Somoza's handling of things did not die easily. One Sunday when he and his wife were passing through the lobby of the Intercontinental Hotel before going to church he took one more opportunity to sneer at Tacho, telling reporters, "When they had him in the hospital after his heart attack, they must have cut his balls off."

Mercenary Echanis also refused to hold back his disgust with the regime's submission and reiterated his friend Alegrett's words. "What did they do? They freed fifty-nine political prisoners. They gave the Sandinistas back all of their generals and political chiefs. Politically it was the only thing he could do. Militarily it was a disaster. It demoralized the troops. I'm sending my commandos back out into the jungle. I'll work them hard, they'll shoot every day and we'll build them back up."

When asked by the Associated Press why he was in Nicaragua, Echanis said for the money and because he hated communism. "Secretary of State Cyrus Vance sent me a letter. He said I was a disgrace to the United States. He urged me not to violate any human rights, and said I shouldn't kill any noncombatants. I took that to mean it was okay to kill combatants." His specialty, he said, was "over-border operations," but he added that the government would not allow him to pursue Sandinistas into Costa Rica. "That's absurd. They [Costa Rica] don't even have an army. I could take the whole country with 150 men." He was in charge of counterintelligence for the guard. At one point he told newsmen at the hotel that "we're after intelligence from journalists. You people are the best intelligence gatherers we've got." He said reporters' telephones had been tapped.[6] Most journalists, aware of that possibility, were careful to protect opposition sources. Most photographers covering street violence and demonstrations did not run photographs of unmasked persons.

Officially, the number of mercenaries in Nicaragua never was very large. Besides Echanis and Sanders there were seven other American mercenaries, five Cuban exiles, a few West Germans and, near the end of the war, six Argentinians. One active Guatemalan major fought for the guard; he was severely wounded later in the Nueva Guinea campaign.

On the surface Echanis and Sanders were two happy-go-lucky Oregon boys cashing in on their Green Beret training and their Vietnam years. They lived in a trailer, had girlfriends by the score, raced around town in their guard jeep and had a high time. But they were killers. Mike, with his wide sideburns and Fu Manchu moustache, was a martial arts expert and wrote about the tactics of silent warfare for *Soldier of Fortune* and *Black Belt* magazines, appearing on the covers of both. He followed a vegetarian routine and seemed to believe he was immortal. Where kids back home practiced karate as a sport—perhaps daydreaming about someday smashing a mugger's windpipe—Mike practiced what he preached. Chuck never said much. He was a great one for shaking hands and grinning but his flat gray eyes never smiled. When he went hunting, he said, he never shot to kill. He preferred wounding.

Echanis told Tom Fenton of the Associated Press he wanted to stay in Nicaragua for "one good fight. I could have stayed in Special Forces, or trained the United States' secret antiterrorist unit," he said, "but what's the point. You train years and may never get to fight. Here I fight all the time. I led the attack against Granada when the Sandinistas seized it in October. I was in San Carlos and Rivas. I've fought all over this country. . . . U.S. officials freak out when they see me in my guard uniform, but there's not a damn thing they can do about it."

Echanis was certain civil war was inevitable in Nicaragua, that President Somoza had no concept of how unpopular he was with the people, and that if he (Echanis) had been born into a Nicaraguan peasant family he probably would be fighting the National Guard. This last line stunned Nicaraguan officials. When Fenton's dispatch was sent from the Intercontinental, Somoza aide Max Kelly "came running into the Intercon trying to get it killed. The thing the old man objected to most were the allegations that if Echanis were a peasant, he'd be fighting Somoza too," Fenton said.

In the same interview, when commenting on the seizure of the National Palace,

Echanis had this to say: "Did you see Cero wearing frags [hand grenades] on his shoulders? Very unprofessional. That guy is a punk who has been watching John Wayne movies. What fractures me is they didn't even hold out for the ten million. Somoza had the cash flown in from New Orleans. It stayed in a plane out on the runway. Some of my guys were guarding it."[7]

The palace attack was timely, coming on the heels of an FAO plan calling for a transitional government to replace Somoza. With its broad range of anti-Somoza movements, the FAO had become the principal opposition. On Friday, August 25, it declared a general strike to continue until Somoza and his family quit the presidency and the National Guard. Spokesmen claimed the general strike in January failed because "it did not have the popular support as this one has." They stressed that the MPU, the United People's Movement, which included leftist organizations such as socialists and communists, seventeen unions, student groups and others, was fully supporting the new effort.

Somoza's only words for the strikers were "good luck to them." Twelve days later he continued to dismiss the strike with a contemptuous half-smirk. "They'll get tired or go broke."

Two presidents in Washington. Anastasio Somoza García (Tacho I) and Franklin D. Roosevelt, May 5, 1939. (UPI)

The sons of Tacho I, Anastasio, Jr. *(left)*, and Luis, at LaSalle Military Academy, Oakdale, Long Island. (The Somoza family's private collection)

Tacho I with Luis *(left)* and Anastasio *(right)*. (The Somoza family's private collection)

The dynasty founder with one of his favorite bulls. (Juan Guzman)

EL VERDUGO DE NICARAGUA

SOMOZA

HOY 21 DE FEBRERO 14º ANIVERSARIO DEL ASESINATO
DEL GRAL. SANDINO

NEGOCIOS PRIVADOS

FERROCARRILES
VAPORES
AZUCAR
ALGODON
GANADO
MAIZ
CUEROS
MADERAS
AJONJOLI
GALLINAS
MINAS DE ORO
EMPRESAS
ELECTRICAS
JUEGOS PROHIBIDOS
AGUARDIENTE
TRATA DE BLANCAS

SISTEMA

PRISIONES
ASESINATOS
TORTURAS
SOBORNOS
DESTIERROS
CONFINAMIENTOS
DEPORTACIONES
LEY FUGA
MUJERES REHENES

EL PUEBLO DE NICARAGUA QUIERE LIBERTAD

A subversive postcard of Tacho I. On one side it lists the private business enterprises of Somoza: railways, ships, sugar, cotton, cattle, corn, leather, lumber, sesame seed, chickens, gold mines, firearms, electricity, forbidden games, alcohol, white slavery; on the other side, the methods he used to govern: prison, assassination, torture, payoffs, exile and *ley fuga*—being shot while attempting to escape.

Tacho I playing billiards with his son Tachito. Both are wearing diamond rings. (Juan Guzman)

Tacho I in a pensive mood, 1948. (Juan Guzman)

A press conference at El Retiro, in January 1967, in which Tacho II came across as much more a "chairman of the board" than the Latin American strongman that he was. (Bernard Diederich)

Tacho II with his American wife, Hope. (UPI)

Early April 1971. Tacho in Washington for a private dinner with President Nixon. Concerned about the reaction to offering a formal dinner for a dictator, Nixon's chief-of-staff Alexander Haig decided to call it a West Point Class of 1946 reunion. (UPI)

Dinorah Sampson, Tacho's mistress, getting out of her pool at her villa just outside of Managua. (The Somoza family's private collection.)

By 1972 Tacho had become seriously overweight. (Bernard Diederich)

After his heart attack, July 26, 1977, Somoza restricted his diet and began jogging daily. (Jean-Pierre Laffont/Sygma)

(ABOVE LEFT) The author with Xavier Chamorro Cardenal, co-editor with his brother Pedro Joaquín Chamorro, of the opposition newspaper, *La Prensa*. Pedro Joaquín's assassination on January 10, 1978, was a catalyst for popular insurrection. (Charles Green)

(ABOVE RIGHT) Matagalpa, August 1978. Student rebels fire into National Guard ranks. (Silio Boccanera)

(BELOW) Cero, Eden Pastora, most popular Sandinista today, who commanded the raid on the National Palace on August 22, 1978. (Karen DeYoung/*The Washington Post*)

Tacho and son at the reviewing stand. (Silio Boccanera)

The National Guard. (Silio Boccanera)

León, September 1978. Rocket fired by National Guard plane enters the ceiling of a church, near the altar. Refugees were hiding inside. (Silio Boccanera)

(OPPOSITE) Havoc in Masaya, September 1978. From top: Sandinistas with "muchachos" flee a burning gasoline tank truck, then seek out defensive positions. (Susan Meiselas/Magnum)

Rosa Gadea and her sister Esmeralda making a grave for their mother in Masaya. (Bernard Diederich)

Author presenting Somoza with newsmen's protest during press conference following the June 20, 1979, National Guard assassination of ABC newsman Bill Stewart. (Ted Cowell / *Life*)

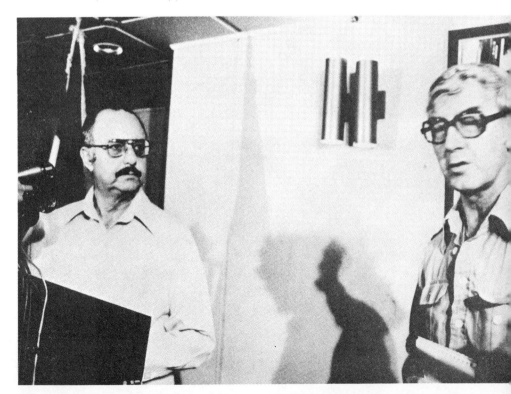

Managua being bombed and rocketed by Somoza's air force. (Silio Boccanera)

The second offensive, July 1979. (Susan Meiselas/Magnum)

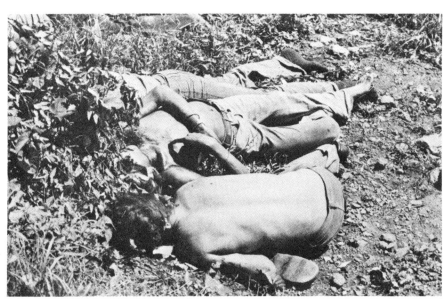

July 1979 executions on the shores of Lake Managua. Executions during the night of youths suspected of being Sandinistas were commonplace. (Silio Boccanera)

Sandinistas occupy Tacho's former Bunker headquarters. (Alon Reininger/Contact)

(ABOVE LEFT) Burning of cast National Guardsman and portrait of Somoza. (Susan Meiselas/Magnum)

(ABOVE RIGHT) Somoza during his last hour in Nicaragua. (Alon Reininger/Contact)

Triumph of the revolution. The sign reads: The One Who Has Abused Us Has Left. (Silio Boccanera)

Somoza's bombed car in Paraguay, July 17, 1980. (UPI)

CHAPTER 13

Los Muchachos

When the call for a general strike was given on Friday, August 25, youngsters in the town of Matagalpa responded by taking to the streets. They soon occupied most of the town, covering streets with broken glass, setting up barricades, and hanging out the red and black Sandinista colors. They collected arms from the citizenry either by stopping people and taking their guns or by gathering them from the surrounding coffee *fincas* (farms) and cattle ranches. Some said they stole the guns; others preferred to say the community donated them. Whatever the source of their firepower the town's boys, or *"los muchachos"* as they were called, had launched a spontaneous uprising they described as the "people's fight against the Somoza regime." Crude signs appeared with such slogans as "This time the fight is definite." The main condition to end the "people's war" was that Somoza "must go."

During the nationwide strike in January *los muchachos* had set up barricades and closed off the town at night. Then they wore masks and were armed with only sticks and stones. Now it was different. On Sunday morning these young people, mostly teenagers, began taking potshots at the National Guard headquarters on Morazán Park. By Tuesday the National Guard garrison had been reinforced with combat troops. The town was then subjected to a three-hour aerial attack. Overnight Matagalpa became front-page news, not because *los muchachos* had taken over the little coffee town, but because it was being bombed by the Somoza forces. When telephone reports were received in Managua from hysterical townspeople—"they are bombing us"—images were conjured up of the Basque town of Guernica, destroyed in 1937 by German planes in the Spanish civil war. But, newsmen reasoned, these are Nicaraguan pilots, not Germans. They found the reports hard to believe. Somoza spokesmen at first denied the use of air power. Later they changed their story to say there had been some limited aerial action.

Early Wednesday morning, August 30, newsmen all headed in the same direction: Matagalpa. At the small town of Sébaco, the crossroad to Estelí and only eighteen miles from Matagalpa, Tachito's black-bereted EEBI troops manned a roadblock, searching cars and trucks passing in both directions.

An EEBI officer with his beret at a jaunty angle made a strange request of a carload of newsmen: "If you have guns you had better leave them here with us because *los muchachos* will be sure to take them off you in Matagalpa." It was the first time we had heard the young rebels referred to as *"los muchachos."*

It was an eerie ride over the eighty miles to Matagalpa. The major highway was empty except for an occasional small car or pickup flying a white flag speeding down the highway away from Matagalpa. The closer to Matagalpa, the more numerous the white flags.

A peasant struggling with a wooden-wheeled cart full of corn and the occasional peasant riding to his fields on horseback were the only signs of life in the countryside. And these peasants seemed both uninvolved and unconcerned.

As we drove into the mountainous valley surrounding Matagalpa we heard, then saw a DC-3 spotter plane droning among the scattered clouds. Soldiers were sprawled out facing the road leading into the picturesque town. A rifle cracked in the distance. At the second road entering the town there were no guardsmen. Before the small bridge there stood the San Vicente Hospital, constructed by the Somoza administration in 1947. Across the road was the Red Cross encampment, the center of emergency relief, refugees and negotiations.

The town was divided between the *muchachos* and the guard. "This is one of Nicaragua's oldest and most rebellious towns," explained Dr. César Amador Kuhl, president of the Medical Association of Matagalpa and a leading neurosurgeon who was working with the Red Cross. "The *muchachos* have the support of the people. They got their arms from the people. But they have only small-caliber pistols and rifles and some shotguns." The guard on the other hand was well armed but could only count on the support of some paramilitary goons and paid informers. Although Matagalpa was the birthplace of the most important Sandinistas, and considered the cradle of their guerrilla movement, the Frente had no control over the *muchachos.* The spontaneous uprising had caught the guerrillas out of town.

"We are giving all services in this emergency," explained the hospital administrator, who along with other Nicaraguan hospital employees had been on strike for weeks demanding better salaries and the ouster of its military director. In the corridor a youthful doctor, Juan Cardenal, reported, "We had three dead Tuesday. A woman of forty-five and two *muchachos,* one fifteen and the other twenty-four years old. The two were killed by rifles and one by a .45 bullet." "These are the arms of the National Guard," explained one of the crowd who had gathered around the reporters. Dr. Cardenal told the ugly truth. "No one knows for sure how many people are dead. There are lots of wounded in the clinics inside town, and who knows how many are dead in different barrios."

A woman, her eyes flaming with anger, approached. "People here are being murdered by the National Guard planes. For three hours yesterday two planes bombarded us with rockets. They fired rockets into the poor barrio of La Chorizo, which is over there," she pointed, "high in the hills. They are killing innocent people. The people hate Somoza." Nobody around her disagreed, a few nodded their heads in agreement at what, for the reporters, was only the first of scores of denunciations of Somoza heard throughout the day in Matagalpa. Time and again people of all walks of life in the pretty little town of old rust-colored tile roofs were condemning Somoza and saying the only solution was his departure.

If the bombing and strafing—which was launched without warning—was designed to have some psychological effect on the population, it appeared to have failed miserably. Much of the town's wealthy population had fled but many townspeople were staying on in defiance. "We know they are going to bomb us again," one besieged resident said. "It shows what a barbaric regime we are living under." For many newsmen it did offer a closeup of the ruthless side of the Somoza dynasty.

A little Franciscan monk in a brown habit walked down the middle of a street into the city holding almost religiously a Red Cross flag and carrying truce proposals to and from the *muchachos*. Archbishop Obando y Bravo had arrived at midmorning with the head of the Nicaraguan Red Cross, Ismael Reyes, to work out a truce between the guard and the *muchachos*. It was proving no easy task. The *muchachos* had no single leader and were widely spread out in at least three barrios besides downtown Matagalpa around the San José Church, which was filled with refugees. The archbishop asked guard commander Colonel Rafael Martínez for a four-hour cease-fire beginning shortly after noon. In an old Red Cross station wagon with a public address system, Obando y Bravo, guided by Sister Marta Frech López of the Spanish Order of Charity who had taught many of the *muchachos* at the Catholic school, visited the various districts occupied by the *muchachos*. It was a long and arduous task. The young rebels were not easily convinced of the cease-fire as guard rifles still cracked around them. When asked their conditions the *muchachos* told the archbishop that they not only demanded the National Guard leave the town but that Somoza leave the country. One masked youth, wearing a baseball cap and standing against a corner brandishing a .38 pistol at the ready, said, "Somoza's leaving is not negotiable. The people want him to go. He must go." As the archbishop talked with a commando in the barrio of Palo Alto, rifle fire from the ranks of the guard broke out. The rebels told Obando y Bravo that the guard was using the cease-fire to advance on them. They wanted no dialogue with Colonel Martínez.

There was no cease-fire. One youth posing in action shots for journalists, said, "We want Somoza out and we are not going to accomplish this by sitting at home. This is the only alternative." Along the city streets it was evident the people were not fear-stricken. Some were smiling, others bitter. "The government is massacring the people," said a woman who owned a little store. "If the *muchachos* don't come out they say they will bomb the city again." In the meantime a distraught woman carrying a baby rushed into the store's doorway for a moment. Across the street her husband backed a late-model white Mercedes Benz out of the garage. They unfurled a newly made white flag and sped out of town.

Piles of lettuce and carrots lay rotting alongside empty stalls of the usually busy central market on Morazán Park. Flies were everywhere. Pigeons strutted near the old gray cathedral picking at the corn husks and other rubbish in the street. The town was desperate for food. One man in cowboy attire standing in a doorway told us there was usually a cease-fire from six to eight each morning, observed by the *muchachos* to allow the people to move about and find food for the day. "A lot of people are now without food but *los muchachos* make this contribution in the morning to show they are for us," the man said. "And people aid them with food when they can."

At 2:30 p.m. the archbishop told reporters, "The situation is more difficult but we are searching for a solution." Obando y Bravo still did not know how many *muchachos* he was dealing with. The Red Cross and others said they could number as high as 500 but no one knew their actual strength. The hard core, those with arms, might number 150.

An hour later gunfire was heard in the little five-room Hotel Soza. A National Guard patrol emerged around the corner looking very much like a United States World War II patrol, uniformed and with flak jackets, walkie-talkies crackling. News of the shooting spread through Matagalpa by word of mouth, from doorway to doorway. The patrol had burst into the Hotel Soza and raked the reception room with machine-gun fire. Bullets ripped into the reception desk, smashed the cash register, and took further toll—four persons in the reception room fell into bloody heaps on the tiled floor. Dead were the hotel owners, Mr. and Mrs. Julian Soza, their seventeen-year-old daughter, Silventa, and twenty-nine-year-old engineer Harold Miranda, a guest. The shooting had taken place an hour before the cease-fire was supposed to end. One of Miranda's arms was torn to pieces by the bullets.

One version said the guardsmen were seeking refuge from gunfire. When they knocked at the hotel to enter there was no answer so they went in shooting. Later in the day the guard commanding officer's post laid out on the floor at the entrance to guard headquarters "evidence" of the Sozas' subversive activity. Along with some Sandinista poems and magazines were a box of nails and one empty Gerber baby food jar allegedly "used to make bombs." There were also a small type set and several shotgun shells. The exhibit was supposedly collected from the hotel where the government later declared four *"extremistas"* had been killed. No witnesses could confirm that the guard had actually removed the pitiful collection from the hotel.

The garrison commander's headquarters on the park was a page from Pancho Villa. The snout of a .50-caliber machine gun pointed out through a slit in the wall; it was aimed at the city. Potbellied old guardsmen, one of whom admitted to thirty years' service, lounged around the steps. Across the street younger troops in combat gear occupied a vacant house. A civilian, a pistol in his belt and carrying binoculars, came down from the cathedral belfry. Colonel Martínez's aide showed off the torn toe of his boot. "A gift from the Frente," he said referring to the Sandinistas. A bullet had ripped his boot.

At 4:45 p.m. the archbishop and Sister Marta Frech López left the colonel's office grim-faced. Inside the office, windowless and lit only by a small desk lamp, a young General Anastasio Somoza Debayle in a white uniform looked out from a cracked glass picture on the grimy walls of the headquarters. Colonel Martínez, unshaven and disheveled snapped when asked about the truce, "We don't have to do anything. We are the constitutional authority. They have to hand in their arms to the Red Cross and that will be it." At the word *"muchachos"* the colonel swung in his chair angrily. "They are not boys, not children. All are adults and they are communists." The arms, he added, "were stolen, robbed from houses." A grimy soldier stood tightly gripping the barrel of a carbine next to the colonel's desk. When the colonel answered the phone, the soldier sprang to life and blurted out his pent-up rage. "International communism has robbed me of my life's work and earning. I'm a victim of international communism." The *muchachos* had burned his home and private clinic to the ground, he said. "I managed to get my family out, thank God, but they burnt my place to the ground. My loss is over two million córdobas. I have saved lives. The U.S. must be warned, this human rights business, this international communism is the real threat to us all." The loyal Somoza soldier was Colonel Augusto Flores Lovo, fifty-six, a military doctor for twenty-eight years and the unpopular director of the San Vicente Hospital. He gripped his gun tighter than ever and looked menacingly at the newsmen as they left the colonel to his little war against "the kids."

As the sun set on Matagalpa, intensely furious fighting was under way in the city. A lull from the firing of the rifles was filled with the almost forlorn pops of the small arms of *los muchachos*. It was beyond anyone's imagination how, armed with their revolvers and light-caliber rifles, they expected to match the special units of the National Guard but "the kids" were far from demoralized. They were spoiling for a fight. We journalists left to return to Managua. Back in Sébaco, fresh-looking EEBI troops searched our cars. One of the eight American mercenaries in Nicaragua attached to the unit told us the force was awaiting word to clean out Matagalpa.

A wealthy woman we encountered, whose son had persuaded her to leave Matagalpa, explained she had had a sniper on her roof and that his spent shells dropped down on the veranda of her two-story home. "The people support them," she said. "Why doesn't he [Somoza] see that the people want him to go? We are capitalists and should be afraid of the Sandinistas, but we are ready to take what comes after Somoza."

Early the next morning Somoza issued orders for the National Guard to retake Matagalpa. It was no pushover. Though armed with M-1 rifles and at least one Staghound armored car, the troops found the *muchachos* didn't run. Rather, they fought back from their barricades with their light weapons and dwindling ammunition. The driver of a large yellow bulldozer, under orders to scoop up the barricades for the advancing troops, was wounded by a shotgun blast in the shoulder and face. He lay bleeding under his big machine for nearly two hours before he was rescued.

The rebellion ended almost as suddenly as it began. In the face of a blazing onslaught by National Guardsmen the youthful rebels took off their masks, hid their arms and abandoned their resistance. Casualties for the five-day episode were set at thirty dead and at least two hundred wounded. Newsmen returning to Matagalpa after the battle of *los muchachos* had ended were often startled to find young men looking them in the eye, suddenly to wink and smile as they brazenly walked through the plaza assuming their ordinary role of kids.

"If a man or even a teenager comes at you with a pistol I think you have the right to defend yourself with the best available weapon," Somoza said from the Bunker shortly after increasing Nicaragua's defense budget from 10 to 20 percent of the national budget. He likened the kids of Matagalpa to "Bronx street gangs, just juvenile delinquents." But to the rest of anti-Somoza Nicaragua they were an example of the guts and tenacity of young people who asked but one thing: "Somoza go."

At the same time Somoza admitted that the nationwide general strike had gotten worse. There were signs the strike was picking up more support in the provinces than in the capital, where it was gaining strength, but only slowly.

The FAO, which had launched the strike, issued a sixteen-point program promising that after Somoza's ouster from power his family's huge business empire and land holdings would be expropriated. The National Guard would be purged of corrupt criminal elements, and social reform would be promoted. A "national government of transition" would hold free elections. The moderate opposition coordinating the strike had no choice but to continue it, saying that it could be their last chance to oust the strongman. If they failed it would only cause a greater swing of the population to the left, they claimed, with reliance on the left-wing Sandinistas to find a solution through violence. "Somoza breeds violence," the opposition said. Speaking for the Conservatives, Adolfo Calero-Portocarrero added, "The Conservatives want it known that in Nicaragua there are democratic forces that represent the great majority of the people who have placed themselves in civil opposition to this government." Alfonso Robelo Callejas agreed. "We feel more than ever the urgency to get rid of Somoza and the government because his presence provokes such [terrorist] actions."

Somoza had given a press conference on Tuesday, August 29, to dispel a tide of rumors that he had fled the country. In a prepared statement to the foreign press he said he would not resign from office before 1981 because, "To resign would be to betray the men in uniform who have defended this society with their lives. To resign would be to open this country to chaos and anarchy." He would not open the way to a civil war by leaving, he warned. "If I resign, I'm going with my people and my arms and something will start which we don't know how it will end." He announced that it would not be the "rifle that will make me go. I say it's the vote that's gonna make me go," and he invited the press to drop in in 1981 to "witness the balloting and tell the world what you found." Again he warned his opposition that the Sandinistas "have pledged to continue the bloodletting until they establish a Marxist state or die trying." The concept that "my resignation will bring peace is false," he said.

The nation's economy was the real victim of the strike. A rush on banks saw frightened Nicaraguans withdraw more than thirty million dollars in savings. One lady, seeing her daughter off to school in the States, complained bitterly to anyone within hearing at Las Mercedes airport about "that man not wanting to leave." Dollars cost her more because there was a shortage and "you have to buy them from *coyotes*" (black-market dealers).

Somoza took a number of strike measures, among them an order to the government-run Bank of Nicaragua to cut off future credit to companies that joined the strike. However, unlike the January strike, when the employers had shut their doors, this time it was the employees who were forcing them to close. INDE, the Nicaraguan Institute for Economic Development, was dissolved and its charter revoked by Somoza. All car dealers except for Tacho's Mercedes Benz auto distributorship had closed. The country's two largest breweries, the Coca-Cola and Pepsi bottling plants and the two major dairies went out on strike, leaving the nation dry at the mouth. But gas stations were still open, and it was unclear if "general" was actually the right word to characterize the strike. According to Somoza, "It's a bourgeois strike. When they begin to hurt they'll return to work."

On September 5 more than 800 members of the opposition and leaders of the strike were reported to have been arrested over the preceding three days. Tacho told reporters that he had done nothing to halt the seventeen-day strike following Chamorro's assassination because it was an "emotional" issue. This time it was "political." He charged that his opposition was "unable to win at the ballot box so now they are resorting to this kind of pressure to try and win power." Rafael Cano, Somoza's new press secretary, told reporters that those people advocating the overthrow of the government "are liable to be arrested, are being arrested and will continue to be arrested."

Two days later at what was normally siesta hour, at the officers' club Somoza was awake and raging. Dressed in a well-tailored pinstriped suit, blue tie, and shirt, with immaculately polished shoes, he stepped before television cameras and gave an aggressive performance for the foreign press. He displayed scorn and arrogance to impress upon newsmen and his viewers inside and outside Nicaragua that he was in charge—in case they questioned the fact.

What particularly angered Somoza was Venezuela's decision to take the Nicaragua situation to the OAS with a call for a foreign ministers' meeting. For the United States, which was looking at some form of mediation as the only possible path to resolve what was becoming a dangerous situation, the Venezuelan initiative was a step in the right direction. The United States backed the Venezuelans.

Unhappy, Somoza had called Ambassador Solaun to the Bunker and in his best manners complained about the United States supporting the Venezuelan move. "Venezuela has for the last year been trying to interfere in the internal affairs of Nicaragua," Somoza subsequently told newsmen. "This last week they went to the United Nations Security Council because of those small disturbances we have here. The president of the Security Council told them they had no room for it. They have gone to the Organization of American States asking for a conference of foreign ministers to meet.

"I'm denouncing that attitude of President Andrés Pérez and his government because there is no precedent in the history of the OAS that any government has gone to the OAS for a situation like we have in Nicaragua. There have been riots and revolutions in other countries and no government has ever had the gall to ask the OAS to intervene like Carlos Andrés Pérez is asking." Tacho told a Spanish-speaking reporter he was considering breaking relations with Venezuela because of Andrés Pérez's actions, warning, "I hold him responsible for a bloodbath which could be provoked in my country by his actions."

The United States was finally casting Somoza adrift after the long years of unquestioning support. But that word had not gotten around nor was Somoza interested in broadcasting the fact. The United States hoped that mediation might make the transition from dictator to democracy possible and was seeking to bring the FAO and Somoza together. Explained a State Department official: "We're trying to avoid any 'U.S. solution.' If we were to suggest that Somoza should take a three-month vacation, that's exactly what Somoza's people would do—and then say that this was what the Americans told them to do."[1] The United States, in a break from the past, now sought a "Nicaraguan solution." The opposition insisted the United States back this up with action by halting eleven million dollars' worth of food, health and education loans that they maintained mostly benefited Somoza's politicians. Said one Conservative party spokesman acidly: "Somoza is part of the American system, not ours." Added Conservative Congressman Eduardo Chamorro Cornel, forty-four, referring to the American military force that had installed Somoza's father in power in 1933: "Somoza is the last Marine."[2]

"After so many years of intervention, you say, 'We don't intervene.' That's the most sophisticated intervention we have seen," said Chamorro Cornel, who wanted to see Nicaragua make the transition to democracy by constitutional means immediately.

UDEL chairman Rafael Córdova Rivas complained, "All of Nicaragua demands Somoza's resignation and the Department of State says 'be patient until 1981,' which I say is intervention in Somoza's favor." While the opposition argued that "U.S. policy is fiction," the United States looked unhappily at the factionalization of the opposition and worried that it couldn't agree on a leader or government in post-Somoza Nicaragua.

Under Jimmy Carter's self-styled "moral and open diplomacy," the United States felt it could no longer resort to strong-arm methods used in the past—neither the big stick nor the unsavory destabilization methods used by previous administrations to get rid of undesirable regimes in Chile and the Dominican Republic. The CIA theoretically no longer had its license to kill. But with intervention ruled out the Americans found it easier to preach than put into practice its new moral and open diplomacy. To sever diplomatic relations or recall the ambassador as a sign of disapproval of the dictatorship would make it impossible for the United States to influence events within Nicaragua. While realizing that support of the Somoza dynasty was no longer possible, Washington wanted to see it replaced by a moderate regime. But the so-called moderate Nicaraguans still suffered from the old "protectorate mentality" and felt it was Somoza's old protectors who should get rid of him by pulling out all the props. The dilemma was complicated even further by a United States Congress in which Tacho could count on many friends.

Earlier in the first week of September the Nicaraguan Congress had approved the $3.5 million loan for rural nutrition and education being debated when the palace was seized by the Sandinistas. The loan was a product of legislative blackmail. Representative Charles Wilson, Texas Democrat, had threatened to hold up the Carter administration's entire foreign aid package in May if aid for Nicaragua wasn't included. The administration acquiesced. All American military aid had been halted —the United States was not signing military aid sales credits for Nicaragua. An embargo on lethal weapons and crowd control equipment sales to Nicaragua had been in effect for two years. The only item the guard received was $150,000 for military training abroad, which the State Department was not supporting. To Tacho the refusal of military aid was a psychological blow. The United States was no longer his ally. He was now forced to shop around elsewhere to find arms and ammunition. He found suppliers of war matériel in Europe and Israel.

On the afternoon of September 9 an Aerocommander airplane crashed in Lake Nicaragua at the mouth of the Sapoa River near the Costa Rican border. Piloting the plane was Brigadier General José Iván Alegrett, often called the most hated member of the guard. Mike Echanis and two other "mercs," an American, Chuck Sanders, and a Vietnamese, Ngoyen Van-Ngoyen, were his passengers. That evening a newsman rushed into the Managua Intercontinental waving a communiqué and shouting, "Mike and his buddies 'bought it.'" When Alegrett's death was announced a woman shrieked, "Great, wonderful, the bastard is dead. They must have killed him."

Throughout the previous week Mike had been a voice of doom, insisting to reporters operating from the hotel that it would be taken by the Sandinistas, warning them to get out in time. When the raid came off, he said, the National Guard would retake the hotel with all the force it could muster, even though Tacho was a major stockholder and might be upset with more bullet holes and destruction. Echanis told reporters a plot was afoot to kill him and Alegrett, but he spun his tale with the understanding that any story to that effect would be published only after his death. When it happened, Somoza was immediately suspected of having had a hand in the crash—some speculated a bomb had been put aboard the plane. The official version was that it crashed in bad weather. The full details never surfaced, however. In his earlier statements, Echanis made vague references to a Panamanian plot to kill him and Alegrett, but he did not know who was planning the attempt. He claimed that it was intended to sabotage the guard's intelligence program and pave the way for a guard coup by unidentified guard officers. "These people were plenty unhappy with the old man [Somoza] for his handling of the legislative palace takeover. My commandos are the only thing standing in the way of a takeover," he said only shortly before his death.[3]

At 6:00 P.M. Saturday, September 9, the Sandinistas launched a nationwide offensive with coordinated attacks on military vehicles and installations in Managua, Masaya, León, Chinandega and Estelí. Weapons were distributed to the population and as soon as the guerrillas' well-planned attacks began, they were spontaneously joined by the *muchachos*, wielding hunting rifles and automatic weapons grabbed from the hands of fallen members of the guard. "I'm no communist," said a nineteen-year-old economics student wearing the black and red colors of the Sandinistas over his face and carrying a 16-gauge shotgun. "I'm a Christian against Somoza, nothing more." Many other young rebels tied handkerchiefs over their faces in the Sandinista fashion to avoid identification. As a result, the fight was soon dubbed "The Revolution of the Scarves."

The garrisons of the four provincial cities were under siege within hours and reports of heavy fighting poured into the capital. Masaya was in flames as five major fires blazed out of control—one covered an entire six-block business district. Citizens were warned by the military to take cover as it would begin bombing guerrilla positions from the air. The Sandinistas occupied most of León, a city of eighty thousand people, and the guard launched intense bombing and strafing attacks there on the barrios of Laborío, Guadalupe and Subtiava. Ciertas Balsas was also hit by a popular uprising. In Monimbó angry rebels who had been battling the National Guard almost daily since February finally overran the local guard barracks and slaughtered its two officers and a dozen enlisted men.

"The hour of insurrection has come," Sandinista radio transmitters broadcast. "All the people into the street." Ironically, the civil war erupted just as the country was preparing for Independence Day, the annual celebration on September 15 of the break by Nicaragua and other Central American states from Spanish rule in 1821. Somoza, directing the war from the Bunker, marked the day with a champagne reception that American Ambassador Solaun declined to attend. The Sandinistas promptly labeled the holiday Nicaragua's Second Independence Day.

As the fighting continued, neither side could really celebrate a victory. It was one of the most savage and confusing wars that Central America had ever seen. Each side predictably deflated its own casualties and exaggerated the number of those on the other side. The Nicaraguan Red Cross, whose members heroically retrieved the dead and wounded and rescued refugees in the midst of the shooting, estimated at week's end that at least five hundred people had been killed and as many more wounded. In some places bodies littered the streets. The bottom line of the insurrection was that it pitted an angry, poorly armed populace against Somoza and his now 8,100-strong National Guard, already well armed and awaiting the arrival of ten thousand new Israeli Galil automatic rifles the following week. With its overwhelming firepower, the guard began slowly, systematically to put down the uprising, first in Managua and then in the provinces, with orders to take no prisoners. Most of the casualties appeared to be civilians.

In Masaya pretty Rosa Pérez Gadea, fourteen, stood inside the broken wooden door of the Casa del Obrero, a Somoza trade union meeting hall on a corner opposite the Don Bosco school. It was early in the morning of Wednesday September 13. I had come to report on the course and effects of the fighting there. The inside of the rose-colored hall was pockmarked by the impact of hundreds of rounds of bullets; wooden chairs stood lined against the wall. Rosa was holding what appeared to be a torn color photo. Her sister, Esmeralda, fifteen, and brother Marlo, nine, stood in the patio. Their two-year-old brother Lester was recuperating from a bullet wound in the head at a clinic. In a shallow depression in the patio area lay the body of their dead mother, thirty-two-year-old María Jesús Gadea. On Tuesday afternoon the children had scraped out the small indentation and laid her on a mattress before covering her with earth, mostly mud. Over the crude grave they had placed wooden boards and some candles they received from a neighbor, but they had not lit the candles. There was no priest across the street in the Magdalena Church and a cemetery burial in Masaya even Wednesday was impossible.

Little Rosa sobbed out her story. "We take care of this workers' house. It is the government. We kept it clean and watched it. We didn't get paid. We lived here. Monday at two P.M. we saw the guard coming. We closed the door when we saw them coming toward us in a *tanqueta* [Staghound armored car]. Mother said, 'They are going to kill us.' They were shooting. 'Everyone quick, into the bath.' We all took shelter here," she said, showing a primitive concrete shower with a little water pipe off the patio. "The *tanqueta* came right into the hall, breaking down the door and firing all the time. They threw tear gas. Then they came into the back. We were all on the floor of this little space. Mother was standing. Suddenly her head fell to one side. A guard shot her through the nose."

She pointed to the two bullet holes in the shower and the dark pool of congealed blood on the floor. Asked what she was holding, Rosa lifted up the remains of a torn portrait of General Anastasio Somoza García and another of the white-uniformed son, General Anastasio Somoza Debayle. "They [the guard] saw the pictures too late," she said. The people from the neighborhood in their anger later came in and tore up the pictures. Rosa and her family had remained in the shower with their dead mother two hours during a fire fight down the street in Vega Matus Plaza, named after a famous Masaya musician.

Why had the guard attacked the home? Above the ruined doorway to Somoza's workers' union was a small red and black flag with the letters "FSLN" the size of a hand. "We don't know who put it there. Maybe the *muchachos* put it there."

A neighbor came up carrying a white flag. "Did you see what the beasts did here?" she asked me enraged. "Come and see what they did to the Don Bosco school and church. They even broke the crown of the Virgin—those guardsmen!"

How many died, no one knew. A young man carrying a flour sack as a white flag, a safety device quickly adopted by the entire populace, said, "Everyone is burying the dead in backyard patios or gardens, wherever they fall or wherever there is soil. I helped bury five today." Newsmen also took to waving white flags, many of these towels from the Intercontinental Hotel. Some unwisely painted "Prensa" ("Press") on them. To the guard this meant the hated opposition newspaper, so the journalists then put up "Periodista" ("Newsman") but that did not always help. Guardsmen often shot first and then asked questions. And no one ran in Masaya. "To run is to commit suicide," explained one man.

A number of us reporters had sneaked into Masaya as the battle there came to an end. Leaving the city presented an even greater problem than getting in. I was in a two-car convoy with Ed Rabel of CBS News. A group of enraged guardsmen on patrol, sweating in heavy flak jackets, ordered us to retreat into the town. The patrol stood in a little circle with guns at the ready. The guardsmen's eyes were red and wild, a combination of lack of sleep and fear. For them the enemy, the people of Masaya, were all around. These guardsmen were clearly an army of occupation.

The only guardsman who remained cool was smoking a cigarette as he held the tip of the barrel of his M-1 rifle to the temple of a youth sprawled out on the grassy edge of the street. Tears rolled silently down the well-dressed youth's face. He knew he was going to die. He had been hauled out of a neighboring house as we arrived. When we refused to retreat into the city, an elderly soldier finally examined our press credentials and allowed us to leave the city. They did not want any witnesses to what was about to happen. But the people who lived across the street were peering out from behind curtains to watch the summary execution of a youth whose only crime was being in the age bracket of the enemy.

By Wednesday the guard's counteroffensive had retaken Masaya. A convoy of EEBI troops left to rest up before going on to retake León. On the outskirts of town a crowd held up containers to purchase milk from a delivery truck, but any semblance of normality ended there. The downtown and barrios of old adobe, mostly single-story buildings with old tile roofs, were in ruins. Around the old *mercado*— the central produce market built in 1891—the scene was one of fire-gutted shops and stores. More than fifty stores and a bank had been burned during the fighting. Some people blamed the Sandinistas for not being more careful with their molotov cocktails. Others said it was the fault of inexperienced youngsters who had joined in the insurrection.

At the corner of Avenue El Progreso and C. Julio Cesar a stream of people jostled their way in and out of the gutted Banco Nacional de Nicaragua, a state bank. They laughingly held up large plastic bags filled with córdoba coins. The fact that they were looting, an offense that could mean a guard bullet, did not bother them. They allowed themselves to be photographed, but when a guard squad moved down the street from Vega Matus Plaza they scattered. Then as soon as the guardsmen returned to their fortified headquarters on the plaza, the people returned to pick over the leftovers at the bank. A body, identified as that of a guardsman, lay burning at the side of the marketplace. No one paid it much heed. It could have been a dead dog as far as anyone was concerned. The guard could count on few friends—only the occasional "sapo" or informer, who served as their "ears."

The Masaya Red Cross Center had hundreds of refugees jammed in its central patio and garage. Adam Sánchez Cerda, the head of the clinic, reported, "We have had over five thousand refugees since Saturday and we have not kept count of the wounded. But what we now want to do is to convert this center into a hospital. It is hard on the wounded with all the noise of the refugees." The Red Cross had not even been permitted to enter Masaya from Managua until Wednesday, when an official protest was filed with Somoza.

In Estelí the rebels remained in complete command. The garrison was caught in their fortress holding a dozen prominent citizens hostage. The guard was launching a counteroffensive to retake the town of León; units were also sent to hold the embattled towns of Sapoá and Peñas Blancas in the south, and violated the Costa Rican border in hot pursuit of Sandinistas. Somoza clamped martial law on the country on September 13.

In spite of such headlines as *Novedades*'s: "Movement Smashed: Somoza," the death toll continued to rise. Every line of *La Prensa* was edited out by censors under the provisions of martial law. After a week of steady fighting, the conflict had taken on the proportions of a bloodbath, and American diplomats met hastily with the government to speed the evacuation of nearly 1,500 United States citizens caught in the fighting.

Saying "You might compare [the September 9 attack] to the Tet offensive in Vietnam," Somoza told a press conference September 13, "They have been defeated." The price was high. Four cities lay war-scarred, their central markets, shops and warehouses charred and gutted by a war machine that left at least 1,500 dead. The lines at guard roadblocks became longer as refugees began to return to their homes to pick up the pieces and go on living. Families grieved the loss of loved ones. There was no way to estimate how many people, like the Gadea family, had buried relatives in their backyards. They spoke of nothing else. In rages and fits of anger they talked of the days of shelling, rocketing and strafing. The entire country seethed with anger and the object of that anger was one man: Anastasio Somoza.

The war-torn appearance of the burned-out and bombed-out towns after the fourteen-day insurrection was only part of the story. More deeply wounded were the people. "Our wounds will never heal," said an elderly doctor who treated the wounded and dying in León, adding, "not as long as that murderer of his people remains." The aerial attacks, with rockets fired from Cessna push-pull loadmaster aircraft of the Nicaraguan air force, left youths dead at their barricades with great gaping holes in their bodies. "They tried to shoot back with peashooters," an eyewitness to the fighting said. The troops moved in behind their armored cars and at least one vintage Sherman tank, indiscriminately spraying the walls of homes and stores with machine-gun fire. The Guard literally went crashing into houses to drag into the street youths whose only crime sometimes was their age. They were executed regardless of whether they had been involved or not.

Los Doce member Miguel d'Escoto said, "When the Sandinistas marched into León, they were applauded and that is when Somoza decided to burn the city. There was absolutely no concern for human life."

The Sandinistas had captured enough radio equipment to be able to monitor Somoza's guard traffic. Radio equipment was used by many others including influential Nicaraguans who thus overheard what Tacho had to say to his commanders. This was often quickly disseminated to the public.

On the night of September 14 a conversation was picked up between Lieutenant Colonel Humberto Corrales in León and Tachito, who was on the outskirts of the city, discussing ways to cover up a helicopter gunning down and killing two Red Cross volunteers manning an ambulance. Corrales told Tachito he didn't know how to report the incident. After a lengthy talk Tachito convinced him to deny reports that helicopters had been involved and to pad his story by saying there were reports the Sandinistas had stolen the ambulance. Corrales later told Nicaraguan Red Cross president Ismael Reyes that the incident "had been a terrible mistake" and sent apologics. The guard had had a convoy proceeding down the highway five miles from León and had opened fire on the vehicle after gunmen began shooting at them from the ambulance, Corrales first said. In reality, they were unarmed volunteers. A member of the International Red Cross who returned to find out what had happened was briefly taken prisoner by the guard. Other Red Cross volunteers who returned to the scene were fired upon by a helicopter gunship. More than two hundred people attended the funeral of the volunteers a few days later in Managua. The coffins were draped with Red Cross flags and with the volunteers' helmets, one of which was punctured with bullet holes.

The National Guard's armored battalion, supplemented by graduates fresh from Tachito's basic infantry training school, recaptured one town after another. Somoza had boasted the campaign would take only a week, but it was taking longer and at a very high price, both in human lives and in property, to say nothing of alienating further an already hostile population.

On Avenida Santiago Argüello in León, Rosamilde DeFranco, thirty-eight, sat in a rocking chair before a large crucifix. Bullet holes perforated the wall, on which hung an old print of the Virgin Mary. Rain beat down on the tin roof as the mother of five told her story. It was short.

"Three families took refuge in here," she said, waving to the rear of the large room. "Then the soldiers came. It was September fifteenth and maybe four P.M., but most people had lost all notion of time. They ordered women over here and men over there. Then they grabbed my eighteen-year-old son Efraím and five others, cursing and ordering them to the door. Right here on the doorstep they killed three boys. Then they put the others up against the wall across the street and shot them. One of the soldiers wanted to take my husband but he pleaded, showing his hair was gray. A soldier said to me, 'You are lovely, I'll visit you.' He took a watch from one of the dead and said 'Wash this' and put it on my wrist. It was covered in blood."

An amateur neighborhood photographer took a picture of the youths' entangled bodies on the doorstep. He sent a copy to *La Prensa* but it was censored out, with the rest of the day's copy.

A total of ten had been executed in this one block, and eight in the next. There were dozens of people to vouch for the veracity of the reports. Farther down the street they told of how the soldiers made a sixteen-year-old youth march to the center of the street and raise his hands in the air. Then they machine-gunned him.

The overworked Red Cross and other relief workers often had no choice but to burn bodies to prevent the spread of disease. Mrs. DeFranco gave her son a real burial. Others buried their dead in their backyards, rather than see them burned.

People in all the battle-torn areas who had seen their cities battered mercilessly by machine guns, artillery, rockets, aerial strafing and National Guard combat troops wanted to know about the United States' position in the matter. As guard soldiers removed an American-made rocket pod and a cluster of unexploded rockets from the backyard of a poor home in the city of León an old man whispered to an American newsman, "What is Mr. Carter doing? What about his human rights?" Much of the anger was directed at Carter and his human rights policy, which Somoza had said was misunderstood by his opposition and had given them muscle to defy his government.

Pointing to two corpses of Red Cross volunteers shot by the National Guard in Estelí, a woman watched an American television crew film the burning of the bodies in the street. "This," she said, "is President Carter's human rights." All around, American journalists were asked why Carter, with all the clout that Washington had always exercised in Nicaragua, did not stop the fighting and bloodshed, most of it shed by troops trained and noticeably equipped over the years by the United States.

As the National Guard continued rocketing and shelling the cities of León and Estelí on September 15, the Nicaraguan church hierarchy sent a letter to President Carter calling on him to help mediate the conflict. In the letter, handed to the American embassy in Managua, the clergymen noted that Somoza's regime was a "death-dealing regime," accusing it of "indiscriminate machine-gunning of the population in different cities; summary killing of captured insurgents; killing by torture of imprisoned persons; illegal raids on a large number of homes, along with physical violence and confiscation of property; torture in public thoroughfares by the National Guard of many persons, especially young people."

The letter added, "Our concern would increase if the regime of General Somoza were to continue in power . . . the only way for it to remain in power is by bloody coercion."

Father Miguel d'Escoto, who was underground in Managua during the fighting, said he was "personally disappointed at the total inability of the U.S. to persuade Somoza to come to mediation. The U.S. has not been able to mitigate the unbridled madness of the man who has been their friend so long." D'Escoto said no one in Nicaragua really believed the United States was sincere in its human rights effort. Carter, he said, was now in a position where he would have to prove himself. "Nicaragua," he added, "presents a good opportunity."

Members of the opposition and businessmen said that Somoza, even though showing little sign of collapse, had lost touch with reality. "He has no idea of the intensity of the anti-Somoza feeling in this country," said an insurance executive who had traveled widely throughout Nicaragua. "It has to be intense when people, ordinary people, are prepared to die for that feeling."

"Tacho is going to leave this country in ashes," the wife of a banker said before revealing that most of the Somoza clan had departed Nicaragua for Miami. "Only Tacho and his son remain."

The aim of the general strike had been to make Somoza quit but both sides were by now admitting that there was no possibility of mediation or dialogue. "Too much blood has already been shed," an opposition party member said. Nicaraguans were beginning to look to mediation from abroad. Leaders of the FAO named three representatives who would mediate in the name of the opposition to obtain "a permanent solution for our problems, which is only possible with an immediate and authentic democratization process." Talk of the FAO preparing to form a provisional government was denied—it would cause further problems with the government. One candid member of the opposition stated, "They would be signing their death warrant."

Named as FAO representatives were Alfonso Robelo Callejas, the wealthy industrialist; Sergio Ramírez Mercado, Los Doce member, and spokesman for the group; and Rafael Córdova Rivas, UDEL president who had helped set off the January general strike. The naming of the representatives was seen as an attempt by the opposition to show it was united and that the delegates could speak for all of the opposition.

The rest of the opposition, the Sandinistas, utilized the lull to rest and regroup their forces for their next military action. They also took the time for intense evaluation and self-criticism. They claimed the fourteen-day war was not a defeat, although they had failed to overthrow Somoza. The war had served them well in gaining battle experience, arms, men and money, but above all it emphasized that to beat Somoza they would have to unify.

CHAPTER 14

Mediation

The United States was seriously concerned about the extent of the anti-Somoza sentiment and the popularity of the Sandinistas. There was also fear that the next round of fighting might internationalize the conflict and engulf all of Central America. In an effort to prevent further violence and polarization, Washington began a belated search for a peaceful solution, an endeavor President Carter called "one of the most difficult tasks which we have ever undertaken."

Following the September insurrection United States Ambassador to Panama William Jorden arrived in Managua as Carter's special envoy to convince Somoza to join a multinational effort to resolve the Nicaraguan crisis. Given Somoza's aversion to the word "mediation," the group was to be christened "The OAS Sponsored Commission on Friendly Cooperation and Conciliation."

Jorden, a Texan and former *New York Times* newsman who, prior to his arrival in Managua, had consulted with the governments of Venezuela, Colombia, Panama and Costa Rica, found Tacho violently opposed to the suggestion that William Rogers, former assistant secretary of state for Latin American affairs, be appointed as a mediator. When Jorden mentioned Rogers, Somoza snapped, "He is not acceptable. He is biased." Somoza claimed that Rogers's law firm had been active in trying to embargo goods to Nicaragua from the United States.

Jorden then proposed that the United States, Colombia and the Dominican Republic could be members of the multinational mediation team. Tacho wanted the United States, Guatemala and El Salvador; the latter two countries were headed by friendly military governments. Somoza quickly rejected Colombia because it had joined Carlos Andrés Pérez of Venezuela in condemning Somoza before the United Nations for a "wave of genocide." The FAO, which spoke for the opposition, rejected El Salvador because its military dictator was sympathetic to Somoza.

The United States embassy had made the initial contact with the FAO with an offer to mediate on September 19. The tall, taciturn William G. Bowdler, who was eventually accepted to head the American side of the three-nation team, recalled, "The FAO didn't want mediation. Neither did Tacho."

One member of FAO summed up the feelings of even moderate Nicaraguans when he said, "A river of blood separates us. How can we sit down and negotiate with a man who has just slaughtered three thousand Nicaraguans?"

Meanwhile, Somoza's faithful lobbyists in the United States Congress, led by Representative John Murphy, mustered seventy-eight signatures on a letter to President Carter warning him that "the campaign of violence, urban terrorism and near civil war in Nicaragua is being carried out by a revolutionary group." Somoza, they insisted once again, "is the bulwark against Communism in Latin America."

On September 30 Somoza officially agreed to the mediation talks in his first nationwide address since the insurrection. His speech was punctuated with the explosions of bombs in various sectors of Managua, despite the 8:00 P.M. to 6:00 A.M. curfew that had been in effect in the city since September 12. He vowed again to remain in office until 1981 and called on the opposition to "make the small sacrifice of losing face" and stop calling for his ouster by any and all means. "This campaign of agitation and idealizing armed struggle must end," he said, reading from a prepared text. He challenged the opposition to "organize a real political party" and contest the 1981 elections at the ballot box. But much of his speech was devoted to attacking those he conceived as his enemies. Venezuela, Panama, Costa Rica and Cuba were denounced for openly supporting the Sandinistas. The media were accused of abusing press freedom and sowing hatred and making "adventurers out of bomb throwers." His criticism was an indication of just how widespread his opposition now was. Businessmen and politicians were accused of fomenting civil strife, and the Roman Catholic church was denounced as "inflexible." As for the mediation, he said he hoped it would begin as soon as possible, as if it were an irritant which he wanted to dispose of quickly.

The United States had once again pressured Somoza into allowing the OAS human rights commission to enter Nicaragua, and they arrived in Managua on October 3. Seven jailed opposition leaders, including Conservative party leader Adolfo Calero Portocarrero, the fifty-two-year-old president of the local Coca-Cola bottling company, were released.

The FAO immediately urged people to organize groups to testify before the OAS and sought guarantees from Somoza that witnesses would not suffer any form of retaliation. Nicaraguan permanent human rights commission president José Esteban González, whose office was decorated with a West German human rights group poster that read: "End the silence of forty-four years of dictatorship in Nicaragua," testified that since the OAS commission's arrival, the number of kidnappings and murders of Nicaraguans by presumed government agents had actually increased. "Last February at least one person was killed a day in political violence, but now, in the aftermath of the fighting, the rate is up to three to eight a day," he stated. There were over 600 political prisoners in National Guard jails, he testified.

Somoza became short-tempered with the commission and defended his National Guard as their commander in chief. As to their committing atrocities during the insurrection he said, "I had to respond to the combat needs of my troops. Of course there was a great deal of destruction, but what did you expect me to do? Hand over power? When there is a war, mistakes are inevitably made." There was no disguising his rage. His face twitched, and he shook his head. Many of the atrocities, he fumed, had been committed by Sandinistas wearing guard uniforms as they had when they seized the National Palace on August 22, 1978. Trying to contain his outburst he delivered his final salvo at Carter. It was Carter's human rights policy that had convinced Nicaraguans, he said, that they "can overthrow my government."

The investigators completed their work on October 12 and left to write their report.

The three mediators arrived in Managua on October 6. Bill Bowdler issued a "no comment" to the press and Admiral Emilio Jiménez of the Dominican Republic, the commission chairman, issued a slightly longer statement, saying he was "happy to be taking part in this friendly cooperation to bring peace and tranquillity to Nicaragua." Never a talkative person, Bowdler en route to Managua summed up the mission in one phrase: "This will be a tough one."

Bowdler was a formidable negotiator and no stranger to Latin America. Completely bilingual, he had worked with Ambassador Ellsworth Bunker to negotiate the end of the 1965 Dominican civil war and United States intervention. He had also served as ambassador to neighboring El Salvador and Guatemala and knew Nicaragua from previous visits. He was a former member of the National Security Council. His height was also formidable. Tacho, who was accustomed literally to looking down on accommodating American envoys because of his six-feet-one frame, found, perhaps for the first time, that he had to look up—to the six-feet-six Bowdler.

The other two mediators were studies in contrasts. Navy admiral and foreign minister of the Dominican Republic Ramón Emilio Jiménez, also tall, was a man without any ideology. Somoza believed Jiménez would be disposed to be sympathetic to "an old friend." But Milo, as the foreign minister was popularly known, played his role correctly and was later added to Tacho's list of people who suggested that he step down. Alfredo Obiols Gómez, former assistant foreign minister of Guatemala, the third member of the team, seemed to be more interested in ecology than politics and was chosen so that his government could take a neutral position in the mediation.

Facing them across the table was the three-man FAO negotiating team: Alfonso Robelo, Sergio Ramírez and Córdova Rivas. It was decided that the FAO would have no contact with Somoza, that all the negotiations would be handled through Bowdler, Gómez and Jiménez. Alfonso Robelo, a United States–trained chemical engineer and wealthy cooking oil manufacturer, was a moderate and anti-communist; Rafael Córdova Rivas was a longtime Somoza critic and a lawyer; Sergio Ramírez Mercado was a university professor, a writer and a member of The Twelve. Ramírez was the unofficial representative of the moderate Tercerista faction of the Sandinistas. Though chosen as a "unified" opposition negotiating team, they proved to be as diversified as the business, political and civic groups that the FAO represented, each coming into the talks with his own project for a post-Somoza Nicaragua. There would be no final solution without Somoza quitting; upon this they all agreed.

As a condition to begin negotiations the FAO called for an end to censorship and the lifting of martial law. Somoza agreed to press freedom, which meant that

La Prensa could resume publishing. But Somoza was unsure of just how far he should go and showed his indecision by agreeing during a cabinet meeting to lift the 8:00 P.M. to 6:00 A.M. curfew in Managua (in the rest of the country the curfew was from 6:00 P.M. to 6:00 A.M.), then changed his mind and merely shortened it to 10:00 P.M. until 4:00 A.M. Martial law was extended through April 1979.

During their shuttle diplomacy between Tacho and the opposition the mediators spent their spare time visiting the country and taking its pulse. "While waiting," Bowdler said, "we talked with all kinds of people and groups. We found the same feeling everywhere; there was no solution without his going. Democracy had been so abused by Somoza they didn't have any confidence left." It was perfectly clear to the mediators that Somoza had no popular support whatsoever. Confined to the Bunker, Somoza seemed to have lost touch with reality and acted more like a businessman negotiating real estate than a chief of state upon whose decisions the life of a nation depended. While he continued to rant and rave and humiliate those around him, even during the negotiation sessions, he was showing signs of tension. His facial tic and shaky hand grew more pronounced.

In early October the mediators were incapable of articulating a way for Somoza to leave without losing face. "Why don't you just resign?" is how Bowdler put the issue to him in their first meeting, Somoza revealed during a postexercise breakfast. "He said his instructions were to advise me to leave, to get out of the country."[1] On that, as on other occasions, Somoza's answer was an emphatic no.

Andrés Pérez sent word from Caracas to the Carter administration that resignation might seem attractive to Somoza if he were permitted to leave Nicaragua with most of the family fortune and offered exile in the United States, where he could live out the rest of his life in luxury. Somoza's "only publicly reported response to that suggestion was reminiscent of a last-ditch stand in a second-rate gangster film: 'If they want me,' he said, 'they'd better come in and get me.' "[2]

After nineteen days of negotiation, on October 25 Sergio Ramírez quit as a member of the FAO negotiating team. He announced that Los Doce, for whom he spoke on the panel, was also officially withdrawing from the FAO as it had become apparent to them that the talks would not accomplish the ouster of Somoza. "We have realized that the mediation commission did not really want to extract the cancer from our society, the ouster of Somoza," Father Miguel d'Escoto, said, minutes before he and five other members of Los Doce took refuge in the Mexican embassy in Managua. The departure of The Twelve also meant that the Tercerista moderates of the Sandinistas had decided that the mediation was not only a farce but an attempt by Washington to seek stability and the establishment of a reformist government which would exclude any participation of the Sandinistas.

Father d'Escoto said that Bowdler and the other two envoys "probably realized that Somoza is a very stubborn man who could not be budged, and therefore they began to make us give in with concessions. . . . We had already at their request presented the mediators with an alternative political program for a post-Somoza government. . . . Our plan was for a three-year transitional government led by a three-man civilian junta." The last straw came, he said, when the mediation team tried to persuade the opposition to accept talks with Somoza representatives and even agree to drop plans to prosecute Somoza officials under a future government.[3]

The Twelve also charged that the United States plan "would leave practically intact the corrupt structures of the Somoza apparatus." They challenged the American "promise" to remove Somoza from the scene, citing its continued support of *somocismo* through arms supplied by countries within the United States "sphere of influence."[4] The Twelve and the guerrillas sought a complete break with the past not only by Somoza's ouster, but also by the expropriation of his extensive business empire and the disbanding of his National Guard.

The next day the mediators and FAO pushed ahead with the talks despite the pullout of The Twelve and ominous signs that a new round of combat was at hand. On the day The Twelve pulled out of the talks, a Sandinista deadline for the anticipated new guerrilla offensive ended, and Somoza called the guerrillas' bluff, saying, "Whatever the guerrillas do won't be successful." The deadline, he said, was "only propaganda." Speaking of the future, Somoza boasted he was going to give Nicaraguans "peace and tranquillity" for Christmas. The passed deadline, a guerrilla source explained, "is part of our psychological warfare. When the real offensive comes, we'll catch him with his guard down."

Washington's timid approach had in fact drawn the three Sandinista factions closer together. Neither the GPP faction nor the Proletarians had been happy with the Terceristas' involvement in the talks, even through The Twelve. All three tendencies were now agreed that only by force of arms could the Somoza regime be removed. They rejected an imposed solution that would retain any trappings of *somocismo*.

Somoza, encouraged by what he saw as the breakup of the opposition, toughened his own stand and objected to the United States peace formula, which called for a national plebiscite on his future as president. But he reaffirmed his formula for a plebiscite which would allow the opposition to share power with him, an old family recourse during a period of crisis. Knowing the opposition's objections to direct talks with him, and hoping it would divide their ranks even more, he sounded a moderate note and offered to hold direct talks with opposition leaders, rather than through international mediators.

Somoza backers released the Nationalist Liberal party report to the mediators, rejecting the so-called Washington plan of a plebiscite under which Somoza would resign immediately and leave the country with his family if he lost. "With due respect," they wrote, "we differ with your proposal because it is unconstitutional since a plebiscite . . . or a referendum is not contemplated in our constitution. The demand that the president and his family leave the country is [also] notoriously unconstitutional because that would involve banishment and that has been excluded from our constitution."

Hours later the FAO also rejected the plan because it did not seek Somoza's immediate resignation. The FAO urged the United Nations and the OAS to apply sanctions against Somoza's regime, isolating him and forcing him from office. FAO negotiator Alfonso Robelo in Nicaragua said a plebiscite with Somoza "not viable."

Patting the thick OAS human rights report, he said, "It is going to be very incongruous having the OAS condemn Somoza for massive violation of human rights. He should be on trial for these crimes and yet they [the international mediators] want to put him in a referendum. Is that logical?"

The OAS human rights commission's eighty-one-page report called upon the United Nations member states to impose effective sanctions against Somoza's regime for the "horrendous crimes he committed" and urged them to take "immediate action to prevent a repetition of these acts of genocide." The strongly worded report gave the opposition new ammunition to hurl against Somoza and attack his flagrant, persistent abuses of human rights, including summary execution, torture, arbitrary detentions, indiscriminate bombing of unarmed civilians and the obstruction of the humanitarian efforts of the Red Cross. The report, described as a "shocker" by the Carter administration officials, was regarded as the most critical ever issued by the commission. Nicaraguan human rights commission coordinator José Esteban González said, after the report was released, that the United Nations charter made it possible to bring formal charges against Somoza for acts of genocide. "There is ample proof of these acts of genocide for which Somoza is directly responsible. The human rights climate couldn't be worse. Five to ten people are being killed daily." Most of them, he said, turn up dead after being apprehended by the authorities.

"Most of them show signs of torture and the women are often raped and found dead with their breasts slashed. Ninety percent of the victims are under the age of 25, and while some bodies turn up in the morgues most are found dead on the country roads. The victims are not necessarily youths who participated in the September civil war; many appear to have been denounced for one reason or other by informers of the regime. As there are no constitutional guarantees under the present state of martial law, the police and soldiers make the arrest by simply knocking on the door or knocking the door down."

From Costa Rica, Los Doce member Carlos Tunnerman declared that the OAS report must be "carefully examined so that international sanctions can be applied to isolate the Somoza regime." Tunnerman said even an economic boycott should be considered but he warned that if all such pacific actions failed to bring down Somoza, there would be no other choice or alternative but "armed struggle."

On October 26 the international mediators made their first public statement since their October 6 arrival, announcing that they had presented Somoza with an opposition document that contained an alternative formula for the peaceful, lasting and democratic solution to the current situation in Nicaragua. Although the mediators' statement did not reveal the exact contents of the document, sources close to FAO said it called for Somoza's resignation to the Congress in a constitutionally acceptable form and the banishment of both him and his family from Nicaragua. His successor would be appointed by the Congress from its ranks and would probably rule until 1979, when a three-man civilian junta would lead a transitional government which would allow a free election in 1981 after reforming the constitution, perhaps in 1980.[5]

"The conditions of the document," Somoza said later, "are conditions that they are asking or demanding that we do. As of today I cannot give you an answer other than what I said before, which is that I'm living by the constitution and those people are asking me to break the constitution. . . . One of the things that I would ask the opposition is that they abide by the laws of Nicaragua."[6]

On October 26 another statement was issued that provoked even more interest than that of the mediators. It was a communiqué signed by National Guard medic Colonel Alejandro Lara and it stated that Somoza had a broken toe on his left foot. Who inflicted this wound? The only clue in the guard statement was that the "fracture stemmed from a blow suffered nine days earlier." Bunker aides found it difficult to suppress the story of Tacho's wound which they joked about as arising from the battlefield of honor.

After presiding over the opening of a new lobster factory in San Juan del Sur, Somoza had attended a party at the beach home of a leading Nationalist Liberal politician. Nicaragua being the land of poets, a local troubadour sang his original composition about a tragic love affair which strangely paralleled Dinorah's situation as Tacho's mistress. The song brought tears to Dinorah's eyes. Soon she was sobbing. Tacho, who had sometime before abandoned his ration of half a glass of wine for daily trysts with vodka, wanted to know why his "Dinita" was crying. When it was explained the singer had upset her, a befuddled Tacho staggered to his feet and in a drunken rage chased the singer out of the house and along the beach. Despite his state of inebriation, Tacho came close to overtaking the unfortunate man, but not quite. He made a last effort to defend his Dinorah's honor by aiming his left foot at the musician's backside. Tacho's kick missed its mark and collided with a rock instead. Nine days later the swelling had become so great that he was rushed to the nearby military hospital for an x-ray, which revealed the broken toe. The foot was placed in a plaster cast and the Bunker society had something to laugh about— behind the chief's back.

The FAO said it was accepting the mediation team's proposal for a plebiscite but made it contingent on a series of thirteen conditions that would be difficult for Somoza to accept. The first demand was that Somoza leave the country during the campaign for a plebiscite and that he hand over the presidency to an interim president for that period. The FAO asked that all Somoza family members with military positions also leave the country because "they are principally responsible for the massacres and other human rights violations denounced by the OAS human rights commission." They demanded that the National Guard be commanded by an officer "not compromised by the repression" and that the guard be confined to its barracks fifteen days before the vote. The FAO also asked the OAS, which would supervise the plebiscite, to establish a mechanism whereby "hundreds of thousands" of Nicaraguan exiles could vote abroad; to study methods of voting fraud used in previous elections by the Somozas and to take measures to prevent recurrence; to control campaign spending and eliminate the automatic 5 percent payroll deduction from all civil servants of Somoza's Nationalist Liberal party. The FAO said it accepted the plebiscite proposal the second time around because it was confident that a referendum would result in a "massive repudiation of the Somoza regime. But, the opposition said, "no fair plebiscite is possible unless the repressive machinery [of the Somoza government] is neutralized."[7]

Somoza spent an entire day meeting with Bowdler and the other two mediators but did not issue a statement. "Time is of the utmost importance here and the mediation efforts continue to drag on and on and on and this is bad," said one mediator.

But there were other mediators nearby in the Hotel Intercontinental. Fifty clean-cut well-groomed young Americans, practitioners of transcendental meditation, had arrived in Managua claiming they would restore peace and prevent further bloody violence by using their brainpower. They claimed their presence had brought about the reduction in curfew hours and the lifting of press censorship. Dressed like wealthy young executives in three-piece suits, despite the oppressive heat, the young Americans, outwardly serene, spent hours each day on mattresses in the Rubén Darío salon of the hotel and behind closed doors meditating and trying to levitate. Levitation, they explained, is the ultimate in the exercise of TM science. Newsmen in Managua awaiting the new guerrilla offensive and covering the mediation talks, were permitted a brief look at the TMers at work. Some of them were sitting in yoga-style positions on white mattresses while others hopped around the large convention room like frogs. The hopping, they explained, was the first stage in levitation, though none of them, they admitted, had ever achieved levitation.

They claimed to have 600 students in Managua who had paid an average of twenty dollars each for a four-day course in TM. "We would like to see President Somoza and sell him on the idea of TM so that he will understand that weapons are not necessary," said group coordinator Jonathan Gordon, of Cambridge, Massachussetts, who added they were sent to Nicaragua by TM world leader Maharishi Mahesh Yogi in Switzerland. He said the group had sent telegrams to Somoza but had not received a reply.[8]

On November 2 there was a stronger than usual report that the hotel would be in the line of fire of a supposed mortar attack by Sandinistas on the Somoza Bunker and guard headquarters complex across the street. The threat was serious enough for the international mediation team to quit the hotel and seek quarters in their respective embassies. They did not return to the hotel. The meditation people called the Maharishi in Switzerland for advice. With unconcealed pride Thomas Zimmer, an assistant to Gordon, recounted how His Holiness gave instructions not only to stay but to move in reinforcements. "More orderliness was needed," Zimmer said. Thirty more TMers moved into the hotel.

Ironically it had been a secret report that the United States intercepted of a Panamanian-Venezuelan plot to bomb the Bunker complex in September that had persuaded Washington of the urgency of the mediation effort to defuse what had obviously become the most dangerous crisis in the hemisphere in many years. The whole idea of a bombing run by one of the Venezuelan Canberra bombers that were briefly stationed in Costa Rica, along with Panamanian helicopters, may have been a plot completely manufactured by Panama's strongman General Omar Torrijos and

Venezulan president Carlos Andrés Pérez to pressure the United States into action. But the United States took the threat seriously enough at the time to summon the Panamanian ambassador to Washington and voice the administration's concern. Panama has not revealed what National Security Adviser Zbigniew Brzezinski told its ambassador in September 1978 at the White House, but Torrijos traces a toughening of the American attitude toward Somoza after that episode.

The mediators took credit for warding off the mortar attack which would have certainly changed the shape of the pyramid-style Intercontinental.

Nearly two weeks later, Somoza announced he had accepted the plebiscite in theory and would share power with the opposition if he lost, but he brushed aside the main opposition demand that he resign and leave the country. By this time the FAO mediators had given Somoza a November 21 deadline to quit or they would pull out of the mediation. A new stalemate had begun on November 12 when Bowdler and his colleagues, exhausted by Somoza's intransigence, had returned to their countries for "consultations."

On November 17 two of Somoza's staunchest supporters in the United States Congress flew to Managua to back up their friend. Sitting behind automatic rifles and a rocket launcher said to have been captured from the Sandinistas, Representatives John Murphy and Charles Wilson agreed with Somoza's version of a plebiscite and stressed that it was the only way in which to test the electoral strength of all parties and prevent further violence. On November 23 it appeared as if both Murphy and Wilson were running for office in a Somoza-type election. In a very different kind of air raid from what the people had become accustomed to in September, low-flying air force planes bombed the city with red-colored pamphlets showing pictures of both Congressman Murphy and Wilson. The pamphlet endorsed Somoza's idea of a plebiscite, which was called a voter's census to see what members of the opposition might join him in power before his term ended May 1, 1981. Somoza explained to one aide that he was encouraged by the visit of his Congressmen friends who had advised him, he said, "to stick around" and not give in to "the goddamned commies, here and there [Washington]."

This was not a new charge. Somoza's trump card was his "anticommunism" and he knew how to play it. In September he had said that Carter was surrounded by "communists and fellow-travelers." He refused to name them, saying, "My American friends know who they are."

The following day Ray Molina, Somoza's close business associate, identified Patricia Derian, assistant secretary of state for human rights and humanitarian affairs, as a "Marxist." He added that Robert Pastor, the National Security Council expert on Latin America, along with Mark Schneider, Derian's deputy, were in the leftist camp. The State Department issued a statement saying the charges were groundless and that "the United States rejects totally these defamations." But Tacho had managed to picture himself as a victim of an international communist conspiracy with contacts even in Washington.

The mediators returned a few days before the FAO deadline but reached no agreement with the negotiators. On November 21, with a few hours left, Somoza refused to resign but did lift the nationwide curfew which had been in effect since September 12 and eased television and radio control. (Radios and television stations had been in a nationwide hookup that banned local newscasts and required them to carry the government news programs.) But Robelo replied that the measures were "not enough. Our deadline stands firm. For us to change our minds would take a restoration of full constitutional freedoms and guarantees plus total amnesty for all political prisoners."

The deadline had made the editorial pages of the leading United States newspapers and the negotiators began eleventh-hour talks with both sides. *The Washington Post* warned, "All guns are on a hair trigger," and said, "One can understand why the opposition feels angered and insulted by the thought of having to enter an electoral contest against a man who, it correctly thinks, has forfeited any legitimate claim to hold power." The *Post* editorial of November 21 ended, "Part of the Somoza strategy is to hope Washington will fear that a free-for-all will lead to a "second Cuba." That is blackmail. Anastasio Somoza is a bloody dictator and he cannot be allowed to hide behind American apprehensions about communism."

The New York Times's editorial the same day noted that "General Somoza has made war against his own civilian population and alienated all the forces whose cooperation would be needed in a democratic society. He seems now to have decided not to submit his regime to a popular referendum and to reject all compromises that depend on the ballot. There is nothing left for a frustrated mediator except to make clear to him that he will be completely isolated if he seeks to retain power by force alone." If Somoza read these editorials he gave no sign. Instead he said he would not respect the "Washington plan" because he favored his own formula. "If it's my personal plebiscite, I have no objection. But if it's a plebiscite on the presidency I will have to consult with my party. I cannot constitutionally put the presidency on a plebiscite."

The FAO walked out of the talks promptly at midnight. "There is nothing more to talk about," Robelo said. "The talks are finished." They were studying, they explained, new nonviolent forms of resistance including a possible new general strike.

The failure of the talks signaled to many the beginning of a countdown for a new round in the civil war. Tension was high and hundreds of wealthier Nicaraguans were trying to leave the country by air, while the poor were crossing into neighboring Honduras and Costa Rica, swelling refugee camps that already held an estimated sixty thousand refugees from the September civil war. A United Nations commission on refugees in Geneva appropriated $525,000 to aid them.

On November 22 Costa Rica broke diplomatic relations with Nicaragua after a border clash in which Nicaraguan guardsmen killed two Costa Rican civil guardsmen (Costa Rica prides itself on having no army) and took a civil guardsman captain prisoner along with a wounded Costa Rican civilian. The incident took place on Costa Rican soil two miles from Peñas Blancas in the first such clash between the two nations' forces since a brief border war in 1955. Nicaragua alleged that the Costa Ricans had attacked its border post first, wounding one soldier. Costa Rican President Rodrigo Carazo demanded a meeting of the OAS foreign ministers and called for the ouster of the Somoza regime from that hemispheric body. Venezuela quickly seconded the Costa Rican appeal.

An energetic man, Carazo demanded that Somoza immediately return the prisoners who were being exhibited in Managua as evidence that Costa Rica was at fault. The Costa Rican president also asked President Carter to intervene in the matter. Meanwhile the 450-mile-long border between the two countries was closed.

Shortly after the border clash, a Somoza ship, the *Managua*, was seized in the Costa Rican port of Puerto Limón, by "enraged Costa Rican workers." Somoza called the seizing of his ship an act of piracy. Costa Rica had at the same time dispatched a special envoy to Caracas to consult with President Carlos Andrés Pérez. Costa Rica had made a mutual defense pact with Venezuela at the time of the September insurrection, when Venezuela had sent war planes and Panama helicopters to help defend Costa Rica against any threat from Somoza.

During October the OAS, with Guatemala, Trinidad and Tobago, Honduras and Paraguay abstaining, had voted 19–0 in Costa Rica's favor censuring the "deliberate violation of Costa Rican air space by the Nicaraguan air force." Costa Rican border towns had been bombed and strafed in September, the nation alleged. Somoza defended these attacks as a "reprisal" against the Sandinistas who were known to be operating training camps inside the Costa Rican border. He was furious with Costa Rica, not only for giving safe haven to the Sandinistas but also because earlier in the year Costa Rica had expropriated his 47,000-hectare Murcielago ranch, which had been valued for tax purposes at only two million dollars. It was to become a national park.

Coinciding with the breaking of relations with Costa Rica was the cancellation of a Nicaraguan request for a twenty-million-dollar standby loan from the Central American Monetary Fund. This loan was equivalent to the one denied Somoza by the International Monetary Fund (IMF), following pressure on the IMF by the Carter administration. The meeting to consider the Nicaraguan loan was to have taken place in Guatemala City, but was canceled when the chairman of the Central American Monetary Fund, who happened to be the president of the Costa Rican Central Bank, said he could not attend. Somoza, who watched in amazement as Carter pressured the IMF against extending any credit to Nicaragua, was even more upset by the actions of the Costa Rican who declined to travel the short distance between San José and Guatemala City and in reality was blocking the Central American loan.

Somoza was ending the year desperately short of cash mainly because of the war and because he was also exporting some funds abroad "just in case." Nicaragua's debts and expenses were growing and income was shrinking. Former Central Bank financial director Dr. Raúl Lacayo told *La Prensa* that Nicaragua's external debt had grown at such a rate that the cost of servicing it in 1978 was $148.4 million compared to $88.4 million in 1976. The cost of debt servicing had risen 237 percent from 1973 to 1978, Lacayo said, while the government's tax income had increased only 129 percent in the same period.[9]

Harvesting of the traditional coffee and cotton crops presented problems—not only was much of the country's population dislocated by the war but seasonal workers from Honduras and El Salvador who helped in the harvests had been scared off by the fighting. There was growing evidence that the opposition might sacrifice the crops to sabotage rather than see the government collect urgently needed funds for guns.

Arms and munition purchases were swelling the government debt as Somoza increased the size of his National Guard from 8,100 to close to 11,000. But the event in which Tacho took pride was personally promoting Tachito to the rank of Lieutenant Colonel for his outstanding service in helping to put down the September uprising in Masaya, León, Estelí and Chinandega. Following Tachito's promotion and a military parade there was a family party at the family seaside villa at Montelimar. Dinita, as Tacho's mistress liked to call herself, acted as hostess.

Foreign weapons salesmen were flocking to Central America in search of high profits from the little arms race already under way. Though he boasted superior firepower and an arsenal of unused American automatic rifles, Somoza went on a buying spree in early 1978. He had decided to change the guard's standard arms, the American World War II Garand M-1, for the modern Israeli Galil assault rifle, he explained. Actually Somoza had decided to seek an alternative arms supplier even before Washington suspended military credits to Nicaragua and banned arms sales. Israel was the logical alternative. The Somozas could trace their pro-Israel stance to the United Nations' vote creating the Israeli state. Israel had an excellent inventory of weapons, and sold to governments no matter what their politics.

The unused weapons in the guard arsenal included five thousand M-16 automatic rifles that the United States government stipulated in the sales contract could not be used for internal police work. Somoza's specially trained 100-man bodyguard detail was armed with M-16s and they were soon issued to other guard companies, despite the prohibition clause. The Galil assault rifle and the lightweight UZI submachine gun from Israel soon began to appear in the hands of the guard. But ground-to-air missiles and high-speed patrol boats, which were part of Somoza's arms deal with Israel, did not arrive—the United States intervened. The Israeli ship had almost reached the Atlantic coast when it suddenly reversed its course and returned to Israel. Aboard the ship, Somoza protested, were "lifesaving arms that could spell the outcome of the war. There was abundant ammunition and more than ten thousand antitank and antipersonnel grenade rifles."

The military governments of El Salvador, Guatemala and Brazil aided Somoza by replenishing his munition supply while Argentina became involved in the sale of more sophisticated weaponry. A month after Pedro Joaquín Chamorro's assassination, Somoza purchased a rocket-launching device along with a supply of four thousand rockets for $2.7 million from Argentina. The purchase was made through Interpac Enterprises, S.A., which had a United States address in Key Biscayne, Florida. The apartment turned out to be the address of Ray Molina.

The Sandinistas and Somoza used the mediation period to stockpile arms and munitions and train fresh troops for the next round of the fight.

Panama and Venezuela had become the principal supporters of the Sandinista cause. Panama's Brigadier General Omar Torrijos was particularly disposed to aid the Terceristas of the FSLN, as was President Carlos Andrés Pérez, the Social Democrat.

The FAL automatic rifle of Belgian make which was also manufactured in Venezuela became the standard weapon of Sandinista guerrillas. With their serial numbers removed, the rifles were routed from Venezuela through Panama to Costa Rica where they were then smuggled into Nicaragua. But the sources of Sandinista arms were many. Some FAL rifles Venezuela had seized in the 1960s en route from Cuba to Venezuelan guerrillas showed up in Nicaragua. Cuba, which ideologically supported the GPP, whose members were all avowed socialists, and at first looked on the unity of the three factions and the various forces with a certain suspicion, was accused of funneling arms through Panama to the Sandinistas, a charge Somoza could never prove.

The Sandinistas' own arms buyers ranged around the world, making deals with even French and German arms salesmen. Some M-1 carbines were purchased from a Florida factory. Mexican authorities allowed Sandinista sympathizers in California to ship a considerable amount of arms through Mexico and on to Nicaragua. The Palestine Liberation Organization contributed arms, and at least one Sandinista was known to have fought with the PLO. Reports that the Sandinistas were obtaining ground-to-air missiles proved to be only part of their psychological warfare against the Somoza forces. They did obtain some small RPG-2 Chinese-made rockets and recoilless rifles for sale on the arms black market.

La Hacha, an old American-owned plantation with an airstrip, and Lano Grande airfield in the province of Liberia became the major links in the supply route into Costa Rica; although some shipments of war supplies, including a 707 from West Germany and a DC-8 from Portugal, landed at the Juan Santamaria International airport in the capital, San Jose.

While Costa Rica was pro-Sandinista and anti-Somoza the government of President Rodrigo Carazo Odio made a pretense of playing neutral. Whenever Sandinistas were caught they were deported to Panama. The trip was called R & R—rest and relaxation. They quickly returned to their camps in Costa Rica. In Costa Rica the Sandinista leadership lived in a twilight zone moving between safe houses and using assumed names. Humberto Ortega, head of the Terceristas, made his wartime headquarters there even though he had a sixteen-year jail sentence hanging over his head for trying to free Carlos Fonseca from jail in 1969. (Costa Rica formally dropped the sixteen-year jail sentence in August 1980 after Humberto became commander in chief of the armed forces and defense minister of Nicaragua.)

The Sandinistas claimed their forces now had swollen to more than two thousand and were placed in command of Eden Pastora, the charismatic forty-two-year-old Comandante Cero, whose gesture of defiance on leaving Managua after the palace raid had conveyed the right image to millions. The Sandinistas told reporters they had had little to do with organizing the "spontaneous rebellion" in September. If they had planned it, one guerrilla leader said, "the people would have been better armed and better prepared." It was only after the extent of the guard's retaliation was seen, they said, that their commandos stepped in to organize and lead the population.[10]

The Sandinistas' secret training camps in Costa Rica and Honduras were visited by reporters. Newspapers throughout the hemisphere began carrying accounts of life in the camps datelined "somewhere in Nicaragua," since a condition the guerrillas imposed on those permitted to witness their training was that their location could not be disclosed. Some overcame this by using the dateline "somewhere in Central America," or as Karen DeYoung did, "at a Sandinista training camp."

Training was conducted by veteran guerrillas, like Pastora, who taught strategy, firing positions and weapons handling. Except for occasional minor strikes at National Guard outposts, the Sandinistas said, they were spending their time "resting, regrouping and training" the new members, many of whom said they had never shot a gun before September's battles.[11]

Pastora said the Sandinistas received a great deal of military experience in their abortive raid over the Costa Rican border in September and said it failed because "the arms came late and we had to walk to the border for a long distance. There were only sixty of us that got across the border, only one of three columns. Initially our plan was to take Rivas but we were too late and [the National Guard] had already sent reinforcements. . . . We were under constant fire for nine hours by tanks, mortars, artillery and airplanes. No Latin American movement has had the kind of experience that we have had."[12]

Besides Pastora, the other Sandinista most sought after by reporters in the camps was twenty-nine-year-old attorney Nora Astorga, a mother of two and three months pregnant. She had been in hiding since March 8 when General Reynaldo (Perro) Pérez Vega, the guard's number two man, was found dead, his body draped with the red and black FSLN flag, in her bedroom. Following two years as a student in Washington and Rome she had returned to Managua where she worked as an attorney for a construction firm and joined the underground. Pérez Vega had been negotiating a land deal through the firm and continually made passes at Nora. She accepted them only because she had decided she could set him up for a kill. Upon arrival at her house he led her to her bedroom where she "embraced him immediately, holding him tightly around the chest." The guerrillas hiding in the house slipped up behind Pérez Vega and cut his throat from ear to ear. Then they dumped his body on the bed and covered it with the flag.[13] The government charged that Pérez Vega was slain after he put up a fight and foiled a kidnap attempt and Somoza issued a formal statement to that effect to the international press.

In the camps Nora taught political classes to the recruits. She also took part in the raid at Peñas Blancas. According to her, she was, like the rest, "a Sandinista first. I studied law in Managua and became an attorney for a large construction company. There is nothing special about me—I spent two years studying in the United States and in Europe. I was part of the privileged class.

"It was easy to see, in my own profession, the way the Nicaraguan government operates. The injustice, the corruption. My own job was to find ways for the company to avoid paying taxes. For years, I tried to change things legally, and I saw that it was all impossible. I realized that, no matter how good, or how dedicated, one person can't fight alone. And I saw the Sandinistas as the only organization that had a chance of succeeding."[14]

Among the recruits in the Sandinistas' camps was an eighty-man Panamanian volunteer brigade "Victoriano Lorenzo" led by former Panamanian deputy health minister Hugo Spadáfora and including volunteers from Costa Rica, Venezuela, Colombia, Honduras, Mexico and the United States.

On November 25 Somoza threw a Sunday evening cocktail party under clear, starry skies for about forty foreign correspondents, serving thirty-dollar bottles of Moskovskaya vodka which were imported from Moscow, and filling La Curvita's backyard with the music of a four-man combo to serenade the guests who were nibbling on shrimp, tiny meatballs and beef dipped in rich sauces and served by waiters in red coats and black pants. Outside was an armored personnel carrier, and dozens of troops in battle fatigues and black berets toting automatic weapons. Somoza's party, said an aide, was a way of telling the foreign press that the man neither expected violence nor would step down as his opponents wanted. And, the aide noted, Somoza could also get some "public relations mileage" out of it. "He loves the American press," said another aide, "even if it criticizes him so much."

The reporters, their cameras clicking and tape recorders rolling as American network TV cameras taped the scene, grilled Somoza, mainly on whether he planned to resign. "Everybody is so interested in pushing me out," Somoza said at one point. "My adversaries, they want all of a sudden to fix up everything so that Somoza can go. But they forget that . . . I am not inflexible in things that can be flexible. If I get sick I can resign or if I get disgusted, I can resign." Quickly, almost in unison, reporters asked if he was disgusted. "Not quite," he answered.

He hinted that almost the only way to decide his future would be his own version of a plebiscite to decide on whether the opposition should be allowed to share power in the government. "Do you think I would stay in power if my cabinet was against me?" he asked. He had previously said that if the opposition won such a referendum he would include opponents in his cabinet. Then, reflecting on the national crisis, Somoza revealed that he had been forced to cancel a planned weekend trip to the United States because of unsettled conditions in Nicaragua. He said he would have gone to the United States "for family matters" had the opposition reached an agreement the previous week.

Asked point-blank if he thought war was inevitable, he said no. But he admitted that guerrilla actions might increase. He ruled out the possibility of war with Costa Rica over the guerrilla camps and also discounted possible Nicaraguan strikes against the camps. "No way," he said emphatically.[15]

By November 28 the mediation team had resubmitted the "Washington plan" and gave Somoza and the FAO seventy-two hours in which to make their decision. If there was no response, the mediators said, they would quit and go home. The ultimatum set off a feverish round of new talks in the camp of Somoza's own

National Liberal party as well as within the ranks of the FAO. For three hours the FAO representatives agonized over the issues before breaking up to give their rank-and-file a chance to react before making a final decision on the plan.

Robelo harked back to the primary objection. No plebiscite with Somoza in power. With Somoza in the country it would be impossible to change the climate of repression, he said. Other opposition leaders complained bitterly that in resubmitting the same proposal already rejected by both sides, the mediators had shown a lack of initiative. To some members of the opposition the almost Oriental patience of quiet Bill Bowdler was getting under their skin. They questioned the motives of the mediators and were now highly suspicious, not wanting to admit that Somoza, playing for time, had made a monkey out of the so-called moderate opposition. The mediators defended their course of action saying "You always return to the central issue, whether Somoza will leave or not. Any way you approach it, you come upon it."[16]

Somoza, meanwhile, was reported in "permanent session" with his cabinet and National Liberal party executive committee preparing a reply for the deadline. His newspaper *Novedades* noted that he had been interrupted by a telephone call from General Alfredo Stroessner, the right-wing dictator of Paraguay, who wanted simply to deliver a personal message of encouragement to Tacho in his "fight against international communism." A beaming Tacho passed on the words of the Paraguayan general who had already established a modern-day record for holding on to power in his South American fiefdom. Both sides then tentatively agreed in principle to the idea of the plebiscite and then again began to tack on mutually unacceptable conditions.

Bowdler saw the mediation attempt begin to unravel again. "We ran into difficulties again," he said. "The FAO wanted on the ballot 'The president should continue in power: Sí or No.' " Then Tacho went back to the October document. "We dialogued and dialogued and thought we had overcome it."

Hanging tough, Somoza said, "Look, I'm willing to go and I'm going to give them a crack at me in the democratic way with a national plebiscite. If I win, I'll stay here. If the FAO gets a majority, then they'll have to run this country.

"The FAO is made up of good, decent people. I'm not fighting the FAO. But they don't know what they are getting into. Whoever wins this popular vote is going to have to fight the Sandinistas. If the FAO wins and I leave before my time is up in 1981, the only way a new government can survive is by joining forces with the National Guard for defending the country and preserving order. And I am the only one who can bless this marriage."[17]

The mediators' next move was to try to persuade the opposition to hold face-to-face talks with Somoza but Robelo quickly overruled that. "I see no chance for getting together," he said. "With the current conditions and with Somoza in power this is going to be very hard for the FAO to agree on. It'd be very unpopular to go to the same negotiating table with them while we have a lot of political prisoners in jail. How could we explain to them that we have gone to the same table with the guys who put them in jail?" Tunnerman agreed, adding, "What the FAO should do is reject the plan and break off the mediation talks."

The plan suggested that the referendum be held in two or three months, or within sixty days of an agreement by the two sides, mentioning January 1 as the target date to begin organizing the vote. Somoza had shown himself more astute in playing with the mediators than the FAO. In early December some people were wisecracking that it was no longer "Somoza-ism without Somoza but a good possibility of Somoza-ism with Somoza."

The Sandinistas meanwhile were taking steps to ensure the war would have another act before the final curtain. On December 4 Tomás Borge showed up in the Del Prado Hotel in Mexico City and announced to a small group of newspeople that the FSLN was unifying its military and political command to include each of the three factions. Leaning forward in his chair he talked earnestly about the unity move. The final step had been taken, he admitted, after Estelí in September where the Frente united and managed to resist longer than in the other towns.

"The three factions have sufficient resources to launch the war in our country," Borge said. "We will never abandon our arms. We won't lay down our arms before or after victory because they are our guarantees of democracy. We have enough resources to carry the war on to its ultimate consequences. The blood that has been shed will not be in vain and will spur on the revolutionary struggle."

It was a different Borge who had emerged from prison after the August palace raid to declare himself a Marxist in Panama. "Somoza painted us as Marxists," said the only surviving founder of the FSLN. "We have some Marxists with us but the Frente is much wider. The concept of the prolonged popular war [Borge's faction] was not Marxist. It is a military concept which will lead to taking advantage of the favorable moment."

Borge was not optimistic that December evening in the Mexico City hotel room. He warned the small group of newsmen present that the war would not be a quick one. "It's not a final offensive that is going to start," he said. "People die every day in Managua. It will be an intensification of the struggle that is going on and it will last a long time."

In regard to United States aid to the dictator he touched a more realistic note. "We have to be realistic and realize that it is in our best interest to have normal relations with the United States, to forget the past," he said. But he believed the United States was playing a dubious role in trying to negotiate a settlement in Nicaragua which he believed was designed chiefly to halt the popular revolutionary process. "Somoza," Borge said, "will never allow such a vote because he knows that he is completely rejected by the Nicaraguan people whom he has bombed and shelled as an enemy and continues to kill daily."

The FSLN rejected mediation, he said, because it was intervention in the internal affairs of Nicaragua. The war would continue and the FSLN would back a patriotic solution of the Unified People's Movement (MPU) which he described as not socialist but democratic, a movement with a broad popular base. As to whether the MPU was Marxist-Leninist, Borge replied, "We are all Sandinistas, and *sandinismo* is revolutionary science applied to the Nicaragua reality. We are neither Marxist nor liberal, we are Sandinistas." The ultimate goal of the FSLN and MPU was the establishment of a national democratic government "which will do what the

Nicaraguan people want and will take the direction that the people demand."

The next day, December 5, in Managua, Somoza, who was celebrating his fifty-third birthday in his Tizcapa bunker, was also in a nationalistic mood saying he would never accept a foreign solution for Nicaragua. "This is why I'm willing to risk my life. The people chose the destiny they now have and now they can choose a new path or they can say if they want to continue as today. I and the National Guard can accept a popular mandate but never a solution imposed from abroad." Speaking to top National Guard officers, Somoza said, "I'm sorry that on my birthday, usually a time of joy, I have to speak to you of things like this. If there is no agreement not all of us will be back in this room. I will never be able to repay the loyalty you have shown under these circumstances, only to respond to you as a man doing his duty as a statesman."

The Nationalist Liberal party proved their loyalty to Somoza with a traditional annual birthday gift, this time the equivalent of fifty thousand dollars. Somoza said he would donate the money with an equal sum of his own to help the children of government soldiers killed in the September insurrection. In previous years, the party had given Somoza such gifts as a mobile home, a yacht, forty-six prize pigs imported from Taiwan and fine horses.[18]

Somoza moved to placate the opposition by announcing the end of martial law, promising a sweeping amnesty for thousands of guerrillas, political prisoners and exiles and revealing that he would eventually order the revision of a hated radio censorship law known as "the black code." Within days some 111 political prisoners were released under the amnesty which covered all civilian and military persons convicted from the time of the last amnesty, March 3, 1967.

As part of the amnesty, seven Los Doce members who had sought refuge in the Mexican embassy left the diplomatic mission. They called on the FAO to abandon the mediation process and join a patriotic front and urged Washington to cut off economic, diplomatic and military ties with Somoza, accusing the United States of trying to "neutralize" the Sandinista struggle.

The announcements were seen as major concessions and led to the first face-to-face talks between Somoza's government and the opposition, a crowning omen for the two-month-old mediation effort. The mediation panel arrived back in Managua a day after the announcement to present a modified plan calling for a Nicaraguan plebiscite authority, supervised and checked by an international commission. No other points in the earlier proposal were modified. Robelo, upon receiving the new plan, said he was surprised the mediators had not come back with a new proposal to break the deadlock. "We thought the mediation effort was finished because Somoza did not accept the proposal," said Robelo, and he later added, "We will not begin direct talks with the Somoza regime until we see all the prisoners out on the streets."

Said Tunnerman, in a telephone interview from Costa Rica, "We reject this amnesty totally. I especially dislike the part of the amnesty about military officers. It means Somoza is giving himself a self-amnesty to clear himself of responsibility for the September massacres." Ernesto Cardenal, also in Costa Rica, said the only solution to the crisis was the armed overthrow of Somoza. "It would be high treason to a nation which has lost so much blood to accept this plebiscite which would be in Somoza's benefit. This plebiscite will be known as the plebiscite of the buzzards because of all the dead in September. The struggle will continue."

Robelo made a trip to Costa Rica to try to push for agreement in backing the talks but failed to persuade guerrillas and radicals to support the FAO. Cardenal said that if the opposition front began negotiations with Somoza still in power "it will become a traitor to the Nicaraguan people and as such it will be condemned by the Sandinistas." As if to prove their point, the Sandinistas intensified their military operations with armed confrontations, bank robberies and other actions around the country. In one action gunmen opened fire on Somoza's private secretary, Edgar Solano Luna, but killed his chauffeur while the two were handing out Christmas toys in Monimbó. "The much awaited offensive has begun," one army officer said. "But it is not a frontal attack, rather it is a war of attrition."

Clashes between the Sandinistas and the guard continued in the north where a mountain war had raged for three weeks with air strikes and ground sweeps in the heaviest fighting since the September insurrection. In the south on December 11, a five-man squad led by the Reverend Gaspar García Laviana, a priest from Asturias, Spain, battled guardsmen in an area known as El Infierno near the Costa Rican border. Father García, a major figure in the Tercerista faction and the best known Sandinista leader in the region, was killed along with guerrilla chieftain Luis Arroyo, the former manager of a hotel in Rivas. The death of the thirty-seven-year-old priest was mourned not only by the Sandinistas but by his former parishioners in the little town of Tola, not far from Rivas. In an interview in October Father García sat inspecting a cache of automatic rifles and told why he had become a firearms expert with the guerrillas. "I tried to save the situation in a Christian manner, in the pacifist sense of social promotion, but I realized that all this was a big trick."

With the mediation at an impasse and with the realization that Somoza had no intention of bending to pressure from the negotiators, the administration ordered to Nicaragua General Dennis McAuliffe, commander in chief of the Southern Command in Panama, on the chance that a high-ranking officer in the United States Army might be able to "talk some sense into Tacho." After all, Tacho was a gradudate of West Point, and while he hated "those striped-pants bastards," he treasured his links with the American military.

But when General McAuliffe arrived for his meeting on December 21, Tacho was disappointed to see that Bowdler was with him. "I knew then it would be the same old crap," Tacho told an aide. Bowdler, he said "began making the same old pitch and complaining about a lack of cooperation. They didn't want to hear what I had to say, but I said plenty and told them it was I who wanted peace. But they said it was too late for negotiations; it boiled down to 'Somoza has to go.'"

McAuliffe had explained the concern of the Joint Chiefs of Staff about stability in the area, Tacho later related to an aide, "and there would be no stability as long as I remained. I was supposed to be the magnet that was attracting the communists." The United States position had not changed. If Somoza stepped down there was a chance of a moderate government taking power and the National Guard could be reformed and then perhaps supported. Somoza's remaining at the helm would continue to polarize the country until a moderate solution would be impossible. The interview with General McAuliffe ended as all the others had. Tacho made no promises, and the meeting only reinforced his private theory that he was a victim of a diabolical conspiracy in Washington.

A few days after Christmas Somoza revealed a clever counterproposal rejecting the key points of the United States plan, but Bowdler told Tacho his plan was again unacceptable. In a nationally televised news conference Nationalist Liberal party spokesman Alceo Tabalada read the government's plan. It accepted OAS supervision of the plebiscite vote, but not full control, which it proposed be kept in the hands of the government party and the opposition. It accepted the president's resignation if he lost but not the self-exile clause and claimed that the American proposal "in many aspects not only violated the republic's constitution, but it also violated the sovereignty of Nicaragua because it proposed to turn over electoral control to the OAS."

Somoza added his own statements later in the day saying, "Their plan proposed that the polling stations be presided over by a foreigner and we propose that the polling stations only be watched over by a foreigner, but he would not have the right to reject voters or become the arbiter of the destiny of Nicaragua." As to State Department criticism of his plebiscite rejection, Somoza asked, "Why does the State Department censure me for trying to defend the national sovereignty of Nicaragua?" He said that "in due course" he would file a protest with the State Department.[19]

Bowdler called Somoza's proposal clearly unworkable and said the responsibility for the failure of mediation was clearly on Somoza's side. All the negotiations were in Spanish but Bowdler had taken Tacho aside and given him some advice in English: "I told him, 'If you decide to accept the mediation, you may not win the respect of your people, you will win their gratitude.' " There was never any doubt, Bowdler said later, about the results of a plebiscite. Somoza could never win such a vote. But at no time did Tacho weaken; he was obstinate, never wavering in his determination to finish out his term until May 1981. He had received additional weapons but he didn't reckon with the help Venezuela, Panama and Cuba would give his enemies. He thought he could repeat his tactics of the September insurrection by holding the capital and moving out and crushing uprisings at his leisure. But he didn't foresee what was coming. His crack units were soon to be tied down by an invasion of Sandinista forces from neighboring Costa Rica.

According to assistant secretary of state for Interamerican Affairs Viron P. Vaky, the mediation attempt "temporarily attenuated the climate of violence," and identified a number of procedures by which a process of reconciliation might develop.[20] But Somoza's fundamental rigidity also demonstrated the tenuousness of hopes for compromise. Intransigence fed intransigence with the relentlessness of a self-fulfilling prophecy. Week by week, Somoza's position deteriorated and his opposition became more radicalized.

Somoza's friends in the United States Congress had not helped matters. Their advice only fueled Tacho's obstinacy and gave him false hope. When Texas Congressmen Charlie Wilson on December 6 issued a statement in Managua saying he had linked the Nicaraguan issue to the Panama Canal treaties, Tacho thought he was more secure than he was and that his friends had President Carter over a barrel. Wilson accused Torrijos of supplying the Sandinistas with guns and with encouraging "Marxist revolutionaries" in Central America. He claimed he had enough House votes to block the Panama treaty legislation which he said he intended to "torpedo." The State Department was furious over the congressman's pro-Somoza press conference in Managua. Wilson responded to their anger by charging the State Department was being run by a "bunch of adolescent anarchists" and said that the policy the United States backed in Nicaragua was "encouraging communism in the Caribbean." He said that the department had "broken its word" to him with its refusal to disburse twelve million dollars to the Somoza government following the civil war. (The aid money had been authorized several months earlier in exchange for Wilson's agreement not to sabotage the administration's entire eight-billion-dollar 1979 foreign aid bill.) The State Department retaliated the next day by saying administration policy was directed toward a "peaceful, democratic resolution" of the Nicaraguan crisis and that such efforts "are not helped, nor is public understanding of the situation improved by statements and charges such as those by Congressman Wilson."[21]

Fighting remained heavy along the Costa Rican border and Somoza was forced to airlift troop reinforcements to the Peñas Blancas area before ordering an indefinite shutdown of the entire southern border "until the government of Costa Rica takes the necessary measures" to prevent Sandinista forays.

"The town of Peñas Blancas has been harassed constantly by subversive elements who have positions only 300 yards within Costa Rican territory," a Nicaraguan foreign ministry statement said. "This situation has created an atmosphere of insecurity in the area, endangering the lives of travelers and hampering the free transit on the Pan American Highway. . . . [Thus] the government is forced to close the border . . . and it will remain alert until Costa Rica stops these attacks."

In Costa Rica, the Sandinistas moved to name Tomás Borge general coordinator of the FSLN forces.

With the year nearly over, Somoza huddled "somewhere in Central America" with the military presidents of Guatemala, Honduras and El Salvador seeking support in the Costa Rican border crisis and the international pressure mounting against his government.

Returning from his trip, his first outside the country since September, Somoza made a New Year's Eve speech saying, "The year of 1978 was one of the most difficult in the contemporary history of Nicaragua but I fervently wish that 1979 will restore reconciliation and [bring] change toward a lasting and permanent peace." Although he said he was still willing to talk to his foes, he warned that the National Guard "is stronger than ever" and is ready to repel any attack on his regime. However, he called on guerrillas and dissidents for a reconciliation.[22]

On New Year's Eve, United Press International reporter Alfonso Chardy and his wife, Sally, an NBC radio stringer, were the only two guests at the Intercontinental Hotel. "In Managua, thousands flocked to discothèques, nightclubs and restaurants to celebrate the new year," Chardy said. "In several nightclubs, witnesses saw that at the stroke of midnight many patrons rose with glasses of champagne in hand and yelled: 'Down with Somoza,' 'Viva free Nicaragua,' and 'Long live the Sandinistas.' At the restaurant of the hotel many young people at a party cheered as a middle-aged man shouted, 'Viva el FSLN.' The patrons cheered louder with each new cry. Young women at a nearby table giggled nervously, as their male escorts cheered and clapped, shouting back, 'Viva.' Egged on, the man yelled in quick succession, 'Viva FSLN,' 'Viva free Nicaragua,' and 'Viva the people.' Just as suddenly as it began it ended when the man sat down again and went back to his dinner and drinks."[23]

CHAPTER 15

Easter in Esteli

New Year's Day 1979 ushered in a fresh round of fighting with skirmishes border to border raising anew the specter of another Sandinista offensive. By the end of the first week of the new year the guerrillas had blown up a Somoza radio station in Managua, attacked one of his rice plantations and assassinated several of his close friends.

Somoza began the year with a rhetorical prayer to "the Lord that He may guide mankind on the paths of love and peace, preventing men and their leaders from plunging the nation into the abysses of hatred and discord." He then ordered his air force to the mountainous province of Estelí along the Honduran border to crush heavy fighting between the FSLN and guard troops. The renewed air strikes with indiscriminate bombing led the human rights commission of Nicaragua to charge that the planes bombed not guerrilla positions but civilian populations. On the ground, the commission charged soldiers with raping women and murdering children and the elderly. A call was issued by the commission "on all democratic nations of the world and especially on the Organization of American States to take immediate measures to prevent the continuing genocide."

Despite United States displeasure with Somoza and the mockery he had made of the mediation effort, Ambassador Solaun was on hand at Somoza's annual New Year's reception for the diplomatic corps.

Weighing heavily on Somoza was the first anniversary, on January 10, of the murder of his archenemy, newsman Pedro Joaquín Chamorro. Diplomatic and political analysts were predicting that the days leading up to the anniversary could be decisive. Somoza also foresaw the potential for trouble and issued a National Guard communiqué warning, "The demonstration or march to the cemetery will not be allowed if the organizing committee does not request a permit in accordance with the laws of the republic, accepting responsibility for law and order in such a march." Organizers said they would hold the memorial march with or without a permit. Somoza replied that troops would be on the alert to disperse them.

Tension mounted when opposition labor leader Luis Medrano Flores was shot and killed the eve of the march while passing out fliers on a Managua street corner inviting people to the memorial services. The thirty-seven-year-old leader of the moderate Labor Unification Confederation, Nicaragua's third largest labor group, was also a member of the FAO. Medrano had just returned from the United States, where he had met with the AFL-CIO longshoremen's union and won a tentative boycott of Nicaraguan ships and goods by the labor group. Conservative party president Alvaro Chamorro Mora called Medrano's assassination "a dangerous provocation to spark violence."

Managua on January 10 took on the appearance of a ghost town. Most stores and businesses closed their doors as a sign of mourning for Chamorro and as an anti-Somoza protest. The city was paralyzed. Buses and taxis stayed off the streets. At the last minute Somoza granted the demonstrators a parade permit and opened the day with, "Well, it looks like everything is going on schedule. They [opposition leaders] have their mass and their demonstration permit. I just hope they behave themselves." Despite claims that more than 100,000 people would take to the streets in protest, many stayed away fearing violence. Ten thousand marched from the church to the cemetery. The first incident of the day was the arrest and three-hour detention of the fourteen-year-old nephew of the slain publisher for tearing pro-Somoza signs off the walls of the church where Archbishop Obando y Bravo, assisted by Miguel d'Escoto and Fernando Cardenal, was to deliver the memorial mass.

A National Guard Piper airplane circled the crowd but troops earlier seen patrolling the streets in jeeps, some with heavy machine guns mounted on swivel tripods, were conspicuously absent. After marching for one mile through a working-class district the crowd reached the cemetery where hundreds more joined it, many carrying signs praising the Sandinistas, one showing a portrait of the now famous Comandante Cero. Outside the cemetery thousands staged a separate rally shouting for Somoza's downfall with cries of "Somoza and his chigüín to the firing squad." "Chigüín," meaning "kid" in Nicaraguan slang, was Tachito's nickname.

At the gravesite opposition leaders and demonstrators smothered Chamorro's tombstone with wreaths. At one point a youth clambered atop the marble cross on the grave and posted a red and black Sandinista flag. Others raised another Sandinista flag atop an archway at the entrance to the cemetery as the crowd cheered and clapped wildly. The crowd around the grave shouted, "Viva el Frente."

As people started drifting home from the cemetery, they were met by troops who began scattering the crowds with gunfire and tear gas. Several persons were shot and wounded. Colonel Aquiles Aranda Escobar, press spokesman for the National Guard, said the troops opened fire because a group of armed persons had fired on a military patrol.

The next day the Sandinista flag still rippled in the breeze at the cemetery and atop the marble cross on Chamorro's tombstone, as well as atop some of the houses in the working-class barrios around Managua. Thousands of new antigovernment slogans spray-painted by the demonstrators still peppered the walls of Managua.

Tacho in the meantime continued his jogging regimen in the presence of two foreign correspondents at the Bunker, relaxed and in good spirits. When asked why his troops had fired on the marchers, he said the soldiers had only repelled fire from an armed group that had attacked a police station near the demonstration site. "I'm very grateful that the [demonstrators] did it peacefully," Somoza said. "[The march] can be considered as a day without incidents."[1]

The United States–endorsed mediation team returned to Managua on January 11 to present a modified peace plan allowing Somoza to control a plebiscite but stipulating that the referendum would be supervised by an international authority. Ambassador Solaun was telling Tacho at the same time that the Carter administration would reassess its relations with Nicaragua if he turned it down. The opposition and Somoza were given a week's deadline to act on the new proposal, in which the other stipulations in the original plan remained intact. Robelo reacted by angrily walking out of an opposition meeting in which the plan was being discussed.

Somoza said to *Washington Post* correspondent Karen DeYoung before the mediators' arrival that he was still open to dialogue and would receive them but as far as reconsideration, "My position on the plebiscite is quite clear. I proposed it and I never thought that my proposal would be deviated into a vulgar intervention in Nicaragua." Somoza referred to sanctions by the United States in retaliation for his "no" vote as "presumptuous" and admitted "relations are going to get cool." The United States had had influence in Nicaragua at one time, Somoza said, "but they've lost it. They've been two years harassing my government. If they remove the military people and lower [diplomatic] representation, materially I would not lose anything else but a few nice gentlemen who are living in Nicaragua." Asked if he knew Washington's supposed plans to withdraw its diplomatic mission Somoza said, "Since it's a unilateral mission, it's for your grace to desire. We're not throwing them out. We're not fighting the people of the United States. It's the administration who has gotten tough against the government." A few days later the Liberal party rejected the new mediation attempt.

With the failure of the new attempt at mediation, Washington's next move was anxiously awaited by the left, right and middle groups in Nicaragua. After three weeks of hesitation, the White House decided to administer diplomatic punishment to Somoza for rejecting the "Washington plan." Long-standing military ties were severed, no new economic assistance would be considered "under present conditions." Twenty-one Peace Corps volunteers, four members of the military mission, eleven Agency for International Development officials and eleven embassy officials were withdrawn. The transfer of these forty-seven persons out of the country sliced by more than half the United States' official representation in Nicaragua.

"The unwillingness of the Nicaraguan Government to accept the group's proposals and the resulting prospects for renewed violence and polarization, and the human rights situation in Nicaragua, as reported by the Inter-American Commission on Human Rights, unavoidably affect the kind of relationship we can maintain with the Government," American State Department spokesman Hodding Carter III said. "The U.S. Government has reassessed its relationship with Nicaragua and has concluded that in these circumstances we cannot continue to maintain the same level and kind of presence in Nicaragua as we have had in the past." Hodding Carter added that thirty million dollars in economic aid projects were all well advanced and would be continued "since they are aimed at the basic human needs of the poor."[2]

Somoza's reaction to the aid cutoff was low-key. He took it in stride, saying only that he regretted that the United States "has taken this decision against its old ally," but added that "here things go on as before." Few thought that the cutoff in military aid would have any effect on the Somoza forces. "The U.S. has so saturated Somoza with weapons," one opposition leader said, "that he will be self-sufficient for years to come."[3]

Observers saw the move as more symbolic than substantive, saying the United States was reluctant to apply additional pressure to Somoza in fear of a radical overthrow of the regime in which the Sandinistas would play a large role. At the same time, the FAO, fast losing support and strength, merged into a leftist umbrella organization called the National Patriotic Front (FPN) of which the backbone was the United People's Movement (MPU) that sponsored its formation. The new organization was forged of an array of "progressive elements" opposed to the entire mediation effort including Independent Liberals, Social Christians, the Conservative party and Los Doce, who had withdrawn earlier from the FAO. The new organization nominally supported the Sandinista effort but not all sectors were committed to FSLN goals, their single objective being the ouster of Somoza. However the group gave no long-range scenario as to what was to follow that event.[4]

The MPU became the political base for nineteen student and labor groups that sympathized with the guerrillas as well as the political arm of the FSLN after the September insurrection. The relative strength of the MPU was shown in the Chamorro anniversary march. Although the demonstration was called by the FAO, 90 percent of the participants represented the United People's Movement. "The problem with the groups that remain in the FAO is that they represent nobody," said one politician whose party was going to leave the coalition. "They exist only because the mediators talk to them, so they accept anything the mediators suggest." The National Patriotic Front, on the other hand, "not only represented the numerous grass-roots organizations that had emerged in previous months but also underlined the growing unity of the three guerrilla factions and their need for greater political preparedness in anticipation of a new military offensive."[5] Preparing for the new offensive the FSLN began selling fifty thousand dollars worth of nonnegotiable "war bonds" in Puerto Rico.

The end of February was proclaimed Sandino week by the FSLN. Skirmishes with the guard stayed limited mostly to brief daily sorties. In one of the more consequential of these, eight guerrillas burst from a lonely stretch of road near Matagalpa and pounded a furious barrage of bullets into a truck carrying Colonel Federico Davidson Blanco, allegedly a member of the hit squad that had executed Sandino. Blanco, sixty-seven, died instantly, as did his two companions. After a jeep driven by Blanco's son rounded a bend and drove into the ambush, the guerrillas stopped it and asked which of the three men was the colonel's son. When Jackie Blanco answered, "I am," the guerrillas put a gun to his neck and shot him.[6]

In early February, Tacho perceived help coming from an unexpected quarter: the Vatican. Pope John Paul II had just visited Mexico where he told the third Latin American bishops' conference in Puebla that the Catholic clergy should stay out of politics. "This is a victory for all of us," Somoza told the Voice of America's Jack Curtiss, apparently referring to his fellow Central American general-presidents also facing church opposition. "Who do you think gets these kids [the *muchachos*] so worked up? The priests! Every time I go outdoors I hold on to my ribs wondering if I'll get blown up with the weapons these kids are getting now."

Sitting alone with Tacho in his dark-paneled private office at the Bunker, Curtiss asked Somoza about the Carter administration's order cutting back the United States embassy staff in Managua. "Yeah, how about those jerks," replied the dictator. "First they send me this," and he took a small envelope from a drawer and tossed it across the desk to the VOA correspondent. It was President Carter's 1977 letter to Somoza praising the suspension of the state of siege. "And then they send an ambassador down here to tell me I have to resign!"

February also marked the departure of Ambassador Solaun, who quietly slipped out of Nicaragua saying he had no idea when he might return. While Somoza said Solaun, as far as he knew, was in the United States for consultations, others put forward the rumor that Solaun was going to be kidnapped or killed by Somoza forces who would arrange to blame it on the Sandinistas. Some said it was the other way around. Solaun himself reportedly believed that he was the target of both sides in the storm and felt superseded by William Bowdler's presence and without any influence with the Somoza government.

Doctors and his delicate health also had little influence on Somoza—he had returned to the bottle as in the old days. For a February interview with *Washington Post* foreign editor Peter Osnos and reporter Karen DeYoung, Tacho invited the two to the El Coliseo Italian restaurant on the Masaya road. They arrived at 11:00 A.M. "There was nobody there, except for the owner who was very obsequious and led us into a back room where a table had been set up," DeYoung said. "Somebody immediately brought in two unopened bottles of Stolichnaya vodka and we politely declined Somoza's offer of a drink, saying it was not yet noon. We started to talk and at about thirty seconds after twelve, Somoza asked was it now okay to drink and was served a big glass of ice, over which he poured straight vodka.

"Somoza ordered a big bowl of pasta, we all ate lunch and pretty soon he had consumed about three-quarters of a bottle. Toward the end, he was inebriated and started railing against the United States, saying everybody was out to get him." Somoza noted he was "angry, but I keep my cool" and said he had no plans to retaliate to the diplomatic and military recalls by ejecting other American diplomats or recalling any of his own diplomats from Washington.

The official merging of the three Sandinista factions into a "single organic entity" took place in mid-March. In Managua and in most cities throughout the country guerrillas were skirmishing with the guard on a daily basis. As Tomás Borge of the GPP had announced in Mexico City four months earlier, the FSLN Ter- cerista, Proletariat and GPP factions were finally uniting to share "the same goals and the same strategy." The announcement was seen as a prelude to popular insurrection. National Guardsmen were placed on alert throughout the country.

Somoza maintained that all the Sandinistas were doing was "attempting to maintain a climate of uncertainty in Nicaragua by these hit-and-run tactics. But we are after them. I would say that the country is at peace and whoever has done anything, we will keep in check." In an interview with me and Don Bohning of the *Miami Herald* at the end of March, Somoza, dressed in a pinstriped business suit, did his best to exude an air of confidence. The interview was held in the Bunker. Somoza claimed that there was no longer potential for another September-style civil war because "the Sandinistas have lost credibility . . . in the sense the people who took up arms in September were left by the would-be cadres to be defeated by the National Guard. They said that their cadre was intact—they hadn't lost any people. And of course the population isn't dumb." Placing the number of hard-core Sandinistas at three hundred, Somoza, trying to keep cool though the veins in his neck swelling with each question betrayed his irritation, described the current situation in Nicaragua as "going through a phase. We are trying to work out what the effects are of the aggression Nicaragua has suffered from all the countries that wanted to change the political situation in this country. I think the people who thought they could overthrow this government are realizing they were playing into the hands of people who were not doing them well. We have a country that is trying to live with full constitutional guarantees. But we have a group of people who are hell-bent in making these guarantees nonexistent by hit-and-run attacks, by assaults, by assassinations, by kidnappings, by guerrilla movements. So we are working it out and we are having a tough time maintaining those constitutional guarantees." As Tacho answered questions in the cool conference room, outside the Bunker young women EEBI recruits were being trained to assemble the Israeli assault rifles. He had no immediate plans to reinstate martial law, Somoza said.

Tacho stressed that American policymakers had been "misinformed. They are putting this country and the people of Nicaragua through undue hardships." He said the newly imposed United States sanctions against Nicaragua had no effect on the immediate situation but "in the long run there might be. But, then again, it's the privilege of the United States to do that," and then he said the United States was ultimately responsible for "what happens if they don't help their neighbors."

When asked again about the United States being misinformed Tacho replied, "Yes, I mean, we have had a continuous offensive of the Communist-backed Cuban and Russian guerrillas and we have had to fight against that offensive. And because we have had to fight against that offensive it would be considered by some of the politicians in Washington that we are violating, willingly, the human rights of the Nicaraguans. And, of course, we have been attacked for that. I think that it is not correct. I think that what we have done is what any government would have done who is attacked by an international ideology through its satellite like Cuba." Carter's human rights policy was in part responsible. "They have applied it to my regime and of course everyone has gotten on the bandwagon. So now we have a lot of people assaulting people with armed robberies. They are pretty sure nothing will happen to them because of their 'human rights.' It's no laughing matter."

I asked Tacho to elaborate on Russia and Cuba's participation and he replied, "You know your question is redundant because I've been asked that a hundred times.

. . . [Look] to the people who have gone and gravitated to Cuba, Czechoslovakia and come back and then they have confessed and they have said they have [been trained by the communists]. I mean I get tired of saying certain things and people just brush it off, especially the news media. They don't understand that if this area is destabilized the United States might have a destabilized country next to its border through Mexico."

The threat to his government from within was as weak as that posed by the Sandinistas. The talk of a coup was "a rumor that I imagine the Sandinistas turned out to see if they could get up some steam, trying to get the schools involved demonstrating against me if there were a coup d'état, but it failed. Nobody paid attention to it."

Though his country was in severe financial straits Tacho was sure he would get a forty-million-dollar International Monetary Fund standby loan despite the fact the United States pressured the group to deny the first loan. "I think they [the United States] have realized that what they did last time was an act that really put in evidence its politicizing the IMF." The first American loan block "kept us from getting one hundred million dollars which we would have gotten in September and we would have paid off our commercial debts. We would be in good stead with all of the banks and we wouldn't be in this situation—where we have to renegotiate the payment of our international debt for part of 1978 and all of 1979—and have access to all of the banks."

Somoza had previously denied all rumors about the córdoba being devalued but was now saying, "I haven't talked with the IMF seriously about it. It's one of the possibilities." It was not impossible, he said, because "the way things are going I think the whole world is going to have to devalue."

Stepping down from the presidency was far from his mind. "I was elected for this period and I don't think I should step down. It's like asking Carter to step down. My plans are we shall have free elections. We are going to invite all the observers we can and all the press can witness the process on the first Sunday in February 1981." After the presidency, "I plan to become a private citizen of Nicaragua— retire to my business." Somoza said his business was "very simple. We are principally farmers, and we develop natural resources and we create opportunity to work in Nicaragua for the Nicaraguans."

Somoza accused Venezuela and Costa Rica of supporting the Sandinistas "by giving them arms, shelter, training, food and money." The Costa Ricans a month earlier had launched "Operation Checkmate" to clean out any Sandinistas from their territory, though the move was unpopular with their citizenry. Some United States officials credited the Costa Ricans with a serious operation but Tacho thought otherwise.

"It's a fallacy—Operation Checkmate. It is not serious." He warned that "the OAS will receive a report from its commission. They will be told what is happening. I think the OAS is going to get itself concerned about the situation because if the OAS cannot solve this situation then there are going to be other cures." The implication seemed to be that he would send his troops into Costa Rica to mop up

Sandinista camps, but then he added, "Well, we might ask for Costa Rica to be sanctioned for becoming a parrot's beak and destabilizing all the Central American states." (The reference is to a Cambodian border area that Viet Cong guerrilla forces used as a refuge and regrouping area during the Vietnam war.) Tacho said he had no problems with the military government of Honduras, that they were doing everything in their power "to keep the Sandinistas from becoming belligerent."

Even as Tacho spoke, barefoot children, old men and women picked over the garbage strewn on a vacant lot next to the Mercado Oriental in Managua in search of something edible among the rotten fruit and vegetables. In other sections of the sprawling city gunmen driven by hunger, revenge, ideology and repression—or orders—chose their victims with less discrimination than the garbage pickers. The social fabric of Nicaragua was unraveling. "The country," an FAO member said, "is a dead-end street without an exit."

When darkness descended, the streets of the capital and streets in provincial towns were deserted. The men with guns took over. Even during the September insurrection there was not the fear that pervaded the streets only seven months later. Nicaraguans would tell you, "Everyone observes his own curfew. The streets are no longer safe at night." Even in daylight there were holdups and robberies. Managua's Intercontinental Hotel no longer had guardsmen on the roof or barbed-wire barricades but at night it was like a morgue. All of its restaurants were closed except for the coffee shop.

The Sandinistas had increased the tempo of their attacks throughout the country but at the same time—with a seeming abundance of arms in the country —common criminals were continually on the prowl, assaulting and shooting people. Robberies and burglaries increased and with the end of the harvest season, unemployment was now around 40 percent and expected to climb even higher—along with crime.

Criminal elements began impersonating Sandinista guerrillas. Then there were those who maintained that the FSLN did not have effective control over its urban guerrillas. Even Sandinista forces suffered from the upsurge in criminal activity. In one case, an FSLN sympathizer whose truck was caught transporting a shipment of arms from Costa Rica in a secret compartment had his gas station attacked the same day by men who claimed to be FSLN.

Arms began pouring into Nicaragua and the Sandinistas stockpiled them in safe houses throughout the republic. In some instances large trailer cargo trucks were backed into garages and other locations where they were unloaded and stored even though the owners of some of their hiding spots were reluctant to have the weapons on their premises. In one instance a major of the guard in charge of the town of Rivas displayed large caches of weapons he claimed were taken from the Sandinistas. Several rooms were devoted to displaying the weapons and rocket launchers captured from the FSLN. There was also a truck, which the major said was carrying arms to the guerrillas, containing 230 American-made M-1 carbines and 124 used FALs, automatic weapons made in Belgium.

During an interview tall, gray-headed Adolfo Calero-Portocarrero, general manager of Milca, the largest soft-drink bottling company in Nicaragua, waved his hand toward the door. "They could come in here right now and hold us up," he said in reference to the violence and abundance of guns. "Only this morning they held up two of my Coca-Cola trucks."

Calero-Portocarrero, who had spent twenty-four days in jail in September for joining the general strike, said in reference to the spiraling common crime, "Some one hundred-sixty of my Coca-Cola trucks have been held up since October, fifty-one in March alone. We are already living in anarchy. The violence on the part of the insurgents, plus the irrational repression of the government, have given rise to all sorts of indiscriminate assaults, robberies and holdups.

"The average citizen doesn't know who is going to hit him over the head or put a gun in his ribs and take the money from his pocket. The common criminals are having a heyday." He added that the moderates were suffering and trying to do their best but as the extremists on both sides continued with violence, civic opposition was very difficult to organize.

On the other hand, people also accused the National Guard of shooting first and then asking questions. One instance illustrating indiscriminate killing by the guard was the March 30 shooting of Francisco Castro Urbina. He was shot dead by soldiers while riding home that night at 9:30. A soldier who inspected the car with his flashlight turned to Castro's brother, Hilario, who was driving the car, and said, "Sorry, brother. It was a mistake." Then they charged him for transporting the body to a funeral parlor, the only business that seemed to be open.

A mother of five in one of the poor barrios that surrounded Managua warned, "The guerrillas now move in groups of thirty and forty. When they attack the National Guard you must be very careful not to be caught in the crossfire." Pointing to her naked, potbellied children, ranging in age from two to ten, she said the guard took any younger men they saw. "If they are believed to be guerrillas you never see them again; even if they are not you still don't see them again." *La Prensa*'s daily editions appeared with a regular gallery of photos of young people who had "disappeared" the day before.

Nicaraguan human rights sources said at least five hundred persons, mostly youths, disappeared in the first three months of 1979. Most of them were killed. The National Guard lost at least fifty soldiers. The largest unified guerrilla operation since the September insurrection came when 120 guerrillas captured the town of El Jícaro in Nueva Segovia where General Sandino once fought. The government admitted six soldiers had been killed in the attack and newspaper headlines reflected the reality that the country was at war. *La Prensa* headlines announced: "Jets Bomb North; Civilians Flee War Zone."

While the guerrilla war escalated, the moderate opposition, mostly in the business community, appeared demoralized and in disarray. And despite the confident face Somoza put on, in an interview in the Bunker, he paused for a moment when he was asked whether the National Guard was still loyal to him. "Yes," he said, "at this moment."

The opposition remained stymied. According to Alfonso Robelo, "the situation in Nicaragua is very confused. Unity among the opposition is not strong. The only point of convergence we have is that we all agree we can't have a solution without getting rid of Somoza. But we can't agree on the next step. The next five months are going to be hell. Economic problems will get worse. We are ending good months and starting bad ones."

Robelo said that the "private sector was fairly aware that there is no solution with Somoza. It is also fully aware that any solution that could lead to radicals coming to power is not desirable. The Sandinistas want to keep Somoza in as long as possible to create the environment for drastic change.

"I have come to the conclusion that if there is a military victory of the Frente, and I think that improbable, we would end up under a totalitarian regime of the communist type." Robelo saw Somoza "as a feudal lord in the Middle Ages sitting in his Bunker which is a fortress. Whatever happens as long as it doesn't bother security of his fortress is not important. It is a very simplistic and very brutal situation. He doesn't care. This has led to economic bankruptcy.

"Somoza has no respect for anything," Robelo continued. "He is there and he is going to stay until 1981, officially and forever. The solution? You have to realize the country is polarizing more and more—people who have suffered and people who want to protect what they have. There are those who are radicalizing and those who want some stability, even if it is Somoza."

Robelo remained bitter about the United States role in Nicaragua. "First the U.S. came and told everyone they would put pressure on Somoza to go. They created false expectations. When Somoza's reaction was to say, 'Come and do it physically,' they backed down. They actually downplayed the process and at the end put little pressure on Somoza and gave him valuable time to build up his National Guard.

"It has a boomerang effect on the civil opposition, on the U.S. image and has created this situation," Robelo said. "Human rights has become a conflict. If the U.S. applies human rights and puts on pressure you have the problem of maybe ending up in the hands of a communist government." A more effective means of pressure, he suggested, would have been for Washington to cancel Somoza's visa to the United States which he was preparing to visit during a Holy Week vacation, or to cancel landing rights for his Lanica Airlines or to boycott his Manenic Lines shipping company.

Fernando Cardenal, who had maintained his close ties to the FSLN, said the "hypocrisy of Carter" was "intolerable" and claimed the United States "is playing with the blood of the Nicaraguan people. Carter's human rights is simply moral, ethical and Christian, but he doesn't follow through. Carter likes to pronounce the words," the Jesuit said, but he is "trapped by these words." He added that the "solution in Nicaragua is a national government of reconciliation of which the Sandinistas should be a part." Cardenal said, "We are not communists. We have all kinds of elements in the opposition. The U.S. should just take its hands off Nicaragua, take all possible support away from Somoza and the U.S. should look for contact with the real forces of the country which include the Sandinistas. Some people will not forgive Carter the deaths of September. He sent mediators down here only after five thousand had been killed. He didn't try and halt the war."

Carter, Cardenal said, was "betting on a sick horse. Iran should serve as an example."

According to Calero-Portocarrero, "We told the American embassy that if the mediators came and left without a solution it would be better not to come at all. It's a Bay of Pigs situation. The U.S. had created expectations but they called off their air support at the Bay of Pigs and failed. It's the same thing in this case. The mediators were here for a long time and left without even getting us to the doorway of a solution.

"I am not one of those who blames the U.S. for everything," the bottling executive said, "but they are partly responsible. They did not use their goodwill to help. I don't see the U.S. doing a damn thing. I'm sorry to say that. It took thousands of lives even to begin the implementation of the human rights program and for the U.S. to come out with firm action—sanctions. People," he added, "are dying like flies here in Nicaragua."

On Sunday, April 8, the day he was scheduled to leave for his Easter vacation, Somoza announced a 42.8 percent devaluation of the córdoba, the first since 1955. Unofficial reports were that the American attitude toward Nicaragua and pressure from the IMF had forced the economic measure. The devaluation caused most supermarket prices to jump by the same margin overnight. A twelve-bottle carton of Coca-Cola costing $1.90 the week before now cost $2.60. Medicines went up by 50 percent and staples like cooking oil, rice and sugar were all vastly more expensive. Inflation had been galloping ahead by 35 percent before the devaluation; the effect of the devaluation was expected to be even more severe inflation, weighing especially on seasonal workers who were returning to the slums after close of the harvesting season.

Somoza, nattily dressed in a dark gray business suit, climbed aboard his British-made, British-piloted twin-engine jet after the devaluation announcement and flew off to spend Holy Week with his children in Florida. After long months of living in his Bunker, Tacho was looking forward to his vacation. He was fairly confident nothing much more would happen on the home front. Tradition was such in Central America that along with businesses and everything else even revolutions usually ground to a halt during Holy Week, with families deserting the cities for beaches or returning home to their native towns. Bloody Nicaragua was no exception. The Sandinistas issued a communiqué announcing they would observe a Holy Week truce.

But it was a truce that was breached within hours.

As Tacho was giving Tachito a good-bye embrace at the airport, nearby Cessna push-pull aircraft were reloading their rocket pods. Shortly thereafter, Tachito was again busily directing his forces in the north by radio from air force headquarters at the airport.

Guerrillas of the Carlos Fonseca Amador column on the northern front slipped into the city of Estelí early Sunday morning. The guerrillas took over the city center and most of the southern section. The National Guard controlled the northern edge of town and used a baseball diamond as an airfield on which to land reinforcements.

Unlike the small town of El Jícaro where seasoned guerrillas wiped out the

National Guard outpost ten days earlier before withdrawing, or the town of El Sauce, which they occupied for six hours the night before, the Sandinistas decided to remain in Estelí after other weekend attacks on the National Guard in Ducali, Achuapas and Condega.

During Sunday's operation against the guerrillas in El Sauce and Estelí, a C-47 transport and a Cessna rocket-launching push-pull aircraft were brought down by the Sandinistas, though the government claimed the planes had made forced landings because of malfunctioning engines.

The battle in Estelí was a replay of the September insurrection. The Cessnas made their rocket runs over the sections of the city occupied by the guerrillas. The National Guard airlifted in their best combat troops in small Spanish troop carriers and helicopters to their makeshift landing strip. Fighting was fierce. A Nicaraguan newsman who managed to slip in and out of Estelí reported that the townspeople were terrified of the bombing and rocket attacks. Three thousand poor people who inhabited the flimsy wooden shacks and tiled roof adobe structures of the southwest section of Estelí were fleeing. People begged a reporter, "Tell them to stop the bombing. It's not the shooting that worries [us], it's the bombs. They blow up whole houses. Entire families are being killed."

The FSLN guerrillas fighting in Estelí looked much more professional than in the past. Most were uniformed in olive green fatigues and boots and sporting either the Sandinista black beret or stetsons and sombreros. They appeared to be seasoned fighters now capitalizing on previous successes in their lightning raids on small towns and army posts in the north. They were also much better armed this time. One squad, which included a woman, sang as it marched along a street to take up new positions behind barricades which had been constructed from street paving blocks.

The guerrillas carried no food, just weapons and ammunition. They were soon reinforced by young men and women of the city. By midweek the guerrillas, still in Estelí, had observers totally confused about their ultimate goal. Though numbering more than one hundred veteran fighters and joined by at least one hundred youths, they appeared no match for the twelve-thousand-man National Guard, its Sherman tanks and armored cars.

Sighed one person, "Holy Week is an incredible tradition here. The guerrillas have the people with them; they have to be careful not to alienate them. Tactically this fighting during Holy Week is not good. Frankly, I don't know what went wrong. Maybe the departure of Tacho provoked them into this."

The Sandinistas elsewhere were wondering whether or not the guerrillas had overplayed their hand and remained too long in Estelí. Might they in fact be trapped in the city? If not, what were they trying to prove? Only seasoned veterans would be capable of retreating through the guard's lines. Those who remained would be slaughtered when the guard eventually retook the city.

The smell of burning corpses filled the air on Thursday. Somoza's combat batallion moved to encircle the city and a guerrilla told a Nicaraguan newsman that "only dead will remain here. We will die but we will take a lot of them with us." He shook his FAL automatic rifle as he spoke.

Eyewitnesses in Estelí reported that the Sandinistas retreated from the city about 7:00 P.M. Thursday with some eighty recruits, most of them grown men. Sporadic fighting continued Friday and Saturday. Shooting was still heard Sunday when the foreign press was admitted for a few hours. The commander in chief of the guard was adamant that the Sandinistas were still hiding in the city; he did not believe reports that they had managed to escape. The guard claimed to have killed thirty-seven guerrillas on Saturday alone, two days after the reported escape. Radio Sandino reports said the guerrillas had slipped through the guard perimeter on Friday and admitted only to losing three of their men during the siege, including a commander named Juan Alberto Blandón who fought under the code name Froylan. The government maintained that more than a hundred guerrillas perished in the weeklong fighting. The National Guard announced a death toll of seventy-seven for the first day of fighting, but did not release any more figures. When asked about the number of dead, Paul Schoch, a Swiss member of the International Red Cross, said, "We have to worry about the living ones."

Clandestine Radio Sandino accused the guard of using civilians as shields in attacks on FSLN positions before the latter began their "orderly retreat" into the mountains. It reported the FSLN as "always on the offensive" now. No one should expect any relaxing of the daily clashes occurring between the Sandinistas and the National Guard.

On Sunday outside newsmen were finally permitted to visit Estelí but an hour later they were ordered out at gunpoint, their film and videotapes confiscated by the National Guard. Upon entering the city they found cars and trucks backed up for more than two miles as the refugees waited in the hot sun for permission from the red-bereted guard troops to enter. Few refugees could leave the city and even fewer were permitted to return. Many of the refugees said they had read the morning paper *Novedades* extra edition in which Somoza declared in huge headlines, "Estelí Liberated from the Communist Hordes," and showed pictures of guardsmen backed by Sherman tanks moving over street barricades. (Until then only reporters from Somoza-owned newspaper and television stations had been permitted to enter Estelí.) Foreign correspondents were told that no one was being permitted to enter or leave the city because the guard was still searching for guerrillas and their sympathizers.

Reporters found the city heavy with the smell of burning flesh even though only two burning bodies near an abandoned Sandinista command post were visible. Buzzards circled overhead. The bodies of two other youths about fifteen years of age lay on adjacent streets filled with rubble, their throats slit, their hands still tied behind their backs.

The city was without light and water. In one street guardsmen were trying to deactivate some fifty booby traps left behind by the retreating Sandinistas. They also collected homemade bombs and found a homemade mortar. Near the city's SOS camp for abandoned children a man had been shot dead trying to reach refuge. The guard commander refused to permit the Red Cross to take away wounded when its convoy left the city. Only one wounded child in a coma was allowed to leave. Some refugees were permitted into the city for an hour but were not allowed to take out members of their families.

The guard was paying particular attention to the footwear of all males in town. At a city shoe store they found fifteen pairs of old combat boots that had been exchanged for city shoes. That made them suspect that some of the Sandinistas were still in the city and would try to escape as ordinary citizens. Anyone with new shoes was being arrested.

A letter allegedly captured by the National Guard from a Sandinista was published in full in *Novedades,* outlining the lessons to be learned from Estelí. It was attributed to Tercerista leader Daniel Ortega, who was confirmed later to have written the letter. In it he warned that "position warfare," such as had taken place in Estelí, was counterproductive. He stressed the need for small-scale, quick attacks, with more highway assaults and a general war of attrition on the National Guard. He laid special emphasis on the capture and reconditioning of arms; otherwise, he warned, the guerrillas would soon be short of firepower and ammunition. The letter went on to praise the FSLN for its recent unification of forces. As if in response to Ortega's directive, the guerrillas quickly followed their Estelí operation with a successful ambush on a National Guard convoy moving toward Masaya.[7]

The Sandinistas were now organizing by geographic sectors of the nation though none of their four armed fronts had a fixed base of operations. To the north was the Carlos Fonseca Amador front; the Pablo Ubeda front operated in the northeast; the south was controlled by the Benjamin Zeledón front; and the fourth front, designed to operate throughout the country without regard to a designated region, was the Roberto Huembes front. The four basic fronts operated primarily in the mountains. In the urban areas militias or brigades were organized in the barrios to hide arms, make bombs and molotov cocktails and harass the guard. Commando units were formed, armed with automatic weapons and with bases in Managua, León, Chinandega, Matagalpa, Carazo, Masaya, Rivas, Estelí and Granada. Suburban forces were organized to operate under the commando units, but these operated with a greater number of men and firepower, conducting forays against the guard in the peripheral areas of the towns. One of their major tasks was to collect arms in combat.[8]

Somoza returned to Managua on April 16 smiling. In an airport news conference he brushed off the attack on Estelí as a "mimicry of an offensive" and referred to the Sandinistas as "a group of people bent on undermining constitutional guarantees, armed by Costa Rica, Panama and Venezuela, who are trying to damage Nicaragua's reputation for law and order." Calling for the guerrillas to lay down their arms, Somoza said that "attacking Estelí for the purpose of putting the government to shame is a criminal act. It was aimed at causing propaganda damage to the government, but politically they [the guerrillas] have lost."[9]

Later that evening one of Somoza's own cousins, Edgardo Lang Sacasa, was killed by the guard as he and a group of Sandinista area commanders were meeting in a house in León. Lang, the twenty-eight-year-old son of Federico Lang whose wife was a cousin of Somoza's mother, was killed with the five other Sandinistas when, according to León commander General Gonzalo Evertz, the guerrillas, hiding in the home of a prominent León resident, opened fire on a passing military convoy. But area residents said the troops, their guns ablaze, had burst into the home while the guerrillas met secretly to plot for León an operation duplicating the Estelí uprising a week earlier. Killed with Lang, whose father was one of Nicaragua's wealthiest men, were Oscar Danilo Pérez Cásar, twenty-six, and forty-year-old Roger Deshon Argüello. Pérez Cásar was a member of the FSLN's general staff and was the son of a prominent León family. Deshon Argüello was one of the early members of the FSLN and had taken part in the 1974 raid on the Castillo residence. Lang was married to Castillo's daughter, María Soledad Castillo, a childhood sweetheart. Three weeks after the attack on her home, he had joined the Sandinistas. Lang went underground on August 20, 1975, was arrested on November 20, 1977, but was released as a result of the palace raid. In one of the ironies of the civil war, María lost her father to the guerrillas and her husband to the National Guard.

A woman killed in the shootout was said to be Dora María Tellez, Comandante Dos in the Palace takeover. In fact the woman proved to be Araceli Pérez Darias, a Mexican psychologist and daughter of a prominent Mexican industrialist.

More than 1,500 persons, some shouting insurgent slogans, attended the burial of Lang a few days later. Witnesses reported that Lang's coffin was draped with a red and black Sandinista flag as it was lowered into its grave in a Managua cemetery. Many of those present were wealthy Nicaraguans who attended because of Lang's father. When asked about the young rebel's mother's connection to Somoza, National Guard press spokesman Colonel Aguiles Aranda Escobar tried to play down the link. A day later, Lang's father vehemently attacked the National Guard, accusing them of assassinating his son and denouncing reports that he had been killed in combat.

On the same night Lang was killed, I obtained an interview with a member of the FSLN national directorate, Carlos Nuñez Telez, an eight-year veteran of the Sandinista movement and leader of the proletarian faction. I had to agree to keep my eyes shut while a beautiful, long-haired Nicaraguan girl drove me to what turned out to be the plush residence of her father, Joaquín Cuadra Chamorro. After the war Berta became Nuñez's wife.

Nuñez began by saying the Sandinistas "no longer identify ourselves by factions, because we have to be the first ones as far as teaching unity." He described the United People's Movement as "a joint effort of all Sandinista factions for the moment. . . . So the MPU is the result of the policy of unity which is being implemented at a national level."

Nuñez characterized the Estelí offensive and the April guerrilla actions "which you are seeing right now" as "a guerrilla offensive within our method of fighting, which is trying to solve the problem here—still not solved—which is the composition of the base.

"We consider that to unleash . . . a general uprising in the country, there is one condition—to undermine, erode and demoralize the military apparatus which right now is sustaining the dictatorship. Right now this is what we have chosen to do. . . . Without a doubt in order to fight a war against a whole army such as the one we have in this country we have been building up our army for some time. We are still building it up. This is the role which is reserved for the forces we have in the mountains, and in the future they will face combat in the south and east. We still believe that the means to overthrow the dictatorship is by insurrection. We are preparing these conditions." At Estelí, according to Nuñez, the world was witnessing "an army being born."

"But what happened?" he went on. "The level of fighting we are reaching in Nicaragua is such that the masses . . . tend to enter into insurrection. In Estelí we are witnessing this phenomenon in a more acute manner. The nearby action of the revolutionary forces, which are trying to fight a war to wear down the guard, stimulates the masses and precipitates the uprising. . . . In Estelí there was a partial insurrection. This cannot be denied. But we didn't plan on staying in Estelí up until the end precisely because of tactics. Rather we maneuvered militarily to break up the guard's encirclement and to avoid . . . that this strategic force be annihilated because of taking fixed positions and defending them—and at the same time, [we have planned] to go on striking so that the army would not concentrate itself on the population. It would have been a great mistake to accept the challenge of the dictatorship to fight a battle of fixed positions prematurely. This is what we want to avoid."

Nuñez felt that the end to Somoza's rule in Nicaragua would come in 1979 —"the political situation in the country tells me so and the international situation also. . . . The end of the dictatorship is irreversible. Nothing worse than the dictatorship can happen here. It's got to be something better."

The much-rumored possibility of a guard coup d'état, Nuñez said, would only serve the purpose of involving all FSLN units in combat throughout the country to abort it, "stripping it of all legitimacy and tending to take immediate advantage of an army no longer centered around Somoza. We believe the major error of the United States at this moment . . . would be to push for a coup d'état. Such a coup d'état would cause serious, uncontrollable fissures within the National Guard which we would take advantage of."

The FSLN's attitude toward the more moderate opposition in the case of Somoza's leaving office would be to incorporate "all the popular, revolutionary and democratic forces including the bourgeois sectors who have not associated with the regime" in order to establish a "true democracy." He rejected any thought of the FAO as a significant element in the opposition. The FAO, he maintained, had stripped itself of popular support by endorsing the United States mediation efforts, which did not seem aimed at a real end to *somocismo*.

The FSLN was still trying to implement its policy of unity and "to promote a greater unity among all forces of the nation against the dictatorship." As to a post-Somoza future, Nuñez said, "We consider that with a provisional government, not only should the forces of the National Patriotic Front be represented but also all the forces which are also struggling against the dictatorship. That is why we have to persuade them that the alternative offered by the FSLN is the most correct one.

If the FAO [which opposed an armed struggle] assumes a subsequent position we guarantee that they will be part of this provisional government. In this we are in agreement. We are at the same time trying to persuade them of the necessity of directing all forces against the dictatorship and to somehow establish a political compromise."

At the end of the interview Nuñez agreed that all prospects indicated a long hot summer ahead for Nicaragua.

On April 18 Tacho addressed the ninth World Anti-Communist Youth League Conference in Managua. Somoza opened the confab at the Rubén Darío National Theater with a speech to the group of mostly obscure, aging, professional anticommunists. There he struck out at his enemies, accusing them again of backing a "Russian-Cuban conspiracy" against his government, explicitly singling out Venezuela, Panama and Costa Rica for condemnation. A manifesto sponsored by the Honduran Democratic Armed Movement (Movimiento Armado Democrático Hondureño) accused those nations of supporting "communism" in Nicaragua and "energetically" condemned Jimmy Carter for putting the Western nations' liberty "in a precarious situation" that "only benefits communism." Both the Panamanian ambassador and the chargé d'affaires left Nicaragua, a further sign of the deterioration of relations between the countries.

At the end of April Ambassador Solaun resigned as American envoy for "personal reasons" and was replaced by Lawrence A. Pezzullo, then ambassador to Uruguay. In a press conference a few days after his resignation Solaun described his eighteen-month tenure as reflecting a three-phase evolution of American policy in Nicaragua—neutrality, mediation and partial withdrawal. The neutrality phase, he said, followed Carter administration guidelines of "disassociating from repressive regimes." It contemplated no covert action and did not aid the opposition, "a policy not of full commitment to either side, but not indifference either. We said publicly and privately we wanted some change" and that, in turn, encouraged the opposition.

The mediation phase developed when the potential for widespread bloodshed became more apparent and Washington "decided to become more active." The final phase, partial withdrawal, was meant to indicate to the Nicaraguan government that "it lacks our support and we no longer have any confidence in Somoza," Solaun said. Solaun conceded that United States policy had not satisfied either the government or the opposition. His assessment of the present situation was one of stalemate —"the government is not strong enough to control the opposition and the opposition is not strong enough to overthrow the government." The result was a process of disintegration, a "situation of quasi-anarchy," Solaun said.

Solaun blamed the mediation's failure on Somoza's awareness of the United States' "unwillingness to go all the way against him. Because we were not willing to use overt or covert force, we were not able to change the government of Nicaragua."[10]

May Day celebrations in Nicaragua opened the way for further violence. Nearly forty labor leaders were arrested on April 30 in an attempt to prevent their participation in May Day gatherings, which had been banned in the capital. Somoza trucked in supporters from the countryside and stationed armed soldiers throughout the resultant crowd before launching into a tirade from behind his bulletproof ticket booth. Again he blamed armed aggression "launched by the capitalists in connivance with the communists" and "economic aggression . . . supported by the Carter government" for many of Nicaragua's problems.

"Nicaraguan capitalists thought they could overthrow my government with the help of unscrupulous politicians in the United States and Venezuela," Somoza said. "They thought I was going to commit treason and abandon the 700,000 persons who carried me to the presidency but they are wrong. If Nicaraguan capitalists want to blackmail me, I'll show them just who Anastasio Somoza is," he said, drawing mild applause.[11]

Only moments after Somoza finished speaking guard clashes with protestors in other parts of the capital resulted in three deaths. The night before the guard had fought a twenty-four-hour battle with an estimated one hundred Sandinistas in León and as many people were killed before the Sandinistas abandoned their positions to the guardsmen and disappeared into the countryside. Once again the civilian toll was high, many of them dying from guard-launched rockets.

At the same time, Somoza, in response to attempts to organize another general strike, arrested FAO leaders Córdova Rivas, Robelo, Julio César Aviles and others, including Front leader Dr. Medina Bravo, Conservative party lawyer and opposition leader Vilma Nuñez de Escorcia, and opposition labor leaders Alejandro Solórzano and Eli Altamirano. No charges were filed and the arrests brought heavy protest from the United States and other countries. United States State Department spokesman Hodding Carter III called on Somoza to release Robelo and Córdova Rivas. The two men were turned over to a civilian court later in the week and charged with "illicit association" and "disobedience of laws." In Washington, Deputy Secretary of State Warren Christopher called on Nicaraguan ambassador Sevilla-Sacasa to express concern over the arrests and told him that "these arrests may be seen by many in the United States, Nicaragua and elsewhere as an effort to stifle moderate opposition which would only serve to benefit those extremist elements seeking a violent solution to the problems of Nicaragua." Christopher expressed hope that the arrests did not signify the beginning of a campaign to repress such moderate opposition.[12]

On May 4 the army confirmed it was moving troops and heavy military equipment to the agricultural region near Nueva Guinea, some forty miles from the Atlantic coast where an estimated two hundred Sandinistas were said to be located. Guard press chief Aquiles Aranda described the operation as "tactical exercises for training the army." Despite his claim, hundreds of agriculturists and government personnel were evacuated from Nueva Guinea and it soon became known that Tachito was personally commanding the operation which involved an estimated one thousand troops, planes and helicopter gunships. By May 7, *La Prensa* was reporting heavy fighting in Nueva Guinea with sporadic skirmishes up and down the coast. On May 10 *Novedades* said "a group of guerrillas—comprised of Cubans, Panamanians, Mexicans, Costa Ricans and Americans—fell after being surrounded by the guard on the Atlantic coast." The article went on to allege the guerrillas had been "paid by the Soviet Union, Cuba, Panama and Venezuela." Earlier the government had denied the presence of guerrillas in the region but now it announced that sixty-one Sandinistas had been killed there between April 30 and May 8. Aquiles Aranda told journalists that 30 percent of the guerrilla force had deserted, 10 percent had escaped dressed as civilians and that a large arms and ammunitions cache had been captured from the "international brigade."

The Sandinista column in Nueva Guinea, numbering 160 men and aided by others, had in fact suffered one of its worst defeats in months. Helicopters swooped down on them strafing the guerrillas with .50-caliber machine-gun fire in what one Cuban exile mercenary involved in the fighting described as "easy hunting." A Guatemalan major, who had decided to stay and fight for the guard in Nicaragua after a visit, was wounded by the Sandinistas in the action.

By May 16, the Sandinistas and the guard were involved in fighting in eight parts of the country. Clashes were reported in Managua, Guasaule, El Rama, Wiwilí, Morrito, Chinandega, Juigalpa and León. In León Bishop Manuel Salazar y Espinoza gave a pastoral message lamenting that "the Nicaraguan youth has chosen the road of weapons because [the government] has closed the road to authentic social justice."

On May 20 a column of five hundred men entered Jinotega in the early morning hours. By daybreak they were in control of the city of forty-five thousand located in a large valley northeast of Managua surrounded by mountains. Roads were blocked and telephone and telegraph lines were cut. One of the first guerrilla victims was ex-Nicaraguan Coffee Institute (Incafé) director Francisco Chavarría whom the guerrillas shot and killed along with his son Bayron. With the arrival of government troops, the combat raged in Jinotega.

The escalating state of war prompted varying reactions from governments in nearby countries. Mexico broke diplomatic relations with Nicaragua on May 20 and hours later called on the United States to end all remaining assistance programs to Somoza. Mexican President José López Portillo made the announcement during lunch with visiting Costa Rican President Rodrigo Carazo Odio and urged other nations to follow suit. Venezuela declined to do so; Colombia said it needed "to study the situation." Panamanian President Arístides Royo said his country could not break ties with Nicaragua because of the need for his Managua embassy to accept political refugees. Mexico's move came only a few days after López Portillo met with Fidel Castro in the Mexican resort of Cancún. Mexican Foreign Minister Jorge Castañeda said the action was taken to isolate the Somoza regime politically and diplomatically. Castañeda also urged the United States to cut off Nicaraguan aid.[13] "We hope our action may lead to other breaks in relations with Somoza and that the diplomatic and political isolation of Somoza will speed the downfall of this bloody regime," Castañeda said as he dispatched two high-ranking missions to South America and the Caribbean urging countries there to follow Mexico's example and break relations because of the "horrendous genocide" committed by the Somoza regime.

In Managua, Somoza was enraged by Mexico's action. When the subject was brought up on June 3 by newsmen, he would only say, "López Portillo is a fucking hypocrite."

He immediately blamed the diplomatic rupture on "Cuban intervention." The leaders of Guatemala and El Salvador gave him moral support and joined him in blaming Castro for insurgency and political violence throughout Central America.

By May 24 the guard had either driven out the guerrillas or they had escaped from Jinotega. An estimated two hundred persons were dead. Partially burned corpses lay rotting in the streets as residents surveyed the results of four days of fighting. At one street corner, a knot of silent people, some clutching handkerchiefs to their noses, stared at a charred figure, its arms reaching grotesquely for the sky. A floppy hat and leather holster lay nearby. Buzzards circled overhead. A lone foot, still wearing a blue tennis shoe, lay in one street. In a demolished house a charred figure could be seen lying on a metal bed. Spent cartridge cases and burned-out automobiles littered the streets. Many homes were pockmarked with bullet holes and a few looked to have been heavily damaged, by tank cannon fire. But despite this damage, most structures were intact. It appeared both guardsmen and guerrillas had spared bystanders somewhat as they sharpened their deadly skills. "Both sides were real gentlemen this time, both seemed to respect the people. They kept the fighting between themselves," said Leonte Pallais, a district court judge in Jinotega and distant relative to Somoza. Pallais said the guerrillas went from house to house asking for weapons and urging people to join them. He said he had feared for his life but was told by the guerrillas he would not be harmed because he had a reputation for being fair. "They warned me they would be back," he said.[14]

One guerrilla who would not be back was Sandinista fighter Germán Pomares, the toughest FSLN warrior of them all. He had been killed. Well known as the top Sandinista soldier on the battlefield, his death was kept a secret to keep morale high in what was becoming a crucial stage of the fight.

CHAPTER 16

The Final Offensive

In the predawn hours of Tuesday, May 29, a well-armed Sandinista column from Costa Rica crossed into the tiny neck of land between Lake Nicaragua and the Pacific Ocean. Unlike the numerous attacks on the well-defended Peñas Blancas border crossing in the past, this was no simple probing action. Following the September insurrection the nine-month gestation period of arming and training had given birth to the final offensive. By daybreak the three-hundred-man column had occupied the farming community of El Naranjo, so small it appears on few maps, near the Pacific coastal hamlet of El Ostional at the extreme southwestern corner of the Nicaraguan border.

The launching of the final offensive was no surprise. In fact, Mexico had timed breaking of relations with the Somoza regime on Sunday, May 20, to the expected beginning of the offensive, which was put off even though Germán Pomares had led his troops the following day into Jinotega in a premature move that cost him his life. Television viewers in Costa Rica had been informed a few days earlier by Tomás Borge, the general coordinator and a member of the nine-man Sandinista directorate, that the last battle was about to begin. Those who could monitor Radio Sandino on its shortwave frequency heard Humberto Ortega, commander of the Sandinista army, call from somewhere in Costa Rica for a general mobilization of all Sandinista forces, because the hour of liberation was at hand.

In major cities arms stockpiled or hidden since September were quietly distributed while defense committees set up by the Frente and its political arm the United People's Movement (MPU) began preparing for the war. Clandestine field hospitals secreted away in some barrios went on a war footing. Food depots for combatants were made ready. Clandestine communiqués were quickly distributed by runners throughout barrios in Managua advising people to leave their lights off at night and doors unlocked to permit fighters to take refuge when necessary in the coming battle.

On the morning of May 29, Radio Sandino declared the Frente had liberated El Naranjo and urged guardsmen to desert with their weapons and join the guerrillas. Coordinating their attack with the strike at El Naranjo a group of guerrillas harassed the southern town of Rivas. It was only a small diversionary action at the city cemetery, but Rivas was an objective of the Sandinista southern front. There they hoped to set up their own government on Nicaraguan soil. Somoza also made the southern front his top battle priority and airlifted additional elite forces to El Ostional. Supported by the M.S. *Managua*, a Somoza freighter with 40-mm Bofors mounted on its decks, standing offshore, T-33 jets and two giant Argentine-made 42-tube 70-mm rocket launchers mounted on the backs of flatbed trucks, the superior firepower and heavy-caliber mortars of the government forces kept the column pinned down in the mountainous coastal strip of the border.

In the initial Sandinista column was an eighty-man volunteer brigade from Panama led by Hugo Spadáfora, a doctor who had resigned as Panama's deputy health minister to aid the anti-Somoza forces. There were also several American volunteers. Two members of the OAS observer team who had been sent to the border area in November were caught in a fire fight between the Sandinistas and guard in Rivas. They spent six hours pinned to the floor of their car until they were finally rescued and helicoptered back to Managua. A guard captain, Manuel Sacasa, attached to the OAS observers, was killed in the outbreak of fighting.

The column held on in El Naranjo despite the pounding. The noise of battle soon engulfed Nicaragua. Guard Comandante Bravo, in charge of the southern front, received his orders direct from Tacho or Tachito. He was advised by Tachito on the use of special paralyzing gases to be used against the Sandinistas entrenched in the Rivas cemetery. A buoyant Bravo replied in Italian, the language he had learned while training in Italy, that the battle of El Naranjo was going "molto bene" and gave an optimistic field report.

From the outset Somoza was concerned that an even stronger force could be expected to invade from Costa Rica. He quickly went on the offensive through the Organization of American States in Washington. He ordered his brother-in-law, wily old Sevilla-Sacasa, to invoke the Rio treaty, the hemisphere's mutual security treaty, announcing that the "new invasion" from Costa Rica was a provocation of "international communism." Costa Rica denied aiding the Sandinistas and a meeting under the treaty provisions was scheduled for the following week. Costa Rica had itself invoked the treaty twice previously since the September 1978 insurrection, alleging that Nicaraguan guardsmen and aircraft had made incursions into their territory.

The Costa Rican government did not deny there were Sandinista camps on its territory. They pointed out that Costa Rica was playing host to thousands of refugees who had fled Nicaragua. Costa Rica claimed it had sought to remove the Sandinistas, and it denied aiding or arming the rebels. It pointed out that Costa Rica was a democracy and had no army; its border was lightly guarded and there were no means to halt the Sandinistas from crossing. They stressed no complicity. But arms shipped even from Cuba were now literally pouring in to Costa Rica for the Sandinistas.

The Nicaraguan government imposed a radio and television blackout. Communications were cut between Managua and León where the guard poured rocket after rocket into suspected guerrilla positions, taking a high toll on civilians who had already been subjected to four major battles in León during the past year. The guard announced that Somoza's cousin, Julio Portocarrero Navas, had been killed when the Sandinistas botched a kidnap attempt on him in a bookstore in the city.

On Sunday, June 3, the guard contended that the Sandinistas were massing troops on the Costa Rican border to launch an attack that was designed to relieve the beleaguered column pinned down at El Naranjo. Somoza decided to use the Sabbath to trade his business suit for green army fatigues, bedecked with five stars and a pistol strapped to his waist, and rally his troops along the Costa Rican border. Flying by helicopter to Rivas near his southern command field headquarters, Tacho briefed his commanders. They in turn warned him that they were no longer battling *muchachos* but hardened soldiers.

The lessons of September had been well learned. This time the guns didn't jam, the pins were pulled from the grenades, mortar rounds were armed before they were fired. The Sandinistas were better organized and there was a clear chain of command and unity. Assaults were coordinated and controlled by trained cadres on orders from Humberto Ortega's radio command post in Costa Rica.

With the exception of the southern offensive across the border, the basic tactics in cities, towns and villages throughout the country were the same: erection of barricades in the street and obstruction of thoroughfares with burning vehicles, piles of rubbish and paving stones; harassment of guard patrols until they withdrew to their garrisons; siege and eventual capitulation.

In September the guard had sent columns to relieve each of the Sandinista-threatened cities. The difference in June was that there were too many cities, too many uprisings, too many trained Sandinistas and a growing popular insurrection.

With the launching of the final offensive the war of numbers began. Each side made inflated claims of casualties inflicted on the other while keeping their own losses secret. The guard, for example, reported it intercepted a Sandinista patrol outside Chinandega and killed fifty-three guerrillas trying to enter the town near the Honduran border. The guard also claimed that guerrillas were mortaring from inside the Costa Rican border but that guard positions remained unscathed as the rounds were off-target and fell short. Only the Red Cross could supply figures on civilian casualties, which were the highest in the war.

Managuans spent the day Somoza was playing soldier in the south stockpiling food because of a new general strike called by the opposition. It was a wise move for those who could afford it because supermarkets were closed the next day, Monday, June 4, and long lines formed at the few stores and gas stations that were open. Residents in Chichigalpa stayed indoors Monday, not because of the strike but to keep out of Sandinista and guard firing lines—the Sandinistas had the National Guard bottled up in their garrison. The guard communiqué for May 31 again had contended that the Sandinistas in all battle locations were being "dislodged" and announced "the situation throughout the country is under the control of the authorities," although it also said that a Panamanian plane unloaded fresh "communist mercenary reinforcements" in Costa Rica. Somoza then threatened war with Costa Rica unless the OAS kept the guerrillas from operating out of the neighboring country.

Somoza did not invade. The OAS met June 4 to rebuff Somoza's call for intervention in what one diplomat called "one of the greatest humiliations I have ever seen." The OAS ministers refused even to consider the Nicaraguan resolution.

Bowdler was in Washington to deliver a special report to Secretary of State Cyrus R. Vance. The report indicated that "the most obvious and tangible manifestation" of the crisis in Nicaragua was "the lack of free participation in the political process" and warned that the escalating violence may "transcend the limits of internal conflict and affect the peace and tranquillity of all Central America."

Despite guard claims to the contrary, the guerrillas soon controlled most of León and once again succeeded in trapping the guard there inside their *cuartel* (barracks). The war of the barricades began shaping up as the Sandinistas, *los muchachos* and the new popular militia *(milpas)* pried Somoza-made concrete blocks out of the street to build barricade after barricade. Barrios became a maze of barricades. It was a tactic from the French Revolution but it worked. The barriers provided the revolutionaries cover while out in the open and impeded the guard's mobility.

A Sandinista patrol made a hit-and-run attack on a guard convoy outside of León, knocking a tank carrier out of service. The Sherman tank itself still made it into town where its 75-mm cannon opened fire at the barricades from outside the guard garrison.

Another Sandinista ambush less than a mile from the American embassy in Managua hit forty men, a troop-carrying half-track, armored cars, trucks and a jeep. The general strike continued, holding closed all but a few gas stations. New fighting was reported in Matagalpa, Diriamba and Jinotepe. Reservists in the guard were called to active duty. In the pitched battles in León and at the southern border, the Sandinistas were making little forward progress but at least succeeded in tying down Tacho's best troops.

On June 6 Somoza imposed a ninety-day state of siege giving the guard authority to arrest persons without warrants and hold them longer than the twenty-four hours specified in the constitution. There was complete restriction of domestic news coverage, and of movement in the countryside. The entire nation was placed under an 8:00 P.M. to 4:00 A.M. curfew.

Criminal elements took advantage of the unstable situation as well. Five foreign correspondents who ventured out of the Intercontinental Hotel prior to curfew one night were robbed at gunpoint at the Rincón Español restaurant, which was still in business. The gunmen destroyed the establishment's food and wine inventory before they were done. Managua at night was deserted. In the day the men with guns ruled.

The government was finding itself entrenched in war at home and in a political war being fought abroad. Mexico had not only broken relations with Nicaragua but taken Somoza's threat to invade Costa Rica seriously. Deeply concerned, Mexican President López Portillo warned that his country would "use every means within international law to prevent or check any act of aggression against Costa Rica."

Luis Pallais and Somoza secretary Max Kelly went on the offensive in Washington, where they testified before hearings of the Panama Canal subcommittee of the United States House of Representatives that Panama was a major Sandinista arms supplier and conduit. They displayed large tables and racks of guns and weapons allegedly taken from the FSLN in battle. State Department official J. Brian Atwood blasted the committee for "permitting a foreign government to present evidence against the nationals of another government," calling it "terribly awkward from a legal and foreign policy perspective" and saying there were "proper forums for presenting evidence of violations of international law."

The motive of the testimony was clear. The hearing was held by the Panama Canal subcommittee of the House merchant marine and fisheries committee headed by Tacho's close friend John Murphy, which was to report before the House the following week. Pallais did his best to sabotage the vote on the Panama Canal, charging the State Department was guilty because of its policy of silence in the face of "this open aggression against Nicaragua," and saying that Panama's behavior "raises the critical question of whether the canal should be entrusted to the current leaders in Panama." He said he agreed with Somoza's contention that President Royo and General Torrijos were "unfit to operate a canal of such socioeconomic importance to the world. Is it possible that these people will comply with the neutrality provisions of the treaty?"[1]

Also testifying before the committee was the United States Army's southern command chief, Lieutenant General Dennis P. McAuliffe, who had come from Panama to tell the solons that "the Panamanian involvement appears directed more against the Somoza regime, which is perceived by Panama as repressive, than toward advancement of the Sandinista cause." He acknowledged some Panamanians were supplying guns to the Sandinistas but stopped short of commenting on whether the government itself was involved.

Supporting the Somoza regime and telling Congress it should not allow the treaties to pass was retired Lieutenant General Gordon Sumner, formerly chairman of the Inter-American Defense Board. Torrijos had told him in 1977, Sumner said to Congress, "of his intention to support rebellion and insurrection in his neighbor republics."

Brandon Grove, a deputy assistant secretary of state, went before the subcommittee to say that the administration felt "it is a mistake to link" the Nicaraguan conflict with the canal vote. "If this is done, the results will be self-defeating. . . . It would be contrary to U.S. interests to allow Panamanian attitudes with respect to Nicaragua to jeopardize the prompt passage of effective implementing legislation. We are disturbed by actions taken by the Nicaraguan government, including the violation of human rights. We are also disturbed by the activities of outsiders— whether Panamanians or of other nationalities—who are feeding the flames of violence in Nicaragua."[2]

In the actual fighting in Nicaragua, the Sandinistas proved better prepared than ever before. They were more numerous, armed with more sophisticated weapons and could count on more backing from the people. The population witnessed firsthand the increase in bloody fighting. The sight of rocket-laden planes screaming down out of the sky was soon all too familiar. Neutrality was almost as risk-laden as combat. Red Cross workers, the heroes of the September uprising, found their job even more dangerous this time, sometimes pinned down in their offices in guerrilla and guard crossfire. In Matagalpa the dead and dying lay only a few hundred yards away from them, but they didn't dare venture forth to give aid, well aware that their Red Cross insignia no longer guaranteed immunity. During one exchange a Sandinista jeep skidded into the Red Cross driveway with a wounded man, his leg torn apart by a shell. The medics screamed for the guerrillas to get away, afraid that guardsmen in the floor above them would open fire. But they didn't and the Sandinistas carried their comrade inside on a stretcher.

The government sought to repeat its September tactics in putting down the fighting in a methodical, repressive manner. But no sooner did they contain fighting in one area than it sprang to life again after they moved on to a new objective.

By June 8 the Sandinistas claimed they held twenty-five towns and villages across the country, among them León, Masaya, Matagalpa, Chichigalpa, Somotillo, Estelí, Chinandega and Ocotal with fighting continuing in Jinotepe, Diriamba and Granada. That same day the war came to Managua, where the guard was bolstering its forces by inducting new recruits into its army of 12,000-plus at the national stadium. Meanwhile the general strike continued strong.

Managua was not particularly suited for urban guerrilla warfare. There was no downtown section to fight in. The poor barrios were astride the highway to the airport or in other areas that did not provide the best terrain for such warfare. But Managua was violently anti-Somoza and the Sandinistas had been parading around the barrios in uniform for months. The little townlike neighborhoods with names such as "Open Tres," "Las Americas" and "San Judas" were linked by excellent streets paved with Somoza's factory's blocks. Overnight on June 8 these barrios erected their street barricades. Old ladies and small children helped erect some barricades; the government charged they were forced to build these fortifications by the Sandinistas.

This was the war of barricades but it had no barriers. Fighting could and did flare up anywhere at anytime. For the populations of many of the poorer barrios it was disastrous, with damage and suffering even more terrible than that inflicted by nature in the 1972 earthquake. With indiscriminate rocket attacks from the skies and mortar barrages into any area suspected of holding Sandinistas or militiamen, there was no safe refuge in the city. Many of the poor population took to the road again, carrying a few belongings and clogging the highways out of Managua seeking refuge in the countryside. As the tempo of the war increased so did the atrocities. A telltale bruise on an arm or leg was sufficient proof for guardsmen that a person had been fighting at the barricades, and the bruised individual could be hauled away to jail or summarily shot, depending on the mood of the guardsmen.

That Friday night the normal amount of shooting in Managua suddenly increased; the battle of Managua was under way. Warned that the battle was about to begin, returning from Masaya we ran into fire fights around the corner from the Hotel Intercontinental. The white flag, the indispensable sign of peace (some cursed it as a sign of surrender) appeared on the streets of Managua and few people ventured out. "The flag is only psychological," said one old man as he walked toward a normally busy vegetable and fruit market that had been closed. "It cannot stop bullets," he said. "Anyway, it has become a sign of hate—hate of war and of Somoza."

Newsmen were taken on a tour of the southern zone by the government on Saturday, June 9. They were shown the small, broken-down barbed-wire fence and border marker separating Nicaragua from Costa Rica. Comandante Bravo, the dashing guard officer in charge of the area, described to newsmen how "an international communist brigade made an offensive into my country from Costa Rica. They were three hundred fifty strong," he said, adjusting his sunglasses and M-16 rifle. "They were equipped with sophisticated equipment and they commanded ten square kilometers of territory. We killed about one hundred twenty of them and the rest are in Costa Rica. We won the battle this morning at nine A.M."

The tour was viewed as a farce by many of the newsmen—they left in an air-conditioned Mercedes bus stocked with picnic lunches. "We only saw what the government wanted us to see; the National Guard controlling the town of Rivas after a mopping-up operation," reported *Newsweek*'s Stryker McGuire. "We were shown a small cache of captured weapons—a few rifles, two small mortars and three machetes—but we saw no prisoners and no dead guerrillas. In the central square of Rivas, a relaxed guardsman told us: 'This has become a routine. We drink coffee, we eat lunch, the guerrillas start firing and we fight again. They are as well armed as we are.'"[3]

The southern zone "was important for a political and military victory because the Sandinistas said they wanted to liberate the area and seek international recognition," one official told newsmen.

Bravo, short, swarthy, moustachioed and immaculately turned out in his fatigues, had arranged a three-stop battlefield tour after the departure from Rivas. First was the border crossing at Los Mojones: a barbed-wire fence, a single wooden customs shed and several square miles of lush grassland covering bluffs on both sides of the border overlooking the Pacific Ocean.

Five corpses, shrunken and dust-covered inside mud-spattered uniforms, were lined up on the ground waiting for the photographers. Shell casings littered the campsite, the Sandinistas' first bivouac in Nicaraguan territory when they had crossed the border at the beginning of the month. Plastic bags full of medicine smashed and sodden from the elements lay open to view. Some were of East German manufacture, some labeled "made in Central America" under the aegis of the Common Market, some Mexican, some American—including Bayer aspirin. Many bottles and vials bore labels from Costa Rican drugstores. Down a short slope two vehicles, one a camouflage-painted armored jeep, had been overturned and deliberately wrecked. They still had Costa Rican license plates, eagerly pointed out by guardsmen anxious to demonstrate Costa Rican complicity.

El Naranjo, the second site, was a rustic hacienda overlooking the ocean with a rambling rough-cut wooden villa made of native timber. "It was a wild, breathtaking, beautiful place, deserted except for three Sandinista corpses discarded in a stable," remembered *Miami Herald* reporter Guy Gugliotta. "There was some metal laying around—cartridge clips, spent brass—and some empty bandoliers and infantry boots, but for the most part it was deadly still. I remember thinking, My God, when this is over I want to find out who owns it and make them an offer, if I ever have the money.

"The big show was at another villa, similar, slightly inland near El Ostional. On a sweeping veranda the guard had laid out a smorgasbord of captured armaments. There were thousands of rounds of live ammo of various calibers, hundreds of Chinese-made RPG-2 rockets, a Vietnam staple and a reminder of a dozen similar exhibits I had seen over the years, boxes of American-made grenades and a gun collector's dream in small arms—Garand M-1s, Mausers, M-16s, Galils, an ancient Lewis gun, slightly newer Thompson submachine guns and a lot of Belgian FAL. Some of these had had their serial numbers milled out, the trademark of the Panamanian shipment. The guard took care to point this out, as they had with the Costa Rican license plates. By this time, nobody seriously questioned that the Sandinistas were getting outside help. No one cared. Somoza, Somoza's staff and the guard never seemed to catch on."

A soldier arrived to tell Bravo in the presence of the journalists how he and his men had blown six Sandinistas off the trail from an ambush. "They came one at a time," he told Bravo. "We blew them off the path and then pulled their bodies away waiting for the next."

"Great stuff," said Bravo, slapping the soldier heartily on the chest.

Neutralizing the southern front permitted Somoza to withdraw some of his elite combat troops, numbered at 500, back to the embattled capital. The failure of the newly constituted Sandinista Atlantic front to pin down any significant number of Somoza's troops appeared to have seriously damaged the guerrillas' plans for Managua. But he still had to keep many of his best troops before the Costa Rican border.

The guard managed to retake the city of Masaya, famous for its handicraft and hammock-making, from the Sandinistas on Saturday. But when reporters visited its debris-strewn streets later that day it was far from pacified. *Los muchachos* were still roaming the poor Indian barrio of Monimbó.

Matagalpa Saturday was being pounded by artillery and aerial attacks by a T-33 jet, a push-pull Cessna and a C-47 "Puff the Magic Dragon" craft whose .50-caliber machine guns mounted in an open door left white-puff trails when fired on the Sandinistas.

The Sandinistas continued to control the streets in León; the guard garrison stayed in its barracks. The guerrillas held fifty-three important prisoners whom they were prepared to turn over to the Red Cross on the condition they were shipped out of the country to Panama.

Even as the Sandinistas' southern front collapsed, the war continued to rage elsewhere. There was intensive bombing by government planes, and a full-scale counteroffensive was launched in the barrios. Many of the youths fighting alongside the uniformed Sandinistas refused to hide their faces this time, saying, "This is the final offensive."[4]

The Sandinistas probed close to the Intercontinental Saturday morning and provoked a heavy response from the guard in the Bunker. Troops moved out manning armored cars and .50-caliber machine guns on jeeps. The sound of war was all around. I was reminded of Santo Domingo during the civil war of 1965 when Dominican rebels faced the United States Marines and Eighty-second Airborne as well as Inter-American Peace Force troops that included units from Nicaragua.

The general strike was fully effective on Saturday and no one cared to go into the streets, even in search of food. The only people in the open were refugees carrying their belongings from the barrios which by now were under attack by the guard. For a time on Saturday newsmen were prohibited by heavily armed soldiers from leaving the Intercontinental. After protests the order was rescinded, but newsmen were warned they went into the streets at their own risk.

The American embassy told its staff members to evacuate their families as a major battle raged near Managua's national stadium, only a mile from the Bunker. The most furious fire fights Saturday were in the middle-class districts of Altagracia and Bolonia. Rebels set fire to automobiles and a school bus a short distance from the United States embassy.

On Monday, June 11, the guard had still shown no sign of cracking or disloyalty to Somoza and the trigger-happy army could still outgun the guerrilla forces. Yet this time the guard had their hands full. Somoza held a Monday morning press conference in the officers' club and was businesslike as he fielded questions, mostly in English, from the growing international press corps. Matter-of-factly he said that it would take at least another two weeks to contain the fighting. His excuse for not retaking León, Chinandega, Matagalpa, Estelí and San Dionicio and the numerous barrios in the capital was "to force them to use up their ammunition first." But the fighting in Managua was so fast and furious that guardsmen were using everything they had just to contain the guerrillas and their supporters. Somoza paused, blinked into the TV lights and made a prediction: "The Sandinistas have decided to shoot their last gun here."

Tacho gave no sign he would seek a political solution, even though he met with the Andean nation envoys in his Bunker on Monday. When he told people on television, "Please don't force me to apply the law, because above all things I love my citizens," his words were interpreted by most as meaning more bloodletting.

In an angry tone he denounced the governments of Panama and Cuba for "the international aggression of which Nicaragua is being made the victim." To prove his case Somoza flashed the Panamanian driver's licenses and ID cards of three Panamanians he declared had been killed in the fighting in El Naranjo. The first documents he said belonged to Dr. Hugo Spadáfora, who had never made any secret of the fact he was leading the "Victoriano Lorenzo" brigade into Nicaragua. He had formerly fought in the western Sahara with the Polisario guerrillas opposing Moroccan rule there. Somoza said the casualties in the new round of fighting could number 300 National Guardsmen killed or wounded along with 1,000 Sandinista casualties.

The only two prisoners the government reported taken on the southern front had been exhibited to the press two days earlier. They gave a poor showing; certainly they were not very convincing. They said they had been trained two weeks in a camp in Costa Rica but they were fuzzy on facts. Neither was able to describe to newsmen the little El Naranjo farming complex.

Tacho said he accepted the presence of the Venezuelan and Ecuadorian foreign ministers but he said he did not have any concrete proposals to discuss with them. The people in the streets had a clearer idea of what they wanted. They openly said that peace would be possible only if Somoza left, but Somoza told reporters Monday for the hundredth time that he had no intention of leaving until his term ended in 1981.

That same day twenty-eight American embassy dependents tried to leave the country together with twenty-eight other Americans trapped in Managua, several of whom were missionaries. When it was discovered that fighting on the airport road had in fact closed the airport, the Americans were transferred from the embassy's consular section to the ambassador's residence where they were shown movies to pass the time. The airport was virtually closed; no ground crews could reach the facility. Ecuadorian foreign minister José Ayala Loza and Venezuelan foreign minister José Zambrano arrived as representatives of the Andean pact countries on a peace mission. They were able to land at the airport but had to be helicoptered from the airport over the fighting to the Intercontinental. By early Monday most of the city's water supply was cut off and electricity was out in many places as well.

The American refugees were the most fortunate—they were leaving the country. Among the few others who did so were some wealthy families and government officials. Most of Somoza's cabinet appeared to be staying and taking meals at the Intercontinental. Then there were the 15,000 Nicaraguans forced to flee their homes in Managua either by direct attacks or from fear of imminent attack. All had horror stories about atrocities committed by the guard. Many stated they had fled the *barrios* because they had been warned the guard was going to begin aerial attacks on the barricaded neighborhoods. Few had any safe place to take refuge.

Tacho's hate for *La Prensa* and all it stood for finally got the better of him. He quietly authorized an operation against the newspaper plant and offices, just a mile from police headquarters on the northern highway, which had become a war zone. Normally foreign newsmen and photographers could penetrate the war zone but on Monday afternoon it was temporarily off-limits. Somoza wanted no witnesses to what he shrugged off as a casualty of war. During the night the word spread quickly: "They have burned *La Prensa.*" And there were plenty of witnesses to testify how "Operation *La Prensa*" had been carried out. Fifteen employees had managed to escape over the back fence to give a vivid account of the destruction of Pedro Joaquín's newspaper to his sons, his wife and his brothers Xavier and Jaime.

A Staghound armored vehicle had leisurely lumbered up from its position before the police station to *La Prensa*. Turning in the middle of the street it fired at point-blank range into the building. Then several guardsmen climbed the still-padlocked high iron fence and were handed cans of gasoline which they emptied over the building—one of the cans still stood in the front driveway the following day. For good measure, and with the excuse that Sandinistas were using the building to snipe at the guard, a Cessna subjected the newspaper offices to rocket attacks.

Ironically, the huge facade of *La Prensa* had recently been reinforced with concrete to protect it and its 230 employees from bomb throwers and machine-gun attacks, to which the newspaper had been subjected in the past. But apart from the heavy facade and the nameplate, nothing remained. *La Prensa* had carried Pedro Joaquín's picture on the front page every day since his death, with the number of days since he was assassinated indicated and a call for justice in each issue. Other members of the Chamorro family had been killed since Pedro Joaquín, including two children of a Chamorro relative killed by the National Guard in May.

As newsmen stood and surveyed the still-smoking remains on Tuesday morning, refugees poured out of the city, waving their white flags to salute a paper they believed in even if it wasn't impartial. "After all," said a neighbor who gave reporters an account of the guard's daylight operation, "it opposed Somoza."

Xavier Chamorro commented on the loss, "A printing press and paper can be replaced but the thousands of people who are dying in Nicaragua and will continue to die cannot be replaced. Many in the flower of their youth. We can rebuild the paper. We have done it before. These good Nicaraguans today can't be replaced. We have to rebuild the paper because the paper will be needed to rebuild the morality of this country."[5]

More embassies were trying to evacuate their nationals from Managua. The city's social fabric was visibly unraveling.

The press sat on wicker chairs, with no drinks but with cameras and binoculars, in search of each night's bloody news. Newsmen could watch the twin-tailed Cessna push-pull aircraft dive slowly out of the clouds to launch rocket attacks. If the plane was close enough, a flash could be seen as it launched its rockets on a suspected target —or in the general direction of a target. Seconds later there would be an explosion on impact. When it hit the flimsy crowded slums with their dirt-floor single-room shanties a rocket could wipe out whole families. In these slums families often included a dozen people.

When the families fled the slums, many went to the more urban areas where they could loot and scavenge for food. The descent toward generalized anarchy continued. Encouraged by the National Guard, a mob broke into the Supermercado La Colonia in the chic new Plaza España that belonged to Felipe Mantica, a well-known, longtime opponent of Somoza. When the mobs became too great and the curfew approached, the guards, themselves drinking looted beer, began firing in the air. The looters didn't even quicken their pace. One man left with a load of toilet paper. The New China restaurant was completely wiped out by people in search of food. Already used to gunfire and driven by hunger, people walked calmly through a fire fight to reach the food. Some could be seen braced against the weight of hundred-pound sacks, struggling away from a giant warehouse only three blocks from the central police station. Some came with pushcarts, others with horse-drawn wagons. "We will exchange what we have for what we need later," a woman with a huge sack on her head explained. "We exchange what we have to live. And we had nothing before." The owner of the warehouse, Constantino Campo, had thrown open the doors, permitting people to carry off bags of cornmeal, flour, coffee and cocoa. One man even carried out a large bag of cinnamon, which he offered to others outside. An employee at the warehouse said that Campo had opened the doors rather than risk looting, which could have resulted in damage to the machinery inside. The guard also helped themselves to some of the goods. Guardsmen stalked one man as he left the warehouse carrying a case of Nicaraguan Flor de Caña rum.

Nearby, people showed reporters a grave in the backyard of a small wooden shack where a fifteen-year-old boy had been killed by "a guard bullet as he slept in his bed Tuesday evening." The tales of woe and anger were all the same. There was almost a chorus directed against Somoza in the streets. Large numbers of angry people were in the streets, including the owner of a drugstore, Pharmacy Union, which he said had been looted by the National Guard. "I lost half a million córdobas," he said. "I have only two hundred córdobas [$20]. I have worked all my life. I am fifty. But all that matters is that I may live with my seven children."

There was also evidence that the Sandinistas had gained considerable military skill. Four blocks from the central police station eight teenagers, all unarmed, pried up paving stones with crowbars and built a barricade. Then they placed empty oil drums across the highway. When a column of National Guard troops arrived in jeeps, the teenagers quickly fled. All but one of the soldiers opened fire on them. The lone exception among the guardsmen sat in his jeep like a wax figure. Suddenly, he slumped forward. He had been expertly killed by a single sniper shot. As a newsman commented later, it was a perfect urban guerrilla ambush less than a mile from the headquarters of the national police.

The streets of Managua presented a study in paradox. I was with a group of reporters who, in one tree-shaded area, came upon men in shorts playing baseball. In a nearby street, a youth, apparently a member of no organization, held his hand up to stop our car. In his other hand, he held a .38-caliber pistol, which he aimed directly at me. We did not stop to see what he wanted.

At 9:30 Wednesday morning, June 13, "Operation Cleanup" was launched by the guard against the community of postearthquake structures in three of the Las Americas barrios located near the airport. "Can you please help? We beg all the world. God help us," was the emotional outburst of a middle-aged man on the highway leading to Las Mercedes. "Take Somoza out of Nicaragua. We don't need him. We don't want him. The American is impossible. Carter is impossible to allow what is happening here in Nicaragua. Nobody wants Somoza. Nobody. Only death. Death. He told us, 'If I get victory, you will remember me.' It will be worse than now. The order is to kill and kill. Shoot everybody. 'You are with me. No? Then shoot him.' All children he will kill. I say kill Somoza. Kill him. Kill him."

Stranded on the airport road was a man who wanted to take his family out of Nicaragua. "I used to be in the Mil [American Military Assistance] group," he said. "I am an American citizen and I have to get my twenty-year-old son out of here because if the National Guard gets hold of him they might shoot him." In an upper-class neighborhood, a wealthy Nicaraguan said, "If the FSLN wins I don't know what our fate will be, but frankly I would rather see Somoza leave now and worry about that later. I really think he is going to kill every able-bodied Nicaraguan in this city and then he has to go off after the other cities the Sandinistas now have. He just wants a victory at any price. This time the price could be too high for everyone."

There was evident suffering among government supporters as well. Fifty-five-year-old Antonio Rodríguez García stood crying before the Intercontinental Hotel one morning. He had six small children with him. "They said I was an 'oreja' [literally "ears"—a government informer]. They said I was a 'sapo' [toad], a paramilitary. I have my school in the *colonia* Luis Somoza and it is the Masonic Institute Benito Juarez." Breaking down into tears and trembling, the short, squat man said, "I escaped with these six children of mine. My wife is trapped somewhere. I have sixteen children. My second son is a captain in the National Guard. He was killed in the north two days ago fighting the Sandinistas. I have three daughters who are policewomen. The Sandinistas put my picture on a barricade. I saw it. It said I was an *oreja.* They forced my children to build barricades in the *colonia* in which I lived. It is the *colonia catorce de Septiembre.* I managed to escape. They did not recognize me." Whether he was, in fact, a "big ears" was anybody's guess, but the strange security types who spent the day lounging around the entrance of the hotel all knew him and shook his hand. They were angry at his story and the newsmen's questions. A taxi driver said quietly, "He is very lucky. He is obviously one who got away. These spies are very dangerous. They have caused others to die." The following days he appeared on Somoza's TV program sobbing out the same story. Later he was found to be working in the Bunker.

Among the strange people in the hotel, now overcrowded and understaffed, was a Mr. Russell Brown, a former United States Marine who had come to Nicaragua with the Marines in 1926 and stayed on, becoming a bodyguard of Tacho and his father. The old man still donned his uniform and stood close beside Somoza when he gave his press conferences.

The small Nicaraguan air force flew more strikes on Wednesday the thirteenth than ever before, bombing and strafing the young rebels holding the slum districts behind the barricades. Somoza's air force was dwindling considerably. One aircraft crash-landed because of a mechanical failure on Wednesday; one pilot defected with his plane to Costa Rica; and only two of Somoza's five Spanish Avicar troop transports were still intact. The Sandinistas claimed they had downed several other planes.

The pilot who defected called on his radio to fellow pilots to stop the bombing of innocent people and stop supporting "that bastard thief." His fellow pilots replied with unprintable curses and damned his mother on the open frequency. Saying he was leaving for Honduras, the defecting pilot fired a couple of rockets harmlessly at the airport and flew to Costa Rica. The order was passed to shoot the pilot and plane on sight but pursuers were too slow and the pilot landed safely in San José.

Aerial rocket strikes in León sought to take the pressure off the National Guard garrison there, besieged by the Sandinistas since June 2. Tacho called the garrison by radio Wednesday. The conversation was picked up from the army band by reporters with scanners. He told the garrison officer to whom he spoke, "Hold on, my friend, we are with you and we are with you all the time." Replied a Colonel Marconi, "Yes, we will act like the French Foreign Legion. We will fight to the last man. We are going to hold on and wait until they make the first move." In the meantime the Sandinistas had captured and repaired an armored car and were on the point of attacking the barracks.

A León newspaper editor reported by telephone Thursday that the air strikes there were "the worst we have ever seen. . . . The guard bombed Wednesday from two until five o'clock in the afternoon and then started again at daybreak." Word spread through the night that León was on the point of becoming a Sandinista city completely. One source in León said, "The guerrillas have five thousand men under arms. They include peasants with machetes and trained guerrillas with heavy machine guns and mortars." It was the mortars that inflicted the final defeat on the garrison. The FSLN burned the garrison and routed the guard. Some fled in their underwear, others dressed as women.

"The 'boys' are well organized and have won the respect of most of the citizens of this town," a lawyer from León said by telephone. "It seems there is more law and order in this Sandinista-held town than in the capital. The 'boys' distribute food from door to door and will not permit pillaging."

By this time, however, there was little left to pillage. The battle for the León *cuartel* had lasted for three weeks and was perhaps the most savage of the war. The front of the barracks had been blown away in chunks, piece by piece destroyed by rockets. The guard had given as good as they got for the apartment houses across the narrow streets where the Sandinistas had launched their attacks were little more than piles of rubble.

The courtyard behind the barracks was ankle-deep in brass, ammo boxes and the empty black cardboard cylinders that had once held individual rounds for the Sherman tank. Two days after the garrison fell, the city was still in shock. The streets were empty, doors were bolted and people waited inside, unable, as yet, to believe it was over. The market was vacant and the city was slowly starving to death. Staple food was thin, terrible-tasting porridge made with sorghum—birdseed—the last edible grain left in the city. Up the street from the *cuartel* was an empty building whose street-floor window had long been shot out. In the big cellar room was a heap of moist black earth, covering the dead of León. The stench was overpowering.

While he did not admit it at the time, toward the end Tacho admitted that the tide of war turned in favor of the Sandinistas when they won the battle of León. Major General Gonzalo Evertz, one of his top guard officers, was wounded in the defense of the León *cuartel* in which they were trapped. A retired guard officer, Brigadier General Ariel Argüello, came forward in that "moment of peril," Tacho noted proudly, and took command. Both Argüello and his son died in the battle for León. Tacho liked to compare his "gallant defense of León to that of the Alcazar in the Spanish Civil War, when Franco forces held out heroically against the republican forces."

The International Red Cross delegate, Ulrich Bedert of Switzerland, said that some 31,000 refugees had registered with the Red Cross in the capital and that he believed the nationwide total could now be more than 150,000. One report said as many as 7,000 Nicaraguan children refugees were crammed into Honduran camps in near-starvation conditions and that there were many refugees in Costa Rica as well. Nicaraguan Red Cross president Ismael Reyes said many refugee centers in Nicaragua did not have adequate sanitary facilities and had no water for sanitary use. "Many of the children already have stomach problems and diseases will begin soon," Reyes said. "This is ten times worse than the 1972 earthquake."

The church was called upon to assume its traditional role as a haven of refuge. At the national seminary a blue and yellow bus with its destination sign saying "Managua–Rivas" was one of several such vehicles in the institution's front yard. Each seat was occupied by a refugee with no place to go. The bus was deluxe accommodation in comparison to the crowded squalor of the seminary, which once trained young men for the Roman Catholic priesthood. Whole families—minus their teen-aged sons—were camped throughout the seminary's rooms and corridors, in every inch of available space. There were more than 11,000 people crammed into even the seminary's chicken coops and animal pens. The yard and gardens, once the pride of the old priests who had used the building as a retirement center since the 1972 quake, were turned into mud. Few of the refugees, who had left the bombing in the barrios, brought any food with them, just occasional personal effects and household objects. Some had brought their pigs and chickens.

Families sat around cooking-fires fueled by a few sticks of wood, boiling rice and beans. Miriam Morales, twenty, had just given birth to a daughter in the chicken coop. "I've called her Diane, and I hope she never hears a rocket in her life." Other children smiled and played underfoot.

As conditions in the makeshift camp became seriously overcrowded, workmen began to construct single wooden rooms with the help of Catholic charity organizations. Before even the tin roofs and some walls had been completed, whole families moved into the new living space.

When the director was told how sad it was to see these people living like animals, he bristled slightly and said, "What can we do, we can't close the doors to anyone."

"The main problem now is food," Bedert said. "We are organizing planes to bring in food from the United States and other countries. There is no distribution. We can't go into places where people need the food." Bedert, with more than ten years as regional director in East Africa, Nigeria and Biafra, said, "This is the worst I have ever seen. It is much less organized than in Africa."

Americans and other foreign nationals were boarding daily flights from Somoza's private jet landing strip at his Montelimar estate. Those trying to leave included 300 Spanish nationals, and members of the Brazilian, Argentine and Colombian embassies and their dependents. More than 301 persons had been evacuated during the week. A Colombian C-130 Hercules with a cargo of relief supplies received incoming fire as it landed at Las Mercedes airport. The news that even a mission of mercy was exposed to hostile action frightened off other planes similarly laden.

The curfew in Managua had been moved progressively forward from 8:00 P.M. to 6:00 P.M. After six o'clock reporters covered the war from the ninth floor of the Intercontinental. Looking down on the Bunker, reporters could see two huge recently installed structures designed to deflect rockets. Fresh sandbag emplacements were erected. When reporters approached during the day, it was clear that all was not peaceful in the Bunker. Guards were bad tempered, reflecting their nervousness. When firing broke out Wednesday afternoon, a paramilitary man in civilian clothes carrying an M-1 snapped abruptly at journalists gathering to cover the day's developments. "There is no entry to the presidency press office. We are on alert. Can't you hear the firing? Get out."

The evening show from the Intercontinental's upper floors was often horrifyingly spectacular. One night black smoke covered the northern horizon as a textile factory went up in flames. The sounds of war contrasted grimly with the sounds of nature all around. The ominous rattle of automatic weapons fire and the duller, heavy "poom, poom" of the .50-caliber guns and armored cars usually began at the same time birds awoke to commence their chirping in the crisp hour after dawn.

Wednesday, June 13, Tacho went on television to deliver a strident speech to the nation and appeal for calm. As customary by now, he denounced intervention by foreign governments. He also morally condemned the Sandinistas for turning over arms to "inexperienced youths." Despite the fact that many relief flights could not land in Nicaragua and that many of the supplies were siphoned off for personal use, Somoza promised the guard would distribute food to residents of Managua.

"I never thought there would be so much disorder and pillaging in our capital," Somoza told his countrymen. "I never thought people would have to face the embarrassment of having to take things that are not theirs in order to feed their children." Again he urged his public not to force him to apply the law because he loved his citizens but his plea brought nothing but jeers.

Nicaraguan foreign minister Julio C. Quintana called the foreign press together on Friday, June 15, in the lobby of the Intercontinental to denounce for the second time in one month an invasion of Nicaragua from Costa Rica. The foreign minister said a column of some 300 Sandinistas, equipped with sophisticated weapons, had penetrated into Nicaragua in vehicles. "I want to make a very serious denunciation to the world," he said and went on to describe how the invaders had crossed into Nicaraguan territory at 6:00 A.M. Thursday. "This new invasion is threatening the peace of the Central American isthmus," he said, adding, "I am ready to go to Washington to present Nicaragua's case to the Organization of American States." Quintana said the aim of the Sandinistas was to capture the city of Rivas, set up a liberated territory and seek recognition from some governments.[6]

Southern front guard Commander Bravo called for reinforcements on Saturday, June 16, after learning that a military convoy of heavy vehicles and weapons had gathered in Costa Rica near the border town of La Cruz. Radio Sandino reported the FSLN had fought a pitched battle in nearby Peñas Blancas and that heavy casualties were suffered on both sides. Somoza forces, taxed with trying to retake León and other towns in which the guard was still fighting the Sandinistas, seemed to have little likelihood of going to war with neighboring Costa Rica. They would first have to clean up the south as well.

Radio Sandino announced that the FSLN had formed what they described as a "temporary government of reconstruction." The government that replaced Somoza upon his overthrow would be made up of five persons, Radio Sandino said: Violeta Barrios de Chamorro, widow of Pedro Joaquín; Alfonso Robelo; Daniel Ortega; Sergio Ramírez; and Moises Hassan Morales. All but Hassan were in Costa Rica and preparing to travel to the liberated boot of Nicaragua at Sapoa. Hassan was at the Sandinista frontline headquarters fighting in Managua.

The makeup of the reconstruction government was left-leaning but a number of Nicaraguan businessmen heard Robelo make an appeal over Radio Sandino for prayers and unity, saying such a government would not necessarily be communistic. "We are prepared to work with such a government," said a banker. "We have assurances from Robelo. Anything will be better than the present senseless bloodshed, chaos and pillaging."

Five South American nations—Andean group members Venezuela, Colombia, Peru, Ecuador and Bolivia—on Saturday, June 16, declared that a "state of belligerency" existed in Nicaragua. Under international law, this move put the embattled guerrilla forces on an equal legal footing with the government and permitted the countries to aid the rebels openly. The action was a serious blow to Somoza's efforts to minimize the Sandinistas' attacks as the work of terrorists. Observers saw the move as an initial step in intervention into the civil war. The basic concept of the OAS was nonintervention but the action taken by the five nations was seen as an attempt to break the diplomatic logjam and circumvent the OAS principle of nonintervention. The Andean pact nations had earlier in the month produced a peace initiative that was lauded by United States Secretary of State Vance, but Somoza rebuffed this peace effort when meeting with the foreign ministers of Venezuela and Ecuador in the Bunker. One moderate source said, "It's a real break politically for the guerrillas." But a government source said sarcastically, "Now they can receive humanitarian aid—rockets." In their communiqué the Andean states said they hoped their initiative would facilitate the installation of a "true representative democracy, justice and freedom" in Nicaragua.[7]

The move was the first concerted international attempt to end the bloody war. Ecuador next followed Mexico's example and broke relations with Nicaragua. The United States expressed its hope that this recognition of the junta would give the OAS the right to seek intervention to negotiate a cease-fire and a peaceful transfer of power—and avoid the destruction of the National Guard and the Liberal party in exchange for Somoza's departure.

On the morning of June 18, Alan Riding of *The New York Times*, whom Somoza had denounced as "a Sandinista spokesman," received a message that the FSLN's top leaders in Managua were waiting to see him deep inside the city's rebel-held eastern slums. He put on a flak jacket and then invited a French and a Mexican reporter to accompany him. They set off in a car, passing the bullet-marked statue of the late Luis Somoza, along a city highway traveled only by occasional refugees carrying their paltry belongings and a white flag, until they could go no farther. Broken glass covered the road leading up to the first barricade. They parked the car and listened to the sounds of battle taking place in the area they were to enter. Overhead, three Cessna push-pull aircraft took turns firing rockets into the slums. To the south, the National Guard, unwilling to penetrate the rebel-held zone, lobbed mortars into the area. And nowhere in particular but always close there was the report of sniper fire. The reporters looked at each other. No one wanted to go on, but no one dared turn back.

They began running into the deserted slums, doubled over, listening for sniper fire, watching the trajectory of the rockets, occasionally hitting the ground as a mortar fell nearby. At one point, a family opened the door of a hut and called them in. "Careful! You'll get killed. Where are you going?" they were asked. Breathlessly, they explained. A young man offered to guide them and they set off again. For more than a mile, they ran along muddy streets, hugging walls and houses for protection, stopping only at crossroads to listen for snipers, until finally they reached the first barricade manned by the *muchachos.* The young rebels, some uniformed, most not, looked at the group with curiosity. The guide quickly explained the mission. The reporters were pointed on their way, beyond perhaps a dozen more combined barricades and trenches. Then they were told to wait beside a house where life seemed to be going on almost normally. At one corner, women and children with pots in their hands waited for food handouts. On wooden verandas, old men sat in rocking chairs observing the war as if the attacking planes were no more irritating than a pair of mosquitoes. Suddenly Riding heard his name called out. He turned around and saw an old friend, Margarita Montealegre, a young reporter-photographer who was now in uniform and known, she quickly whispered, as Marta. "Come along," she said, leading the way down three more streets to a simple wooden house with a guard at the door. "In you go," she ordered.

Inside the hut's single room sat Moises Hassan, who only the previous day had been named to the junta that would govern Nicaragua, and Julio López, a leader of the United People's Movement. A few minutes later, Carlos Nuñez Tellez, a member of the FSLN's national directory, and Joaquín Cuadra Lacayo, later to become army chief of staff, arrived. The two men embraced Riding. They had known him for some time. Cuadra laughed when he felt Riding's flak jacket. "What's happening?" he asked. "You don't need to feel nervous here." He was wearing an olive green T-shirt and a shoulder holster with a pistol. He had placed his Belgian-made FAL automatic rifle at the door. "We're in very good shape," he said. "The guard daren't come in here. Their morale is broken. By the way, are you staying in the Intercontinental Hotel?" Riding nodded. "Get out, get out immediately. It's a target for us. It's full of *sapos.* Why don't you stay with us?"

Moises Hassan, wearing a dirty sport shirt and ten days' growth of beard, sat on the edge of a metal-frame bed. He was unabashedly surprised to find himself in the provisional junta and he had little idea about what it was up to. He was the only junta member on the front line; the others were all in Costa Rica. But he spoke confidently, as if the battle were already won, of the new Nicaragua that would soon be constructed. He seemed an unlikely politician—a thirty-eight-year-old quantum physicist with a doctorate from the University of North Carolina who had spent the past few years teaching in the National University. But he had gained some prominence in recent months as an organizer of the United People's Movement, the coalition that served as the political arm of the FSLN. Although he had even won the reputation of being a hard-line leftist, he assured Riding that he was not a Marxist. "We want socialism for Nicaragua, but our kind of socialism," he insisted. "We have carried out our own kind of revolution and we'll build our own kind of socialism."

Outside the hut, with its thin walls and tin roof, the war went on. Occasionally rockets fell nearby, but the rebel leaders merely raised their voices to be heard. Perhaps they were numbed by the continuous noise and violence; perhaps they were so sure of victory that they felt immune from danger. In the tiny muddy patio at the back of the hut, the owners, who were proud to lend their home to the FSLN leadership, had dug a hole and improvised a bomb shelter. Inside it lay two tiny children, while nearby their mother stood over an open-air oven preparing a watery bean soup. Overhead, the planes still droned, the pitch of their engines rising every few minutes as they went into a dive.

The reporters, nervous again at the thought of having to leave the relative safety of the rebel stronghold, looked at their watches and at each other. "You'd better go," Cuadra said, "It's usually worse in the afternoons." Marta led them to the main highway and handed them back to their guide. "Vámonos," he said. But at the fourth barricade, the *muchachos* stopped them. "You can't go on," one said, "there's a guard sniper blocking the way." Every few seconds, a shot rang out and dirt jumped on the path they were to take. "You may be better off that way," he said, pointing beyond an open sewage canal. The guide set off, followed at an interval by each of the reporters. They half jumped, half forded the canal and, crouching while running, headed into a deserted area of slums. They turned a corner and almost bumped into a young guerrilla with a pistol in his hand. He held up his hand and they stopped. "We're carrying out an operation," he whispered. "There's a guard around. Go that way." The group headed off again. Half an hour later, perspiring, exhausted, they reached their car. They embraced their guide with gratitude. "Let's get the hell out of here," Riding said. They drove off in silence. In the rearview mirror, Riding watched the guide wander slowly back into the war zone.

Somoza was distressed at developments and showed bitterness in interviews that the United States was not supporting him in his hour of need. As the third week in the "final offensive" began on Tuesday, June 19, aides in the Bunker were increasingly quick-tempered, showing the fatigue and strain of the nineteen-month civil war. There were shouts and barking commands, the slamming of phones. Tacho, in an open white shirt, was jowly and his eyes red and heavy-lidded. In a meeting with an interviewer much of the optimism and certainty of victory that he had voiced over previous months was gone. He predicted victory but qualified it with "when the will of the people weakens, then it could go either way. Maybe we win, maybe they do."

He was a man gripped with paranoia—a day earlier he had told another reporter, "At least I have one friend left [myself]." He lashed out at the merchants and businessmen whom he singled out as among major inciters of the insurgency, took a shot at the United States once again for not coming to the aid of an old anticommunist partner, assailed Panama and Venezuela for supplying aid to the guerrillas, and reiterated the well-worn theme of an international communist plot to take over his country.

He retracted his prediction that he would put down the insurgents within two weeks. Because of the second "invasion" from the south, he did not know how much longer it would last. "As long as the communists continue to supply weapons, there will be a battle," he said. "They've [the guerrillas] practically outgunned my government," he asserted, citing alleged outside arms flowing into Nicaragua and displaying a variety of foreign-made arms to make his point.

At times Tacho sounded confused and contradicted himself. At one point he blamed the merchants themselves for bringing on the rampant looting and pillaging that had left hardly a store or factory in Managua unscathed. Then he put the onus on the "communists." He vowed, "There will be a military solution. . . . I think I'm winning. Right now I think I am moving ahead." He sounded uncertain. He tried to explain away popular support for the uprising, contending that it had no backing from the citizenry, that the "reds" were forcing the people to erect barricades and fight the guard.

Somoza once again rejected negotiations with the Sandinistas, declaring they had wrought too much damage to permit the opening of a dialogue. He scoffed at the idea of talks with representatives of their new "temporary government of reconstruction," branding a majority of its five leaders as people with "known communist records."

If he sounded more muted, his strategy had apparently not wavered: "We must defeat the insurgents." He claimed to have the second front invasion "contained" and to be recovering Managua "yard by yard." But as shells burst around the city and rocket planes dived on dense barrios that statement was hard to accept at face value.

Again he appealed for United States help—not specifying exactly what—in this battle against "communists trying to take over my country." He was a bitter man, lamenting what he termed the ingratitude of the United States failing to return the aid he had given in the past. "I helped them for thirty years to fight communism. I'd like the American people to pay back the help we gave in the Cold War. The U.S. can't afford to lose a good partner. I am transitory but the reds are not."

On one point he was adamant. Under what conditions might he consider quitting? "None. I won't go unless they throw me out."

Somoza's latest offensive began in the capital on Tuesday the nineteenth. In a replay of his successful September strategy, companies of crack troops began the drive to clean out Managua. The question was whether it was too late. Were the guerrillas too well entrenched?

A vast section of the capital, several square miles of sprawling barrios in the northeast section of Managua, was completely in the hands of the guerrillas.

Somoza's plan was to uproot them fast. Then he'd move to the south with his best men to halt the second invasion and clean up Rivas, a city of 50,000 only sixty-eight miles from the capital which had seen sharp fighting for days. And then finally he'd go after the northern towns, including León, which was wholly Sandinista now.

The thud of 120-mm mortars, whistling rockets from the Cessnas, and the crackle of the .50-caliber automatics from "Puff the Magic Dragon" signaled the drive on Managua's barrios Tuesday morning. Somoza's men, about 1,600 tank-led soldiers, were throwing everything they had into neighborhoods where many still lived, despite the massive refugee outflow. Thousands of innocent civilians were involved. Arrayed against the guard were 300 hard-core guerrillas, with their own .50-caliber machine guns, makeshift mortars and rockets. They were well dug in. Colonel James McCoy, the United States military attaché at the embassy, in a deep-background report Tuesday morning, estimated that the guerrillas had numbered 800 in the sector of the city now under attack. Many had slipped out, possibly heading down to Rivas where the Sandinistas had the guard under attack in the central barracks, or they were possibly regrouping on the outskirts of Managua for an attack from another direction on the capital.

Somoza's security people spread word that the guerrillas intended to hit the Bunker. The Intercontinental next door would be right in the middle of the war. The ninety-seven-member foreign press corps housed there waited in tense expectation.

The focal point of the attack by the guard in the barrios was but three miles from the Bunker. The sky was thick with black smoke; the thunder of shells and the whine of attack planes and helicopters bringing in the wounded from other fighting around the country were constant.

Somoza's predicament was that his forces were being spread increasingly thin. He was not getting significant replenishment of arms and ammo because of United States pressure on his allies. Reliable estimates had it that the guerrillas had already destroyed half his air force and armor. He had but two old Sherman tanks left, he had lost four of his push-pull aircraft and a main assault low-level aircraft. Planes he did still have were staying increasingly higher because of the Sandinistas' better weaponry and expertise in use of it against low-flying aircraft. He now had only five push-pulls and three Spanish-made troop transports. His most modern planes were the T-33 jets. He had but three of them and only two could fly.

There was the troublesome south where Somoza's success or failure in the long run would rest on how quickly he could win back Managua—if indeed he could. He was devastated as well by the fatigue of his men and the inexperience of many of his troops. Some reservists were as young as thirteen, with no more training and with none of the zeal of *los muchachos.* Somoza's intelligence gathering was poor and lines of communications vague. Many of his senior generals didn't have the faintest idea of what was going on.

The long-range prospects were increasingly grim. The guard was still holding loyal to its leader, but some were openly asking, "What is the solution?" and began to question more and more as they saw their countrymen die in greater numbers.

Could a military victory be won? Even if Somoza pulled this one off, they considered it inevitable that the Sandinistas would regroup and attack again.

Heavy mortar and aerial attacks on the Don Bosco barrio thwarted an attempt I and several other journalists made to interview Sandinista commanders in Managua. We were forced to return through small dirt lanes and backyards filled with people. They helped by opening their homes, pointing out what streets were dangerous and where the fire fights were taking place. Many families had dug their own air raid shelters in the soft soil in their backyards or, like the Viet Cong, right under the flooring of their little homes.

One very young militiaman, manning a barricade with twenty-five companions, all armed with an assortment of weapons, told us, "We are holding this point here, as are hundreds of our companions, waiting for other troops of the Sandinista National Liberation Front to come from the north and south and then take over here. We are not strong enough to take over the government ourselves." Deeply entrenched behind rugged concrete barricades and waist-deep foxholes and tank traps, they had been fighting a standoff sniper war with the guard for days and in doing so had tied up Somoza's much needed troops.

Elsewhere in the war-weary country fire fights raged in a half-dozen cities. In the south the guerrilla force numbering nearly 700 dug in near the village of Sapoa. In León the Sandinistas, fully in control, organized a revolutionary municipal council, the first such rebel governmental apparatus in the nation.

CHAPTER 17

Death of a Newsman

"Buenos días—you see, I'm making progress," ABC's Bill Stewart said in English to a Nicaraguan woman and her young daughter in the elevator of the Intercontinental the morning of Wednesday, June 20, the second day of Somoza's big offensive to clean up Managua. I was riding down to the lobby with him that morning. It was easy to see Stewart was trying to improve his nonexistent Spanish. He had been in Managua since June 10, after most recently covering events in Iran. For Stewart, his four-man crew and some ninety other foreign correspondents, it was just the beginning of another routine day of terror covering the Nicaraguan war.

The ABC network team—Stewart, cameraman Jack Clark, sound man Jim Cefalo, interpreter Juan Francisco Espinoza and driver Pablo Tiffer López—was only one of many groups (reporters seldom if ever ventured off alone) that were setting out to cover the aftermath of Tuesday's bombing in one of the northeast barrios of the capital. The guard had made progress in cleaning out many of the Managua barrios but their advance was slow. Heavy losses were inflicted among the civilian population. However, the Sandinistas suffered few casualties as they remained entrenched behind their barricades. Rockets and mortars began raining on the area again at the first crack of dawn.

The morning started inauspiciously for the ABC-TV crew, motoring toward the heart of the fighting. "In the first area that we entered," Cefalo said, "the National Guard was quite pleasant and assisted us in getting shots of them, showing how the guard's morale was up. There was a fellow there with a guitar and a group of soldiers got together to sing a couple of songs. We filmed all of this. The guard also told us that there were some other [guard] outposts several blocks further into the barrio, so we took a road and went through the area."

It was shortly before 11:00 A.M. The team moved on in their small blue Mazda van with sliding doors and "TV" and "Foreign Press" signs emblazoned on all sides. "We came upon [a guard] outpost," Cefalo said, "and Bill felt that, rather than driving towards them and making them nervous, he would get out of the car with the interpreter and together they would walk towards the guard and explain to them what we were doing." Cefalo and Clark stayed in the truck and began recording the encounter.

A battle was being fought farther ahead, but the street was quiet where Stewart left the van. The few trees provided little shade from the morning heat. A short distance away a woman in a small house beckoned to him to come in. She stood at the door and tried to tell Stewart, "They are killing people down there." Her seven-year-old son pulled at her skirt. "Mother, he doesn't understand Spanish," the boy tried to explain. The thirty-seven-year-old reporter smiled and shrugged and, carrying a white flag, continued past them toward the guard his press card held above his head. Espinoza inexplicably walked on the other side of the street, out of earshot.

Stewart, dressed in a white and blue checked sport shirt, immaculate white trousers and shoes—perhaps the cleanest-looking person in Managua that day—moved onward to the fifteen- to twenty-man guard patrol scattered and lounging at a roadblock at the end of the street. A lone soldier walked between him and Espinoza. The woman and her son, both sensing what was going to happen, re-treated into their house and peered out from behind a small curtained window. At that moment Cefalo looked down to adjust his tape machine; the boy watched the guard order Stewart on his knees.

"When I looked up again I saw Bill on his knees," the big, heavyset Cefalo said. "Whether the guard told him to do that, I don't know. I think Bill may just have been making a gesture." The guardsman motioned for him to lie down on the street and Stewart complied, his hands stretched in front of him. He stayed in that position "for thirty seconds or a minute" and "wasn't making any overt moves. We still at this point thought that the situation wasn't that serious," Cefalo said. Then the guardsman approached Stewart. "Mommy, they kicked him, they kicked the man," blurted the youngster audibly in Spanish. Killing had become a way of life but kicking the ribs of a newsman lying prostrate in the street seemed to shame even the little boy.

"We realized that this was more serious than we thought it would be," Cefalo said. "The soldier stepped back and motioned to Bill as if he wanted him to put his hands behind his head." Stewart started to comply, but then the soldier suddenly took a step forward, calmly leveled his M-14 rifle, and shot him behind the right ear.

"We saw Bill's head bob, couldn't believe it and still weren't quite sure of what we had seen," the sound man said.

Clark's camera lens shot up into the air and focused on trees through the van's windshield. The words "Let's get out of here" were recorded on Cefalo's machine. The driver cautioned them it was better not to move.

"After a few minutes, the guard soldier motioned to us to come forward with the van, which we did," Cefalo said. "We drove past Bill's body to the right-hand side of the street where there was a last house before a field and a barricade. The guard soldiers had us get out and show our identification. While we were out of the car, I noticed our interpreter's body lying on the left-hand side of the house. He had also been shot in the head."

It was quick thinking that got the ABC crew out of its tight spot. The credit went to the fast-talking driver, Tiffer, who told the guardsmen a lie so bold it apparently saved his own life and that of Cefalo and Clark. The driver said the soldiers first "asked me if I knew that 'dog.' " Tiffer replied that the crew was from Managua's Channel Six, owned by Somoza. Cefalo and Clark presented their government-issued press credentials. One of the soldiers told the driver, "We've stuck our foot in it this time." The guardsmen then asked Tiffer if he knew Espinoza. Tiffer answered that Espinoza was an interpreter. "What do you mean?" one soldier said. "He's an interpreter—that son of a bitch? I know him. He's a porter at the airport." Espinoza was indeed a porter. He was also bilingual and reportedly had been dismissed from his job because he was becoming too chummy with incoming Americans. Stewart's crew had met Espinoza at Las Mercedes and hired him shortly after their arrival.

The soldiers first insisted they would have to kill the witnesses, but then let them go after Tiffer told another lie, promising to blame the incident on Sandinista snipers. The guardsmen were mildly irritated and indignant at the situation but the crew was allowed to leave. The guard was unaware that the execution had been videotaped and that they were letting the news crew go with the evidence intact.

As the crew got back into the van, Tiffer asked them if they wanted to take Stewart's body back to the hotel. They said they did. "The driver and I backed up, put Bill's body in the van, and came back here to the hotel," Cefalo said.

It had been a cold-blooded execution, starkly filmed by the veteran crew in the van. After making and hiding extra copies of the video cassette in case it was seized by the government before it could be transmitted to the United States, the crew sent the footage via satellite to New York to be shown on the evening network news. Asserted the shaken Cefalo to reporters, "There was no reason for the shooting." The sequence was run on all three networks that evening, CBS leading its newscast with it and ABC reserving the Nicaraguan war story for the last five minutes of its program, devoting the time to the memory of Bill Stewart. Television stations across the United States and around the world reran the horrifying footage of Stewart's death several times a day for the next few days "until you just couldn't watch it anymore," as one newsman in the States said at the time. "People were numbed by it, and when the numbness wore off they were outraged. Public opinion quickly registered that Somoza had to go." The few minutes of videotape did more to injure Somoza's reputation around the world, even among conservatives, than perhaps any single incident in the decades-long family rule.

President Carter called the newsman's killing "an act of barbarism that all civilized people condemn." A group of United States senators and congressmen signed a declaration labeling Somoza "the Idi Amin of Latin America."

The murder outraged the ninety-seven foreign newsmen covering the war, most of whom promptly signed a strongly worded letter of protest that I handed to Somoza at a press conference eight hours later at the military casino, the officers' club. The letter was written in both English and Spanish so that it would be disseminated in Nicaragua. It flatly contradicted an assertion by the government's Radio Nacional made shortly after the murder that Stewart had been killed by a Sandinista sharpshooter.

Tacho had a love-hate relationship with the foreign press. The ham in him was evident in the way he styled his press conferences after those at the White House. As he entered a guard would announce: "The president of Nicaragua." Congressmen and local newsmen in his pay always rose and applauded his entry. The day Stewart died his meeting with the press corps was a heated session. A photographer hissed as Tacho's lackeys applauded on cue. But Somoza cheated. This was one press conference that was not broadcast live.

Facing the television lights and some seventy members of the foreign press, Tacho, dressed in a light blue *guayabera* with gold cuff links, appeared shaken. His eyes showed he was a shattered man. He had still not seen a copy of the videotape but had heard so much about it that he had to believe in what had happened. The carnage of the war didn't seem to move him as much as did the death of one man, Bill Stewart. He realized the impact documentation of that would have on the world.

"Members of the press," Tacho began,

> I am going to read this statement and I ask you as president of Nicaragua and as supreme commander of the armed forces of this country to accept my most deep condolences on the sad and tragic event that resulted in the loss of the life of an American newspaper [man] *(pause)* . . . Bill Stewart and his Nicaraguan interpreter, Juan Francisco Espinoza.
>
> I have already ordered a full investigation of this painful and dreadful incident and I assure that the individual or individuals responsible for it either by actions or omissions will receive the full weight of the law.
>
> The army has already formed a military court of investigation that will hear this incident with the objective of bringing those responsible before a court-martial. This unforgivable and isolated happening has moved me and everyone very deeply and it does not belong to the framework of my government's policy on information and relations with the press which has been one of continuous and friendly relations with you all.
>
> I have been advised that film of this tragic incident has already been exhibited in the United States and perhaps the rest of the world. Therefore I ask those companions of Bill Stewart to supply a copy of this tape to the military authorities as well as a sworn statement and full cooperation to do justice.
>
> I also want to give my deepest sympathies to the companions who were with Bill Stewart during the incident. I also want to extend my condolences through you to the American people, to Mr. Roone Ardledge, president of ABC News, and to Mr. Bill Leonard, president of CB [CBS] News.
>
> It is with deep regret that I have received this news for I wanted your stay in Nicaragua to be as open as the way we have dealt in the past. I assure you that we are going to investigate this case fully and those found guilty will be punished. I am open for questions.

He never once mentioned sympathy for Stewart's family in New York City. When Tacho ended his apology, I handed him the copy of the protest note we had written even before watching vivid replays of the killing on the ABC video monitor in the Intercontinental. I asked if it could be read out loud. Somoza's eyes narrowed.

I handed ABC producer Ken Lucoff a copy of the note and he stepped forward. In a booming voice full of emotion that needed no microphone he angrily read:

> Mr. President. We, the undersigned members of the international press, wish to protest in the strongest possible terms the execution today by the National Guard of Bill Stewart, ABC correspondent, and his interpreter, Juan Espinoza. Attached is a copy of the statement made by ABC sound man, Jim Cefalo, who was an eyewitness to the shooting. It flatly contradicts the assertion by Radio Nacional that Bill Stewart was killed by a Sandinista sharpshooter.
>
> We also wish to protest the inflammatory media campaign in *Novedades* and on Radio Nacional projecting us as "part of the vast communist propaganda network." This is a blatant lie. It foments hostility towards us and makes our work even more dangerous than it is already. Even though Nicaragua is under state of siege, your government has issued us formal press credentials. Mr. Stewart was carrying such a card when he was shot. We insist that the Nicaraguan government fully honor its obligations implicit in our official accreditation. We also demand an explanation of the execution by the National Guard of our colleague, Bill Stewart, and his interpreter, Juan Espinoza.

Lucoff then asked for Somoza's personal assurance that he would not impede the removal of Stewart's body from the country on Thursday.

In the hope that the press conference was being broadcast live to the nation, and in an effort to make sure the Spanish-speaking press, especially *Novedades*, got the message, a translation of the complaint was read by a reporter from the Mexico City daily *Excelsior*. Some eighty-nine reporters had signed both versions of the journalists' protest.

Somoza replied with assurances that the killing "was an isolated incident which I never wanted it to happen in Nicaragua." A guarantee was given Lucoff that the government would permit and assist in the removal of Stewart's remains. When asked how the press and world could believe Stewart's killing was an "isolated incident," Somoza replied that "you have to believe my good faith and the good faith of the Nicaraguan people." Somoza retorted to charges that his people were being massacred by his air force with "I feel very bad about that. But the people who will be hurt between the fight of the guerrilla and the regular armed forces of this country are hostages of the guerrillas and they've been forced to stay with the guerrillas. We have made radio announcements to evacuate the areas where we were gonna operate and we already have received the testimony of people who have escaped saying that the guerrillas have kept them under threat of death and sometimes execution so they will become the shield of their intentions, so this is a very difficult situation."

Reporters besieged Somoza with query after query concerning allegations of guard brutality and excesses. Questions such as this one posed by a film crew were typical: The guard rounded up four civilians on the street and took them into a warehouse for "questioning." A few shots rang out and the guardsmen exited alone. What happened? Somoza's answers were simple. He had no specific knowledge of that or any other atrocity. Send him the details and he would check into the matter.

There were questions in Spanish, with responses that made one feel the answers were rehearsed beforehand, the reporters from Somoza's paper and radio stations playing the part of shills. The answers were quick and had none of the pauses and disjointedness of his replies in English. Somoza was quick to say in English that he would give assurance the guard would not kill another journalist—he would promptly order them not to.

One reporter then asked why the press was no longer being issued credentials. Somoza asked how many journalists were without credentials and a person in the back yelled "I am." The matter was referred to one of Somoza's men in the audience and a three-way shouting match began in English and Spanish, the topic quickly changing to Stewart's death until Tacho stepped in to referee. Speaking over the other voices Somoza began to order, "I am going to ask you . . ." but he was drowned out and he tried again.

"You," he started in a high angry voice that he forced down an octave in midword, "you are getting very emotional, and I am too. But neither you nor I know the circumstances unless you were present at the incident."

The reporter replied, "We have all experienced similar if not all of the tragic circumstances at one time or another."

"I said I'm not going to get into an argument," Tacho retorted. "I'm listening to you."

"Thank you," the reporter answered.

Tacho attempted to be a little apologetic and fatherly. "And, uh, I'm sorry that you go through this. But you know that newspaper (*pause*) men, is one of the most dangerous businesses in the world whether you're in peace or in war. One thing. And, uh, the other thing is that those Nicaraguans fighting also have to look after their life. They, they don't know you. You, you get into crossfire to get your picture and to do your journalism.

"I'm aware of the risk that I have of allowing all of you to go everyplace," Somoza said. He then put in a good word for his soldiers. "But it really seems the Guardia Nacional who has been, uh, very comprehensive to have you visit them. I think that you, some of you have very good experiences with the soldiers so it isn't really an overall attitude."

Commenting on the Nicaraguan press branding foreign reporters as "communists" Tacho said he would speak to Radio Nacional about broadcasting these "rumors" but as far as *Novedades* was concerned, "[You can] go to the editor. Because I cannot tell the editor 'you can do this; you can do that.' "

Gone was Tacho's humor—which had at times been macabre considering what was happening beyond the Bunker complex. Usually, despite his grammatical mistakes, he was able to use his everyman's English to play to the average family in middle America just as did some of his United States congressmen friends. The Tacho hokum often went over. What the American viewer saw was not the megalomaniac but the friendly dictator from Central America who was just a regular guy.

But this time he botched his performance. He was inarticulate, confused his lines and was sloppy. He showed only contempt for his sycophants and sometimes ignored their deferential questions, asked in Spanish. (Many of his own people, including his press secretary, Cano, understood very little English, even Tacho's English.) This proved to be his last press conference at the military casino.

Early in the morning of June 21, government spokesmen awoke reporters to tell them they had taken twenty-seven-year-old guard Corporal Lorenzo Brenes as a suspect. Brenes maintained he was merely the commander of the platoon allegedly responsible for the murder and declared that he was innocent.

A court of inquiry opened amid a bizarre atmosphere that Thursday morning as interrogation started in a small room in the guard complex. The suspect, instead of the usual promise to tell the truth, said, "I promise not to tell the truth." And this incredible remark set the scene. The swarthy Corporal Brenes sat on a steel chair in the air-conditioned office, in combat-camouflage uniform and boots that still carried the mud of the barrios. He fidgeted with his hands and on one arm was a visible scar. Brenes's defense lawyer, a personable, bright United States–trained Major Arturo Vallejo, said he was not being charged with the murder of Stewart. "He is just rendering a statement."

"I was half a block away from where the gringo died," Brenes told the court. (He called Stewart a gringo throughout the testimony.) "I saw them talking; I walked over and heard a shot. We are in combat. I think the man who shot him died in combat around three or four in the afternoon. I was a block away." But the next time the question was asked, he said, "Unfortunately, when I started towards them, I only got about ten steps when I heard the shot. I asked what happened. The journalist was already dead. The others said they were friends of his and had come to take the bodies, and I continued my mission." When asked to describe the body, he said, "It was there with its head up."

Tiffer, the ABC driver, said that he couldn't identify the executioner, because "I didn't get a good look at his face." Tiffer had been detained by the guard after the shooting Wednesday and was badly beaten while in custody.

The sound of the northeastern sector of the city being steadily pounded to rubble by artillery was audible inside the courtroom, where typists were busy taking down the questions of prosecutor Colonel Felix P. Sanchez and the responses of the various witnesses and suspects. Judge Colonel Manuel M. Sandino sat at another desk as head of the court.

Said Major Vallejo, trained at a number of American military bases, after he also listened to the description of the film showing how Stewart was kicked and then shot in the head: "I am sorry to say, but executions are now part of our daily life."

Another officer admitted, "No side is taking prisoners. This is a war without quarter." When told that the Sandinistas were holding guard prisoners in León, he said, "For how long will they hold them? They also could be killed."

Vallejo added, "Nobody gives an inch in this war, they [the FSLN] don't withdraw." When asked when this killing could stop, he answered, "The current round could cease in two weeks or maybe a month or even more. But when it stops both sides will rearm and we will be fighting again in three months or so, just like before."

A C-130 military transport left Managua that morning for the Panama Canal Zone with Stewart's body, about twenty-five foreign newsmen and all but one of the American television networks' twenty-four representatives. Most cited lack of safety. "No story is worth a man's life," Ken Lucoff said. (Lucoff died four months later in the October 31 crash of a Western Airlines DC-10 in Mexico City while en route to cover the aftermath of a coup d'état in El Salvador.) The evacuation brought a sharp criticism from a number of journalists—notably CBS's Walter Cronkite—who felt the war needed to be covered and pointed out that the deaths of correspondents in other wars had not brought the same evacuation response.

About 1:00 A.M. Thursday a small Sandinista airplane made a bold attempt to drop nine concussion grenades on the Bunker. They missed their target. The grenades fell instead on a residential district three miles away injuring one woman and damaging two houses. The Sandinistas announced on Radio Sandino from Costa Rica that the Intercontinental was situated next to a "military target" and recommended that its guests check out. Foreign journalists and Nicaraguan congressmen and their relatives made up the guest list at the hotel. Its staff had dwindled. Only thirty-five valiant employees remained and they were scared. One waiter's brother had been killed by a bomb and a woman in the laundry room had lost her husband. The staff held a secret meeting with journalists that night in the hotel's restaurant and warned them that they were going to disappear as soon as curfew ended the next day. A *sapo* tried to crash the meeting but was warned by the journalists to "get the hell out."

It was clear during the session that the workers could no longer keep the hotel functioning. Food was scarce and the hotel had little if any hard cash to buy provisions. A few journalists decided quietly to pay their bills but many did so with credit cards, which was no help to the hotel. The congressmen did not pay their expenses and all banks were closed. Prior agreements had been struck with the hotel employees whereby the journalists agreed to make their own beds and accept fewer changes of linen as well as assist in arranging buffets to feed the press corps when they could. A resourceful Dutch chef helped out the best he could. Pineapple was abundant and became a staple diet for many correspondents—but one can prepare pineapple in only so many ways. Beer and most other alcoholic beverages were gone.

The tension and strain finally got to the telephone switchboard operators. Now they fled, too. They had spent countless hectic days and nights waiting for hours just to get the Telcor overseas operator to answer. They never lost their tempers and despite the yelling and pleading around them they were always kind and considerate. In that room behind the front desk, no matter what the hour of the day, there were always newsmen screaming stories to stenographers in various parts of the world, with one newsman banging out his story on the lone telex while dozens waited their turn at the machine. The Intercon, as it was called, was home, mainly because its staff was tolerant, concerned and kind. Stewart's death affected them as much as anyone.

But the demands of the congressmen on the hotel employees had been too much. They refused to keep order of any kind in their rooms, made incessant calls for room service, demanding the luxuries they felt their rank afforded them. When not sitting in their rooms eating and drinking contraband food and booze, they could be found roaming the hotel asserting that all the newsmen should be taken out and shot, declaring openly they were happy to see Stewart killed, and wishing there could be more treated just like him.

By morning the staff had completely evaporated. As representatives of the management, they left a letter to the hotel's guests saying that after being 270 employees short for the last seventeen days they were forced to close. Max Kelly, the chubby Somoza aide, was awakened. He rushed around asking "What happened?" and made hurried trips back and forth between the Bunker and hotel, sweating and giving assurances he would find ways to keep the hotel open. The press would have none of it and put as much distance between themselves and the hotel as they could. Those who were leaving the country headed for the Montelimar landing strip to wait for evacuation flights, while the others looked for scarce lodging elsewhere. By afternoon the hotel had become a ghost of its former self. A man cut another's hair in the lobby as guards lounged around. A few newsmen ventured back to use the precious telex machine, often their only link with the outside world because of the erratic telephone service.

The Ticomo Motel on the León highway outside the city near Dinorah's mansion became headquarters for some of the press. Others, myself among them, rented a "safe house," although there was no such thing as a safe place in Managua then. On Friday, June 22, Somoza announced a major military offensive for Managua, vowing that his troops would reopen the Pan American highway linking Managua with Las Mercedes. "In Managua we advance and the Pan American highway to the airport will be opened this afternoon," Tacho said in an interview. "In the south we smashed two probing attacks from Costa Rica–based guerrillas."

The tension was high throughout the day. Journalists at the Ticomo found that its location in the open countryside left it exposed to many hazards, most of all to ordinary gunmen who preyed on the motel's guests. The stories of danger and discomfiture were countless. A French reporter for Le Monde was stopped in his jeep on the way to the motel; thieves stripped him bare, taking every belonging including his passport. Reporters knew that a knock on their door at any hour of the day or night was likely to announce a gunman.

Brushes with tragedy were frequent for journalists even before Stewart's death. A grenade landed next to photographer Susan Meiselas and fizzled but miraculously failed to explode. CBS correspondent George Nathanson was robbed at gunpoint and photographer Matthew Naythons was slugged with a rifle butt. Guard riflemen fired on Time's Richard Woodbury and two Associated Press newsmen, although their car was covered with press markings. Free-lance cameraman Carl Hersh was driving in the city of Estelí when National Guardsmen opened fire without warning; his passengers were wounded. The Washington Post's Karen DeYoung, the Chicago Tribune's Mark Starr and Silio Boccanera of Jornal Do Brasil barely escaped a mortar attack on the guerrilla-held town of León. In Managua three other reporters and I were caught in an artillery bombardment as we attempted to keep a rendezvous with Sandinista leaders. Said the *Baltimore Sun*'s Gilbert Lewthwaite: "It's Russian roulette. You don't know where your enemy is or whom they're firing at."[1]

To get any solid assessment of how the fighting was going correspondents had to make regular and frequent visits to the battle zones. Frustrations abounded for those trying to gather the facts. The government maintained a press office, but all that the National Guard issued were fragmentary communiqués on the fighting that could never be taken at face value. On the other hand, the Sandinistas maintained no press office. Their headquarters were unreachable, their leaders scattered and virtually inaccessible and official spokesmen were just about nonexistent.

Then there was the unreality of the Bunker and the usually poised Somoza addressing the press like a Rotary Club president, as if nothing were really happening outside. Yet much of the barbarism was taking place just a bit farther up the hill where security forces under Colonel Giron tortured youths suspected of any involvement with the rebel forces.

The widespread nature of the fighting, spread in all directions in many cities, compounded journalists' frustrations and placed a premium on the exchange of information. Until the major fighting moved to Managua itself the week of Stewart's death, the mode of reportage was for correspondents to pick a town each day, join up in groups of three and four for security and whisk off to take in a few hours' battle. Then they would return to the hotel and swap information. With the battle spread over a vast section of Managua itself on Friday that format still held.

In and near the fighting one was, of course, in ever-present danger, particularly so because it was a small-arms, sniping war, both sides increasingly weary and trigger-happy. There were few firm areas of control by either side. One might feel he was safe deep within the guerrilla ranks only to be strafed by a guard plane. Then when one rode with a Somoza platoon, he was also a target of potshots from the guerrillas.

There were no battle freaks among the reporters, none who got a kick out of the release of their adrenaline. There were atrocities all around that were not easily forgotten. The horrors and stench of the war were vivid. We saw dogs tearing the remaining flesh from rib cages of bodies half-buried after execution by the guard at León. We witnessed the despair of the Red Cross worker in Estelí who, upon receiving word that his wife had been wounded by a rocket, was prevented by the guard from rushing to her. When he finally reached her side he found her dead, the dogs gnawing at her. Then there were the numerous small children who had been wounded, lying in "safe" churches, trying to play but the pain not allowing it.

There were other problems: some reporters didn't speak Spanish and didn't know their way around a city not easily navigated because it had become so spread out after the 1972 earthquake. And many of the newcomers didn't know how to go about dealing with the guard. These problems were all especially evident in Stewart's case. Alan Riding of *The New York Times*, who had been reporting on Nicaragua since 1971, said that Friday, "I think it's irresponsible to send into this situation anyone who doesn't speak Spanish. Bill Stewart might have been able to save his life if he had been able to speak it."

Another important aspect of the war was the Somoza government's paranoia about the foreign press. They confiscated boots and bulletproof vests from reporters at the airport for fear they would fall into guerrilla hands. It was true that most of the press was hostile to Somoza. Indeed, government officials complained bitterly that the press hadn't mentioned that Sandinistas had executed *Novedades* reporter Pedro Espinoza earlier in the week. The Somoza people believed that the foreign press made a point of blasting the Nicaraguan president while giving the Sandinistas the benefit of respectability. The government spokesmen harped repeatedly on the Cuba analogy, citing *The New York Times'* Herbert Mathews, who had interviewed Castro in the Sierra Maestra when he was believed dead and who was blamed forever after for resurrecting Cuba, as an example of procommunist leanings in the press. There was marked contrast between Somoza's public air of friendliness toward the press and the inflammatory local media campaign that assailed the foreign press corps as part of the red conspiracy against him. A lot of Tacho's own press hacks were planted in the Intercontinental and joined directly in the foreign press baiting. Some carried pistols in their waistbands, others were followed by their UZI-carrying bodyguards. Most had nothing to do but sit around the hotel and drink morosely, and send the tab to Somoza.

The dangers in covering the conflict—the reporters agreed—were real and ever present. But each there had resolved the question in his or her own mind by remaining behind after the exodus of the others.

A shortwave radio broadcast tuned to the Voice of America aired a report filed by its correspondent in Managua, Jack Curtiss. The report included the voice of Jim Cefalo recounting the horror of Stewart's execution and Somoza's hollow apology. Then the correspondent reported to VOA listeners:

> In covering this war foreign reporters have found that what President Somoza terms an isolated incident—a summary execution—is one of the most frequent accusations leveled against his government troops by Nicaraguan citizens. The local human rights commission has files bulging with testimonies of such acts. It is one of the ironic tragedies of this cruel civil war that the first time the international press could irrefutably document such a crime the victim was one from its own ranks.
>
> The international press, whose representatives were temporarily stunned by the brutal murder of correspondent Bill Stewart, and scattered by threats against the Intercontinental Hotel, has now regrouped and reestablished a base of operations from which to follow the war. As the decisive hour of the Nicaraguan crisis draws near, despite threat and dangers, the foreign reporters are determined that the eyes and ears of the world shall not be closed to what happens here.

Comparing Nicaragua with five other wars, Lewthwaite said that it was the

> most dangerous situation I have ever been in. The difference between war and civil war is that in the former you know who the enemy is and where he is. In the latter

you don't. You can be shot at any time. The real danger here is that both sides have become extremely tense. Too many people are all too ready to fire too many guns at too many moving targets. In my first seven days here I have been involved in shooting five times. That's five too many times.

According to Somoza's television channel this couldn't be further from the truth. One would hardly have known a war was raging all around. The Three Stooges were shown often, sometimes followed by an old film. Even during night bombings the station would run an hour-long propaganda film purportedly showing "all is normal." One program featured only a white dog walking around a neighborhood as the commentator kept saying, "This place is coming back to life."

CHAPTER 18

Popular Insurrection

"This is Alfa Sierra Delta, stand by," a voice said on the National Guard's ultrahigh-frequency radio network at 10:30 P.M. Saturday, June 23. The few privileged Nicaraguans and Sandinistas listening to the National Guard transmission on radio-scanner monitoring devices recognized Tacho's voice and code name, the first letter of each word standing for his initials. A majority vote in the OAS had just called upon him to resign.

Tacho's voice was firm, loud and clear. In a military fashion, which he obviously enjoyed, he said, "I ask each of you to acknowledge," and then addressed each of his field and area commanders by numbers. The numbers were not called in order. The highest was nineteen. Each commander replied, "Yes, sir, understood, sir." In a performance worthy of George Patton, Tacho then reported: "Instead of promoting a real peace, the OAS is encouraging us to continue the fight. I want to tell you since I last talked to you in the meeting of commanders, it was understood that we could come to this." He added, "I'm willing to continue to fight to defeat the enemy."

He characterized the OAS resolution as a "flagrant intervention into the internal affairs of Nicaragua," and added in a more strident tone, "This means that we will have to fight only with the resources that our country can give us, that is, our own resources—the men that this country can provide."

His radio briefing ended with, "Okay, boys, the National Guard must remain united and cohesive to maintain order and the constitution of the republic. It doesn't matter to me what some countries that don't know the reality say. We know the reality and we must go forward. Roger and out." The "okay" was in English.

The OAS resolution was a defeat for Somoza as well as for the United States. The latter was still determined to leave the Sandinistas out of a final agreement to establish a government that would retain the framework of the existing regime. Calling for a "clear break with the past" in the United States' relations with Nicaragua, Secretary of State Cyrus Vance had asked for the emergency OAS meeting on June 21. The United States had put forth a six-point plan calling for Somoza's resignation but the proposal was defeated because one Vance proposal included sending an inter-American peace-keeping force to Nicaragua with the help of American air, naval and logistical units, although no American combat troops. It was the first time the United States had failed to gain approval for an intervention proposal in the OAS.

Other elements of the United States plan were: formation of an interim government of national reconciliation acceptable to all major elements of the society; dispatch by the OAS foreign ministers of a special delegation to Nicaragua to assist the people to achieve a political solution without Somoza; a cease-fire; cessation of arms shipments to either side; an OAS peace-keeping presence to help establish a climate of peace and to assist the interim government in establishing its authority and beginning the task of reconstruction; and a major international relief and reconstruction effort for Nicaragua.

Nicaraguan foreign minister Julio Quintana said his country would be happy to open a dialogue and have a cease-fire, but he pointedly made no comment about Vance's unequivocal declaration that the United States was now dedicated to replacing Somoza.[1]

Mexican foreign minister Jorge Castañeda led the vote against the Vance proposal, joined by his colleagues from Panama, Jamaica, Grenada, Brazil and Peru, all of which had broken diplomatic relations with Nicaragua in the previous weeks.

The ministers of those countries put forth a new resolution calling for Somoza's resignation and specifically denouncing intervention. The military governments of Chile, Guatemala, El Salvador, Honduras and Uruguay abstained in the 17–2 vote endorsing the resolution. Paraguay joined Nicaragua in voting against Somoza's resignation. The United States voted with the majority and conceded the peace-keeping force proposal was now dead.

Carter administration hard-liners such as National Security Council adviser Zbigniew Brzezinski, his assistant, Robert Pastor, and Defense Secretary Harold Brown continued to echo Somoza's claim that Cuba was heavily involved in aiding the Sandinistas and continued to favor intervention to avoid "another Cuba." But Stewart's killing tarnished much conservative support for Somoza in Congress. Legislation implementing the Panama Canal transfer passed the House despite efforts to portray Panama as a Cuban agent in the Nicaraguan crisis.

The Cuban intervention allegations once again reflected Washington's inability to understand the dynamics of the structural crisis of Latin America. Instead of recognizing the Nicaraguan rebellion as a clear reflection of the Nicaraguan people's desire to be rid of a tyrant and be governed by a system that provided some hope of economic improvement, Washington responded first to the narrow concept of human rights violations—torture and assassination—rather than considering as well the widespread hunger and unemployment. The bottom line of the United States attitude that weekend was determined by the suspicion that the insurrection had heavy Cuban backing. Cuba's involvement had in fact been peripheral until the final offensive, when it stepped up arms delivery to the winning side. Five Costa Rican pilots who participated in the transportation of arms and ammunition to Costa Rica during the Sandinista offensive against Somoza told an official board of inquiry in San José on March 24, 1981, that toward the end of May and on July 17, 1979,

31,000 pounds of munitions came from Cuba on each of twenty-one flights. Half those flights had been flown by Costa Rican crews, they explained, and the others were flown by Panamanian crews.

Washington failed to understand that the political unrest stemmed overwhelmingly from internal conditions and could not successfully have been provoked from abroad. This was a worrisome failure of long-term United States policy toward a region convulsed by social and economic pressures.

Cuba had recognized the need for certain internal conditions to prevail before a revolution could take place. In the 1960s it "exported revolution" by training guerrillas from all over Latin America but none of these movements flourished because local conditions were not propitious. Cuba paid little actual attention to the Sandinistas beyond giving some of them training and safe haven and allowing Radio Havana to beam anti-Somoza propaganda to Central America.

Further, for reasons of Marxist orthodoxy, Cuba opposed the alliance the Tercerista faction made with bourgeois groups until it was evident a major insurrection was under way. Because of the lack of a disciplined, unopposed Marxist cadre in the vanguard of the revolution, many intelligent Nicaraguans were now maintaining that the time was ripe for the United States to help create an option between the extremes of military dictatorship and radical government. But Washington felt it had to talk about Cuban involvement to justify intervention. And Senate Foreign Relations Committee chairman Frank Church was saying intervention was out of the question because of the desire to avoid "another Vietnam," while Secretary of Defense Brown was saying it was "not inconceivable."

The FAO's seven-group coalition gave its backing to the Sandinista junta on Sunday, June 24, calling it the only viable alternative to Somoza. "The junta is the only option for a solution," Jaime Chamorro said, "but we must make sure when the junta carries out its program that all opposition groups are represented, as well as members of the important economic and social forces of the country." The junta's composition worried other Nicaraguan conservatives who wanted guarantees it would not radicalize once in power.

Somoza read a statement on national television Sunday that was much more moderate in tone than his briefing of his commanders the day before. He declared himself "open to dialogue," expressing willingness to "receive the initiative of member governments of the OAS which have a real interest in the resolving of the Nicaraguan crisis through democratic, just and permanent formulas." He did not condemn the United States resolution as he had done Saturday, simply calling the new resolution a by-product of "strong communist influence."

The government radio called on the population to join the army now spread thin around the country against guerrilla forces which could count on popular support in most areas. Guard ranks were being augmented with women and even thirteen-year-olds. The announcer pleaded, "Your country needs you, we must join to defend it. Report to the National Guard commander. Have faith in Christ." Then he condemned the communists, charging they converted the youth with an orgy of blood, sex and drugs.[2]

Despite Sandinista efforts to promote desertions and guarantee soldiers' personal safety, the cracks that appeared in the guard were very minor. It remained loyal to Somoza like a faithful but ferocious Doberman. The guard commander in chief, like so many Latin American dictators before him, stayed isolated in his Bunker, pronouncing with his usual bravado, "I am ready to resist until my death." Few who knew Tacho believed him.

On Monday, June 25, a Sandinista in FSLN headquarters in the Managua barrios suddenly stirred his companions with a startled, "Look." He pointed to a helicopter hanging still in the clear morning sky. "They are taking aerial photos of us. My God, the photographer has fallen out. Look!"

The other Sandinistas, including Moises Hassan, now a member of the junta, watched fascinated as the black object lazily tumbled down out of the sky. "It's a bomb," someone shouted. A 500-pound bomb had been pushed out of the Huey helicopter toward its target—an entire barrio. The explosion on impact was deafening and shook homes four miles from the target, sending up a giant cloud of red dust that could be seen rising over the poor barrios of the city. Elsewhere families, including businessmen with drinks in their hands, crowded onto verandas of their homes. Some watched the horrendous show using binoculars for a better view. From then on the helicopter was referred to by the Sandinistas as "the photographer" whenever it appeared on its bombing run, hanging in the sky like a vulture.

Somoza was still making it clear he intended to "clean up Managua first" before trying to recover cities in the interior. Despite his promises that the sprawling city would be in government hands ten days earlier, the Sandinistas continued to hold a dozen northeastern barrio neighborhoods and resisted fierce government attacks to dislodge them. Their tenacity held many guardsmen in the capital while Sandinistas advanced in the countryside.

As it turned out, "cleaning up Managua first" was exactly what the Sandinistas had in mind for Somoza and the guard. The battle for the barrios in the capital was not designed as a final killing blow, or even as an offensive thrust. Instead, it was a limited holding operation undertaken to make Somoza expend maximum time, effort, manpower and armament on an objective the Sandinistas did not consider essential. Meanwhile, the guerrillas, relatively unmolested elsewhere, were sweeping up pockets of resistance and conquering cities all over the country.

As Tomás Borge described it later, the strategy was bound to succeed because Somoza could not afford to ignore the Managua insurgents. They straddled the highway leading to the airport and turned the capital into a killing zone for the first time, shattering the appearance of normality that the general had to maintain for international propaganda purposes.

"The only thing we didn't expect," Borge said, "was that we would be able to hold out for so long. The Managua rebels did much better than we thought possible. It was a tremendous success."

Arms shipments to the FSLN continued through Costa Rica from Cuba, Panama and Venezuela. A Nicaraguan Lanica 727 was hijacked by its flight crew after leaving Miami and diverted to San José, where the crew asked for asylum. But though Costa Rican support for the FSLN was obvious, allegations of Cuban involvement were denied vigorously. Junta member Sergio Ramírez from his home in San José complained that the United States "had to talk about Cuba to justify military intervention in Nicaragua." The United States and the CIA knew the charges were false, he said, and he reiterated the Sandinista claim that they would have already won the war with genuine Cuban involvement. Cuba would not intervene to give just a few old rifles.

United States Ambassador Lawrence A. Pezzullo arrived in Managua from Panama on Wednesday, June 27. His orders were precise: get Somoza to resign and arrange a transfer of power, and try, at this late date, to save the country from the extremists and chaos. It was a tall order and Pezzullo lost no time in getting to the point. Upon arrival he went to the Bunker. Tacho was not alone. To the Bunker, to bear witness at this meeting he judged crucial, Tacho had invited his long-time friend American congressman John Murphy, foreign minister Julio Quintana, and his cousin Luis Pallais, vice-president of congress.

The initial meeting with the tough, businesslike envoy began on a frivolous note, with Tacho establishing his American credentials by saying the conversation would be conducted in English because, "I'm a Latin from Manhattan," and, "I grew up in New York with John, here," pointing to the congressman. Pezzullo established that he had in fact grown up on Staten Island and could have been one of the congressman's constituents if he had remained there.

But there was a lot of procrastinating on the part of Tacho at this and the many subsequent meetings he was to have with Pezzullo. His bitterness welled up and he spent much of the precious time denouncing the State Department, and even "that Baptist" (Carter). Pezzullo told Somoza that what he had to say was from the highest level of government and that because of the long and friendly ties with Somoza and Nicaragua the matter had been given the highest attention. The United States, he explained, saw no solution without Somoza's departure. At the same time the United States wanted to preserve the institutions that could be preserved and wanted to avoid chaos. Time was short, he noted, but the United States wanted Tacho to be able to leave in a dignified manner. It might take four or five days, but they had to move quickly before the whole "goddamn thing comes down on our heads." Sensing that time was still needed to arrange what he referred to as his own "coup d'état," Tacho answered, "Okay, what if I leave tomorrow?" "We still need a little time," answered Pezzullo and they made a date for the following day. Tight-lipped Pezzullo said later that night to a reporter that he did not expect any dramatic happenings in the near future.

In Panama, Pezzullo had huddled with Bowdler to discuss negotiating Tacho's resignation. But as is often the case with United States diplomacy, Pezzullo had arrived too late. COSEP, the large umbrella organization that included most of the private business sector, now joined the FAO in backing the new junta. And both groups ruled out the involvement of *any* Somoza forces in a final settlement, in opposition to the new United States package which advocated gradual constitutional change with continuing involvement of some of Somoza's people.

COSEP called for Somoza's "immediate" resignation. The reins of government should be given to the junta which, COSEP said, should be a transitional government until one which "will include all opposition forces in the productive sectors of the country" could be formed. And, in the setting of a conflict where children shot children and summary executions were by now a way of life, COSEP said, "As a guarantee of respect for human rights of all Nicaraguans without exception, we ask the new government to respect from this moment, the lives and physical integrity of public officials and members of the army and that it be given to those believed guilty and charged to face a legal process and that no type of summary executions be permitted."

The plea was seen as a direct response to the death of former congressional president and longtime Somoza top aide Cornelio Hueck on his hacienda San Martín located forty-five kilometers northwest of Rivas in the jurisdiction of Tola. The sixty-four-year-old Hueck had fallen out with Somoza and retired to his 10,000-manzana coffee and cattle farm. As recently as September 1977 he had represented the then-sick Somoza at the Panama Canal treaty-signing ceremony in Washington. There he received a strong whiff of anti-Somoza sentiment brewing in the White House. Somoza, no longer trusting this family courtier, soon thereafter cast him adrift. Hueck had already fought off one Sandinista attack on his hacienda when his son contacted him by ham radio from Masaya telling him, "Come Papa, your passport is ready." But the Sandinistas returned for a second attack. Hueck escaped from his house, ran into the nearby Pacific and tried to hide in water up to his neck. He was followed, captured, summarily judged and executed in Tola. Tacho shrugged at the news of Hueck's death. "He was a fool. He moved too late," he said.

COSEP also affirmed its "determination to particpate actively in the great task of national reconstruction within the context of the free enterprise system" and expressed confidence that "in spite of the material destruction of the great majority of businesses, if it is to rebuild the country, it could begin as soon as a new climate of peace, order, justice and liberty is established." Wealthy Nicaraguans who had fled the country were asked to return and help with the reconstruction effort. So many had left Nicaragua that one large company held its annual board meeting in Miami.

Bowdler remained in Panama where three junta members arrived from Costa Rica to a hero's welcome. Meeting Chamorro, Ramírez and Robelo at the airport was President Royo, his entire cabinet and thousands of Panamanians. Bowdler was assigned the task of establishing contact with the junta and attempting to persuade them to broaden its base in the direction of moderation. The Sandinistas had earlier rejected a so-called Brzezinski plan calling for Somoza to resign in favor of his handpicked Senate leader, Pablo Rener, who would turn over the country to an unnamed "council of notables" in which the rebels would have only a nominal role. Bowdler's new plan was sticky: induce an agreement that would include the Sandinistas to a greater extent but still involve pro-Somoza elements. It appeared to have little chance of success once the FAO and COSEP gave their unequivocal support to the junta.

In Managua, Pezzullo's message to the National Guard was that their best chance for surviving in the post–civil war period was to help expedite Somoza's departure. It was part of what State Department spokesman Tom Reston called "a procedure for removing Somoza promptly and [we] are discussing with all sides a means that may lead to a cease-fire. We do not want a set of competing forces or a vacuum."

The United States recognized that no political solution could succeed until Somoza left. "The trouble is that you cannot take away from the Sandinistas at the conference table what they have won on the battlefield," one administration official said. No American official had any realistic idea as to whether the guard would take a hand in removing Somoza or whether there was any solution the United States and the OAS could put forward that would satisfy the Sandinistas when they were so close to victory.[3]

There were some signs that the guard's loyalty was finally beginning to waver. Enlisted men and officers alike had begun to reassess their position. The heavy bomb destruction of Managua and mounting international and domestic pressure for Somoza's resignation were leading many guardsmen to wonder aloud if they and the country would not be better off without Somoza. Officers said that when they were fighting their only alternatives were to kill or be killed but now they were pondering whether their futures were tied to Somoza's. But there seemed no escape. It was already too late.

Somoza's position was fast eroding. On Thursday, June 28, the rubber-stamp Nicaraguan Congress was called to an extraordinary special session by Tacho but could not muster a quorum. Conservatives remained in hiding while Liberal congressmen were also unwilling to attend for unknown reasons. Rumors circulated the session was called for budgetary matters while others said it would be an attempt to find a constitutional solution to the crisis. Somoza told reporters by telephone while waiting for the session to begin that "I will stay in power at all costs, and if Congress asks for my resignation, I will dissolve it." They had no such initiative or intention.

Later that day, a rump session was held at the Intercontinental involving only four of the forty opposition members and twenty-eight of the Liberals. The session proved anticlimactic. The Conservatives demanded a prior guarantee that the session would "solely deal with Somoza's resignation." Chamber of Deputies President Francisco Urcuyo Maliaño said, "In no manner will this session treat Somoza's resignation. We intend to treat budget matters." Even so, speculation persisted as to whether Somoza would continue to fight or offer a constitutional solution that would include his resignation and departure from the country.

When Pezzullo returned on June 28 for their second meeting, Tacho was in a more caustic mood and spent a lot of time placing the blame for his predicament on the United States, while Pezzullo countered that it was he, Somoza, who had polarized the political forces against himself. The same little group including Murphy listened sympathetically as Tacho tried to "illustrate," as he referred to it, the wrongdoings of the Carter administration and the communist peril.

At one point Tacho changed tactics. "Okay, I'm ready to go. I have no conditions. I'm not in a position to have conditions." He then followed up by warning Pezzullo, "From now on, the United States will be responsible for the blood that is spilled in Nicaragua." Pezzullo snapped back, "We will not accept that." But even steering the conversation back to the subject of preserving some part of the National Guard, needed to maintain law and order, proved impossible. The second meeting ended with Pezzullo saying he would return the next day to talk specifics.

With ammunition running low on the morning of June 28 the Sandinistas in Managua's barrios moved out of the city at dawn in buses and trucks and on foot. Air drops behind Sandinista lines had failed to provide them with the necessary supplies to hold their territory. The decision was for a strategic retreat to Masaya to regroup in that town, already in rebel hands.

It was perhaps the most audacious act of the war. Pilots spied the Sandinista columns lined up and down the highway for miles, excitedly reporting, "They are everywhere—they are like ants." But only seventeen people were killed in the retreat. Hassan was among the wounded.

The Sandinistas had become excellent snipers while defending the barrios. They even succeeded in killing a top antiguerrilla expert, a major appointed by Somoza. Tacho then tried to recruit one of the country's top marksmen to head an antisniping squad but he found an excuse to decline.

After the FSLN retreat, newsmen found evidence throughout Managua of the guard brutality that had taken place. Besides the usual bodies dumped, after torture and execution, at the *cuesta de plomo* (lead cliffs) near the Esso refinery, newsmen discovered, only 500 yards from the National Palace, the corpses of eleven young men and a young woman. Their hands were bound and they were blindfolded. One of the dead was wearing the black and red Sandinista neckerchief. They had been executed beside the little ledge at lakeshore. The ground was littered with shell casings.

Other groups of Sandinistas were found in the northeastern sector of the city, also executed. At 11:00 A.M., three hours before the Congress had originally been scheduled to meet, the guard called fire brigades to burn the bodies.

By Friday, June 29, speculation concerning Tacho's resignation was rampant. "We Nicaraguans want to know one thing from you American newsmen," said a motorist who drew up alongside a car filled with journalists. "Is Somoza going or not? If he doesn't go, then we are dead," he said, making a cutting sign over his throat. With the fighting dying down in the capital the question uppermost in people's minds was whether the United States could persuade Somoza to resign.

Pezzullo found it just as difficult to pin down Somoza on specifics at their June 29 meeting, which was attended by Tachito and former intelligence chief General Samuel Genie. Discussion of the transfer of power wandered to a point when Tacho suddenly, with a hint of self-pity, said, "My life is now worth nothing, and if I remain longer it will be worth less."

Tachito was more businesslike and touched on the problem of how to keep the guard together once the Somozas had left. He noted that most of the officer corps were at retirement age and that as power had always come from above (the Somozas) it might need the assistance of a United States military group to help in the transition period. He pointed out, "Frankly, the leadership of the guard is the president, myself and General José Somoza." The meeting ended with Somoza confessing again that he feared assassination and with Pezzullo reassuring him he could take care of himself.

Somoza aide Max Kelly said on Friday that a major offensive was planned against the southern front; meanwhile the United States warned Cuba, Panama and Costa Rica against gunrunning into Nicaragua. State Department spokesman Reston said, "We have received intelligence reports indicating that various aircraft, some with Panamanian air force markings, have made flights from Cuba to Panama and Costa Rica. I'm not saying their denial is credible or that our intelligence report is correct. We see a variety of intelligence assessments of varying reliability." Air drops *were* made to Sandinistas in the countryside as well as in Managua, where weapons were parachuted into the barrios at night. Once that operation backfired. One night a plane with its lights out flew over the Sandinistas' positions and waited for a signal from below. When that signal was forthcoming, it turned out that the aircraft was a National Guard plane, and it bombed the unsuspecting guerrillas.

Congressman Murphy reported on his latest visit with Somoza in Managua at Tacho's invitation. He gave Somoza no advice, he said, but pointed out the heavy odds against him and was present in the Bunker when Pezzullo asked Tacho to resign. Murphy and Pezzullo conferred together later before the solon moved to Panama to meet with Bowdler.

"The issue isn't Somoza but Nicaragua and the security interests of the U.S.," Murphy said. "This Sandinista uprising is a Cuban, Venezuelan, Panamanian, Costa Rican operation. It's another Vietnam and it's in this hemisphere."

Bowdler's visit in Panama was drawing to a close. He now planned to move to San José where the junta had indicated it would negotiate the new government's composition and the role of the National Guard once Somoza had resigned and a cease-fire was in effect. Somoza by this time was ready to step down. But only if the guard and Liberal party were preserved, both terms unacceptable to the rebels.

Pezzullo met with newsmen on Friday, June 29. Reporters were curious. Did his diplomatic skills equal his toughness? The press corps knew Somoza could be tough and was especially aware of his political ability to maneuver around his opponents and of his talent to buy time and weaken the momentum of the opposition. In an off-the-record session, the shirt-sleeved Pezzullo was more than taciturn. Negotiations surrounding Somoza's departure would be kept fully secret, he said. Reporters were complimented for their coverage but Pezzullo called for understanding, saying that press reports speculating on Tacho's departure were not helping the negotiations. Somoza would go, he said, but refused to speculate on any time frame.

Pezzullo was just as closemouthed and stubborn in private. His toughness showed when he told several reporters the following day that he had taken exception to a reporter's question as to whether the United States ambassador was in touch with reality. The reporter had noted that the American embassy in the past had been notorious for being out of touch with reality. "I felt like telling him to kiss my ass," Pezzullo said.

Pezzullo and Bowdler flew to Washington for consultations on July 1 and were back in Managua on the Fourth of July to begin a new, intensive negotiation period. Rumors began floating back and forth, across the border from Costa Rica and in the lobby of the Intercontinental, that Somoza would leave the following Saturday, July 7. Close aides denied heatedly Tacho would depart. Kelly agreed however that Somoza could not leave until the guard's future was assured.

The Sandinistas were in control of more than twenty cities and towns. The only two of any importance they had failed to take in the north were Estelí and Chinandega, where the guard had armed civilians and was using paramilitary units. But Sandinista control over the north was consolidated with the overrunning of the garrison of Sébaco, a small town at a strategic junction on the Pan American highway. The Sandinistas were stalled on the southern front where the guard force under Comandante Bravo had the best troops and support. It was still Tacho's priority front. Government troops as well as the Sandinistas were dug in across much of the little neck of land between the Pacific and Lake Nicaragua. Local rebel forces almost took Rivas on July 3 and guard reinforcements were airlifted to the embattled town to take pressure off the besieged guard headquarters. The Sandinistas talked of moving the junta to León instead of Rivas but ruled out the idea in light of Somoza's air power.

Tacho's security and intelligence service were his weak points. His broadcasts under "Alfa Sierra Delta" permitted the Sandinistas and press corps to read his moves. Even Tachito's "Alfa Sierra Papa" was often heard on the guard network. One time, calling Bravo in the south, Alfa Sierra Papa told the commander to keep an eye out for the Costa Ricans, or "Ticos" as he called them. "When you get to the front lines poke your tongue out," Tachito advised, "because the 'Ticos' are the señoritas of the Americas."

On Tuesday, July 3, Tacho was heard again loud and clear as he ordered the commander of Rivas to hold tight while he sent reinforcements which the officer had earlier asked for but José Somoza had turned down. Colonel McCoy, the tall military attaché serving at the United States embassy, said that the National Guard's inept intelligence service had given the Sandinistas the edge in the "final offensive." There was now no thought of the National Guard recovering the cities firmly in the hands of the Sandinistas, he said. The guard was losing the war and it was only a matter of time before they lost it completely.

Only fifteen of Tacho's forty aged British Staghound armored cars remained operative; at least three had been captured by the Sandinistas and put into service against the guard. The air force had lost almost half its aircraft and there was no way Somoza could purchase more planes or even the ammunition he needed. The National Guard, with a reputation for having absolutely no fire control, had used up its ammunition in enormous quantities and was ordered to be more selective. The well was running dry. The Sandinistas, on the other hand, had increased military options. Somoza's dictatorship remained sloppy and careless. An example of the way

Somoza ran his war was an early morning call on Wednesday, July 4, for an air strike from "Massachusetts," the code name given to the commander of Fort Coyotepe, overlooking the rebel-held town of Masaya. Massachusetts called "Buffalo," the code name for General José Somoza, requesting an immediate air strike against a twin-engine plane that had landed on the Masaya highway. The excited commander said the *jeikos* ("jackals"), as they called well-trained and well-armed Sandinistas, were unloading the aircraft. When the commander was told Buffalo was asleep, he requested to talk to Alfa Sierra Delta. The president, too, was asleep. The commander then asked that Tacho be awakened, but again the orderly replied he could not. So the plane's cargo of ammunition was unloaded unopposed by Sandinistas using trucks and jeeps. They then promptly destroyed the aircraft because a rough landing had left it damaged.

It was possible to pick up a phone in Managua and talk to members of the junta in Costa Rica. As Bowdler was arriving in San José on July 4, a phone call to Sergio Ramírez revealed that the junta was not about to change its position on anything. Said Ramírez, "We are not in any position to make concessions to the *Somocistas*, or to enlarge the junta. We know that the [United States] State Department is very interested in such an enlargement, but we are already representative of all the anti-Somoza forces in the country. Perhaps they don't consider us pro-American enough. But we see no need to go along—and we also see a very serious danger. It would be taken as a sign of weakness if we added one or two new members, not only in terms of international opinion but among our own people. At this moment all sectors of Nicaraguan society accept our political formula. The U.S. is trying to create dissension where it does not exist."

The junta knew a military solution was possible. Though they were viewed as overly optimistic at the time, the junta members already felt Somoza was beaten. "Somoza has already lost the war," Ramírez said. "It's impossible for him to take the military initiative again. He can't take the forces he has in Managua elsewhere. The moment he does, the Sandinista columns that left there will return. His elite forces at La Virgen [just north of Rivas] cannot move from there. In fact, all of his elite forces are in Managua or Rivas. There is no other important *Somocista* force in the north or west of Nicaragua. We have control. The National Guard can't survive."

The Sandinista junta was also laying plans for their eventual assumption of power. They would establish a thirty-member council of state to represent more than twenty political, business and trade union groups. The junta would retain executive power with the council acting as a legislative arm.

The junta was aptly named a government of national reconstruction. The war had obliterated Managua's industry and reduced food supplies to dangerously low levels. Businesses and warehouses were empty, looted or cannibalized by mobs—not only for food but for any object they could later use for barter as many of the poor no longer had any money. The war damage along an eight-mile strip of factories on the northern edge of Managua was reminiscent of World War II. Now there were only gutted buildings of twisted steel and charred hulks where once stood thriving factories producing for export. Even more destructive to the nation than this loss of industries and business was the loss of its professional class. Most of the wealthy owners of industry and business had fled before the fighting, mostly to Miami. The young managers that remained complained that the proprietors had not paid their workers and with the banks still closed there was no way to manage them. More than 40,000 people who had worked in Managua's industry now faced unemployment, as did nearly 100,000 who were employed in commerce. The only food available was from looted stocks which were bartered or sold from door to door or in the open-air markets. From early morning on the vegetable and fruit markets were swamped with buyers who paid inflated prices. The Nicaraguan córdoba, devalued in April from ten to seven dollars, was now commanding twenty to the dollar on the black market.

Tacho remained indifferent to the street looting and was in fact angry at the capitalists whose properties were being looted. "I'm still the storekeeper for those sons of bitches who left the country with their money. And they expect me to watch over their goods? Baloney."

The nation's agricultural sector was at a standstill; it was the crucial planting season. Commercial farmers were frightened off the land as poor peasants occupied farms and slaughtered cattle. One Somoza aide who lost his own farm during the week to angry peasants said, "This is no longer an anti-Somoza war, it is also a class war. Suddenly the poor want what the rich possess."

Late the evening of the Fourth of July a phone call from Congressman Murphy got through to Tacho in Managua. "We're in a quandary on the diplomatic front," Somoza told Murphy. Somoza had had "a very friendly meeting" that day with Pezzullo but nothing had happened to break the impasse. Somoza had told the ambassador that he was ready to quit the presidency, taking Tachito and his half-brother, José, with him, if a government could be installed that would ensure the safety of his 800 American-trained guard officers and the members of his government. "You see my cards," Somoza told Murphy. There was no immediate confirmation that asylum in the United States was one of those cards; however, there was little doubt it was. It was not difficult to see United States officials suggesting to the junta: "We'll take Tacho and Joe and Tachito off your hands if you promise not to kill those who stay behind."

The junta was becoming increasingly wary of United States motives. Bowdler's third round of talks with the junta in San José failed even to take place. The Sandinistas and the American embassy did not know what was going on. The junta was inclined to be cynical about the resignation rumor, Ramírez said. "Our feeling is that it is only a rumor. It may be that the U.S. now has Somoza's resignation in its pocket, but if so they're going to play with it. It's only part of the negotiations." If the rumor turned out to be true, he added, "We must then consider the situation over again entirely. It's very hard to say what we should do." One of the options would be the junta's move to Nicaragua which Ramírez called "one of our immediate goals." In the meantime the Sandinistas remained in Ramírez's house in San José going over the situation. One of the problems the Sandinistas had hashed out was turning down a Cuban offer to supply heat-seeking surface-to-air missiles that might have the power to neutralize Somoza's air force. After much soul-searching the Sandinistas declined the offer, feeling the use of socialist bloc weapons would be too much of a provocation to the United States, possibly inciting unilateral intervention.

While heavy fighting in Jinotepe augured the fall of yet another city, American assistant secretary of state Viron Vaky tried to persuade Venezuela to pressure the junta to broaden its base. On Thursday, July 5, Vaky left for San José with a list of five names compiled for him by Caracas officials. Vaky was preparing to ask the junta to add as many as four of the people to the provisional government. At the same time, hoping to build support for the proposal among other Latin American nations, he visited Colombia and the Dominican Republic to persuade them to recommend the plan to the junta. Ramírez said late that night that the imposition of four new members would be unacceptable to the junta. He indicated they would reject the imposition of the four, that the whole idea was absurd and was certainly impossible because it would be imposed by a foreign government. Ramírez added that any broadening of the government would have to be done by the Nicaraguans themselves.

Ramírez and the other junta members were taking note of press reports saying that Somoza was almost sure to step down. They were certain they could buy time the same way Somoza did, simply by stalling United States attempts to pressure them into expanding the junta. It was clear they were winning on the battlefield and that the guard's commander in chief was not much of a tactician.

Despite failure on most battlefields a desperate Tacho ordered a strong counteroffensive on July 6 against strategic guerrilla positions in hope of bolstering the guard before his pending departure so as to break the Sandinista noose tightening around Managua. Commanders were busily reporting from the field that they were under heavy pressure and pleaded with the Bunker for precious .50-caliber ammunition and air strikes. It was finally getting through to Somoza that he was being beaten on both the battlefield and the diplomatic front. More than 800 guard troops, a Sherman tank and an armored car surrounded Masaya, where approximately 1,000 Sandinistas were entrenched, but the city remained relatively quiet despite the concentrations of both forces. The guardsmen merely camped outside the town and never made a serious effort to retake it. The opposite was true in Rivas where more reinforcements were sent in and a furious battle was fought. One reporter who had spent time in Rivas reported the Sandinistas were "fighting like tigers" though suffering heavy casualties. The guard succeeded in burning down the city's hospital. The same day Jinotepe, along with the nearby town of San Marcos, fell to the FSLN after only forty-eight hours of fighting, cutting off Somoza's southern land supply line. Somoza nevertheless reported that fighting on some fronts, particularly Masaya, was going "fairly well." Furthermore, a shipment of ten T-28 airplanes was expected, Tacho said, but he would not be specific about their arrival.

About this time Somoza gave *The Washington Post*'s Karen DeYoung his first interview to an American publication in weeks: DeYoung had a habit of calling the Bunker each evening and asking for Tacho. Usually she was asked to wait and politely put off. But on the night of July 5 he himself answered the phone and invited her to come the following day. The message he gave in the interview, which was marked by long pauses before each sentence and between phrases, confirmed the rumors which had been denied all week—Tacho had agreed to quit and the timing of his departure was up to the United States.

"I am like a tied donkey fighting with a tiger," Somoza said. "Even if I win militarily, I have no future." Somoza said he had told Pezzullo upon the ambassador's arrival, "All right, I'm ready."

Somoza was subdued and calmer during the interview than at most points during the five-week offensive, a stark contrast to the normally aggressive and animated dictator, always full of challenges and charges. This time he was a defeated man who said he did not know where he was going or what he would do in exile. "I've got my education. I might find a job someplace. What can a retired general, a retired president, do?" Not only was he losing on the battlefield but he saw a virtual international embargo on supplies to his faltering National Guard, and the OAS was demanding his resignation. Tacho said that refusing to leave would mean "just lengthening the bloodshed in the country."

Tacho said that the imminent Sandinista victory had not greatly influenced his decision. "That's not my attitude. There are only two alternatives. One is to leave in an orderly manner, and the other is to take what [we] think we should and move out of here. Arms, goods and money. Make a tactical retreat. Instead of holding a lot of small, unimportant towns, we gather everything up, put up in a section of the country and we stick it out.

"What I'm trying to do," he said, "is lessen the suffering of the Nicaraguan people by getting an arrangement where everybody would feel secure. Right now, nobody feels secure, because the junta has been adamant about . . . wanting it their own way. I am the fly in the ointment but I cannot leave unless there's some kind of democratic government formed here."

Early in the interview Tacho said he feared the junta would not provide this. "The way I understand it, the junta doesn't want anything to do with the United States, not because they like or dislike [the American diplomats dealing with the situation] but because they dislike the way your country lives." He then warned that the junta would turn Nicaragua to communism. "It might not happen in this century but it will happen. [The United States] is not able to create the democratic and capitalistic incentive in them." Other Latin American countries had more influence over the junta, Somoza said, because "the only thing the junta will understand is if whoever is supplying their arms says no more arms unless you make a deal."

COSEP and the FAO, Venezuela, Costa Rica and Panama were all participating in negotiations with the junta. Even with the democratic involvement, Somoza maintained the Sandinistas were determined to establish a Marxist-Leninist government in Nicaragua. The distraught Tacho added that the United States had its own strategic reasons for wanting an expansion of the junta. "Your national interest is that Nicaragua keeps on going like it is, with different faces running it, with different attitudes. But not to fall in the hands of the Marxists," he warned, "because you have problems if you let that happen."

The negotiated settlement "is not my bailiwick," Somoza said, adding the guard would continue to fight until the deals were put together for a transitional government. "I feel that I have given a pretty good and fair battle. What can you do when you get everything cut off? The best you can do is make an honorable settlement."

Part of the settlement was still guaranteeing the safety of the guard after his departure, the resignation forthcoming "providing . . . the institutionality of the National Guard" and the Liberal party and an orderly transition of power. He was reportedly affected by the mass executions of army officers after the shah left Iran and, as one source put it, "He knows he would be a real cur to run out on his loyal army." He was, however, "in no position now to impose anything. I am not negotiating." An agreement had been hammered out, he said, while negotiations with the junta continued. The junta was to be induced to add at least two more politically conservative members and abide by his wishes concerning the guard and Liberals. After that a cease-fire would be forthcoming. "That's the whole idea. If we get an agreement, we get a cease-fire." Without an agreement with the junta, if Somoza left and the guard decided to continue the fight, it would mean "every man for himself," Tacho said.

Asked when he had decided to leave Somoza replied, "From the moment the OAS made that decision. Look, I'm a realist. What role do I play when I have the OAS down my neck? The only thing I can do is fight a retreating battle and try to get the best for my people.

"I feel that in my conscience I have done whatever I have had to do according to the laws of this country. People might have different ideas about me, but my conscience is clear."[4]

The Sandinistas were irked that Bowdler left San José a day before he was to hold talks with the junta but it was revealed later he was hospitalized in Panama for an undisclosed illness. Observers had speculated the Panama trip was to persuade Royo and Torrijos to withhold recognition of the junta—the only other nation which had recognized the junta was little Grenada. The junta was holding all-night sessions in San José. They were stalling for time. Sandinista troops were advancing on all fronts, and "if the Sandinistas continue advancing," Ramírez said, "we won't have to broaden the junta." The junta was anticipating moving to a free zone within days, Ramírez said, "and anyone who wants to negotiate with us will have to find us there."

On July 7 a break came in the Stewart murder case. Guardsman Santiago C. Carrasco, seventeen, testified before the National Guard board of inquiry that he had accidentally killed Stewart when his M-16 rifle fired because the safety was not on. An illiterate orphan who had been in the guard for only three months and who eventually escaped when the war ended, Carrasco had originally testified he was standing guard when he heard a shot, turned around and saw the dead Stewart. "I asked who killed him and the other guards said the dead man was a journalist and a soldier named González had killed him." It was the same story guardsman Brenes had told the military board of inquiry.

Board president Colonel Manuel Sandino Mendoza said Carrasco had changed his story and confessed after the board of inquiry said it would show him a copy of the ABC videotape of the shooting. According to Carrasco's confession, "He had his hands over his head. I ordered him to his knees and then to lie prone. I kicked him in the side and was going to hit him in the head with my rifle barrel when it accidentally went off." The board became suspicious of Brenes's tale, Sandino said, after a check showed no soldier named González was a member of the unit involved with Stewart's killing. Now the board had gathered enough evidence to turn the case over to a court-martial to try Carrasco who was being held in a Managua military prison. The trial would begin as soon as Carrasco's court-appointed attorney was ready.[5] (Carrasco was never convicted. Had he been, the most he could have gotten was a thirty-five-year sentence. Ironically, in Nicaragua, a country in which there were executions on both sides, there was no legal death sentence.)

The Sandinistas meanwhile were fuming over United States arm-twisting in negotiations on Sunday, July 8. "The only way to characterize this is blackmail," Father Miguel D'Escoto said in Costa Rica. The priest, now the junta's foreign minister, held the United States responsible for threats by Costa Rica and Venezuela to cut off war supplies to the FSLN. "They're [the United States] trying to bargain with the blood of our people. This can only result in prolongation of the war and anarchy." D'Escoto said that if the junta conceded to Washington's demands to broaden the junta and preserve the guard the Nicaraguan people would reject them. "If we give in, the junta will have signed its death warrant. The majority of the people will feel betrayed." Washington still insisted that Somoza would leave "within days" and said the United States was not trying to impose a solution on the junta, only to broaden its representation. A new trump card Washington was trying to play in its role of arbitrator was the threat of withholding desperately needed foreign assistance to reconstruct the nation. The money would be contingent upon a moderate outcome to the civil war.

On Tuesday, July 10, the United States began to alter its strategy again. A United States AID team flew to Managua to evaluate assistance programs, promising as much as forty-five tons of food daily in an effort to check future threats of mass starvation. Bowdler met with the junta in San José in round-the-clock sessions on broadening the junta. Phone calls continued to the junta from a series of Latin American nations on behalf of the United States initiative. American diplomats were active throughout Central and South America in hopes of twisting the Sandinistas' arm. While Bowdler was in Costa Rica, Viron Vaky toured Venezuela, Colombia and the Dominican Republic, and American ambassador to Panama Ambler Moss dealt with Torrijos and Royo. The increasingly restive junta not only had to deal with pressure to expand, but with the United States' desire for preservation of part or all of the National Guard, for guarantees on human rights and for judicial and electoral systems that would be in line with the kind of constitutional government the United States wished to see established.

According to Robelo, he saw "no reason why the United States should lay down conditions on how we should run Nicaragua. It irritates us to be told to do things we've already said we'd do. We see no logic to broadening the junta. . . ." After all, it had the support of Nicaragua's largest moderate opposition political and business groups. As to the guard, Robelo said, "We're fighting to eliminate Somoza—and they're trying to maintain parts of the National Guard."[6] Junta resentment of pressure exerted by the United States through intermediaries was apparently somewhat alleviated by Bowdler's personal attention.

Two other critics of American policy, but from an opposing point of view, surfaced in Managua on a quick, one-day trip Tuesday. Congressmen George Hansen, an Idaho Republican, dripping with perspiration and accompanied by his ever-smiling wife, and Larry MacDonald, a Georgia Democrat, carried with them fourteen boxes, five of which contained baby food. They announced they were on a humanitarian mission. If their humanitarian aid was small, their rhetoric was considerable. The congressmen, who met with Somoza and visited a refugee center, denounced what MacDonald termed "unbelievable distortion of the news about Nicaragua in the U.S. media."

MacDonald, standing before the Hotel Intercontinental clad in a blue seersucker suit, charged the press with playing up the Sandinistas as "Robin Hood angels" while they painted, he said, "the authority element, the elected government, as some kind of brutal, oppressive dictatorship." His statement brought an invitation from ABC correspondent Tom Shell to "walk down here on the beach at the lake and look at the bodies with their hands tied that [the National Guard] is burning in the morning. And you come down here and accuse us of distorting? Where the hell have you been, sir?"

Next the two addressed members of the Liberal party lodged in the hotel. With Luis Pallais doing the translating, Mrs. Hansen said, "The truth will prevail and ultimately Nicaragua will be a country free from the slavery of communism. I do believe that God-fearing and freedom-loving people of the U.S. will assist you." Mrs. Hansen took exception to newsmen referring to Somoza's nearby headquarters as "the Bunker" and told them it looked like any office in Washington. When she was told the name was an invention of the Somoza people and not the newsmen, she smiled.

MacDonald told the Somoza faithful, some sixty congressmen and cabinet members, that he knew what was happening in Nicaragua, and he reemphasized Somoza's own charges that the country had been invaded by communist forces. He said, "Our administration's response to these threats is a human rights program based on kissing the enemy and slapping our friends." He said he hoped Washington would "quickly reverse its policy on arms sales to your country. Take heart, keep your courage and stand fast. The American people are beginning to understand your plea. I know these have been lonely days for you, but you have a growing number of friends in the U.S. Keep up your guard. We are coming to your assistance."

Another critic receiving much press attention was Archbishop Obando y Bravo. In a Sunday sermon two days before, he alleged that the United States was agreeing to stretch the fighting as an extra element of pressure to persuade the Sandinistas to accept a political solution more beneficial to Washington. "We are thankful to the understanding and collaboration of those governments who have shown interest in our people's situation," Obando y Bravo said, "but at the same time we lament the ambiguity of those governments who have thought or continue to think of their own political interests before the common good of the Nicaraguan people."

The archbishop condemned the bombing of churches by Somoza's forces and the seizure by the National Guard of youths in hospitals and refugee centers. "The raids on churches, places of refuge and hospitals must be considered criminal. . . . The indiscriminate killing of women and children, even when there is simple suspicion that they have collaborated with the adversary, must be considered a war crime. War action that leads to the destruction of cities together with their inhabitants is a crime against humanity and God. . . . War cannot have as a goal the breakdown, and much less the annihilation, of the adversary for seeking vengeance against the adversary. To make war for vengeance is essentially immoral and contrary to the teachings of Christ."[7] His message was read in churches throughout Nicaragua.

By the tenth it was becoming doubtful that Somoza's forces could continue their war on their own people. Arms shipments remained blocked, supplies dwindled and the future of the guard remained uncertain. The morale of "Somoza's beasts," as Nicaraguans called the guard, was low. Their ammunition supply was even lower. The guard had ammunition enough for only three more weeks' fighting, reported tall, youthful and cool United States embassy military attaché Colonel James McCoy. The guard was low on mortar and .50-caliber machine-gun ammunition and had depleted its reserve stock. What ammunition remained was the limited quantity left in the hands of units fighting the Sandinistas. The guard could no longer hold the country's major highways.

"The battle appears to be won," McCoy said. After five days of heavy fighting on the outskirts of Masaya and despite continuous air attacks with incendiary bombs and napalm the guard had still not retaken the town. McCoy noted that the Sandinistas had the option of a major offensive to push northward or trying to capture Rivas. His opinion was that they would try for a military victory, and he felt there was a strong possibility of guerrilla forces converging on Managua.

McCoy said that if Somoza left, the guard would crumble. They would have no one left to assure their logistics. The only resupplying of the guard at the time was via clandestine flights of unmarked Nicaraguan air force DC-6s to neighboring Guatemala, Honduras and El Salvador, where Somoza contacts assured some support.

Over the weekend, the guerrillas finally captured the *fortín* in León which Somoza's father had captured decades before in his struggle to obtain power. Government troops besieged there were finally rescued by a Sherman tank and helicopter.

Many guardsmen were not trustful of the guerrilla claims that they would be respected if they had "no blood on their hands" or if they had "shown honesty and patriotic conduct in face of corruption and intrigue." Even moderate nonleftist Nicaraguans, appalled by the indiscriminate bombing by guard pilots, by artillery barrages directed against the civilian populace, and by the summary execution of youths, believed the guardsmen who had participated in these should be judged and punished. Many suggested the firing squad.

On most days during the past week, citizens leaving Managua were stopped by soldiers and made to roll up their trousers and sleeves. Any sign of bruises on knees or elbows indicated, as far as the guardsmen were concerned, that they had fought on the barricades. This led to summary execution for many. Now fear of possible guerrilla firing squads made some guardsmen determined to fight to the death, as with the guard in León, which was finally overrun by the guerrillas only after weeks of stubborn fighting. But eventually exhaustion and low morale had their effect. Guerrillas entering the *fortín* found soldiers hiding, not wanting to fight their own people anymore. Five guard officers, feeling the same way, appeared at a Sandinista press conference in Costa Rica saying they had defected.

The United States' desire to see the guard maintained as a deterrent to any armed communist takeover disturbed many Nicaraguans. These said they felt the United States could still be helping the guard in their counteroffensive against the guerrillas in order to allow the guard more bargaining power in the post-Somoza era. The same Nicaraguans said the United States was still listening to Somoza's propaganda machine which described all Somoza's enemies as communists and the war as an "international communist conspiracy" against his regime. Sure, the United States had also mentioned it would like to see the guard purified or sanitized of bad elements and perhaps its high-ranking officers retired, but that was easier said than done.

Top officers in the guard were keeping an "eye on the door," one military source said. At the same time some of the younger and moderate elements of the guard were discussing whether they could live with a guard that would have Sandinista guerrillas integrated into it. But, as one guardsman told me, the prospect of a National Guard that would be part of a Sandinista army was "too tough for them to swallow."[8]

CHAPTER 19

The Offensive Is Final

Early Wednesday, July 11: buzzards circled the shores of Lake Managua; dogs scavenged for human flesh. Shortly after curfew expired, women arrived, handkerchiefs pressed to their faces, to search for lost relatives among the freshly dumped bodies and charred human bones littered among the reeds.

It was common practice during the war for youths to be rounded up and shot at the edge of Lake Managua or at the *cuesta del plomo*, where fat buzzards filled the trees. The executions were as systematic as garbage disposal and carried out with as much emotion. At 8:30 one morning three pickup trucks were seen driving out of Giron's security compound carrying a cargo of young men naked to the waist, their hands tied and eyes blindfolded. The night before at 6:30 P.M., a half-hour before curfew, a squad of National Guardsmen had captured some of them as the government soldiers shot their way into the compound of the Nicaraguan Red Cross headquarters, which also served as the refugee camp in Managua. The guard seized seven young men between the ages of eighteen and twenty-two, relatives of Red Cross workers living in the compound, who had been playing cards when the soldiers opened fire, wounding three people.

Red Cross President Ismael Reyes said he didn't know why the guard was harassing his overburdened Red Cross workers. Six had already been killed in the war. The previous Friday the guard had seized a Red Cross truck and its driver. The next day they had commandeered a Red Cross bus used to transport doctors to the hospital. Three paramedics and the bus driver were taken prisoner and disappeared.

Two days later, Sunday, the bodies of nine young men, including one fourteen-year-old, lay on the shores of Lake Managua before the National Theater. Most had their hands tied and were blindfolded. They had been shot through the chest and head. Nearby, smoke still curled skyward from the remains of bodies from earlier executions that had been set afire for disposal. At 1:00 P.M. Reyes drove up to check the identity of the nine bodies to learn if any were his missing people. He was followed by a National Guard detachment in a truck that had a .50-caliber machine gun mounted on it. A uniformed fourteen-year-old smiled with satisfaction as he fired single shots at reeds on the lake's edge over the heads of newsmen and Reyes. "I am just test-firing this gun," the National Guardsman said. Reyes ignored his order to leave and climbed down to inspect the corpses. None of the bodies were his people and he continued his search of detention centers.

Others arrived in search of lost relatives. One lady said her son had been dragged from their home the night before by the guard and she couldn't find him.

On the other side of the war, "people's tribunals" often tried the "ears" and "toads." For an informer who was convicted or found to have caused the deaths of Sandinistas whom he had informed against, the sentence was immediate execution. Then there were the loosely controlled "popular militia" and other undisciplined groups over which the Sandinistas often had a minimal influence. They were known to kill guard informers without the niceties of a popular trial and judgment. For many it was a war of hate and revenge.

Suddenly, out of fear for their safety should the Sandinistas gain control, generals had become farmers and high-ranking government officials assumed the role of industrialists. Their ordinary skyblue passports carried photos not of men in uniform but of civilians. The chief of immigration, a general, had a new profession: office worker.

Only a few days earlier the Casa Presidencial had sent out a pile of thirty-five passports to the United States consulate so that visas could be obtained for the men who had so quickly obtained new professions. The passports, made in Nicaragua and carelessly stapled together—unlike the British-made passports of the past—were given priority treatment.

Tacho's own new passport had his line of work down as industrialist, as did the one given Tachito, also pictured out of uniform. Half-brother Joe had become a farmer. All of the documents were stamped with American B-1 and B-2 tourism and business visas. Tacho also had an A-1 visa in his official passport, which had been renewed December 14. He was taking no chances. Because of his wife's American citizenship he would have no trouble obtaining immigration status in the United States and the right to permanent-resident status. But the barrel the United States had him over was the possibility of extradition. That threat might pressure him to quit. Somoza knew full well that extradition into the hands of a new government would mean trial and prison, as Nicaragua had no death penalty. Dinorah also had a new passport and occupation. Earlier documents had described her as an executive assistant at the Casa Presidencial. She had wanted an A-1 visa, which could only be issued to a member of the president's immediate family. As the United States had no contingency covering the presidential mistress, she finally got the A-2 visa normally issued to bodyguards.

The passports were either proof of Tacho's intention to leave or part of a cruel charade played on the suffering nation. Somoza continued to abide by previous statements that he *was* leaving, that he was only waiting for the Americans to make the next move and advise him when he should depart. Max Kelly reminded newsmen throughout the week that "the ball is now in the U.S. court." But, in the game now being played in San José and Washington, the United States was having trouble getting the ball back over the net. Some were even wondering whether the United States had any strings in its racquet.

Bowdler was still conferring with the junta after leaving his sickbed in the Canal Zone. While the junta said it was firm and resolute that it would not buckle under American pressure, there was growing fear that perhaps it might. If it did, the stigma of American influence would render the junta without influence in the post-Somoza era.

"The junta will need all the muscle it has to control the left," a Nicaraguan business executive said. "There is only one Sandinista on the junta and we all understand that a strong Sandinista presence in the junta is necessary to control different factions. What the U.S. is trying to do is give the junta a little cosmetic dressing, which will only weaken them. They should be working on the four nonextremists of the junta and trying to help them instead of weakening them by compromise."

In a fierce sixteen-minute speech Wednesday before some 100 members of the government and national liberal party, observing the party's eighty-eighth anniversary, Somoza once again charged that Cuba, Venezuela and Panama were behind a "diabolical conspiracy" to turn Nicaragua into another Cuba. Somoza, raising his voice and gesturing with a finger, vowed to continue the fight against what he called "international communist aggression." The president issued a call upon "every man and woman who believes in democracy, free enterprise and individual freedom to stand up and fight for his home, his property, his family and the liberty of the Nicaraguan people." Once again the guard was praised for giving "its blood, generously, so that our country can determine its destiny peacefully."

The fighting was waning, with both sides obviously using restraint to conserve their dwindling munitions. But Somoza went on a public relations offensive, giving a series of interviews in the Bunker. He accused some foreign reporters of distorting facts and speculating negatively about what was happening, and he threatened to impose press censorship on foreign dispatches. In fact, United States television networks sometimes did find that the ground station used for satellite relay of their film from Managua had been closed.

In an interview with the American television reporters, Somoza proved once again he was a master at using the media.

"This is the first time in the history of the Americas that an organization such as the OAS has made a victim of a government without giving any protection to the citizens of that particular state. This is a situation which the United States should look into," Somoza said. "Especially the people of the United States who know that the Nicaraguan people have been along my side. I have been the friend of the United States, and the people who are fighting against me are no friends of yours."

The war could only be settled, Somoza said, when "the conditions of the OAS are met. The conditions have been met and that has satisfied me. We cannot fight seventeen countries in Latin America. I'm realistic. I am a politician. But I have to fight for the integrity and the safety of the people of Nicaragua who have nothing to do with this political fight that I know would be victims of the viciousness of the communists."

The war could go on for a long time, Somoza predicted, because "I'm trying to guarantee the constitutional rights of the Nicaraguans who are on my side and I think there will be no more bloodshed. That's all I'm trying to do."

Leaving the country was another matter. "Look, it all depends. Do you think it would be humane to leave the country and leave people who have maintained the peace in this country in such a manner that they have no guarantees? I think it would be terrible. Look, we still have a lot of the country under our control."

Miami was mentioned by a reporter as a possible place of exile but Tacho wasn't divulging his plans. "That's the first port of entry I ever went to in the U.S. in 1936. I have thousands of friends there. I'm not saying where I'm going." New York was then mentioned—he had once called himself the Latin from Manhattan. Laughing he replied, "I've been that for years, but I'm not saying where I'm going because of the implication."

Somoza's answers were often pure rhetoric. As to his resignation he replied, "Well, the OAS resolution said that the member states should take initiatives to see how that particular resolution should be implemented. Since our relations traditionally have been good with the people of the U.S. throughout this government, we have been discussing it with the U.S. government. Since also the resolution says that the government that takes over should be democratic, I think they have not found a democratic line in the government, and I also think that the factions of the communists in the guerrillas have a majority.

"Therefore all of this implies that there must be a stabilizing force like the National Guard and also a democratic party like the Liberal party in existence in order to ensure that there will be democracy in Nicaragua." Throughout the interview Somoza reemphasized, "I think that the National Guard and the Liberal party are part of a guarantee for the Nicaraguans. I think that the U.S. realizes this."

Tacho also contended the guard was not safe because it did not have adequate supplies. "Nicaragua has never been a warring country. As a matter of fact we were spending ten percent of our budget on the guard, air force and navy. Just like the U.S. used to do before the First World War. So really, we don't have the amount of ammunition. However, the resolution of the OAS has not been complied with by the other countries. The rebels have been resupplied from Costa Rica. So our resources are limited."

The guard had only enough ammunition for three more weeks, Somoza claimed. "Men we have; ammunition is lacking. We are trying to buy ammunition on the open market. Or maybe we will make another decision. We then would turn the table around and then become the guerrillas. And this is what I'm trying to avoid by talking to the U.S. and I would like to appeal to the people of the U.S. to see that a democratic government is installed here, because the government that is pretending to be the new government is communist-dominated.

"The leaders of the guerrillas are communists trained in Cuba," Somoza charged, "and the last thing I want to see is a Nicaragua that goes communist. I am not delaying this to keep myself in power. I am saying this to keep myself in line with the idealism which I learned in the United States when I went to school, a democratic government, a Western way of living and freedom for all the people."

Throughout the interview he reiterated claims and charges made dozens of times before. Again in response to further questions about his leaving, he was vague. When he did leave, Somoza said, he was thinking "of getting a job and calling that job my retirement because I think a person who retires and does nothing just deteriorates. I plan to be productive, with a job, any kind of job, that keeps me busy and I can contribute to the community." Asked what a former president or ex-general could do, he said, "Whatever a man who is full of humility can do and have the respect of the community."

Even as Somoza was speaking, in San José the junta was stalling Bowdler while its members worked on a transitional plan to serve as a counterproposal to Washington's effort. A session with Bowdler the day before was "the first satisfactory meeting we have had," D'Escoto said. "We began doing what we should have started doing in the first place: clarifying objectives before we started making proposals."

As Bowdler was not giving interviews, D'Escoto outlined the fundamental American concerns in three main points: (1) the need for Somoza's speedy resignation, (2) the need to make any transition as orderly as possible, and (3) the need for the new government to enjoy the "widest possible" international support. "It wasn't so much what was said as the way it was said," related D'Escoto. "We could immediately say that those were our objectives too."

The United States plan did not differ much from one presented the week before. Washington still insisted on a continuing role for the guard and the broadening and moderation of the junta. Bowdler had included that in a fourteen-point proposal read to the junta. While Washington called for replacement of the top leadership in the guard, there was little alteration suggested other than the integration of some Sandinista elements into the organization. "We said that their plan seemed to be aimed at maintaining the institutionality of the guard," junta member D'Escoto said.

The junta presented a four-point plan that was released to the press about four hours later. The first point was the immediate resignation of Somoza, to be accepted by the Nicaraguan Congress. The Congress would then hand over power to the government of national reconstruction. Point two was the installation of the government on Nicaraguan soil. To be immediately taken afterward was step three, a call for all OAS members to officially recognize the government.

Step four called on the new government to (1) abolish the *Somocista* constitution of Nicaragua, (2) establish a new constitution that would "provisionally" allow the government to rule, (3) dissolve the Nicaraguan Congress, (4) order the National Guard to cease hostilities and return to barracks, with guarantees that guardsmen's rights and lives would be protected. Selected officers and guardsmen would be allowed to join the new national army or return to civilian life. Sandinista forces would freeze in the positions occupied at the cease-fire.

Further, designated "sectors" of the guard would join with Sandinista fighters in maintaining order. D'Escoto explained, however, that these guardsmen would not all necessarily come from the ranks of those in uniform at the cease-fire. He said that a substantial number of guardsmen who had recently retired from the service were now collaborating with the junta and likely to be given the leading roles.

Other provisions in the program called for promulgation of a law allowing for new state institutions, implementation of the new government's just-published program covering political, social and economic areas and the guaranteeing of safe conduct out of the country for all military and bureaucratic *Somocista* functionaries who wanted it except for those involved in "grave crimes against the people."

D'Escoto said Bowdler's reaction to the program was that it was "quite a bit different from the one that we [the United States] were thinking about" and that he would have to communicate with Washington before replying. Bowdler added that in his personal opinion "I don't see that this really gives us [the United States] an opportunity to contribute" to the Nicaraguan political situation.

In a bit of byplay, Ortega suggested that it was "not too fair" of the United States to be pressuring countries to quit supplying arms and matériel to the Sandinistas. Bowdler denied the charge and then said, according to D'Escoto, who swore it was an exact quote, "As long as there is no cease-fire, the U.S. is not making any effort to prevent either side from receiving supplies." If the statement was true then he had contradicted the official American position of an arms embargo against Somoza.

The situation remained ambiguous. Either a political situation in which a compromise was possible had been achieved that Wednesday or neither side had changed its position very much. That was the main effect of the junta's latest initiative, until the situation otherwise clarified.

Bowdler returned to the negotiating table with the junta at 10:30 Thursday morning, July 12, and three hours later D'Escoto called to tell reporters he was "leaving town." He added, "Something very big has come up. This may be it. Say a prayer."[1]

Progress had been made. Within hours the United States National Security Council was saying, "In two or three days Somoza will leave Nicaragua, and this is neither wishful thinking nor naïveté." The main trouble, the council spokesmen said, was the Nicaraguans themselves: the political struggling between the main opposition groups, the junta and the guerrilla fighters. "The Sandinistas demand full control, or at least a greater share of real power, and we are not going to let that happen," the official said.

Somoza supporter Congressman Wilson was already conceding the end. "We lost Nicaragua a long time ago. We are fighting our last battle there. El Salvador and Guatemala will come next. We will see the Cubans, the PLO and Russians on our borders at the Rio Grande." The Texas congressman had little sympathy left for Somoza. "The killing of the ABC journalist was a terrible thing. And it became really difficult to support Somoza and his National Guard after that horrifying event. Yet, it is our interest not to let the Sandinistas take over Nicaragua. This is our backyard and if we lose there, how should the rest of the world regard us, not able to handle our basic backyard business?"[2]

The State Department was also saying, "We are in a real mess. We were predicting for the last two or three weeks that Somoza would resign and that we would manage to help establish a new national unity government which would carry on until the 1981 general elections. All our predictions turned out to be wrong."[3]

United States officials were still reluctant to spell out the details of the compromise the American government had offered the junta. "Any public statement we make is regarded by them as part of our campaign and as the final terms for a compromise. This is why we cannot be precise and cannot give out the details," a State Department official said.

The seizure of a Boeing 707 in Tunisia, loaded with arms from the Palestinian Liberation Organization, en route to Nicaragua, gave more fuel to assertions of a substantial communist role on behalf of the Sandinistas. Conservatives and government officials in the United States were quick to capitalize on it. CIA intelligence experts were giving out evidence to anyone who asked for it showing the growing role Cubans and the Russian-backed PLO were playing in Nicaragua. According to one CIA source, "When the Sandinistas failed during their first offensive, the Cuban African corps commander, General Requiros, was called in and sent over the Costa Rican border into Nicaragua. He helped and planned the successful offensive. And when recently the Sandinistas were running out of ammunition and heavy arms, the PLO was asked to stretch its own aiding arms and to send arms, weapons and ammunition from its bases in Lebanon and Libya."

Wilson was also predicting that when Somoza was forced out and the radical forces took over, a public debate would start in the United States on who lost Nicaragua. "Let me give you my answer to that," Murphy said. "We played a passive role in Iran, refusing to act against the anti-shah revolutionary forces. This is not the case with Nicaragua. There we played an active role, destabilizing the regime. We pushed the entire world to abandon Somoza, economically and politically, and unfortunately we succeeded. Now we have to face a worse reality, to encounter a fanatically radical government. A real clever game."

The CIA continued to back with facts Wilson's allegations of Russian, Cuban and PLO dirty tricks in Central America. "It took Castro almost eighteen years to take revenge for the Bay of Pigs operation, but in the end he succeeded," one CIA man said. "Enjoying a secret base in Costa Rica, supplied with plenty of arms from Cuba, getting money and training from the PLO—the Sandinistas' objective became relatively easy."

"Twenty years ago we believed Castro when he stated that he was neither a communist nor a socialist," Wilson said bitterly, while showing New York Times clippings from those days. "Look, we were wrong from the beginning to the end. We sympathized with the Castroites because of the human rights issue and we destabilized Somoza's regime because of the same issue. Now we are condemned to lose both. On the one hand our friend and ally and on the other hand the Nicaraguan people will not enjoy human rights."

Meanwhile, in Cuernavaca, Mexico, former President Richard M. Nixon was paying a visit to the exiled shah of Iran and saying he deplored the situation in Nicaragua. "The choice that we face at the present time, possibly, in Nicaragua is not between President Somoza and somebody better, but between President Somoza and somebody much worse." According to Nixon, who said the United States should not "grease the skids" for the ouster of friends like Somoza and the shah, "I think it is crucial that every possible step be taken to make sure that a Castro-type government does not come to power in Nicaragua because that would be a threat to every free nation in the Western Hemisphere."

Thursday night it was revealed the Sandinistas were taking their case to OAS secretary-general Alejandro Orfila. They sent him their peace plan and a letter clarifying their stance in "preserving the right of self-determination of our people." The document carried five major points designed to allay the fears of any OAS members that human rights would not be respected. It extended an invitation to the OAS human rights commission to visit Nicaragua when the junta was installed; invited the OAS ministers to come to the country as a gesture of solidarity; claimed the new government's right to hold trials for those accused of crimes against the people; announced Somoza associates not responsible for the "genocide" could leave the country under Red Cross and OAS human rights commission supervision; and promised free elections "for the first time in this century" for local officials and a constitutional assembly.

On Friday, July 13, Tacho left Managua aboard his blue and white Lear jet for Guatemala. He returned a few hours later, before most people realized he had been out of the country. Many speculated Somoza had gone to beg arms and ammunition, but instead he asked Guatemala, Honduras and El Salvador to supply troops to help disarm the Sandinistas once a cease-fire took effect. Nicaragua was a member of the Central American Defense Council created in the mid-1960s as a mutual defense pact in which the Central American military governments would assist each other if faced with "an international communist threat." His request was politely turned down. In fact, his request was considered extremely unrealistic in Guatemala. He was furious at the brush-off by his colleagues but he was told it was also due to United States pressure. The visit came amid reports Somoza was toughening his stand, that he was no longer prepared to step down when the United States suggested.

Also on Friday an airlift of American food arranged by the United States government arrived in two chartered aircraft. The Southern Air Transport line flew in food from Houston, Texas, as did a separately chartered DC-8. Because of the possibility that the United States might otherwise be accused of bearing arms to the Somoza government, no Air Force planes were used in the airlift which was to reach five planes a day carrying ninety-two tons by the following week.

Meanwhile, the government advised the foreign correspondents that censorship was in force and that the government was planning to monitor the news. If there was any violation—what the government considered a lack of objectivity—the offending reporters would be asked to leave the country.

In San José, the junta said that the United States had not withdrawn "irreconcilable demands" and that they were turning instead to the OAS for support in their plan to install a new government in Managua. The rupture in what had been described as promising discussions between the rebels and the United States occurred Friday morning when a session between the two sides was called off because of Bowdler's absence. United States ambassador to Costa Rica Marvin Weissman told junta members that Bowdler was too ill to attend. Progress in talks with Bowdler earlier in the week and word that Washington viewed the junta's latest proposals favorably had encouraged them to believe that the United States was about to make good on its promise to remove Somoza. The Sandinistas were holding off their march on Managua to await the outcome of the crucial negotiations in Costa Rica. Even in Masaya the mood was close to a national holiday.

Ramírez said the principal "irreconcilable" demand was the insistence of the United States that the group be expanded beyond its membership of five.

Junta member Robelo said, "No Nicaraguan sector is asking for expansion of the junta. They all feel properly represented. This request is a foreign one." Ramírez then released the text of the letter sent to the OAS and extended the same invitation to the foreign ministers of all Latin American nations.

Violeta Chamorro also used Friday to blast Bowdler saying his negotiation attempts were "completely finished." Nevertheless they held a surprise meeting together late Friday and another on Saturday, July 14.

Saturday, on the public relations front, Tacho met with a group of European reporters whom he told the government was in charge of "eighty percent of the country. Our troops in the south are driving back the invaders from Costa Rica. In the department of Rivas we have people doing mopping-up operations of people who tried to take the city of Rivas. We are launching an offensive in Masaya. Managua is completely in the control of the government. They [the Sandinistas] have taken the initiative to attack Chinandega but are meeting the resistance of the National Guard."

Asked if he could win militarily he said, "It all depends. The international law has been, uh, so elongated like a rubber band that, uh, frankly, we are now moving internationally in a jungle in the sense that they also have the political world stretching the law to its convenience and that's what's happening to Nicaragua. The international law has been stretched to the convenience of the Sandinistas who have invaded Nicaragua and that is why we have not been able to, uh, quell this offensive. They get munitions and they get them free from governments . . . from Panama, from Costa Rica, the Dominican Republic and Cuba. This is really an aggression.

"Yes, we are running out of ammunition and we're trying to get some ammunition. I think that the free world should realize that this government has aligned itself traditionally with the Western democracies. There is the danger this government will fall into the hands of the leftists. The communists."

While denying the stranglehold the guerrillas were putting on Managua, Somoza said that a political solution could not come about unless "the institutionality of the National Guard is respected and that the Liberal party also be respected." Not only security for their lives but in the case of the Liberals, "the right of them to organize and to do politicking. If they [the junta] are as democratic as they say they are," Somoza said, they would allow the Liberals' existence. "You see, we don't maintain, we *know* the Liberal party has the majority in this country. But if they outlaw the Liberal party then we, they will not have a chance to work politically."

Somoza said he would not accept the junta's conditions for his resignation and the offer of amnesty for guardsmen not involved in crimes against the people because "they are too generalized. You must understand that the National Guard has been the army and has been the local police force and the local cops and I don't think there is any guardsman who cannot be accused of having put somebody in jail for having committed a misdemeanor or a crime. . . . Therefore, I must insist upon the protection of the people who respect law and order in Nicaragua since the inception of the National Guard."

Tacho refused to answer a question about his recent trip to Guatemala. He was keeping the leaders of the other neighboring countries advised of the military situation by telephone, he said, but they were not yet willing to help him in the war. "I think they are going to have to see more communism installed in Nicaragua to be able to determine themselves. We have three cities now organized as communist cities—that's León, Matagalpa and Masaya."

Help would be welcome from CONDECA [Central American Defense], Tacho said. "All of these people are grown men and they should know when is the appropriate time to defend their own interests. I'm defending mine right now." The pact was "precisely" set up for this purpose, he said, but it was not working "because the OAS made a resolution and the pact is under the OAS and so the OAS right now is opening the way for the takeover of Nicaragua by the communists."

Nor was Tacho happy with the American efforts to negotiate his departure. Pezzullo held the last of a score of meetings with Tacho on Saturday, July 14, and Sunday, July 15. The Bronx-born ambassador finally pinned Tacho down to a departure date. Tacho had been drinking vodka heavily but managed to pull himself together for the meetings. Always crafty and calculating, Tacho knew how to play people, but now despite efforts to evince calmness, he was visibly shaken, a victim of the bottle as much as depression. Those last hours were the toughest for Tacho; he was obsessed with the fact that someone would kill him before he left. When Pezzullo met on Saturday with Tacho and Francisco Urcuyo Maliaño, the speaker of the lower house whom he was designating his replacement, the whole transition to the junta was understood. The next day Pezzullo asked Somoza where he would like to go in the United States and at what airport he would like to arrive. Tacho said, "Homestead Air Force Base," Florida. Departure was set for 4:00 A.M., Tuesday, July 17.

CHAPTER 20

The Last Hours

Squinting into the glare of the afternoon sun, Tacho Somoza contemplated the group of foreign newsmen in the street outside, their video cameras trained on him and their microphones outstretched as he stepped into the garage from the Bunker's back door. Somoza, who had always enjoyed sparring with the foreign press, suddenly lost his verve. Instead of walking across the street to the military casino (officers' club) where he held his press conferences, he inclined his head and, even though he was out of microphone range, whispered instructions to Tachito. Father and son stood alone inside the garage a minute longer before Tacho's last appearance before the press in war-torn Nicaragua.

Dressed in a light gray suit and tie, his graying black hair carefully combed back, Tacho looked like an affluent middle-aged businessman, not at all like a president-general of the longest family dictatorship in Latin America. Usually an arrogant man, he was a closet coward on that Monday, July 16, 1979. He tried to give newsmen the impression that nothing abnormal was happening; at the same time he was assuring his followers and the army that they could rely on help from the United States once he had departed into exile. To ring down the curtain on this last act Somoza had ordered his field commanders to report to the military casino. While the day was cloaked in secrecy, the activity around the Bunker suggested this was the end; but, given Somoza's penchant for press conferences, newsmen were convinced he would not leave without a last hurrah and the chance to denounce his many enemies.

With a last word to Tachito—the heir-apparent who might otherwise have extended the family rule into the twenty-first century—Somoza turned and entered the Bunker. The tall, pasty-faced Tachito, clad in crisp camouflage fatigues, crossed the street to the casino at a trot.

Newsmen surrounded the younger Somoza. "Are you going to leave?"

"Who? Me or these officers?" He opened the door at the top of the steps and called to a group of officers waiting inside. Two dozen men filed out from the casino. Most were haggard, some wore filthy, torn fatigues. One had his arm in a sling; his shirt was torn off at the shoulder, and his pants were caked with blood. The eyes of some were red from lack of sleep. Tachito, holding the door open, greeted each as he stepped out. He had a word for each. He shook hands with some, slapped others on the back, and for several he had a warm embrace, addressing them laughingly by their noms-de-guerre. "These are a bunch of active duty officers. I suppose this is an operational meeting to find out how things are going," Tachito said in English as he ushered the last of the twenty-four officers across to the Bunker while newsmen continued their barrage of questions.

"What are your plans?"

"That depends on the chief of the guard. The president has to pick a new chief of the guard."

That seemed to clinch it. For forty-six years a Somoza had ruled Nicaragua—not always as president, but always as chief of the National Guard from the day in January 1933 it had been bequeathed to Nicaragua by the United States Marines.

Then Tachito added to the confusion by saying, "I don't know if there is going to be a new chief of the guard."

"Will you be leaving with your father?"

"As an active duty officer, it is a matter of the authorities deciding what I do. The army." He made no denial that his father was leaving. Newsmen laid siege to the Bunker. Gunfire crackled in the distance.

Despite his years of education in military academies and running the National Guard, the insurrection had shown that Tacho was not a real soldier. The National Guard for decades had the reputation of being one of the toughest armies in Latin America, but it had never really been tested. Over the years the officers had grown fat on corruption and the recruits were usually illiterate, poverty-stricken *campesinos*. Tacho was more like a gang leader surrounded by his gunmen than an army general. The difference was that most of his hired *pistoleros* were in uniform.

Tachito had tried to get his father to revamp his headquarters staff and get rid of a lot of the "old fat asses" upon his return from Harvard. Somoza had done the same thing to the guard when he returned from West Point thirty-three years earlier. But after spending most of his life running the guard, he had not wanted to get rid of men he felt he could still trust.

The guard had lasted as long as it did during the insurrection because Tachito had founded the Basic Infantry Training School and graduated some classes of black berets, who replaced the old General Somoza García Battalion as the guard's elite troops.

The guerrillas had numbered only 300 a few years earlier, and Tomás Borge said they had had only 3,000 well-armed and trained regular guerrillas when the "final offensive" began. As the offensive progressed the guerrillas' ranks swelled to about 10,000 men and even Borge admitted he really did not know how many troops they had under arms in the end. The guerrilla fighters had been highly motivated as was the population. Prominent were the thousands of *muchachos* with an assortment of small-caliber and old weapons who fought and formed part of the guerrillas' logistic apparatus.

Combined, the population and the guerrillas proved more than a match for the guard in one city after another. Guardsmen feared the people as much as the

Sandinistas. Somoza feared his own fate might be a bullet from his once loyal guard. On Saturday, with a nervous tic in his neck, he looked straight at Pezzullo and was not joking when he said, "You've got me in a hell of a position—it's now open season to shoot me down." The scene in those last days inside the Bunker complex was described by one mercenary as an incredible moral collapse with "a lot of promiscuity, sex and booze. Tacho became very morose and even stopped cursing his officers and aides." The situation in the Bunker didn't resemble Hitler's last day. "There was nothing gutsy about these guys—they wouldn't take poison. They ran like rats," said the mercenary.

The world—or at least, that part of the world which cared one way or the other —had turned against Somoza. In the end, his few friends, the military rulers of Guatemala, El Salvador and Honduras, declined to provide even moral support. Sunday evening, July 15, the five Andean pact foreign ministers met in Caracas to decide the next step for a political solution to the Nicaraguan situation. In communiqués released on Monday they neither formally recognized the junta nor broke with Somoza, preferring to work toward the immediate transfer of power from Somoza to the junta. They told Somoza bluntly, "You should understand that the countries of America can no longer remain inactive in face of [your] continual contempt" of the OAS resolution.

Pezzullo, who had spent three and one-half years as deputy director of Central American affairs in Washington, intended to oversee the junta's plan for turning over power to the new regime.

Over the weekend Ramírez declared, "Our patience with the United States has been used up." The junta however proved flexible enough to allay most of Washington's fears. It appointed an eighteen-member cabinet dominated by moderates, which satisfied American insistence that the new regime should represent all shades of Nicaraguan political opinion. Among its members were corporate lawyer Joaquín Cuadra Chamorro; Carlos Tunnermann Bernheim, former rector of the National University; and Arturo Cruz, a former officer of the Inter-American Development Bank. There were only two hard-core radicals: Sandinista commander Borge, appointed interior minister, and Reverend Ernesto Cardenál, named minister of culture. The rebel junta also agreed to provide "safe conduct" for any Somoza henchmen who wished to leave Nicaragua; only those charged with "grave crimes" or "genocide" would not be covered by that pledge.

To back up that guarantee the junta also agreed to a proposal originated by Washington's special envoy, Bowdler, that the OAS be invited to monitor the protection of human rights. Satisfied with the junta's promises, Washington pledged to support the new regime. That weekend Bowdler, not a man given to dramatics, quietly announced to the junta, "You are now the government of Nicaragua."[1]

On Monday all guard officers with more than thirty years' service were retired, including most of the general staff. The retirement of the officers, who included more than 100 generals and colonels, said one government source, will "benefit the guard, and the ones who are fighting will be those who will run things in the future."

At 1:20 P.M. Somoza left the Bunker in his black presidential limousine for the short ride to La Curvita, his bungalow in the compound farther up the hill. He ignored the newsmen as he passed but waved and smiled broadly to newswoman Karen DeYoung of *The Washington Post.*

A few minutes later aide Max Kelly emerged from the Bunker. Grinning, he exchanged a few wisecracks with the newsmen, insisted nothing was happening, and then breezed away in his little red car. Kelly, who acted as chief Nicaraguan government spokesman in those last days, liked to spend time at the bar with newsmen, scrapping over their coverage of the regime, emphasizing that he had returned his graduation ring to West Point in protest of the Carter administration's policies towards Somoza.

At 2:00 P.M. it was the myopic doorkeeper who, albeit prematurely, announced the end.

"There's no one here."

He wore a shabby blue chauffeur's uniform; an automatic pistol in a webbed military holster was strapped around his scrawny waist. As long as anyone could remember, he had been a fixture of the Somoza regime.

Vexed by the insistent knocking, he opened the mahogany portal a crack, his leathery face reflecting fear. "I told you, there's nobody here. Look for yourselves."

The place from which Nicaragua's dictator had ruled—the Bunker—was empty. The fleet of cars normally parked around the Bunker garage was gone. Missing as well was the large deluxe Winnebago-style recreational vehicle which Somoza had used in prewar days when sneaking out to meet his mistress. Boxes and cartons of paper had been whisked away earlier in the day, along with five brightly colored parrots. "They are going to Miami," their handler declared bluntly.

But then, within the hour, Somoza suddenly reappeared at the Bunker in his heavily armored limousine. Its license plate, which read "Presidente de la República," had been removed. Unknown to surprised newsmen, the return visit was for a round of farewells to his retiring officers who were now free to leave the country. Not publicly announced were the president's orders for military pensions to be paid both his wife and mistress. The orders giving Hope and Dinorah the same lifetime pensions accorded military officers appeared on top of the pile of pensions on the desk of Colonel Manuel A. Sandino. When the early morning decree was issued retiring the guard high command Somoza appeared briefly before the Bunker and displayed what he described as a Chinese-made recoilless rifle shell, which he said had been given to the guerrillas by Cuba. For the last time on Nicaraguan soil, Somoza condemned what he termed "the international communist conspiracy" against his government.

After a forty-minute meeting with Somoza, his field officers left the Bunker by the front door. Their expressions were glum. They glared menacingly when newsmen tried to press them for information. Some of them cursed newsmen under their breath. One did confide that Somoza was leaving, and that they had been told help would now be forthcoming from the United States. Munitions were dangerously low. In some cases the necessary supplies had been completely exhausted, such as the mortars, the 105-mm artillery pieces and those used by the armored units. In all, there was hardly enough left for two more weeks of fighting.

Top Somoza aides left next, scurrying through the front door, briefcases in hand. Elfish foreign minister Julio Quintana almost ran from newsmen in his haste to get to his car. "I can't answer anything," he shouted over his shoulder.

The promised aid was clearly a device to hold the troops together, a desperate attempt to forestall panic in the ranks. Yet some questioned whether the officers would have permitted Somoza to leave had he told them no such aid was forthcoming.

Earlier in the day Urcuyo had met at the Bunker with Somoza who was profoundly disturbed while being bidden farewell by members of his army staff. His last words to Urcuyo were: "Chico, do not forget that you must negotiate, negotiate and negotiate with Pezzullo, until you make the junta disappear from his mind. Do not forget that this junta is a communist threat to Nicaragua and you have to make Pezzullo understand this. He is wrong!"[2]

A little after 5:00 P.M., eight trucks carrying Infantry Training School black berets, who had recently been fighting to retake Masaya, drove in and out of the Bunker compound. The young soldiers, both men and women, shouted "Masaya" and gave the "V" for victory sign as they passed by the newsmen. Others lifted their Galil assault rifles in the air. The tough drivers of the trucks were grim-faced. It was a macho farewell to their commander in chief who had no way of seeing or hearing it.

Newsmen continued their watch over the crumbling of the dynasty.

His black beret at a jaunty angle, Major Pablo Emilio Salazar walked down the street in front of the Bunker. "The National Guard will stand firm and continue fighting to maintain democracy even without Somoza," the much-quoted Comandante Bravo said rhetorically.

"Will you join the new army?"

"I would have to wait and see if it were going to be democratic first."

The story wafted about that what was left of Somoza's rubber-stamp Congress, lodged next door in the Intercontinental Hotel, would be called into session there at any moment. Somoza was about to resign. Newsmen darted from the Bunker to the hotel and back again. No longer were there aggressive guards at the gate or in the new concrete sentry box to detain them. An old soldier lifted the yellow and black boom without interest.

Afternoon rains threatened but never came. Darkness fell and, in the blacked-out compound, an elderly sentry used a flashlight to guide visitors to the sidewalk. The feeling of crisis had passed. There were no tears. None of the visitors showed their feelings. There was a lot of false bravado. It was as if the inevitable had finally happened.

Seconds before 7:00 P.M., newsmen lounging on the dirty white sandbags outside the Bunker door were politely shooed away by a security agent in civilian dress who warned that for their own safety they must return to the hotel. It was curfew time. "Nothing is happening," he said.

The lobby of the Intercontinental was equally unreal. Old senators sat before a television set watching a dubbed version of "Gilligan's Island." When, in accordance with emergency war regulations, the hotel lobby lights were turned off, the solons continued to sit in a semicircle, facing the blank screen in the dark.

For Somoza's people, all the news was bad. The town of Estelí had fallen to the guerrillas after weeks of siege. The Somoza family's ancestral coffee plantation, El Porvenir, near San Marcos, had been pillaged. Chinandega and Rivas were the only major towns the guard still securely held. Granada was under siege and about to fall.

Rumors mounted that the sixty-five members of Congress at the hotel, including nine members of the nominal-opposition Conservative party, would be called into special session to hear Somoza's formal resignation. The evening dragged on as they waited. Small groups of men formed, dissolved and formed again. They spoke in low, hushed tones. Many slipped off to their rooms to consume liquor they had purchased from looted stocks peddled in the lobby earlier in the day. Before long, some were noticeably drunk.

Finally, at 1:05 A.M., they were hustled into the Rubén Darío *salón*. The speaker of the lower house, Francisco Urcuyo, slipped out of the service elevator and rushed into the room in suit and tie. Some congressmen, hurrying in Urcuyo's wake, muttered obscenities at the foreign newsmen crowding into the hallway. The foreign press had increasingly become the object of their fear and hatred.

One-legged congressional press secretary, Umbert Sanchez Uriza, told correspondents they might as well go to bed, that the meeting was being held merely to arrange procedures for the next day's session.

But behind closed doors the resignation of Anastasio Somoza Debayle, Tacho II, was read to bleary-eyed congressmen. Addressed to the Congress and the people of Nicaragua, it stated: "Having consulted the governments which are interested in the pacification of the country, I have decided to accept the resolution of the OAS, and by this means, I resign the presidency from which I was popularly elected. My resignation is irrevocable.

"I have fought against communism, and I believe that when the truth is known, history will say I was right." It was signed "A. Somoza, president of the Republic."

After the statement was read during the noisy and drunken session, Urcuyo was unanimously elected to succeed Somoza as a constitutional buffer between Nicaragua's bloody past and its uncertain future. The blue and white presidential sash was draped across his chest, placed there, ironically, by Luis Pallais Debayle, a member of the family that had monopolized it since January 1, 1937.

Meanwhile, newsmen had ears and tape recorder microphones pressed against the door of the room. They overheard a Conservative senator ask in a squeaky voice what the new president would do about the American plan for turning over the government to the victorious rebels. The Liberal senators raucously shouted him down.

Urcuyo had been selected to manage the transition of power to the Sandinista-backed provisional "national reconstruction government." The United States had worked out the formula, arranging political asylum for Somoza and his aides. Hawk-faced Urcuyo was saying nothing about this.

Most of the congressmen didn't care. It took them little more than half an hour to hear Somoza's resignation, elect his successor and endure Urcuyo's inaugural address. He promised the nation peace, justice and freedom in formal, stilted language. The group applauded dutifully. The majority of them left the meeting and rushed to their rooms to pack to join their families, long since flown to safety in Guatemala and the United States.

Some diehards, overcome with emotion and/or liquor, followed Urcuyo into the corridor, shouting that they would remain and fight communism. As the new president moved to the elevator, he startled newsmen by declaring that political negotiations could take as long as three months.

At 3:30 A.M. a thirty-two-car convoy left the hotel under heavy guard for Las Mercedes airport. It was crowded with congressmen, top-ranking military officers and Somoza aides. The moon peeked through the clouds, lighting the slick wet streets as the motorcade sped away. The rain had finally come to wash away the dust of the day.

At 4:15 A.M. two blue and white helicopters, a Hughes 500 and a larger Sikorsky, lifted off the EEBI grounds and landed on top of La Loma de Tiscapa on the rim of the volcano, next to the ornate concrete wall across from where the Casa Presidencial had once stood. A few minutes later, four cars, led by Somoza's black limousine and followed by the white Checker Airporter that always carried his bodyguards, climbed the winding road from the Bunker to La Loma. Moments later four jeeps made their way to the rendezvous.

From there Somoza could look down on the black shapes of the Bunker and the military base, the seat of power for more than a hundred years.

At 4:45 A.M. Somoza boarded the smaller helicopter. As the chopper took off for Las Mercedes and exile, the pilot switched on the landing lights. For a brief instant the Bunker was sharply illuminated, then it was again pitched into darkness. Somoza broke into tears. But at the airport he had a last burst of anger when Tachito arrived half an hour late and kept them all waiting. He feared Tachito might have decided to remain with his troops.

At 6:00 A.M., July 17, only five hours after having been elected president, a sleepy Urcuyo was awakened at La Curvita to find Pezzullo and two other members of the United States embassy paying an unforeseen visit. The ambassador opened the conversation saying he had faith that Urcuyo, according to an agreement between Pezzullo and Somoza, would turn over the government at nine that morning to Managua Archbishop Miguel Obando y Bravo and two members of the junta.

"According to Pezzullo's plans," Urcuyo remembered, "the junta was to enter Nicaragua from Costa Rica and we were all to meet at the Camino Real Hotel. There I was to deposit the presidential sash in the hands of Archbishop Obando y Bravo, who would then direct a message to the nation. I was to deliver another message explaining that freely and spontaneously, and to attain peace in Nicaragua, the government was now in the hands of the Junta of Reconstruction.

"After all of these 'instructions,' Pezzullo asked me to give orders to General Mejía González [the new commander of the guard] about the plan to meet with the Sandinistas to arrange the transition, and the general told me: 'Mr. President, I hope that you realize that these men are our enemies, and that, upon arriving in Puntarenas [Costa Rica], they will make me their prisoner and will hold me hostage in order to blackmail you, which is why they won't kill me. Why don't they come to Peñas Blancas? If you order me to, I will. I'll go there and meet with them.' And I answered him: 'You are right, General. They must come to Peñas Blancas. And if necessary, I will go with you.'

"Of course, Pezzullo and his companions did not accept our proposal.

"Controlling my anger, I told Pezzullo that I had no qualms about meeting with Archbishop Obando y Bravo in an effort to seek solutions to the grave problems facing the nation; however, I was definitely not prepared to hand over the power that the people had invested in me through their duly elected representatives. If he and General Somoza had arrived at any understanding regarding the instructions that he had so disrespectfully communicated to me, they were null and void for two reasons. First, because neither he, nor General Somoza, had indicated anything to this effect previously. Second, as I was at that moment the constitutional president of the republic, they had to negotiate with me. I was not willing to betray those who had unanimously elected me, by dissolving the Congress, or, by surrendering my power to the junta, which amounted to the same thing. I also made it known that it was necessary to take the army into account, which had fought so valiantly. I told him that at noon I would deliver a message to the nation outlining plans for the well-being and peace of Nicaragua."[3]

Black zanata birds roosting in laurel trees began their chorus early on July 17. They had been disturbed by Managuans forming the now common food lines. No one in the long line across from the National Palace knew that *el hombre* had finally gone. In Ciudad Jardín, National Guardsmen arrived in trucks and dragged young men out of line by their hair. Beating them with gun butts, the guardsmen threw them into the back of the vehicles like cord wood.

The government's Radio Nacional, the lone haranguing voice under martial law, sounded strangely subdued. No longer was the announcer lambasting the populace on the evils of communism. There was a sober, belated call for youth to use their arms to build peace. And a quote from the Bible: "Blessed be the peacemakers."

Among the reeds on the shore of Lake Managua groups of poor women continued searching for relatives. There were no fresh bodies. Flies crawled over three blindfolded and bound youths killed two nights before. Only ashes and bones remained of the other victims.

During the night somebody had placed a new wreath on a wooden lamppost on the corner of a deserted downtown Managua street. The fresh flowers were in memory of Pedro Joaquín Chamorro, killed a year and a half earlier at the same intersection. Of the two lifelong enemies, one was dead and remembered as a martyr and the other, now banished, was to be recalled only as a hated despot.

Then came a communiqué signed by the new head of the National Guard, Brigadier General Federico Mejía González, who, the day before, had been assistant chief of police. It was not conciliatory, not in accord with the "peace plan."

In announcing publicly for the first time that Somoza had resigned, he said: "For political reasons that will benefit the fight against communism, the president has resigned his post." Guardsmen were ordered, "Redouble your efforts in the current fight, maintain the unalterable spirit that has always characterized the National Guard as the only constitutional armed force in the country."

Francisco Urcuyo returned at noon to the Intercontinental. Surrounded by guard officers, under glaring television lights, he read a strident speech praising the guard. Making sounds like a real president, he said, "The difficult era we have endured is over. . . . I assume this high office with a clear conscience and a calm heart . . . as supreme chief of the armed forces, I order an immediate cease-fire. As president of the republic, I call on all irregular forces to lay down their arms . . . the time has come to bandage the wounds made by Marxist terrorism . . . we shall work together to rebuild our republic from the ashes. . . ."

The moustached old Somoza politician left what was billed as a presidential press conference refusing to answer any questions and returned to the Bunker to the applause of a group of Somoza aides who had remained and cast their lot with Urcuyo. There he proceeded to name his cabinet.

A native of Rivas, Urcuyo had served as Somoza's vice-president from 1967 through 1972, as well as been minister of public health. He appeared oblivious to the fact that most of the country was in the hands of the guerrillas and that the National Guard was in the process of disintegration, telling the nation, "We must forget the past in the name of the present, with our eyes fixed on the future."

Somoza's *Novedades* appeared Tuesday afternoon with a banner headline: "Urcuyo President" and devoted five of its twelve pages to the new president, mostly to photographs of his installation. The only newspaper then published in Nicaragua, it carried a three-paragraph story on the arrival of exiled Somoza in Miami.

The American State Department issued a four-page statement on Somoza's arrival at Homestead air force base in Florida, blaming Somoza for the months of fighting and stating that his resignation marked "the end of the most prolonged remaining system of personal rule in the modern world." But did it? Throughout Tuesday, July 17, there was a growing feeling in the ranks of the opposition with ties to the Sandinistas and the junta that what they had always feared had happened. Somoza had gone but the dynasty remained intact. With guerrillas poised to move on Managua, there was also fear that a bloody battle for the capital city could not be averted. Nor did the opposition trust the United States. The feeling was that the United States was capable of a last-minute double-cross in order to prevent a guerrilla victory, especially since it was deeply concerned about keeping some element of the National Guard intact.

Only a few days earlier Bowdler had told the guerrilla-backed national recon-struction government, "You are the government of Nicaragua." Pezzullo, after meeting with Urcuyo in the Bunker, reported back to opposition leaders that Urcuyo had in fact "violated" the agreement worked out between the United States and Somoza, and that Washington could no longer play any further role in the negotia-tions.

Radio Sandino was already declaring what they had long forecast: *somocismo* without Somoza was taking place. It was not acceptable.

Urcuyo's tenacity caused a hitch in Costa Rica's plans to give three members of the new government a full-fledged presidential send-off on Tuesday, July 17, from San José to Managua. A Costa Rican Lacsa Bac II jet, with a red carpet leading to its door and a brass band standing by, waited in vain. Managua's Las Mercedes airport was closed to them.

But shortly before 2:00 A.M. on Wednesday, July 18, two small Piper Navajos landed at Godoy airport in León after a clandestine flight from San José. On board the first plane were Violeta Chamorro and two aides. The second plane carried junta members Ramírez and Robelo. They were reunited with Comandante Daniel Or-tega who was already in León. The one junta member who had been in the country the whole time, Hassan, was with guerrilla forces besieging the guard garrison in Granada.

Shortly after the junta's arrival in León, Costa Rica—the ninth country to do so—officially recognized it as the legitimate government of Nicaragua.

Nicaraguans, who throughout the seven-week rebellion received most of their war news from Costa Rica, learned Wednesday morning that the junta was estab-lished on Nicaraguan soil. Radio Reloj announced that the new seat of government was León. The death rattle of the Somoza dynasty continued.

At 8:00 A.M., July 18, Pezzullo called Urcuyo at the Bunker dining room.

"Are you ready to meet with the advance team sent by the Junta of Reconstruc-tion to work out details of turning over the government?"

"No," was Urcuyo's reply.

"Then," Pezzullo continued, "you will be the only one responsible for what will happen in the country. I have nothing to do here and I will leave with the embassy."[4]

Shortly thereafter, some twenty members of the United States embassy staff left for the airport. Pezzullo, dressed in a dark suit and accompanied by his own bodyguards armed with riot guns and wearing bulletproof vests, followed them shortly after 9:00 A.M. The embassy issued a three-page statement accusing the interim president of not carrying out the transitional plan. It pointed out that Urcuyo had been personally involved in the creation of the transitional plan which included the following elements:

- Immediately after assuming power, the interim president will call for a cease-fire, with opposing forces remaining in place.
- The interim president will arrange an early meeting between the leaders of the National Guard and the Sandinista army, in order to facilitate the

transition and begin the process of reintegrating opposing forces in Nicaragua.

- Within seventy-two hours, the interim president will transfer power to the Government of National Reconstruction.
- The Government of National Reconstruction pledges to avoid reprisals, to provide sanctuary to those in fear, to undertake the immense task of reconstruction, to respect human rights and to hold free elections.
- Organization of American States foreign ministers and representatives of the Inter-American Human Rights Commission will be invited to come to Nicaragua and observe the entire transition process.

"We have been hopeful that the plan described above could bring an end to Nicaragua's tragic civil war and could enable all Nicaraguans to begin the difficult process of reconstruction in peace and freedom. Unfortunately however, interim President Urcuyo has thus far not carried out his solemn commitments. He has not called for a cease-fire; he prevented the timed meeting between leaders of the opposing military forces; and he has indicated his intention to retain power indefinitely. Mr. Urcuyo's actions threaten to bring Nicaragua into another cycle of violence and destruction at the very time when an end to the bloodshed had finally seemed to be in sight."

In Washington, Deputy Secretary of State Warren M. Christopher spoke by telephone with Somoza in his Miami Beach residence throughout the morning to persuade him to get Urcuyo to play by the rules of the agreement. Off Nicaragua's east coast was the United States helicopter carrier *Saipan*.

Representative Hansen, who in Managua just days earlier had vehemently denounced the Sandinista communist threat, charged that the administration had threatened to deport Somoza if he did not persuade Urcuyo to surrender his authority within twenty-four hours. But the State Department said that Christopher had made no direct threat and had set no deadline. He had only pointed out to Somoza, they said, that the agreements, including the one permitting Somoza to come to the United States, were part of a package, and that Urcuyo's actions could invalidate all other commitments.

"It's obvious that Somoza got the point—that he is welcomed in this country only as part of the overall plan and that we expect him and Urcuyo to carry out their part," State Department officials stressed. Somoza, in a huff, called Urcuyo at 7:00 A.M. on July 18.

"Chico, I am lost. I am a prisoner of the State Department. I was just called by Warren Christopher, assistant secretary of state, to tell me that if you don't give up power to the Junta of Reconstruction, they will give me up to the Sandinista Front. That you can definitely not count on any class of aid from the North American government."[5]

The following day Somoza said he was going on an extended tour of South America. "I am afraid of being asked to do other things," he maintained, referring to the State Department pressure to persuade Urcuyo to step down. He called the request by Mr. Christopher a "tremendous political mistake" and said he had protested it but had then been told if he did not intercede with Urcuyo he would not be welcome in the United States, and that the demand came from the "highest level."

By midmorning Wednesday Urcuyo finally realized the futility of his actions and decided to quit. There was no way that the National Guard could hang on without outside help. And none was coming. Overnight the garrison of Granada, the third largest city in the country, surrendered. Sandinistas moving toward the capital from León were meeting little resistance.

Panic set in. It was as if the National Guard, leaderless for the first time in its history, had suddenly begun to believe all the propaganda about the "bloodthirsty communist hordes," as Somoza's Radio Nacional used to call the Sandinistas.

When the pilot noticed a large crowd of guardsmen on the runway at Las Mercedes, the regular Nicaraguan Lanica jet overflew the airport and continued on to San Salvador. One hundred and forty-seven soldiers in full battle dress, some wounded, and accompanied by their families, seized a Red Cross chartered DC-8. After food supplies were unloaded, the American crew was forced to fly the panic-stricken group to Miami. A British Royal Air Force plane, also bringing in food, saw what was happening and managed to take off before the guardsmen captured it.

That same afternoon Somoza's air force defected en masse, with their families, to neighboring Honduras via fourteen-odd Nicaraguan planes.

The Sandinistas were now demanding the unconditional surrender of the National Guard but they promised that the lives of guardsmen who accepted the cease-fire would be respected.

While Managua was a city still gripped by fear, León, by contrast, was relaxed and jubilant. The Sandinistas, who had controlled the old colonial city for more than a month, were in a triumphant mood since the arrival of the junta.

Tomás Borge, standing in front of a yellow Cherokee wagon, said to a crowd on a street in León, "We want unconditional surrender from the stupid puppet, and an end to the war. It will mean the total destruction of the National Guard."

But to newsmen who had driven up from Managua, Borge said, "You will want to see this. We are going to set free all the prisoners we have in León." Borge wanted to make it clear that the Sandinistas' slogan, "Implacable in battle and generous in peace," was not merely words.

Addressing the citizens of León at a rally, junta member Ramírez ridiculed Urcuyo by stopping in midsentence to ask his name. Could anyone give him the name of the man who wanted to be their president? The crowd roared with delight.

Borge, dressed in an olive uniform with the black star on the matching cap, also poked fun at Urcuyo.

Newsmen standing around at the new Sandinista sheriff's office, kibbitzing with the holiday crowd, were invited to come to León's main square at 2:00 P.M. and meet the junta at a news conference. *Miami Herald* reporter Guy Gugliotta described the scene:

> At 2:00 P.M. we gathered in León's bullet-riddled main square where a smooth-talking Sandinista in his early thirties met us and guided us to the news conference a few blocks

away at the University of Nicaragua. We were taken to a lovely, old wood-paneled, second-story meeting room and invited to sit down.

The junta arrived with Sandinista suddenness and no fanfare. Violeta de Chamorro, Alfonso Robelo and Sergio Ramírez, the three junta members who had been talking in Costa Rica, were on hand as was Daniel Ortega, a Sandinista chieftain who had come from the battlefield. . . .

It fell to Borge to present the junta, a task he performed with delicate expertise and great emotional effectiveness. As the world's ranking Sandinista, Borge's role was important, almost priestly. He laid hands on each member as he introduced them. Here they are, he seemed to say. I give them my blessing. It was the first time the government had met together in Nicaragua and the significance of the occasion could be found in the tears of some of the local Sandinista leaders.

Even Dora María Tellez, the twenty-two-year-old woman who governs León as 'Comandante Patricia,' seemed impressed. She is short, dark, not particularly attractive or unattractive, and speaks in the same monotone as Ortega. A national heroine, she was second-in-command to Eden Pastora, the famous "Comandante Cero," during the takeover of the National Palace in 1978. I tried and failed for a second time to have a meaningful conversation with her. She answers questions like a movie star, giving pat, useless answers that offer no hint of the person beneath the black beret. Chain-smoking is her only discernible human failing, otherwise she hides herself well. She is arguably the most powerful woman in Nicaragua.[6]

Sandinista units controlled most of the highway to León. The young guerrillas were friendly and good-naturedly posed for pictures. Some cockily fired their guns, demonstrating that they no longer had to worry about their precious ammunition.

Along one section of the highway lay the bodies of twenty guardsmen who had been killed during fighting that morning. The guardsmen's unseeing eyes stared out of boyish faces—faces that seemed much too young to wear the large Israeli-made steel helmets that had failed to protect them. Their corpses, with limbs bent at strange and awkward angles, marred the beauty of a lush green field.

At Nagarote, on the old road to León, the mood was much more festive. The guard garrison there had surrendered after only token resistance.

Meanwhile, in Managua, the last remaining mercenary still on the job with the National Guard was a short blond West German youth who called himself Mike. He had spent most of Wednesday riding around in a jeep checking troop units now stationed on the edge of the park in front of the Bunker which had become the front line. Five other guns-for-hire, four Argentines and a Cuban exile from Miami, had left days earlier. Mike threatened the photographers, warning them not to take pictures of the troops. The soldiers themselves no longer wanted to be identified in guard uniforms. This young German bully who chose to stay behind gave a clue to what was happening. When asked whether the president was going to give a press conference, he snarled, "What president? There is no president."

Urcuyo found himself totally alone in the Bunker on Wednesday, July 18. The sound of silence drowned out the trumpets of ambition. Urcuyo telephoned Guatemalan president General Romeo Lucas, an old friend, and begged him for help to flee the country. Lucas advised him to seek asylum in the Guatemalan embassy but Urcuyo said it was unsafe to do so. At 8:00 P.M. a DC-6 and two C-47s of the Guatemalan air force paused briefly at Las Mercedes, then departed quickly carrying Urcuyo and his family and aides into a hasty exile. He left behind the chaos his inane bid for power had created. He had not even bothered to resign, saying later that General Mejía had told him, "Mr. President, I am not in agreement with this procedure [of surrender]. Leave in exile as president of Nicaragua. Someday we will return to the country and reinstate you to office."[7]

Nevertheless, throughout Wednesday, the National Guard radio network continued to issue orders as if the war would continue forever. Private citizens with scanners overheard the network advise commanders not to surrender. One guard commander was told that things were actually improving and that he should boost the morale of his troops. What troops?

True, at nightfall on Wednesday, soldiers had been seen entering the Bunker in a variety of vehicles, even old water trucks. But although shooting continued throughout the night and into Thursday morning, it was finally apparent to everyone that the guard had ceased to exist as a fighting force. When the Sandinistas began broadcasting during the night from radio station ABC (not affiliated with the American ABC network) in downtown Managua, it was an emotional moment for those who had favored the guerrilla cause and had been subjected to years of censorship. Suddenly they heard an inspiring rendition of "La Tumba de los Guerrilleros" ("The Tomb of the Guerrillas").

Latin America witnessed, perhaps for the first time in history, the total evaporation of an army. At midnight on July 18, General Mejía met with the National Guard hierarchy and, realizing that only twenty days' worth of ammunition remained, they too decided to flee. They were on their way out of the country by 1:00 A.M. on July 19. When the guard enlisted men awoke to learn that they had been deserted by their officers, they became instant civilians.

At 6:00 A.M. an outbreak of gunfire began at the Bunker compound. It lasted for thirty minutes; then silence. A short while later, scores of guardsmen invaded the lobby of the Intercontinental. They dumped their weapons in a heap, stripped off their uniforms and left, clad in civilian clothes. Many were wearing civvies under their fatigues, others had had them stuffed in their packs. One soldier came in from patrol, unbuckled the radio from his back, threw it into a corner and fled.

A little after seven the lobby was again invaded, but this time by a group of barefoot urchins, the oldest about eight years old. Their chief occupation to date had been begging from hotel guests in the parking lot, but they now had a new source of amusement. They quickly armed themselves with the discarded automatic rifles, almost too heavy for them to lift. Further encumbered by battle helmets that almost touched their skinny shoulders, they happily staggered outside to stage their own private war behind the old Roosevelt monument nearby. Bullets flew wildly until, because the children could not reload the deadly weapons, the guns fell silent. Then, pausing for a second to regroup, the kids began running toward the Bunker. Carrying their empty rifles at ready like real soldiers, they charged the once formidable building. Much to their disgust they found the Bunker empty. In the compound yard several abandoned motorcycles caught their attention. They managed to get the big machines started but each rider promptly fell off. Unable to control the mechanical monsters, the kids lost interest in the whole affair and wandered away. The only casualties: a couple of walking wounded with skinned knees.

Normally cautious newsmen made their way into the compound and began exploring the Bunker's rabbit warren of ten windowless rooms.

The Bunker was a male sanctuary. The color scheme was in earth tones, the colors of stability. All the walls were painted tan, accented by the rich brown shades of the leather upholstery and the mahogany of the furniture and woodwork.

The large waiting room was too well known to the newsmen to hold any interest. The next office was far more intriguing, if equally uninformative—it was knee-deep in shredded paper . . . documents Somoza had wished none to read.

The door of the presidential office was open, one wall dominated by a wooden panel into which a huge replica of the Nicaraguan seal of office had been carved. The desk below was covered with photographs taken during the two-month rebellion. All other papers had been removed.

There were four doors leading off a foyer. Two led again to familiar territory: a conference room and the war operations room, where Somoza held cabinet meetings and gave frequent interviews to the foreign press. The third and fourth led to Somoza's private office and living quarters, which consisted of a lounge, a dining room, a kitchen, bedroom and bathroom.

A large bottle of Tabasco sauce stood in the center of the table in the dining room. On Somoza's unmade bed lay his army fatigues. Next to them was a book in English, *Beat Inflation.* In the bathroom shaving gear was strewn around. There was a scale in the corner, which he had used daily since his heart attack in 1977.

Two photographs and a poster had been left behind: a large photo of Somoza's father, Anastasio Somoza García, a framed picture of Pope John Paul II and an orange poster mounted on wood of the Argentine comic strip character Malfalda, the chubby little girl known throughout Latin America. On the poster were the words: *La cosa que es*—"That's how it is."

Shortly after the correspondents left, Comandante Santo and his young urban guerrillas arrived and removed a number of automatic weapons from the compound. Then at 11:30, Comandante Oscar, a veteran of the battle for León, formed his column into tactical files to occupy the Bunker. These seasoned guerrillas took no unnecessary risks. They treated the operation as an offensive. They had spent the last six days fighting their way from León to Managua and a few hours earlier had fought against soldiers dug in at the power plant in a section of the city called "Open Tres." The inhabitants of this postearthquake barrio renamed it "Ciudad Sandino" the following day.

The junta appointed National Guard Colonel Fulgencio Largaespada provisional commander of the guard. He set up headquarters away from the center of the city and at noon Thursday, July 19, he announced the guard's surrender. But there were few guardsmen left to heed the call to lay down their arms and hand themselves over to the Red Cross.

Earlier in the day, small overloaded planes were being flown off by inexperienced guardsmen. One went bumping down the runway until the wheel carriage collapsed. Thousands of guardsmen also fled into neighboring Honduras where they replaced war refugees, who were already returning to Nicaragua.

At the Red Cross headquarters, where other refugees had been living in fear of the guard, the tables were turned. Now guardsmen were the refugees. Government officials and former military men crowded into the corridors; few had luggage. Several were accompanied by their wives, some by small children. Many appeared to be in a state of shock, their eyes red, full of fear. They filed into a room where a Red Cross official simply took their names and, asking no questions, handed them a number. When that number was called, the person was told he could go to an embassy. Forty-eight soldiers in civilian clothes were taken by bus to the Argentine embassy, which had rented an additional house to lodge them.

Later a man shouted to a group of ex-members of Tachito's EEBI, "The Guatemalan and Colombian embassies are full. Should we go to the Argentine embassy?" A lieutenant said he would like to go to the American embassy, but was told the Americans wouldn't take refugees. A second-lieutenant then stated flatly: "We were deceived into thinking that the U.S. was going to help us win the war as soon as Somoza left. When our officers all disappeared we realized all was lost."

Senator Adolfo Altamirano, sixty-three, a member of Somoza's Nationalist Liberal party from the province of Nueva Segovia, said he had fled the Intercontinental Hotel at 6:30 A.M. along with several other congressmen. "I'm going away, but I will return if the country doesn't turn communist," he said. Another congressman said that two of his colleagues had remained at the hotel, apparently too drunk to understand what was happening.

A thirty-year-old soldier, who had been among the troops that hadn't wanted their picture taken while they were stationed near the hotel, was now saying that he was a police corporal named Modesto Vaca. Red-eyed and in a sport shirt and slacks, he privately admitted his identity. "My unit changed into civilian clothes and took off this morning when we realized there were no officers around. When we found out that the general staff had left for the airport early, we had no other choice but to go to the Red Cross," he confessed.

The young West German mercenary had finally abandoned the cause the night before—but not until he had held up three newsmen in their hotel rooms. He took their tape recorders and almost a thousand dollars in cash from their wallets before he made his escape.

Word spread through Managua from house to house, from barrio to barrio, from rich district to slum, "The Frente is coming." This phrase brought most of the population pouring into the streets shouting, "Viva Nicaragua Libre," and the Sandinista slogan, "A Free Country or Death."

There was a sense of fraternity everywhere. Young guerrillas, their uniforms splattered with days of mud, wore an odd assortment of headgear. Some had rosary beads around their necks and gold medals on their berets. They came in all shapes and sizes. Most were young and many were women. Some fired their guns in the air.

For thousands of Managuans the arrival of the Frente meant that an enormous weight had been lifted from their shoulders. It meant an end to months of war, an end to the deadly indiscriminate bombing by the guard, and an end to years of repression and nervous tension. Even apprehension about the future was swept aside by the wave of euphoria.

The white flags that had been flown on cars and houses and carried by pedestrians as a sign of a noncombatant, were replaced by the red and black flag of the Frente. In one upper-class district a wealthy old couple wore red shirts and black pants, and their Mercedes Benz bore the spray-painted letters FSLN. A man played drums on the roadside in front of his home. The streets were strewn with the cast-off uniforms of the National Guard.

Throughout Thursday, Sandinista radio communiqués reflected concern for private property and compassion for the former enemies. The local ABC station, renamed the Great National Liberty Network, urged people to remain indoors, use restraint and not commit any offenses or pillage. They stressed that the job of reconstruction was now at hand and that nothing should be destroyed. The guerrillas publicly appealed to foreign embassies not to close their doors to guardsmen seeking asylum.

Managuans would not be denied a victory celebration. Thousands lined the streets applauding, embracing the armed youths who responded with the "V" for victory sign. Jubilant crowds dragged the large equestrian statue of Anastasio Somoza García down from its pedestal at the sports stadium. His son, Luis Somoza Debayle, larger than life in metal a few kilometers away, was also hauled down.

Days earlier, on July 15, hundreds of *campesinos* and people from nearby San Marcos had gotten a head start on the festivities. They flocked under the old masonry arch which had held the words *"El Porvenir* Anastasio Somoza, 1918" on it. The area had been occupied by the Sandinistas, but the guerrillas paid little attention to the old coffee plantation. The people did. Hundreds streamed back out from under the arch with roofing, wood, tin, any part of the plantation that they could dismantle with their bare hands. Not much was left of the place where Anastasio Somoza García, the founder of the dynasty, had been born in 1896.

The Somoza dynasty, in the end, had collapsed completely. Attempts by the United States to preserve at least part of the National Guard were stymied by none other than Somoza himself and his longtime faithful aide, Francisco Urcuyo. The guard had always been a personal army, loyal only to a Somoza, who destroyed it with his last vain attempt to stay in power, bringing about the total disintegration of the dynasty. The Sandinistas' "final offensive" was truly final. Somoza was driven from power by the first true popular insurrection in modern times in Latin America.

Reality was not always a strong point of the old regime. Even when it could no longer flex its muscles, on Wednesday, July 18, leaflets printed on yellow paper were handed out from the Bunker—after Somoza's departure.

"Patria libre . . . o morir? Sandinistas: Your situation is untenable. Your unpopular and inhumane movement, destructive and bloody, is discredited and rejected. Capitulate! And thus you will avoid useless bloodshed. God and history will judge you! People, unite with the National Guard of Nicaragua."

Reality will not be denied. It had finally caught up with Somoza.

Guided by a comparatively small group of guerrillas within months after the death of Pedro Joaquín Chamorro, an event that acted as a catalyst, all sectors of Nicaraguan society were in some way involved in the movement to oust Somoza and end the dynastic dictatorship.

Somoza, like many Latin American dictators before him, finally slipped away in the dead of night, without any fanfare or final boast. He had held his own people in such utter contempt that he had completely underestimated their ability to win the final offensive. A few hours after Somoza had departed a young officer of the EEBI who had arranged the departure of the convoy to the airport, stood at the Intercontinental Hotel desk and shrugged his shoulders. "I'm going too. There is no way we can defend ourselves against the people." He confessed, "It's not the guerrillas I'm afraid of but the people. I know they hate us and they could overwhelm us."

In the last days Tacho tried to sound like a statesman, but in fact he was a man who had committed mass murder of his own people. He never once mentioned the thirty to forty thousand Nicaraguans—no one will ever know how many—for whose deaths he was responsible. They had lost their lives only because of his giant ego. And in the end it was this utter disregard for Nicaraguans that brought him to his knees. Except for a few congressmen and a few guard officers, Tacho Somoza in the end was totally rejected and repudiated as no other dictator in Latin America before him. The rejection was absolute. The insurrection, guided by the Sandinistas, had become entirely and utterly popular.

Somoza's legacy to the Nicaraguan people was an industry destroyed by his ruthless bombing, a staggering foreign debt of $1.5 billion and a looted treasury which left the nation with only $3 million. "It was an ingenious thing," said Arturo José Cruz who became head of the Central Bank. "For years Somoza ran this country like a private enterprise. It was a mechanism to produce hard currency to invest abroad." Somoza put his booty at $100 million; the Nicaraguan economist put it closer to $500 million.

If Tacho's ego bothered him he did not show it. His "extended tour" of Latin America when he left Florida on July 19 for the Bahamas meant flight to Paraguay where he felt safe from extradition with General Alfredo Stroessner, the longest reigning dictator in Latin America, in power since 1954. But Nicaragua was now Free Nicaragua. Somoza's Bunker became headquarters for the Sandinista army and was quickly renamed the *Chipote* after the mountain headquarters of Sandino. The entire complex was christened after Germán Pomares Ordeñaz.

Radio Sandino broadcast from Managua that "the genocidal dictatorship of Somoza has been overthrown and the people of Nicaragua are free. The National Guard has been annihilated." In fact, it had evaporated.

At a giant rally before the National Palace on Friday, July 20, thousands applauded their new government and saw for the first time the celebrated guerrillas and members of the junta. Norma Elena Gadea sang,

March forward my companions
Victory will never be denied us
Never again will we be defeated. . . .

An announcer cried above the roar of approval of the crowd in the new Plaza of the Revolution, "The sons of Sandino are going to build the country the general dreamed about." Consigned to an unmarked grave by assassins forty-five years earlier, the avenging spirit of the legendary Augusto César Sandino had indeed arisen to haunt the Somozas and finally topple their arrogant, bloodstained dynasty into the rubble of history.

EPILOGUE

Somoza was in high spirits on Wednesday morning, September 17. Having overcome a bout of influenza, he had resumed his physical fitness routine and was planning to visit his 19,200-acre cotton plantation in the Chaco region of western Paraguay. During his thirteen months in the indolent country wedged in the heart of South America he had scandalized his host, General Alfredo Stroessner, with his outlandish behavior, providing Asunción society with more gossip than it had known during Stroessner's entire twenty-six-year reign.

Stroessner—the last of the old-style caudillos—and his Colorado party kept a tight hold over Paraguay's 2.9 million inhabitants. Everyone's name was in the party's computer files. The son of German immigrants, Stroessner shared Somoza's thirst for power, wealth and women but their personalities were very different. The old general was a dour individual who lived unobstrusively, enjoying the solitude of river fishing. He frowned on Tacho's bawdy barrackslike brawling with his friends. He shared prudish Paraguayan society's rejection of Tacho's profanity in public. The stories of Somoza antics, including food fights and drunkenness, together with gossip about the rude manner in which he treated his Paraguayan bodyguards, soon made Tacho an outcast.

Somoza—slimming—breakfasted on fruit and a boiled egg. During the night an associate, Joseph Baittiner, an Italian-born American who lived in Colombia, had arrived for a daylong business visit. He and Somoza were going downtown to see Somoza's banker. Kissing Dinorah good-bye and promising to return for lunch, Tacho climbed into the back seat of his white Mercedes Benz, the car that he had instructed César Gallardo, the family chauffeur for thirty-five years, to bring around. In the garage of Somoza's rented mansion, number 436 on treelined Avenida General Genes, sat the specially armored yellow Mercedes Benz which he had ordered from Germany to ensure maximum security. But in this quiet, anticommunist nation, where even former Nazis had found safe haven, Tacho felt secure.

At 10:05 the white Mercedes left the secure high walls of the mansion and headed toward the city's center, followed by a red sedan with four Paraguayan plainclothesmen who served as his bodyguard. At the same time, a hit team was alerted by walkie-talkie four blocks away. The team of four to six gunmen waited.

As Somoza proceeded down Avenida España, a blue Chevrolet pickup pulled into the avenue. It obstructed the Mercedes as it approached the intersection with Calle America. Suddenly the mild early-spring morning was rent with the deafening sound of automatic rifle fire from the pickup and from a two-story house near the corner of the street. Seconds later there was a swooshing sound followed by an earsplitting explosion.

The top of the Mercedes was ripped apart. The decapitated, armless torso of driver Gallardo was ejected twenty yards into the street by the force of the explosion. Somoza, seated on the rear right side of the car, had eighteen bullets in his body. By the time the rocket struck the car he was dead. The projectile entangled his remains with the car wreckage. Baittiner, seated behind the driver, was shredded by the blast. The battered car rolled to a halt on the sidewalk, its motor still running. A second rocket exploded harmlessly in the street as the bodyguards in the follow-up car tumbled out and opened fire on the assailants who sped away in the blue pickup. The entire operation had lasted perhaps two minutes.

Two blocks away, three members of the hit team held up a motorist, architect Julio Eduardo Carbone, an Argentine, at gunpoint. They shouted, "Get out, get out quick." Later he told reporters that the gunmen had the lilting, accented Spanish of the River Plate, characteristic of Argentines or Uruguayans.

The house from which the hit team had launched two Chinese Communist–type, small B-50 rockets was empty when the police moved in. In one room a walkie-talkie crackled with what sounded like a female voice. Barely audible, it was giving instructions, the police believed, to the fleeing gunmen. A loaf of black bread and three packs of cigarettes were on a kitchen counter. Weapons and camouflage clothing were spread about the house.

A Paraguayan television crew got to the scene early and filmed the grisly wreck, as officials arrived and inspected the remains of the Nicaraguan strongman whose facial features were relatively untouched by the bullets and rocket blast. While they stood around in little groups, discussing the impact of the assassination that had shattered Paraguay's immunity from terrorism, Dinorah suddenly appeared, running down the street, crying, "Let me see him, let me see him, I want to see him." Her eyes were hidden behind dark glasses but her voice was full of anguish as she tried to reach the wrecked car. Portly interior minister Sabino Agusto Montanaro, in charge of security and police, took her by the arm and held her away from the car. "The car flew into pieces and General Somoza has died," he said, trying to comfort her. But the distraught Dinorah refused to believe the truth. "That's not right, what you're telling me. For the love of God, tell me it isn't true." She was led away and the car was hauled off so that the bodies could be extracted from the tangled wreckage.

The hit team had prepared their work well. They had carried out the attack with meticulous precision and speed, making good their escape. The greatest manhunt in Paraguay's history was soon under way, but it only succeeded in compounding the mystery of the identities of the assassins and their motive.

The police furnished reporters with a scenario almost immediately. On August 29, they explained, an attractive, young, fair-haired woman appeared in Asunción in search of a house for the Paraguayan branch of a group she called "The Associated Argentine Artists." Her passport identified her as Argentine national Alejandra Renta Colombo. She registered at the Hotel Premier, a moderate Asunción hotel favored by businessmen, where she remained only two days in room 605.

Miss Colombo, police noted, found what she was looking for on the very first day of her search, a vacant old two-story, balconied house near the corner of Avenida España and Calle America. It was ideally situated. It was within walking distance of the Olympic Sports Club, one of the capital's best athletic clubs. The American embassy and the Presidential Palace were also nearby. Four blocks away was the white-walled compound where Somoza, the city's most talked about resident, lived with his mistress. His mansion was well guarded and had the best alarm and security systems money could buy. Inside the compound, Somoza had set up a military-style Bunker system much more secure than the one he left behind in Managua.

Miss Colombo, police said, paid the September rent of $1,500, deposited the customary two months' rent as a guarantee, and then disappeared. Her picture was filed away, as are the photographs of most visitors to the tightly controlled country. Within five hours of the assassination the Paraguayan police began circulating her photograph, naming her one of the prime suspects in the killing of Somoza. The other suspect was identified by police as a dark-haired, moustachioed young man named Hugo Alfredo Irurzun. Miss Colombo, they said, was Silvia Mercedes Hodges and both she and Irurzun belonged to the Argentine Trotskyite People's Revolutionary Army, popularly known by its Spanish acronym, ERP.

Pastor M. Coronel, head of Paraguay's criminal investigation office, claimed that Irurzun had fought with the Sandinistas in Nicaragua against Somoza. Allegedly, Irurzun had crossed into Paraguay from Brazil with an Uruguayan passport in the name of Rogelio Hernández Garrido. In Asunción he had been living quietly in a rented house in the San Vicente district, for a while with his "wife," whom some neighbors believed might have been the mysterious Silvia Hodges. At the end of August, Hodges had disappeared. While "Hodges" was house-hunting, Irurzun, police said, had gone to the town of Luque and, using a false identity, purchased the blue Chevrolet pickup that was to be used in the assassination.

A veteran of thirteen years as head of the investigation division of the Paraguayan police, Coronel had sixty suspects under arrest within hours of the assassination. Police agents, soldiers and an army of informers were combing the city. There was a house-to-house search and all suspicious foreigners were interrogated. General Stroessner international airport was closed and efforts were made to seal off the usual escape routes over the Paraguay River into Argentina. It was a difficult time for Paraguay's professional smugglers who make contraband one of the nation's most profitable industries. The smuggling industry came to a temporary halt. The Argentine and Brazilian police quickly offered their full cooperation. The Argentines were just as interested in learning the identity of the killers and capturing any of their own subversives who might be hiding out in Paraguay, having escaped their intensive antisubversive campaigns that had almost wiped out the leftist terrorist organizations such as the ERP.

It was not revenge but a sense of professionalism that drove Coronel to use all his resources to try to catch the killers. The police were infuriated by Somoza's treatment of the bodyguards assigned to him. At times he had ignored their existence and other times he berated them. "He didn't even provide them with coffee," said a wealthy neighbor. As the months passed many of the plainclothesmen assigned to his protection were not particularly interested in his safety. Coronel had a reputation as a tough cop who felt it was his duty to safeguard his country's image as a quiet right-wing dictatorship that had managed to escape the ravages of terrorism. That image had been shattered on Avenida España and it was proving an impossible task to mend it. Even so, Somoza's death was not mourned in Paraguay. The spectacular food-throwing incidents, drunken scenes and abusive language used in public had eroded any sympathy that even the most fervent anticommunist had felt for the Nicaraguan.

Police said that Irurzun, alias Captain Santiago, had been located on Thursday night, September 18, adding somewhat fancifully that he was quietly seated at a table eating a plate of rice and reading Karl Marx when they knocked on the door of his home on the western edge of the capital. He had refused to surrender and died as he attempted to escape over the back fence—with two bullets in his chest. One of the reports the police issued said there had been a "ninety-minute gun battle."

The contradictions in the police stories led many to believe that the famous Irurzun had not been involved in the actual assassination. But the Paraguayan police were determined to produce results. They failed. The identities of the assassins and their motive may remain a secret.

As far as the Paraguayan government was concerned, the Sandinistas in far-off Nicaragua were responsible for the killing. Government spokesmen said the weapons had come from Nicaragua and had possibly been smuggled into the country in the diplomatic pouch. But this theory collapsed when it was learned that the two-member Sandinista mission was not permitted a diplomatic pouch. The envoys, a woman and a man, had arrived by bus from Brazil, and in the formal starchy diplomatic circles of Paraguay were as much misfits as boisterous Somoza. On August 20, the Paraguayan government had ordered the closing of the Nicaraguan embassy and asked the two shirt-sleeve diplomats to leave the country. No reason was given for the closing of the mission, but at the time it was believed to be in line with a general crackdown after the right-wing coup d'état in Bolivia.

Whether the Sandinistas had more to gain with Somoza dead is open to speculation. While Somoza lived, the Sandinistas always had a bogeyman. They probably could have assassinated him in Managua but for political reasons they elected against it.

There was no shortage of motives and terrorists to commit the deed. Even dictator Stroessner was not above suspicion. The theory was that Stroessner had become embarrassed by the presence of Somoza, who attracted undue attention to his little fiefdom. Somoza had not invested his huge fortune in Paraguay, as was expected of him. His land purchase there had drawn sharp criticism from various quarters who held that Somoza was trying to re-create his little Nicaragua in Paraguay.

A *crime passionnel* could not be ruled out. Somoza's licentious ways always made him a target for a jealous lover. In fact the first major Somoza scandal in Paraguay involved his flirtation with the former Miss Paraguay, María Angela Martínez, who was also connected romantically with Humberto Dominguez Dibb, editor of *Hoy* and onetime son-in-law of Stroessner. Amid the titters provoked by the affair, the editor became so angry that he began publishing anti-Somoza diatribes in his paper and at one point sent a bulldozer against Tacho's Mercedes. Miss Paraguay soon returned Somoza to Dinorah and the sparring with Dominguez Dibb ended. Ironically it was Dominguez Dibb's photographer who was the first to arrive at the scene of Somoza's death. His exclusive color photos of the assassination aftermath were sold abroad by Dominguez Dibb. The package of pictures was expensive, and *Hoy* profited.

When the news of Somoza's death reached his homeland on Wednesday morning, people at first did not believe it had finally happened. They crowded around radios waiting for confirmation. As it finally came, spontaneous celebrations broke out in Managua and cities around the country. Bars were soon crowded and the depth of hatred many Nicaraguans felt for Somoza was apparent as they saluted his demise with Flor de Caña rum. Thousands spent the afternoon and evening at July Nineteenth Plaza, christened for the day the war ended. Next to the old cathedral and near the place where the remains of FSLN leader Carlos Fonseca are now buried, Somoza was once again burned in effigy, as during the first anniversary celebrations of the revolution. It was a true catharsis.

The nine members of the National Directorate of the FSLN joined a motorcade through the streets acknowledging the cries of the people who cheered Somoza's death. Some bystanders set off firecrackers. Radio commentators likened Somoza to other tyrants in history. The country's three newspapers rushed out special editions after calling Asunción for any details that were available. As the noisy motorcade passed before *La Prensa*, where a new print shop was rising out of the rubble, Sandinista Jaime Wheelock, in charge of the Agrarian Reform, told newsmen, "Pedro Joaquín Chamorro has been avenged." That afternoon *La Prensa* appeared with the headline: "They Killed Somoza." *El Nuevo Diario*, published by Xavier Chamorro, brother of the slain publisher, had a headline that said simply: "There Was a Party." The Sandinista daily *Barricada*, whose editor, Carlos Chamorro, is Pedro Joaquín's son, had a longer headline: "Popular Vindication: Somoza Debayle Has Paid. He Died Like a Dog on a Corner."

Pedro Joaquín's widow, retired from the junta, said at her home, "Now I can only say that thirty months and seven days later, what Somoza did to Pedro, someone has done to him."

In their official statement the Sandinistas called the assassination "a heroic action" and stated that it satisfied their "desire for justice and popular revenge on the person who massacred more than 100,000 Nicaraguans and kept our country in misery and ignominy." They added, "Exactly fourteen months after having fled revolutionary justice, Somoza has paid for his crimes."

When Tomás Borge, interior minister and the last remaining founding member of the FSLN, was asked who might have killed Somoza, he quoted the Spanish Renaissance poet Lope de Vega: "Everyone killed him."

"I'm full of energy and courage to fight. I will return and conquer Nicaragua," was the last boast Somoza made, to the German magazine *Quick*. Just hours before he died, television news programs and newspapers were quoting Somoza's statement in *Quick* that President Carter was a "bastard" who had betrayed Nicaragua.

On the thirty-fourth anniversary of his father's assassination Somoza was buried in Miami. In death he was welcomed back by the country he loved. He returned in a Paraguayan coffin, with large wooden rosary beads around his neck. His children who had flown to fetch his body had arranged with Dinorah for his return to the United States. Dinorah, grief-stricken, wept over his coffin in which lay a wreath of red flowers with a note: "Tacho adorable, only death can separate us. Your love, Dinita." To newsmen she added, "I have been destroyed by the loss of my friend of eighteen years. . . . I feel very lonely." She chose to remain behind in Paraguay and manage his last business venture, the cotton plantation.

Somoza's burial in Miami's Woodlawn Cemetery turned into a political rally for Republican presidential candidate Ronald Reagan, with Nicaraguan and Cuban exiles shouting, "Down with Carter," whom they accused of "betraying Nicaragua." All their "vivas" were for Reagan, upon whom they placed their hopes for a better future. Some Reagan supporters distributed leaflets at the funeral service.

Cuban exiles, veterans of the Bay of Pigs 2506 Brigade, turned out in uniform to form an honor guard at the funeral home. The crowd refused to permit a hurried trip from the funeral home to the cemetery by automobile, shouting, "On foot." The funeral cortege wound slowly through Miami's Little Havana, along Calle Ocho, where Cuban storeowners stood respectfully on the sidewalk and said, "Adios, Tacho."

In his graveside eulogy, the last Somoza mayor of Managua, Orlando Montenegro, stated, "In this afternoon of pain and anguish and tears of the Nicaraguan and Cuban exiles, I may quote the words of two American congressmen in relation to Somoza's death. They said dramatically that the blood shed by Somoza is sprinkling the steps of the White House. They blamed the Chief of the [United States] government for the death of Somoza." Montenegro nodded to the two elected United States officials and friends of Tacho who attended the funeral, former Congressman John M. Murphy of New York and Larry McDonald, Democrat from Georgia. Manolo Reboso, former city commissioner of Miami and a close Somoza associate, eulogized his friend as the bulwark against communism and criticized the Carter administration and the media for their treatment of the Nicaraguan leader.

One of the mourners turned to Tachito, who stood alongside his mother, Hope, and his eighty-eight-year-old grandmother, Salvadora (Yoya). He said to the new Tacho, "You are our leader now, Chigüín." If El Chigüín, the kid, replied, it was lost in the murmur of prayers for the soul of his father.

NOTES

CHAPTER 1. A FOLKSY DYNASTY

1. *Time,* November 15, 1948, p. 38.
2. Harold Norman Denny, *Dollars for Bullets: The Story of American Rule in Nicaragua* (New York: Dial Press, 1929), p. 66.
3. Floyd Cramer, *Our Neighbor Nicaragua* (New York: Frederick A. Stokes Company, 1929), pp. 4–5.
4. *Time,* March 5, 1934, p. 16.
5. Arthur Bliss Lane to Willard Beaulac, July 27, 1935, in the Arthur Bliss Lane Papers, Yale University Library, New Haven, Connecticut, cited hereafter as the Lane Papers.
6. *Time,* September 9, 1929, p. 32.
7. *Time,* March 5, 1934, p. 18.

CHAPTER 2. TACHO I

1. *Time,* May 15, 1939, p. 15.
2. *Time,* November 15, 1948, p. 38.
3. *Time,* May 15, 1939, p. 15.
4. *Time,* July 17, 1944, p. 43.
5. *Time,* August 7, 1944, p. 38.
6. *The New York Times,* August 26, 1946, p. 6.
7. *Time,* John Stanton's February 1948 report.
8. *Time,* February 4, 1946, p. 38.
9. *Time,* John Stanton's February 1948 report.
10. Ibid.
11. *Time,* November 15, 1948, p. 39.
12. *Time,* February 10, 1947, p. 39.
13. *Time,* John Stanton's February 1948 report.
14. *Time,* June 30, 1947, p. 34.
15. *Time,* January 19, 1948, p. 40.
16. *Time,* John Stanton's February 1948 report.
17. Ibid.
18. Ibid.
19. *Time,* November 15, 1948, p. 40.
20. Ibid.
21. Ibid.
22. Ibid.
23. Ibid.

CHAPTER 3. ASSASSINATION

1. *Time,* December 4, 1950, p. 34.
2. *Time,* December 20, 1948, p. 34.
3. *Time,* December 11, 1950, p. 26.
4. Ibid.
5. Nancy Beth Jackson, "Tropic Magazine," *Miami Herald,* September 13, 1970.
6. *Time,* February 9, 1953, p. 9.
7. Bernard Diederich, *Trujillo: Death of the Goat* (Boston: Little, Brown & Company, 1978).

CHAPTER 4. THE BOYS IN POWER

1. *Time,* May 5, 1958, p. 34.
2. Daniel Waksman Schinca, interview in *El Día* [Mexico City], April 17, 1979.

CHAPTER 5. TACHO II TAKES COMMAND

1. Peter Wyden, *Bay of Pigs* (New York: Simon & Schuster, 1979), p. 84.
2. Ibid.
3. Ibid, p. 63.
4. Arthur M. Schlesinger, Jr., *Thousand Days* (Boston: Houghton Mifflin, 1965), p. 269.
5. Wyden, *Bay of Pigs,* p. 195.
6. Schinca, interview in *El Día* [Mexico City], September 9, 1979.
7. Ibid.
8. Ibid, September 18, 1979.
9. Ibid.
10. Ibid.
11. Ibid.
12. *Time,* May 25, 1962, p. 36.
13. Jackson, "Tropic Magazine," September 13, 1970.

CHAPTER 6. BEGINNING IN BLOOD

1. *The New York Times,* January 25, 1967, p. 6.
2. Jackson, "Tropic Magazine," September 13, 1970.
3. Schinca, interview in *El Día* [Mexico City], April 4, 1979.
4. Ricardo Morales Aviles in "Pancasan: Punto Definitorio," *Gaceta Sandinista* (Comisión de Información en La Habana, Cuba), no. 9, August 1976, p. 18.

CHAPTER 7. THE EARTHQUAKE

1. Jay Mallin, interview in *Time,* January 8, 1973.
2. Ibid.
3. DeVoss, *Time,* January 15, 1973, p. 20.
4. Ibid.
5. Associated Press, dispatch from Managua, January 24, 1975.
6. Don Bohning, *Miami Herald,* February 28, 1975.

CHAPTER 8. THE PARTY'S OVER

1. *Frente Sandinista, Diciembre Victorioso* (Mexico: Editorial Diogenes, S.A., 1977), p. 23.
2. Ibid.

3. Alan Riding, *The New York Times*, January 3, 1975.
4. Laszlo Pataky, *Legaron Los qui no estaban invitados . . . La Sombra de Sandino* (Managua: Editorial Pereira, 1975).
5. Ibid.
6. *Diciembre Victorioso*, p. 35.
7. Ibid, p. 37.
8. Alan Riding, *The New York Times*, December 31, 1974.
9. Alan Riding, *The New York Times*, March 23, 1977, p. 3.
10. Ibid.
11. Schinca, interview with Tomás Borge, *El Día* [Mexico City], April 14, 1979.
12. Tomás Borge, *Carlos: El Amanecer ya no es una tentación* (Sindicato de Empleados Nicaragua Machinery Company [Senimac]), n.d.
13. Guy Gugliotta, *Miami Herald*, June 17, 1979, p. 21A.
14. Humberto Ortega Saavedra, interview, *Newsfront International*, October 1978, pp. 9–10. Reprinted as "Crisis in Nicaragua," *NACLA Report on the Americas*, 12, no. 6 (1978): 22–23.

CHAPTER 9. A VICTIM OF HUMAN RIGHTS ?

1. *Gaceta Sandinista* [Mexico D.F.], Año 1, Numero Especial, n.d., pp. 17–21.
2. *Gaceta Sandinista* [San Francisco, California], 1, no. 11 (July 1976), p. 13.
3. Associated Press, dispatch from Managua, August 17, 1977.
4. Alan Riding, *The New York Times*, August 16, 1977.
5. *Time*, March 14, 1977.
6. Ibid.
7. *AIM Report* 6, no. 20 (October 1977), part 2.
8. Karen DeYoung, *The Washington Post*, July 28, 1977.
9. "For the Record: Somoza's United States Lobby," *Latin American Political Report* [London], August 26, 1977.
10. Ibid.
11. Associated Press, dispatch from Managua, August 17, 1977.
12. Ann Crittenden, *The New York Times*, October 12, 1977.
13. Max Holland and Cressida McKean, "Out of the Public Eye, Nicaragua's Washington Lobby Wins Again," *Los Angeles Times*, August 21, 1977, p. 11.
14. Jackson, "Tropic Magazine," September 13, 1970.
15. Norman Wolfson, "Nicaragua Notes," *National Review*, May 1979, p. 907.
16. Wolfson, "Nicaragua Notes" (unpublished) pp. 25–27.
17. Wolfson, "Nicaragua Notes" p. 915.
18. Ibid.

CHAPTER 10. THE HEART ATTACK

1. Bard Lindeman, *Miami Herald*, July 31, 1977.
2. *Miami Herald*, July 30, 1977.
3. Lindeman, *Miami Herald*, July 31, 1977.
4. Ibid, August 14, 1977.
5. Ibid.
6. *Miami Herald*, September 9, 1977.
7. Alan Riding, *The New York Times*, February 19, 1978.
8. Ibid.
9. Alan Riding, *The New York Times*, August 16, 1977.
10. Ibid.
11. Ibid.

12. Solaun speech, April 1979.
13. Ibid.
14. Ibid.
15. "Jornada Heroica do Octubre '77," (Managua: Ediciones Patria Libre, Serie Discursos, Publicación 1, 1979), Dirección de Divulgación y Prensa de la Junta de Gobierno de Reconstrucción Nacional, p. 22.
16. Alan Riding, *The New York Times*, October 21, 1977.
17. "Jornado Heroica de Octubre '77."
18. Alan Riding, *The New York Times*, October 20, 1977.
19. Ibid.
20. "Nicaragua: Return of the Rebels," *Newsweek*, November 7, 1977.
21. William R. Long, *Miami Herald*, November 6, 1977.
22. Ibid, November 2, 1977.
23. Ibid.
24. Solaun speech, April 1979.

CHAPTER 11. PEDRO JOAQUÍN CHAMORRO

1. *Time*, January 23, 1978, pp. 18–19.
2. Pedro Joaquín Chamorro, *Estirpe Sangrienta: Los Somoza* (Editorial Diogenes, S.A., 1979; 1st ed. 1957), p. 260.
3. Norman Wolfson, "Selling Somoza: The Lost Cause of a PR Man," *National Review*, July 20, 1979, p. 913.
4. Ibid.
5. Viron P. Vaky before the Subcommittee on Interamerican Affairs, Committee on Foreign Affairs, House of Representatives, Washington, D.C., June 26, 1979.
6. "World Beat," *Atlas World Press Review*, January 1978.
7. *Time*, January 23, 1978, p. 19.
8. Alan Riding, *The New York Times*, February 19, 1978.
9. *Time*, January 23, 1978, p. 19.
10. Alan Riding, *The New York Times*, February 14, 1978.
11. Wolfson, "Nicaragua Notes," p. 913.
12. Alan Riding, *The New York Times*, February 14, 1978.
13. Ibid.
14. Alejandro Bendana, "Crisis in Nicaragua," *NACLA Report on the Americas*, 13, no. 6 (November–December 1978).
15. Solaun speech, April 1979.
16. Alan Riding, *The New York Times*, January 16, 1978.
17. Bendana, "Crisis in Nicaragua," p. 24.
18. Solaun speech, April 1979.

CHAPTER 12. THE PALACE CAPTURED

1. *Time*, September 4, 1978, p. 22.
2. Gabriel García Marquez, "Crónica del Asalto de la 'Casa de los Chanchos,' " *Editorial La Oveja Negra* [Bogotá], 1979, pp. 42–43.
3. Ibid, pp. 35–36.
4. Tom Fenton, Associated Press, September 9, 1978.
5. *Barricada* [Managua], August 23, 1979, p. 1.
6. Tom Fenton, Associated Press, September 9, 1978.
7. Tom Fenton, Associated Press, September 9, 1978.

CHAPTER 13. LOS MUCHACHOS

1. *Time*, September 25, 1978, p. 32.
2. Ibid.
3. Tom Fenton, Associated Press, September 9, 1978.

CHAPTER 14. MEDIATION

1. Karen DeYoung, *The Washington Post*, January 14, 1979.
2. *Latin America Political Report* [*London*], 13, no. 42 (October 27, 1978).
3. Alfonso Chardy, United Press International, October 25, 1978.
4. Bendana, "Crisis in Nicaragua," p. 34.
5. Chardy, United Press International, October 26, 1978.
6. Ibid.
7. Van Bennekom, United Press International, November 30, 1978.
8. Chardy, United Press International, October 29, 1978.
9. Karen DeYoung, *The Washington Post*, October 15, 1978.
10. *This Week* [Guatemala City], 1, no. 32 (November 6, 1978), p. 253.
11. DeYoung, *The Washington Post*, October 15, 1978.
12. Ibid, October 19, 1978.
13. Jack Anderson, "A Dead General in Her Bedroom," *The Washington Post*, November 16, 1978.
14. DeYoung, *The Washington Post*, October 15, 1978.
15. Chardy, United Press International, November 27, 1978.
16. Ibid, November 28, 1978.
17. Jeremiah O'Leary, *The Washington Post*, December 2, 1978.
18. Chardy, United Press International, December 5, 1978.
19. Chardy, United Press International, December 27, 1978.
20. Viron P. Vaky before the Subcommittee on Interamerican Affairs, June 26, 1979.
21. DeYoung, *The Washington Post*, December 7, 1978.
22. Chardy, United Press International, December 31, 1978.
23. Ibid, January 2, 1979.

CHAPTER 15. EASTER IN ESTELÍ

1. Chardy, United Press International, January 10–11, 1979.
2. Graham Hovey, *The New York Times*, February 9, 1979.
3. *Newsweek*, February 26, 1979, p. 22.
4. "Nicaragua: Diplomatic Slap," *This Week*, February 12, 1979, p. 45.
5. Alan Riding, *The New York Times*, January 12, 1979.
6. *Newsweek*, March 5, 1979, p. 30.
7. "Nicaragua: the Sandinistas' Military Review," *Latin America Political Report* 13, no. 16 (April 27, 1979), p. 124.
8. Guillermo Mora Tavares, *Uno Más Uno* [Mexico City], April 25, 1979.
9. Chardy, United Press International, April 16, 1979.
10. Don Bohning, *Miami Herald*, May 7, 1979.
11. *Miami Herald*, May 2, 1979.
12. *Miami Herald*, May 12, 1979.
13. Alan Riding, *The New York Times*, May 22, 1979.
14. Tom Fenton, Associated Press, May 25, 1979.

CHAPTER 16. THE FINAL OFFENSIVE

1. Graham Hovey, *The New York Times,* June 7, 1979.
2. *Miami Herald,* June 8, 1979.
3. *Newsweek,* June 11, 1979, p. 16.
4. *Washington Star,* June 16, 1979.
5. Ibid, June 18, 1979.
6. Ibid, June 16, 1979.
7. Ibid, June 18, 1979.

CHAPTER 17. DEATH OF A NEWSMAN

1. *Time,* July 2, 1979, p. 60.

CHAPTER 18. POPULAR INSURRECTION

1. Jeremiah O'Leary, *Washington Star,* June 22, 1979.
2. *Washington Star,* June 25, 1979.
3. O'Leary, *Washington Star,* June 29, 1979.
4. DeYoung, *The Washington Post,* July 7, 1979.
5. *Washington Star,* July 8, 1979.
6. DeYoung, *The Washington Post,* July 11, 1979.
7. *Washington Star,* July 9, 1979.
8. Ibid., July 9–10, 1979.

CHAPTER 19. THE OFFENSIVE IS FINAL

1. George Russell interviews for *Time,* July 11–12, 1979.
2. David Halevy, *Time,* July 12, 1978.
3. Ibid.

CHAPTER 20. THE LAST HOURS

1. George Russell, *Time,* July 30, 1979, pp. 34–35.
2. Dr. Francisco Urcuyo, *Solos: Las Últimas 43 Horas en el Bunker de Somoza* (Guatemala: Editorial Académica Centro Americana, 1979), p. 117.
3. Ibid, pp. 119–20.
4. Ibid, pp. 137–38.
5. Ibid, pp. 132–33.
6. "Tropic Magazine," *Miami Herald,* September 13, 1979, p. .
7. Urcuyo, *Solos,* p. 141.

INDEX